T0248003

THE TRANSITION

THE TRANSITION

INTERPRETING JUSTICE FROM THURGOOD MARSHALL TO CLARENCE THOMAS

DANIEL KIEL

STANFORD UNIVERSITY PRESS
Stanford, California

Stanford University Press
Stanford, California

Printed in the United States of America on acid-free, archival-quality paper

Library of Congress Cataloging-in-Publication Data

Names: Kiel, Daniel (Law professor), author.
Title: The transition : interpreting justice from Thurgood Marshall to
   Clarence Thomas / Daniel Kiel.
Description: Stanford, California : Stanford University Press, 2023. |
   Includes bibliographical references and index.
Identifiers: LCCN 2022030621 (print) | LCCN 2022030622 (ebook) | ISBN
   9781503630659 (cloth) | ISBN 9781503635661 (ebook)
Subjects: LCSH: Marshall, Thurgood, 1908–1993. | Thomas, Clarence, 1948– |
   United States. Supreme Court—Officials and employees—Biography. |
   African American judges—Biography. | African Americans—Civil rights. |
   Discrimination in education—Law and legislation—United States. | Race
   discrimination—Law and legislation—United States.
Classification: LCC KF8744 .K54 2023 (print) | LCC KF8744 (ebook) | DDC
   347.73/2634—dc23/eng/20221115
LC record available at https://lccn.loc.gov/2022030621
LC ebook record available at https://lccn.loc.gov/2022030622

Cover images: Public domain photographs of Thurgood Marshall (left)
   and Clarence Thomas (right)
Cover designer: Gia Giasullo
Text design: Elliott Beard

To M, S, and B,
who keep me
grounded,
and also help me fly

"What is important is a goal toward which we are moving, a goal that is the basis of true democracy. . . . That goal is that if a child, a Negro child, is born to a Black mother in a state like Mississippi or any other state like that, born to the dumbest, poorest, sharecropper, if by merely drawing its first breath in a democracy, there and without any more, he is born with the exact same rights as a similar child born to a white parent of the wealthiest person in the United States."

THURGOOD MARSHALL (1988)

"[I] refuse to have my ideas assigned to me as though I was an intellectual slave because I'm Black. I come to state that I'm a man, free to think for myself and do as I please."

CLARENCE THOMAS (1998)

CONTENTS

PREFACE

On a Thursday morning in June 1991, Thurgood Marshall took his place among the nine seats of the justices of the United States Supreme Court for what would be the final time. That morning, the Court was set to announce the final rulings of its 1990–91 term and then recess until October. For half a century, Justice Marshall had influenced the working of the Court, first as an advocate, then as the U.S. solicitor general, before being named the nation's first Black justice and serving for twenty-four years on the Court.

Thurgood Marshall's first case before the Court had been argued in 1943. At that time, he was 34 years old, less than a decade out of graduating first in his law school class at Howard University. At that time, Marshall cut a tall, lean figure. As head of the newly formed NAACP Legal Defense Fund (LDF, later the Legal Defense and Education Fund), his work left him scant time and funds for eating. In the case, *Adams v. United States*, Marshall was challenging death penalty sentences of three Black soldiers convicted of rape at their base, Camp Claiborne in Louisiana. The soldiers had been charged with rape as a *federal* crime, which was unusual, and the question before the Supreme Court was a technical one—whether

Camp Claiborne was properly considered federal land at the time of the crime. Marshall would argue far more broadly significant cases on far more broadly significant issues of civil rights law over his career, but his early civil rights career often involved challenging the convictions of Black defendants, particularly those sentenced to death. These were among the only cases he could get. *Adams* provided his first victory at the Supreme Court; the justices concluded that the camp had not been "federalized" in compliance with statutory requirements. The defendants' convictions and death sentences were dismissed.[1]

On that June morning a half century later, Thurgood Marshall sat as one of the justices on the other side of the bench. He was 82 years old and hadn't been lean in decades. He had suffered a heart attack more than ten years prior and had been hospitalized with pneumonia in 1987. However, though he used a cane to get around, he remained quick-witted and sharp-tongued, if a bit crotchety. He could be excused for being ornery as he often found himself, as he was that morning, on the losing end of the Court's decisions. In contrast to his storied career as an advocate before the Court, Marshall was regularly unable to convince a majority of the justices of the correctness of his positions as he neared the end of his career. His dissent in the case of *Payne v. Tennessee* would be his last, and, like the *Adams* case of 1943, it involved a Black defendant sentenced to death. Again, the question before the Court was a technical one— whether testimony of the impact of the crime on a surviving victim was properly admitted or whether it should have been excluded for being unduly prejudicial. Marshall believed that the evidence should not have been admitted, but six of his colleagues voted against him, allowing the death sentence to stand. Marshall's dissent in *Payne* spoke beyond the case at hand though, engaging more broadly about the future of a body of law he helped build as both lawyer and justice.

"Power, not reason, is the new currency of this Court's decision making," he began. In a style he had honed over decades and perfected in recent years, his passionate dissent mixed a methodical review of the Court's previous decisions on "victim impact" testimony with a biting and broad critique of the forces at play in society and on the Court. In the *Payne* dissent, he found the Court's majority inviting challenges to established constitutional principles so that they could be overturned. The *Payne* case was "but a preview of an even broader and more far-reaching assault upon this Court's precedents," he warned. "Cast aside today are those condemned to face society's ultimate penalty. Tomorrow's victims may be minorities, women, or the indigent."[2]

Marshall was angry; his frustration at finding himself increasingly marginalized among his colleagues leapt from the pages of his dissent. He found himself powerless and lamented in the conclusion that the case would "squander the legitimacy of this Court as a protector of the powerless."[3]

It was a fitting conclusion to Thurgood Marshall's work in the Supreme Court that the final phrase he used was "protector of the powerless," for he stood atop the list of lawyers who had pushed the Court in the 1940s and 1950s to take on that role, particularly for African Americans. And his work as a justice was built on a foundational belief in the power of the law—and of the Supreme Court in particular—to remedy the deep and persistent inequalities and injustices that plagued the nation. *Payne v. Tennessee* was a case about victim impact testimony, but Justice Marshall's dissent was about the broader shift of the law and the Court away from Thurgood Marshall and what he represented.

And Justice Marshall did not leave any doubt about what he saw as the cause of this shift: "Neither the law nor the facts supporting [our previous decision on this issue] underwent any change in the last four years. Only the personnel of this Court did."[4]

The *Payne* opinion was announced on Thursday, June 27, 1991. Thurgood Marshall notified President George H. W. Bush of his retirement later that day. By the following Monday, there would be a further shift in the personnel of the United States Supreme Court, for on Monday, July 1, President Bush stood outside his family retreat in Kennebunkport, Maine, to introduce Judge Clarence Thomas as his nominee to succeed Marshall on the Supreme Court.

MR. JACKSON'S CLASSROOM

In the summer of 1991, I was a rising seventh grader in Memphis, Tennessee. And while it might make a strong preface if I could claim that I was attuned to the events unfolding at the Supreme Court, that would be grossly untrue. I'm sure that I was concerned primarily with enjoying summer vacation and improving my jump shot as part of my ill-fated dream of a professional basketball career. I probably knew vaguely who Thurgood Marshall was, but I had no reason to know of his poor health, his disagreements with President George H. W. Bush, or the impact his retirement would have on the Supreme Court.

I do recall hearing of Clarence Thomas that fall. Some of the details circulating in the discussion of his alleged sexual harassment of Anita Hill were astonishing to a middle schooler, and my school's daily news program, *Channel One*, provided us with quick, student-aimed reporting on the news of the day. This was the first I had heard about sexual harassment, and I recall being aware of discussions of the topic even though I could not comprehend the details of the drama or the stakes of Thomas's confirmation hearings.

At my school, *Channel One* was shown during fourth period. At the appointed time each day, the television in our classroom would magically turn on, and we would get ten minutes of news before moving on to our regular class instruction. I remember fourth period in particular because for fourth period, I had Mr. Jackson.

In Memphis, I attended what were called Optional Schools. Optional Schools (which might be called magnet schools elsewhere) were designed to offer special services and opportunities, such as an advanced academic curriculum, to draw students. Though I did not know it at the time, Memphis's Optional Schools were created as a reaction to a decade of extraordinary white flight, in which white families fled the city's schools for private schools or the adjacent suburban district. Optional Schools aimed to induce families with means, particularly white families with means, to attend Memphis's public schools. In other words, they were aimed to induce families like mine to send students like me to city schools.

One distinctive feature of Memphis's Optional Schools was that they operated as "schools within schools." Thus, within my elementary and middle schools, there were two distinct tracks—the optional track and the traditional track. These tracks separated those students who had access to the advanced academic curriculum ("optional") from those who did not ("traditional"). I was in the optional track, which meant that I did not have classes with students in the traditional track. In my elementary school, the tracking was largely physical as well: there was an optional hallway and a traditional hallway.

What makes this setup more jarring in retrospect is that the tracks were largely racially distinct: the optional track was made up mostly of white students, like me, while the traditional track was mostly African American students. Thus, when looking at a report of my schools' demographics, they were wonderfully diverse—like Memphis itself, the student populations were roughly evenly split between Black and white students. But when looking at the classrooms and hallways, they were certainly not "integrated" in a meaningful way. While there were always four or five Black students in my classes, I was educated in majority white classrooms. I was unavoidably aware of this dynamic at the time, but it was not until years later, in law school and after, that I would begin to unpack how it came to be and what impact it had on me and my community.

But I'm getting ahead of myself. Back to fourth period and Mr. Jackson. Mr. Jackson taught social studies, and he had the reputation of being the most difficult teacher at the school. And indeed, Mr. Jackson was one of the most rigorous teachers I had. But I think Mr. Jackson's reputation was outsized because he was so different. For starters, Mr. Jackson was a Black man teaching in the optional track. While Black teachers were not unusual, Black male teachers were—indeed, Mr. Jackson was the only Black male teacher I had outside of P.E. and art between kindergarten and twelfth grade. But Mr. Jackson was different in all sorts of other ways as well. He opened his class each day with a rhythmic clapping routine that doubled as a sort of call-and-response between students and teacher. For taking roll, he had the student at the front of each row report "all present and accounted for, sir" or identify if a student was missing. I cannot confirm, but the rumor was that Mr. Jackson had served in Vietnam; either way, there was a military essence to his classroom. And when it was time to begin class, Mr. Jackson would signal that we should get serious by reciting a rambling, nonsensical monologue that I still remember by heart.

So Mr. Jackson was unusual. But as a teacher, he was extraordinary. He was not afraid to expose us to difficult and controversial material: as we prepared for our class trip to Virginia and Washington, DC, he told us to ask the guides at Monticello about Sally Hemmings. He deliberately pushed students through not only course content but in-class discussions. I had never felt so uncomfortable in class. But he was meticulously fair. He spared no one and played no favorites. He stood apart. He knew it, perhaps even relished it. It must have required great courage to be a Black male teacher choosing to assign things like *The Autobiography of Malcolm X* to a group of majority white students in Memphis. And while he was dreaded by a great many students, there were others who found the challenging environment and material exhilarating. I was in that group. He set a model for asking questions of how the world we encounter got to be the way it is and for not being satisfied with easy answers to those questions.

I am sure that Mr. Jackson had opinions about Thurgood Marshall and Clarence Thomas, but I don't recall discussing them. He did, however, emphasize race in his teaching of American history. Memphis is a city with deep racial wounds and persistent racial divisions. The dynamics within my schools reflected that history. And Mr. Jackson's classroom forced me to start thinking more deeply about it.

While Mr. Jackson's class got me thinking about racial justice, my primary interest in middle school remained basketball. I can now see that I was approaching the high point of my basketball "career" at that time, but I can also see that playing middle school basketball contributed to a broadening understanding of the world that Mr. Jackson was encouraging.

Through elementary school, I had played basketball entirely with people I had grown up with; my dad had been our coach more often than not. We played all our games at the Memphis Jewish Community Center against other teams of almost entirely Jewish kids. So when I made my middle school basketball team, I was in for something different. This was not just any middle school team, but a team that won the city championship in eighth grade (no small feat in a basketball-mad city like Memphis) and sent nearly half the team to college on basketball scholarships. As in Mr. Jackson's classroom, I was being pushed outside of my comfort zone.

My fondest memory of middle school basketball is of the relationships I built—some of which continue to this day—with my teammates. Though our school was actually separated based on the optional/traditional tracking, the team crossed that divide. Thus, I was building relationships with peers whom I would not have encountered otherwise due to the structures within our school. But my most lasting memory from those seasons was of our trips to other schools.

Since I had had a stable schooling experience in elementary and middle school, I had simply assumed that most schools in the city were pretty much like mine—that is, racially diverse in the cafeteria even if not in the classrooms. What I encountered upon visiting other schools was something different. In many of the schools we visited, there were no white people at all. This was jarring for all sorts of reasons, but most relevant here, it suggested that stories I had been told about the triumphs of the civil rights movement and the American future of racial harmony were missing something. My schools may have reflected the legacy of racial segregation in a somewhat nuanced way, but here, in the 1990s—a time I had been led to believe was far distant from the world of Jim Crow—I was encountering what looked very much like outright school segregation. That reality may not have shocked every middle schooler in Memphis. I am sure that Black students would have been more keenly aware than me of the persistent legacies of oppression in this allegedly post–civil rights world. But it was shocking to my sheltered impression of things.

I was unsure what to do with these observations at the time, but these experiences occurred in a moment of my life in which I was being encouraged by Mr. Jackson to think more critically, particularly about race in America, and at a moment in American history when riots in Los Angeles after the acquittal of police officers who had beaten Rodney King were forcing others to do the same. Looking back, I can see that the questions I started to identify then set me on the path to study two Black Supreme Court justices.

GRAPPLING WITH 'BROWN'

The more direct impetus for this book can be found in other classrooms at two different law schools. I was in law school in 2004 at the fiftieth anniversary of *Brown v. Board of Education*, the case that had declared racial segregation in schools unconstitutional. The anniversary forced an evaluation of the impact *Brown* had made in dismantling the systems of racial oppression the Court had declared unlawful. The record in 2004 was decidedly mixed. It seemed that the further we got from the decision itself, the more ambiguous *Brown*'s legacy became. There were no more explicit Jim Crow laws that mandated racial segregation, but many schools and neighborhoods retained their racial character. I knew this well from my own experiences in Memphis. And in terms of educational opportunity, racial disparities were easy to find everywhere—from which students were being taught by more highly qualified teachers or had access to more advanced curricula to which students were suspended or expelled from school more often. Yet, despite these systemic disparities, there had been several generations of African American students who had individually excelled and reached the heights of American success.

At Harvard, where I was a law student, it seemed that there were weekly speakers approaching these questions from diverse perspectives. By this time, I had reluctantly given up on basketball and instead imagined myself following in the model of Thurgood Marshall, utilizing the law to eliminate barriers for vulnerable members of our community. I was thus fortunate that my third year of law school allowed for a full immersion in reckoning with the legacy of *Brown v. Board of Education*. I took courses at both the law school and the educational school that focused on race, law, and education and wrote a capstone paper driven by my curiosity about how the schools in Memphis—my schools—came to look like they did. This was when I learned about the history of Optional Schools and began to comprehend the reasons why most of Memphis's schools were made up almost entirely of Black students, even though my schools were not.

That paper ultimately led me into a different type of law school classroom. In 2008, after my wife and I moved home to start our family, I was hired to teach at the University of Memphis School of Law and did not hesitate to create a new course based largely on the questions that had been asked during *Brown*'s fiftieth anniversary. My aim was to do for law students what Mr. Jackson had done for me—push them to think more critically about the role of law in shaping society and evaluate various strategies for change. In the course, which I have been fortunate to teach every year since, we focus on the buildup to and aftermath of *Brown* as a case study for examining other educational disparities connected to law. I utilize not only the primary opinions of the Supreme Court through the desegregation era, but also dissents and concurrences that present alternative perspectives. In the very first iteration of the course, I fortuitously paired a dissent from Justice Marshall (*Milliken v. Bradley*) with a concurrence from Justice Thomas (*Missouri v. Jenkins*), and the class discussion was among the best of the semester. I have been working on this project in one way or another ever since.

The initial question that drove class discussion that day—and in each iteration of the class since—was how these justices had reached such different perspectives. The differences were noteworthy because both framed their arguments as efforts to create a relationship between citizens and government that would lead to fuller Black citizenship, yet they seemed to push for diametrically opposed legal results. And, of course, there was the surface similarity: while many justices had disagreed throughout the Court's history about appropriate results, these two were the ones whose lives had been most directly and personally impacted by the desegregation narrative.

It is likely that many students who choose my course are predisposed toward skepticism about the wisdom of Justice Thomas's positions, as am

I. So what was perhaps most surprising for students was that his perspective—that the better path toward fuller Black citizenship was through less government intervention rather than more—could not be easily dismissed. Instead, it triggered engaged debate that exposed the complexity of these most vexing national topics. As a teacher, I tried to lean into this dissonance in a way that would make Mr. Jackson proud. But as a learner, I began to grapple with the ways in which the ideas of Justice Marshall and Justice Thomas represent the most personally informed perspectives on some of the most difficult questions Supreme Court justices encounter about the most confounding challenge in the American experiment: how to create a society in which diverse individuals all have access to the opportunities of full citizenship.

This book is the product of that grappling.

CONSTRUCTING 'THE TRANSITION'

There is much that this book is (or aims to be) and much that it is not. Although it juxtaposes the lives and careers of Thurgood Marshall and Clarence Thomas, it is neither a full biography nor a simple compare-and-contrast exercise. Pointing out that two justices have different judicial philosophies and citing examples does not require a book. Further, one might critique the focus on two African American justices as superficial or opportunistic, particularly for a white author. But, I argue in this book that their lived experiences as African Americans, unique among Supreme Court justices until the 2022 confirmation of Ketanji Brown Jackson, make an exploration of *these two* contrasting judicial philosophies instructive beyond the mere fact of disagreement, in at least two ways.

First, this book is an exploration of American citizenship, considering the relationship of Americans to one another as dictated by law and embodied in the relationship between citizens and their government. This is a broadly American exploration, but one that is brought into fullest relief by the experience of Black citizenship. The relationship between law, government, and citizenship (or, for African Americans during significant periods of American history, non-citizenship) has been most contested for African Americans. Both Thurgood Marshall and Clarence Thomas navigated these dynamics as citizens in ways virtually no other Supreme Court justice ever had to. Second, this book argues that the 1991 transition from Justice Marshall to Justice Thomas reveals a range of thought that is extraordinary among contemporary Supreme Court transitions and is representative of the broader social, legal, and political debates that have defined the past century, but that both justices have been underestimated in their performance on the Court precisely because of their shared race.

Thus, the book seeks to look at the two justices' contrasting jurisprudence through the lens of a single issue with outsized importance to their own lives as well as to the significant constitutional issues they have encountered. That issue is education, and the lens includes both the justices' personal schooling experiences as well as their professional, primarily judicial, work on schooling. This lens is of utmost importance to the question of citizenship because for most Americans, their most impactful and lasting contact with government comes through the school system. Further, while all Supreme Court justices grapple with questions of law, education, and citizenship, the role of schools as a focal point of contested citizenship is most directly connected to the African American schooling experience.

Admittedly, Thurgood Marshall and Clarence Thomas are not the only voices, Black or otherwise, to be heard. Through 2022, they were the only Black Supreme Court voices, but generations of others—including teachers, citizens, lawyers, and lower court judges—are a part of this conversation. The choice to focus only on these two men misses the way lived experiences of African American women might inform a jurisprudence on education and citizenship. Whether that will be evident in the work of Justice Ketanji Brown Jackson or any other future Supreme Court justices remains to be seen. Justices Marshall and Thomas have extensive records on the topic and thus provide a rich jumping off point. The hope is that this book is an invitation to discussion, not a conclusive account.

Indeed, it could not be wholly conclusive given the range of work implicated in a meaningful study of citizenship. The focus on education necessarily excludes other spaces where the interaction of government and citizen are of great significance, such as within the criminal justice system or at the ballot box. The focus on race similarly excludes the justices' records on other identity characteristics, including sex. Again, those omissions are a choice driven by the desire to present an accessible manuscript and the fact that education and race have prompted more frequent, more personal, and more passionate writing from Justices Marshall and Thomas.

Just as the full scope of the justices' professional work will not be explored, neither will every part of their lives be presented. In particular, there will be little of the justices' personal lives, complex and worthy of examination though they may be. One exclusion of particular note that straddles the personal-professional line for Justice Thomas and that is a significant part of the 1991 transition is his controversial Supreme Court confirmation, a topic that has been examined thoroughly in many places. However, the details do not implicate the subject matter here except where they amplified strained relations between Thomas and the broader Black community or solidified Thomas's disaffection and animosity toward Democrats and the policies many Democrats have pursued. I hope that exclusion of a deeper focus on the confirmation hearings and the allegations of sexual harassment are not understood to minimize the gravity of those claims.

There is no shortage of discussion and critique of *Brown,* the Supreme Court, Thurgood Marshall, or Clarence Thomas. Though much of that will be presented here, those looking for a vindication of the perspectives of Justice Marshall or a demonization of Justice Thomas (or vice versa) will be disappointed. I am aware of the strong feelings Thomas in particular elicits, especially as he continues to play a key role in the work of a contemporary Court that is rolling back some of the very rights Marshall had warned of in his *Payne* dissent.

I will confess my own disagreement with most of Justice Thomas's perspectives and my disappointment in the extent to which he increasingly seems driven exclusively by an ideology aligned with the Republican Party. Perhaps a critic might have once made a similar complaint about Justice Marshall. I am certainly not without bias on questions of the role of law and courts in protecting and bolstering Black citizenship in a nation with overwhelming and widespread racial disparities. But my disagreement with Justice Thomas's approach to these challenges does not change the fact that his jurisprudence is rooted in an American (and African American) conservatism that is central to the legal, social, and political debates of the past American century. To dismiss these ideas because of one's loathing of the messenger (or even the message) overlooks that the ideas appeal to many and perpetuates a winner-takes-all approach to confronting national problems. To me, such an approach only pushes the central American project of coexistence in a diverse society, governed by law, further out of reach.

The aim of the book, then, is to connect two justices' lives to their work and their work to some of the nation's most significant constitutional questions. It uses a unique constitutional event—the replacement of one Supreme Court justice with another—to demonstrate how significantly one such transition can affect how those questions are answered. The differing philosophies on either side of the Marshall–Thomas transition implicate a range of legal and social issues that animate much national discussion, including government responsibility for remedying prior legal discrimination, the proper approach toward educational equity, the relationship between the federal government and states, the presence and continuing effects of conscious and unconscious racism, and many others. The book uses one topic in particular, race and schooling, to bring those issues to life, connecting back to the justices' own schooling experiences. It seeks to braid these varied strands together to explore how law impacts the relationships Americans have with one another and with their government, the foundations of citizenship.

Just as I argue that the lived experiences of Thurgood Marshall and Clarence Thomas shaped their work later in life, my own lived experiences have shaped me. I've already mentioned the ways in which Mr. Jackson and my own schooling pointed me in a certain direction. My professional work, too, connects me to this project.

Between my two immersions in law school, first as student and then as professor, I did practice law, though most of what I did was not in the manner of Thurgood Marshall. One case, however, did connect me to his legacy. *Payne v. Tennessee*, the dissent that marked the conclusion of Marshall's career on the Supreme Court, concerned a defendant from Millington, Tennessee, a town ten miles north of Memphis. The defendant, Pervis Payne, had been represented in his appeal to the high court by lawyers from Burch, Porter, and Johnson, a Memphis firm best known for its representation of Dr. Martin Luther King Jr. during his fateful visits to Memphis in April 1968.

Following Pervis Payne's 1991 loss at the Supreme Court, he returned to Tennessee's death row and awaited execution. As fate would have it, Tennessee amended its law in 2001 to allow for DNA testing of evidence even after an individual had been convicted and sentenced. Eventually, the federal public defenders who had been working on Payne's case reached out to the Memphis firm that had represented him in the past with the hopes of obtaining DNA testing of several pieces of evidence involved in his case. When this request came in, I was working as a lawyer at Burch, Porter, and Johnson, and I was assigned the task of representing Mr. Payne in his appeal at the Tennessee Court of Criminal Appeals. So it was that I stood before a panel of Tennessee judges in 2006 representing the very same person whose case had inspired Justice Marshall's final dissent.

Our appeal was rejected. The court concluded that the evidence against Payne was so overwhelming that even contrary DNA evidence would not have changed the outcome, a position I found utterly ridiculous. I drafted a petition to the Tennessee Supreme Court and, when that was rejected, the U.S. Supreme Court, but we did not receive a hearing. I continued to explore possibilities for ensuring that Payne was not put to death but had not made any progress by the time I left practice and turned toward a career in teaching law.[5]

Meanwhile, Payne continued to fight to avoid execution. For most of the twenty-first century, Tennessee has not proven particularly eager to execute individuals on its death row; from 1977 through 2017, only six people were put to death in Tennessee. However, beginning in 2018, the state began to accelerate executions, with seven taking place between 2018 and 2020, a number that ranked it second only to Texas in executions during that period. I had followed the Payne case even as I moved into teaching, worrying that my failure to win on the DNA question (not to mention Justice Marshall's inability to convince his Supreme Court colleagues to exclude certain evidence) might ultimately result in his execution. It was thus with despair that I read in February 2020 that an execution date had been set for December 3, 2020. By that time, the best avenue for rebuffing Payne's death sentence was based on the argument that he was constitutionally ineligible for execution due to intellectual disability. After being put in touch with the relentless lawyers representing Payne, lawyers whose work is very much in the spirit of Thurgood Marshall, I wrote several articles arguing that moving forward with his execution without providing an opportunity to be heard on the intellectual disability question would be unconstitutional.[6]

By that time, I was immersed in the writing of this book. As I worked, I felt connected anew to that final case Justice Marshall heard decades earlier. He had lamented that the Supreme Court would abdicate its role as a protector of the powerless, but the Court had in 2002 (over Justice Thomas's dissenting vote) created space for individuals like Payne when it declared that the execution of individuals with intellectual disabilities violated the Constitution. In 2020, Marshall's final fight was still ongoing.[7]

By the time I had completed the book, I had testified at the Tennessee General Assembly in support of a change in law that gave those in Payne's predicament at least the opportunity of a hearing. When that statute was passed, it gave Payne the chance to argue for the first time that he could not be executed due to intellectual disability. His lawyers insistently pushed his case forward, and in November 2021, prosecutors revoked his death sentence.[8]

So it was that the outcome Thurgood Marshall had argued for in his final dissent—saving the life of Pervis Payne—was ultimately accomplished at a moment when the Supreme Court seemed to be heading in an altogether different direction, led by Justice Marshall's successor.

THE TRANSITION

RACE, SCHOOLS, AND THE JUSTICES OF THE SUPREME COURT

"Sixteen."

The interjecting voice was a new one amid that morning's argument in 1982. It was uttered with a characteristic note of certainty, as well as a hint of disgust. Justice Thurgood Marshall had a low tolerance for injustice that could be openly apparent when he engaged with lawyers arguing at the Supreme Court.

Moments before, Marshall had been listening to the arguments of Frederick Merkin, the lawyer for the City of Los Angeles, who was trying to persuade the justices to lift an injunction against the use of chokeholds by the Los Angeles Police Department. Adolph Lyons, an African American man who had lost consciousness after being put in a chokehold by police during a traffic stop for a busted taillight, had won an injunction that aimed to stop police from using the practice absent urgent need. In front of the Court in November 1982, Merkin was arguing that such an injunction would only be appropriate if the Court concluded that chokeholds "shocked the conscience," a very high threshold.[1]

Marshall's colleagues pressed Merkin, noting that chokeholds had caused deaths. Certainly, *that* would shock the conscience, they implied. "You had a number of deaths here, didn't you?" asked Justice Harry Blackmun. "A number of them, aren't there?" Justice Byron White followed up, after Merkin conceded that, yes, the LAPD had killed people when employing chokeholds.

As Merkin dithered, Marshall spoke up.

"Sixteen."

Thurgood Marshall knew precisely how many deaths LAPD had caused by chokeholds between 1975 and 1982. And when Adolph Lyons's case reached the Supreme Court, Marshall took the opportunity to put the chokehold on trial. In his dissent from the Court's decision that the city's voluntary chokehold moratorium made the case moot, Marshall was aghast that the Court would remove chokeholds from judicial oversight and left no doubt about who would bear the brunt of this outcome. He highlighted that twelve of the sixteen people killed by police chokehold were Black males in a city where Black males made up only 9 percent of the population. Adolph Lyons survived his encounter with LAPD, but sixteen people had not in the years since, and that group was disproportionately Black and male, like the dissenting justice.[2]

Among the Americans to serve on the Supreme Court, Thurgood Marshall must have been the most familiar with the potential for injustice when African Americans encountered law enforcement. In addition to simply living life as a Black man, Marshall's lawyering career led him to defend many Black men accused of crimes. Marshall argued against all-white juries in capital cases, forced confessions, and wrongful arrest. In one case, Marshall argued that a confession could not be relied on since it had been secured after an eight-hour interrogation during which police dumped the victim's bones into the defendant's lap.[3]

On the Court, Justice Marshall used his experiences as a lawyer to inform his work on matters of criminal justice. He was the Court's most passionate opponent of the death penalty, and he argued urgently that its discriminatory implementation further undermined its constitutionality. In the *Lyons* case in 1982, with the disproportionate effect of LAPD chokeholds on Black men fueling his revulsion, Marshall provided a detailed and clinical picture of the way chokeholds lead to deaths: "Depending on the position of the officer's arm and force applied, the victim's voluntary or involuntary reaction, and his state of health, an officer may inadvertently crush the victim's larynx, trachea, or thyroid. The result may be death caused by either cardiac arrest or asphyxiation."[4]

Marshall was describing a disturbing scene, one that foreshadowed another, nearly forty years later when a Minneapolis police officer was captured on video kneeling on the neck of George Floyd, killing him. Characterizing the Court's decision in *Lyons* as an abandonment of judicial responsibility for restraining law enforcement and its potentially deadly tactics and highlighting the racial disparities in chokehold deaths, Marshall was arguing, essentially, that Black lives matter.

AN EVOLVING COURT

The racial justice protests of 2020 were a vivid reminder of how much of Thurgood Marshall's work remained. Whether Black citizens in their encounters with law enforcement and the criminal justice system, Black students in their encounters with the nation's education systems, or Black voters in their demands to have their voices heard, Marshall's fight was for full inclusion of and fair treatment for African Americans in the American system. His career reflects an urgent demand for full Black citizenship. Moreover, the 2020 reckoning with the nation's racial injustice elevated themes Marshall had frequently highlighted, such as structural racism and unconscious bias. As Marshall had always insisted, the 2020 demonstrators connected contemporary racial disparities to the nation's long history of discrimination against and subjugation of African Americans and demanded remedies. Marshall had never been thrilled with the tactic of mass demonstrations, but he would undoubtedly have identified with the sentiments of those who took to the streets in the summer of 2020.

Marshall spent the final twenty-four years of his career as a Supreme Court justice applying a jurisprudence he had first constructed in his pioneering legal work to the wide range of contexts encountered on the nation's highest court. Having seen the law construct a system of oppression, he developed an expansive view of the responsibility of law to *de*-construct the nation's persistent disparities. That included enabling the federal government broader latitude in overriding the behavior of individual states as well as providing federal courts with the tools to craft effective remedies to stubborn social problems. And at its center was a belief that America's constitutional structure depended on an equal citizenship that could best be produced in an integrated society in which diverse citizens engaged with one another. Marshall was an integrationist, yes, but on the grounds that affirmatively reversing the legally imposed distances between Americans was a requirement for the democratic structure embedded in the Constitution to function.

But by 2020, this was far from the prevailing vision on the Supreme Court. Thus, although they embraced his mission and his outrage, twenty-first-century demonstrators for racial justice did not see the tactics Marshall had placed at the center of his work to reshape the Constitution as particularly viable. Marshall's undying faith in the law and the Constitution might have even seemed naïve. The Supreme Court certainly did not seem a place where racial justice was likely to be pushed forward, at least not in the way Marshall had envisioned it.

In the twenty-first century, the Court had prioritized a jurisprudence of colorblindness that was skeptical of efforts to pursue racial justice through law. The most frequent victors in civil rights cases were white plaintiffs arguing that they were being discriminated against due to their race when governments took affirmative steps to pursue racial justice in classrooms and workplaces. In 2007, the Court struck down school diversity plans that sought to maintain racially integrated classrooms. Two years later, the Court ruled in favor of white firefighters challenging a city's decision to discard a test that had severely disadvantaged Black firefighters seeking promotion. Then, in 2013, the Court declared portions of the Voting Rights Act, a landmark bill passed during the height of the civil rights movement in 1965 and renewed several times in the decades since, unconstitutional.

In that case, *Shelby County v. Holder*, the Court emphasized how much progress had been made on voting discrimination as justification for discarding Congress's judgment to renew the act, an argument Justice Ruth Bader Ginsburg characterized in dissent as akin to "throwing away your umbrella in a rainstorm because you are not getting wet."[5]

These were not decisions in line with the jurisprudence of Thurgood Marshall. But a leading voice pushing the jurisprudence of colorblindness was Justice Clarence Thomas, Marshall's successor and, to that point, the only other African American to sit on the Supreme Court. The *Shelby County v. Holder* decision embraced a position Thomas had taken several years earlier, arguing that "the lack of current evidence of intentional discrimination with respect to voting" made the Voting Rights Act unconstitutional. In *Shelby County* itself, Thomas wrote a concurrence, noting that he would declare portions of the act untouched by the Court's opinion to be unconstitutional as well, a directive the Court largely acted upon several years later. Even when the Court delivered a result cognizant of persistent racial discrimination, Thomas demurred. In 2019, the Court vacated the conviction of a Black defendant on the grounds that prosecutors had unconstitutionally stricken Black jurors from participation in his trial. In dissent, Justice Thomas chided the Court for ignoring the race-neutral justifications for excluding the Black jurors, finding no problems where a 7–2 majority of the Court found discrimination.[6]

The evolution of the Supreme Court from a body Thurgood Marshall, the lawyer, saw as the best forum for confronting the nation's state-sponsored racial discrimination in the 1940s and 1950s, to one that racial justice protestors in 2020 would have been reluctant to approach for fear of how it might further roll back civil rights protections, has many causes and countless reverberations. One undeniable cause is the change in identity of the justices on the Court over time, and no transition has contributed more to the Court's transformation than that in 1991 from Justice Marshall to Justice Thomas. Moreover, the range of thought captured in the jurisprudence of Justices Marshall and Thomas vividly demonstrates the wide-ranging consequences resulting from a shifting Court. Those effects implicate legal, social, and political topics that go well beyond race and touch on foundational tensions of American citizenship.

On the structure of the government created by the Constitution: Where is the appropriate balance between federal authority and the autonomy of states and localities? Do judges have a responsibility to protect the rights of minorities who have limited influence on the elected branches of government? And if so, how much discretion ought judges have in crafting such protections?

On the tension inherent in working to promote equality among a diverse population: Does the Fourteenth Amendment's equal protection clause prohibit only legal discrimination or also circumstances, often the result of private choices, that have discriminatory effects? Can classifications be used by the government to benefit previously disadvantaged groups, or must the government be colorblind and neutral altogether? And how direct must the line be between present disparities and prior discrimination to make affirmative remedial action appropriate?

And on the best strategies for pursuing social change: Are Americans better off working within systems that have historically been oppressive or working to create alternatives? Given persistent racial disparities, where is the appropriate balance between taking individual responsibility for personal uplift and vigorously pursuing systemic change?

These are questions that strike to the heart of the American experiment and the Constitution's negotiation of the relationship between a people and their government. And while all Americans must negotiate that relationship, the intensity of the work has historically been greater for African Americans, whose very citizenship has been contested from the Constitution's earliest drafts.

In their lives, Thurgood Marshall and Clarence Thomas have experienced the challenge of living and learning in a world and system that had enslaved their relatives and that continued to subjugate members of their racial group. In their early careers, each sought to eliminate racial stereotypes and barriers that held the nation's racial caste in place, albeit in very different ways. And on the Court, Justices Marshall and Thomas have had ample opportunity to encounter the vast questions presented in this space and, with the power that comes with being one of only nine justices, have engaged the questions shrewdly.

The 1991 transition from Justice Marshall to Justice Thomas will forever tie these two jurists together, but it is their work, their contrasting visions of citizenship, and the broad effects of those visions that make that transition a crucial turning point in the transformation of the Supreme Court.

SUPREME COURT TRANSITIONS

Remaking the Supreme Court is an exceedingly gradual process. Of the branches of American government, the federal judiciary is the most stable. Justices to the Supreme Court are appointed with life tenure, so turnover is infrequent. Between 1953 and 2020, there was a Supreme Court appointment, on average, every two and a half years, but each appointment only changes the identify of one of nine justices. Changes on the Court happen infrequently and at unpredictable intervals, and each one has less consequence in the direction of the institution than any presidential or congressional election.

And Supreme Court transitions are not created equal. While every transition brings a new perspective into the conference room where the justices discuss cases, many transitions do not fundamentally alter the dynamics on the Court. Justices are well aware of the workings of the Court, and many time their retirements so that the president who will replace them will do so with a successor largely sharing their philosophy. Even in those instances where a transition brings a justice who differs markedly from a predecessor, such a shift will only lead to different outcomes on a closely divided Court. Further, some transitions that at first appeared to shift the Court's balance have turned out to be less impactful due to shifts in the justices themselves over time.

It thus takes a perfect storm for a single transition to remake the Supreme Court. But by every measure, the transition from Thurgood Mar-

shall to Clarence Thomas was just such a storm. It featured the replacement
of a justice appointed by a Democrat (Lyndon Johnson) with a justice appointed by a Republican (George H. W. Bush). That difference actually
translated into contrasting jurisprudence among the predecessor and successor justices. Indeed, the swing from one end of the ideological spectrum
to the other that occurred between Marshall, one of the Court's most liberal justices, to Thomas, one of the most conservative, was the largest such
shift among any transition since 1953. Further, Justice Thomas has not wavered in philosophy over his three-decade tenure, consistently rating as one
of the more conservative justices, just as Justice Marshall had consistently
been one of the Court's more liberal.[7]

The transition occurred at a time when the balance of the Court was
fluid, and such a shift would truly remake the Court and many of its outcomes. The Court of the 1980s was somewhat paralyzed by its parity and
often seemed to contradict itself in cases that ought to have been similar.
This was precisely what Justice Marshall was complaining of in his final
dissent when he noted that the Court was overturning a similar decision
made only four years earlier. Thomas's arrival established a conservative
majority that has persisted as he has passed from the Court's most junior
justice to its most senior. Despite eight Court appointments between 1991
and October 2020, the Court's ideological landscape remained largely unchanged from that established upon Justice Thomas's arrival: the most significant potential disruption of that balance was averted when Republican
senators refused to hold hearings for nominee Merrick Garland, whom
President Barack Obama had picked to succeed the conservative Justice
Antonin Scalia in 2016. The death of Justice Ginsburg in 2020 and her
quick replacement by Justice Amy Coney Barrett (an election-year replacement that Republican senators *did* allow in a reversal of their position for
replacing Justice Scalia) has further strengthened the conservative hold on
the Court.[8]

Thomas's confirmation created an enduring conservative tilt to the Supreme Court that has had an impact beyond the mere counting of votes
and ideologies among the justices. Since the earliest days of the nation,

there has been an American tendency to convert social and political questions into legal ones. As Alexis de Tocqueville observed in 1835, "There is
hardly any political question in the United States that sooner or later does
not turn into a judicial question. . . . Thus, judicial language becomes, in
a way, the common language."⁹ Thus, even though the Court is primarily
confronted with narrow legal questions about constitutional and statutory interpretation, its decisions both reflect and shape the most pressing
social questions of the moment. Given that influence, the nine justices who
occupy the seats at One First Street have great power in defining the evolving meaning of American citizenship. This is one of the threads braided
into the narrative of this book.

THE AMERICAN DILEMMA

While the Marshall-to-Thomas transition was ideologically impactful, it
was also historically unprecedented. At the time of Thomas's nomination,
only 105 Americans had served on the Court in the nation's two centuries,
all of whom were white males except Thurgood Marshall and Sandra Day
O'Connor. Replacing the nation's only Black justice made the moment
historically unique and fraught with the legacy of a nation where law had
subjugated African Americans and where the relationship of race and law
was ever contested. The American dilemma of race has presented the most
confounding tests of the meaning of citizenship for courts and society.

Race cases implicate an array of legal and social issues that underscore
the judicial role in defining citizenship, and both Marshall and Thomas
regularly use race cases to expound on their political and judicial philosophies. That they are able to do so informed by lived experiences as Black
Americans adds a dimension to their work on these topics that further ex-
poses the complexity of the challenge.

Affirmative action was one of the topics the Court had been waver-
ing on through the 1980s. Thurgood Marshall had made his position in
favor of both the wisdom and constitutionality of such measures to remedy
historical racial discrimination clear from his seat on the Supreme Court.

Meanwhile, as head of the Equal Employment Opportunity Commission (EEOC), the federal agency charged with oversight of workplace discrimination, Clarence Thomas had shown great skepticism of such practices.

The topic haunted the Marshall-to-Thomas transition—both as a potential legal issue that would come before the Court and, more directly, in the very selection of Marshall's successor. Less than a year before nominating Clarence Thomas to replace Thurgood Marshall, President Bush had rejected a proposed civil rights statute on the grounds that it improperly encouraged racial "quotas" in hiring. Yet Bush could hardly avoid the perception that race had played a factor in his selection of Thomas. Meanwhile, the sizable Black opposition to the Thomas nomination seemed also to contradict a prior position that race ought properly be a salient factor in filling jobs: having sanctioned consideration of race in hiring, Thomas's opponents were left arguing, essentially, "not *this* African American!"

The transition was thus not only impactful and complex but bursting with irony. At the center of this moment were two Americans who, despite a surface commonality as African American judges, had reached the same pinnacle of American law with vastly different experiences and perspectives. Thurgood Marshall, a product of a life of segregated schooling, argued for the imperative of integration for guaranteeing better educational opportunities for Black students; Clarence Thomas, who came of age within predominantly white environments where he was among a small number of African American students, extolled the benefits of single-race educational options for Black students. Marshall, a lawyer whose entire pre-judicial career involved bringing suits *against* the government for its mistreatment of African Americans, put the responsibility for solutions on the government and was willing to empower courts to use a wide range of tools to remedy prior discrimination; Thomas, a lawyer whose pre-judicial career involved working almost exclusively *for* the government, expressed deep skepticism about any government practice utilizing an individual's race—even to provide a benefit—and sought to restrict government power generally and judicial power in particular.

Such a transition, including its lasting and still unfolding consequences, demands attention. Yet these two justices, different as they are, have been chronically underestimated. Through shallow criticism of their performance on the bench and oversimplification of their judicial perspectives, both Thurgood Marshall and Clarence Thomas have often been reduced to caricature. As a result, the transition from Justice Marshall to Justice Thomas is often portrayed as a simple story about Mr. Civil Rights ceding his seat to a racial sellout; or, from another perspective, a story about a results-oriented judicial activist being replaced by a disciplined adherent to the Constitution's first principles. Neither fans nor critics tend to capture the complexity of these two Americans and their judicial philosophies.

Race is at the root of the chronic underestimation of Thurgood Marshall and Clarence Thomas. The belittling of their intelligence reflects racist assumptions of Black intellectual inferiority. Their subjugation to superior white colleagues replicates the nation's traditional racial hierarchy. The oversimplification of their work—by both enthusiasts and detractors—reflects a resistance to engaging with the breadth and nuance of Black thought and enables the coopting of ideas expressed by Black thinkers for others' self-interest.

The range of legal, political, and social ideas represented in the work of Justices Marshall and Thomas is extraordinary. On a central question of American citizenship—the extension of professed ideals to an increasingly diverse group of Americans, including those once subjugated through law—Marshall and Thomas offer contrasting testimonies with deep roots in the nation's history. In their work on the Court, their perspectives are filtered through the prism of the cases they have encountered, but their judicial writings on narrow legal topics, and often in concurrences with or dissents from the Court's primary opinions, grapple with foundational challenges for a nation still working to deliver on its founding promises, particularly for African Americans.

Some of the issues encountered are unavoidably connected to race, such as school and housing segregation, the value of Black institutions as opposed to integration or diversity, the connection of prior discrimination to present disparities, and the purpose of the equal protection clause of the

Fourteenth Amendment. But others are not, such as the size and scope of the federal government, the appropriate role of the federal judiciary, and the proper method for interpreting the Constitution. Through American history, Supreme Court justices have confronted these issues across various types of cases, but there is one area where questions of race, citizenship, law, and belonging have triggered particularly fertile investigation by courts generally and particularly passionate writings by Justices Marshall and Thomas in particular. That place is schools.

THE NURSERIES OF DEMOCRACY

When courts talk about schools, they are primarily talking about citizenship. In a recent case, Justice Stephen Breyer referred to schools as the "nurseries of democracy," a sentiment that echoed the Court's 1954 assertion in *Brown v. Board of Education* that education was "the very foundation of good citizenship" and "a principal instrument in awakening the child to cultural values." To access Marshall and Thomas's jurisprudence on crucial legal and social issues—and thus measure the profoundness of the 1991 Supreme Court transition—the book will utilize school decisions because while these cases are about education, they touch on so much more.[10]

In addition, in no area are the connections for Marshall and Thomas between personal experience and foundational constitutional questions more robust than in education. This is not unique to these two justices. According to legal scholar Justin Driver, "the public school has served as the single most significant site of constitutional interpretation within the nation's history."[11] More specifically, in the enduring effort to navigate the difficult relationship between American government and *African American* citizens, schools have proven a central forum. Marshall's most famous triumph, *Brown v. Board of Education,* is the most visible example, but because of education's potential to either limit or expand the future of individuals, schools have occupied a prominent place, both symbolically and practically, within the African American freedom struggle.

For both Marshall and Thomas, their own schooling experiences were similarly impactful. Marshall's experiences in the segregated public schools of Baltimore and the all-Black campuses of Lincoln University and Howard University law school drove his work as a lawyer and informed his judicial philosophy. Clarence Thomas entered first grade the fall after *Brown v. Board of Education* and thus experienced an education system in transition, beginning in Savannah's all-Black Catholic schools before entering predominantly white environments for high school in Savannah, college at Holy Cross, and law school at Yale. Thomas's experiences, too, would shape *his* worldview, though in a very different way.

School cases, then, provide an especially fertile source. They intersect with foundational constitutional questions; they are central to the African American freedom struggle; and they provide the opportunity to trace the way the two justices' lives informed their philosophies on the bench. School cases offer a lens with outsized importance to the lives, careers, and legacies of Thurgood Marshall and Clarence Thomas, whose judicial work on school cases reverberates well beyond the classroom. As the justices write about school segregation, affirmative action, or racial diversity, they are at the same time confronting some of the biggest questions in American citizenship and constitutional governance.

THE THOMAS COURT

September 2020 was a most explosive moment in modern American history. The transformative energy of global racial justice protests triggered by the suffocation of George Floyd continued into the fall. But even before the protests, the world was deeply in the throes of the upheaval brought by the COVID-19 pandemic. The pandemic had only intensified a polarization within American society that had divided families and communities into hardening ideological factions, which seemed to find it increasingly difficult to even speak to one another. Indeed, the paralysis caused by fundamental disagreements about basic facts had shattered the nation's response to the pandemic. No figure had done more to accelerate this deterioration of community than Donald Trump, who was facing reelection in November. For Trump supporters and opponents alike, the election seemed an existential moment for the country.

Into this tinderbox arrived yet another shock. On September 18, Justice Ruth Bader Ginsburg passed away after having battled multiple episodes of cancer over two decades. Ginsburg's death produced another of those most unpredictable of constitutional moments: the replacement of a Supreme Court justice. The stakes were immediately apparent and brought to mind stakes similar to when Thurgood Marshall retired nearly three decades prior.

If Ginsburg were replaced by Trump, it would be the first Supreme Court transition since 1991 that would flip a Court seat ideologically and thus held the potential of disrupting the Court's balance for the first time in three decades, as it could create a 6–3 supermajority of reliably conservative justices. It was an opportunity Republican leaders could not pass up, particularly with great uncertainty about who would win the White House. Just over a week removed from Ginsburg's death and less than a month before the presidential election, Trump nominated Judge Amy Coney Barrett to succeed her. After four days of hearings and a failed boycott and filibuster by Democrats, Barrett was confirmed on October 26. The presidential election was held a week later, and Democrat Joe Biden won.

The confirmation of Amy Coney Barrett could be viewed as a culmination of the Court's transformation, a crucial moment of which had been Thomas's 1991 succession of Marshall. But it also created for Clarence Thomas a situation somewhat akin to that Thurgood Marshall experienced upon his own confirmation in 1967. Marshall had joined a Court dominated by like-minded justices, a supermajority under the helm of Chief Justice Earl Warren. For Marshall, this experience was short-lived, as President Nixon appointed four justices between 1969 and 1972, which began the Court's movement in a more conservative direction. Indeed, the first justice appointed by a Democrat after Marshall would not come until Justice Ginsburg in 1993, two years after Marshall's retirement.

However, when Marshall joined a supermajority in 1967, he was the

Court's most junior justice; in 2020, Thomas was the Court's most senior. Over his three decades, he had staked out conservative positions that the Court seemed to be moving toward. His skepticism regarding the Voting Rights Act was just one example. As early as 1994, in a case about voter dilution (circumstances in which the relative value of votes seems to differ due to the way districts are drawn), Justice Thomas wrote a concurrence criticizing efforts to increase the number of African American elected officials, lamenting that federal courts had been encouraged through the Voting Rights Act to "segregate voters into racially designated districts to ensure minority electoral success." A guiding principle for Thomas, and a very personal one, was a rejection of any assumption that all members of any group think alike, and he opposed even remedial efforts like the Voting Rights Act for giving credence to such assumptions. Nineteen years later, a Court majority struck down portions of the act in *Shelby County v. Holder.* Then, in Justice Barrett's first term, the Court went a step further, narrowing the applicability of provisions of the act *Shelby County v. Holder* had left intact. Notably, Justice Elena Kagan—a former clerk of Justice Marshall—dissented in the case, *Brnovich v. D.N.C.*, observing that "the Court decides this Voting Rights Act case at a perilous moment for the Nation's commitment to equal citizenship."[12] Given Thomas's role as a leader among the conservative justices, some have begun to refer to the newly constituted nine, including Justice Barrett, as the Thomas Court. It is a dynamic unlikely to change even with the 2022 arrival of the Court's third African American justice—and first Black woman—Ketanji Brown Jackson.

The transformation of the Court that led inexorably to the Thomas Court of 2020 and beyond began before Thomas's confirmation in 1991. But it was the replacement of Justice Marshall with Justice Thomas that tipped the process. At the center of the Court's remaking are two Americans whose lives informed their work and whose work has both reflected foundational tensions in the American system and pushed that system in contrasting directions from its highest court.

In Marshall, one can find the cocky lawyer eager to prove himself as good as if not better than any white peer. Having made his reputation tearing down systems of discrimination, Marshall easily found long-lasting effects of the historic subjugation of African Americans and was eager to charge government with the responsibility of crafting remedies, even when that process seemed ineffective. He always applied the Constitution in the context of the real world that citizens encountered and focused on the ways systems impacted groups of individuals.

A generation younger than Marshall, Thomas came of age in a world Marshall had help remake. In his work as a justice, one finds in Thomas the fiercely independent and stubborn individual raised by his self-made grandfather who still bristled at the snubs and condescension of others. Having experienced life within largely white institutions and finding a more subversive form of racism than Marshall had encountered, Thomas was deeply skeptical of all government efforts to confront discrimination or promote equality of opportunity. Instead, he favored self-reliance and individual responsibility over systemic change, seeing contemporary disparities as the effect of individual private decisions rather than as legacies of a subjugating past. Thomas believed in fixed principles, such as color-blindness, even when applying them seemed to perpetuate inequality and to distance himself from the Black community for which he professed to be working.

This book first introduces its central figures, their distinct educations, and the ways in which they are bound together by history, including their status on either side of one of the Supreme Court's most impactful transitions. Then, in separate parts, it uses school cases to unpack the underlying legal, social, and political issues impacted by the justices' contrasting worldviews. These include a fundamental question facing advocates confronting racial subjugation and denial of full citizenship: whether to prioritize access to institutions that had excluded African Americans or to strengthen existing Black institutions. From their differences on this question, differences that echo generations of work by Black advocates, Justices Marshall and Thomas formed radically distinct visions for the Constitution and the nation that are reflected in their broader jurispru-

dence. Through the school cases, the book explores the contested mean-
ings of Black citizenship; and by exploring Black citizenship, it examines
American citizenship and constitutional governance more broadly—topics
like the balance of state and federal governments, the appropriate role of
courts among the nation's system of checks and balances, and the responsibility (or lack thereof) of government to remedy historical discrimination.
In conclusion, the book will return to a broad concern raised in Justice
Marshall's final dissent, in which he foresaw a "far-reaching assault" by the
Court itself on the rule of law, an assault furthered in part by changes in
the Court's personnel.

Though not a school case, *Lyons*—the police chokehold case that prompted
Justice Marshall to remind the lawyer for Los Angeles of the potential for
death and the disproportionate risk faced by Black men in police cus-
tody—illustrated the stakes of a shifting Court. As a legal matter, Marshall
lamented that "the Court's decision removes an entire class of constitutional violations from the equitable powers of a federal court."[13] But it was
not the narrow legal question that truly bothered Marshall. Rather, it was
the sixteen lives, mostly Black lives, lost in encounters between citizens and
representatives of their government.

The choice of how courts would evaluate such encounters touched on
social issues that remained urgent decades later and triggered the racial justice protests of 2020. It is a choice that effectively defines the boundaries
and rights of American citizenship. As arbiters of those boundaries, the
justices of the Supreme Court have an extraordinary role in our society.
For more than a half century, one seat on that Court has been occupied by
two men whose lives and work vividly capture the importance of navigating those questions of citizenship and a wide spectrum of possible answers.

PART I

BECOMING JUSTICES

ONE

BRETHREN, OF A SORT

In 1925, amid the norm of Jim Crow racial segregation in virtually every aspect of American life, a thousand African Americans had achieved the distinction of being admitted to the practice of law. However, in keeping with the racial separation given constitutional blessing in *Plessy v. Ferguson* in 1896, and consistent with the reality that separation often meant exclusion, there was no professional organization open to Black lawyers. The American Bar Association (ABA), which had admitted and then expelled its only African American member over a decade earlier, did not admit Black lawyers, and the interracial National Lawyers Guild was still more than a decade from its creation in 1937. The period marked a nadir in American race relations as the gains for African Americans of the Reconstruction era were met with violent legal and extralegal resistance. The *Plessy v. Ferguson* decision provided license for a full battery of Black Codes to be written into state and local laws, while the film *Birth of a Nation* had ignited a resurgence for the Ku Klux Klan. Lynching, which peaked toward the end of the nineteenth century, remained a scourge and led to the be-

ginnings of organized resistance, including the founding of the National
Association for the Advancement of Colored People (NAACP) in 1909.

Within this moment, twelve African American lawyers gathered in
Des Moines, Iowa, and having been excluded by the ABA, founded an organization for Black lawyers, the Negro Bar Association, later to be named
the National Bar Association (NBA). In addition to providing professional
links and development for the tiny cadre of Black lawyers, the NBA sought
to increase legal services for Black communities that were largely un- or
underserved. At the same time, the organization aimed at the very top of
the American legal profession, evaluating judicial nominees on the basis
of their commitment to or hostility toward racial equality. By 1930, the
association played a role in blocking the Supreme Court nomination of
John Parker on the grounds of his outspoken opposition to civil rights and
voting rights.[1]

By 1991, membership in the NBA had reached 13,000 members, and
the association served as the preeminent bar association for Black lawyers.
However, when President Bush nominated Judge Clarence Thomas, the
NBA faced a somewhat perplexing question as it undertook its traditional
role as evaluator of judicial nominees on the basis of their commitment
to racial equality. Though Thomas, who had served as head of the EEOC
under President Reagan, was African American, his positions, particularly with regard to affirmative action, were unpopular within much of the
Black community and ran counter to mainstream positions surrounding
racial equality. After the NBA's judicial council, the body that initially
rates nominees, voted 6–5 against endorsing Thomas's nomination, the association's larger board of governors declined to take any official position
on the nomination amidst intense internal divisions.[2]

Regardless, Thomas was ultimately confirmed. His confirmation hearings began with the types of ideological questions that split the NBA and
evolved into one of the most public, political, and divisive Supreme Court
confirmations in American history. The allegations of Thomas's sexual
harassment of Anita Hill further divided and intensified opinions among
African Americans about the nomination.

Seven years later, Justice Thomas again triggered division within the National Bar Association. Thomas had been invited to speak at the association's annual meeting in Memphis in 1998 by Judge Bernette Johnson of the Louisiana Supreme Court, the head of the judicial council. Then, Thomas was disinvited. Due in part to an effort by retired judge Leon Higginbotham, who had been one of Justice Thomas's most vocal critics within the Black legal community, members of the NBA's judicial council voted to rescind Thomas's invitation, a result that mirrored other protests of the justice and led him to limit public appearances. However, Thomas considered himself still invited and let his intention to address the NBA convention be known, setting the stage for an address later that summer.[3]

The ambivalence from the nation's preeminent association of Black lawyers surrounding the nation's only Black justice reflected a chasm between Clarence Thomas and many African Americans. Indeed, for some, ambivalence had become antipathy amid a belief that Justice Thomas's positions in government and now on the Court were actively making things worse for African Americans. As Judge Higginbotham charged, there was a belief that Justice Thomas had helped "turn back the clock on racial progress."[4] Such claims stemmed from Thomas's performance during the Reagan Administration as head of the EEOC from 1982 through 1990. He had been criticized in that role for failing to aggressively enforce antidiscrimination laws and for allowing a significant buildup in cases, many of which were dropped due to expiring statutes of limitations. Once on the Court, Justice Thomas continued to draw the ire of civil rights advocates, particularly for his positions hostile to affirmative action. But Thomas was certainly not alone in these positions. Chief Justice William Rehnquist and Justice Antonin Scalia, members of the Court when Thomas was confirmed in 1991, consistently took similar positions, and his conservative colleagues who have joined the Court in the twenty-first century have similarly voted against the positions of civil rights advocates. But Thomas, the only Black justice and operating in the shadow of his predecessor, was a special target for ire.

The vitriol from elements of the Black community toward Clarence

Thomas has been consistent and vicious throughout his tenure in public life. He has been called "Judas," a "sellout," and "Uncle Tom."[5] During Thomas's confirmation hearing, Congressman John Lewis, hero of the civil rights movement, distilled the critique into a sentence: "What you have is a nominee who wants to destroy the bridge that brought him over troubled waters."[6] In 2014, Representative Bennie Thompson of Mississippi referred to Thomas as an "Uncle Tom" and subsequently stood by the comment amidst criticism, explaining that issues like voting rights and affirmative action "are very important, and for someone on the court who's African American and not sensitive to that is a real problem."[7]

The theme throughout has been betrayal. According to scholar (and former law clerk to Thurgood Marshall) Randall Kennedy, who devoted an entire chapter in his 2008 book *Sellout* to Clarence Thomas, the justice is "the most vilified black official in the history of the United States" for the crime of "supporting the enemies of black folk, subverting Black America, being a race traitor."[8]

Anita Hill's allegations of sexual harassment by Thomas when the two worked at the EEOC furthered the estrangement between Thomas and the Black community. This was particularly due to the aggressive criticism Thomas's defenders lodged toward Hill, a Black woman, and to how Thomas utilized race to portray himself as the victim in the controversy, referring to the charges against him as a "high-tech lynching." The juxtaposition of the nominee's use of racial imagery (when his own character was challenged) with his positions against consideration of race in employment and education decisions struck many critics as inexcusable.

The antipathy between Thomas and much of the Black community is rooted in this perceived disconnect between Justice Thomas's jurisprudence, which seeks to impose an extreme colorblindness, and the facts of his own life, which have been impacted by skin color. In arguing on Thomas's behalf at the time of his confirmation hearings, the poet Maya Angelou observed that Thomas "has been poor, has been nearly suffocated by the acrid odor of racial discrimination, is intelligent, well-trained, black and young enough to be won over again."[9] Implicit in Angelou's observation was a belief that because Thomas had felt the sting of racism, as a justice, he could identify its presence and work against it. Others pointed out that Thomas had not only felt the sting of racism but had enjoyed the benefits of race-conscious affirmative action in his schooling and professional career. Judge Higginbotham, again, asked how Thomas, having had opportunities afforded to him by affirmative action, has any "moral basis to become hostile to such options being made available to the present generation of African-Americans."[10] The same sentiment was present in Representative Lewis's lament that Thomas was destroying the bridge that brought him over troubled waters. In both the hopefulness of Angelou and the outrage of Higginbotham is a sense that Thomas's life experience ought to have brought him to judicial positions different than those he took on the bench.

The years since his confirmation have not produced much change from Justice Thomas as his positions have remained counter to those of the majority of twenty-first-century civil rights advocates. Undoubtedly, Thomas's scarring confirmation made moderation even less likely. The experience seemed to have permanently alienated Thomas from the liberal politicians and civil rights leaders who so vehemently attacked his character. While the confirmation likely hardened Thomas's ambivalence toward mainstream civil rights positions, it also normalized his demonization. Though, at the time the Thomas–Hill confrontation may have split the Black community, that opinion has shifted against Thomas as the years pass.

The result has been that controversy and protest have followed Thomas virtually every place he goes, stemming largely from within the Black community. In 2001, even an attempt to name his childhood library in Savannah after him led to protest, including the resignation of a member of the library's board. Thus, the controversy surrounding Thomas's 1998 speech to the National Bar Association was typical.[11]

JURIST OF THE CENTURY

The National Bar Association had no such controversy with Thurgood Marshall. Ten years earlier, the association gathered for its annual meeting in Washington, DC, in August 1988. Amid a five-day program of seminars and receptions was the association's annual awards luncheon, at which the award for "Jurist of the 20th Century" was presented to Justice Marshall.[12] The award was only the latest in a countless collection accumulated over decades. In contrast to Thomas, Thurgood Marshall's pre-judicial career was defined by civil rights advocacy. Even before achieving fame for his victories at the Supreme Court, Marshall had been battling for human rights in local courtrooms, often where a Black defendant was on trial for his life. Indeed, Marshall biographer Gilbert King noted that in his early career, Marshall felt "the representation of powerless blacks falsely accused of capital crimes [was] his opportunity to prove that equality in courtrooms was every bit as vital to the American model of democracy as was the fight for equality in classrooms and in voting booths." As his reputation grew, local African American citizens in small Southern towns would flock just to see him at work. "All they wanted to do—if they could—was just touch him, just touch him, Lawyer Marshall, as if he were a god," recalled Alice Stovall, Marshall's secretary at the NAACP.[13]

He would go on to lead the legal assault on segregation, a campaign that turned him into a frequent presence at the Supreme Court in the 1940s and 1950s. He achieved victories in voting rights, housing rights, and, most famously, education. In 1944, he won the case *Smith v. Allwright* (1944), declaring the all-white primary unconstitutional; the following year, in *Shelley v. Kraemer,* he convinced the justices that covenants in housing deeds that prohibited African Americans from buying property were not constitutionally enforceable. Before the most famous triumph in *Brown v. Board of Education* in 1954, he led the NAACP's effort in graduate school desegregation cases, including *Sweatt v. Painter* at the University of Texas law school, and *McLaurin v. Oklahoma Board of Regents* at the graduate school of the University of Oklahoma. In all, Marshall had won twenty-nine cases at the Supreme Court and dozens more in lower courts, a body of work that redefined the American Constitution and its relation to African Americans. The work earned him the nickname Mr. Civil Rights, and John Lewis called him a Founding Father of the New America. Even if he had never become a judge, in Marshall's legal practice, he perhaps did more to transform constitutional law than any other lawyer in American history.[14]

After becoming the first African American Supreme Court justice in 1967, Marshall continued to advocate for the rights of the most vulnerable Americans. For example, he grew into a leading voice against the death penalty, providing a vote in 1972 in the 5–4 case *Furman v. Georgia*, which declared it unconstitutional.[15] As a justice, he also continued his work on issues of voting rights, housing, and education. All of this earned Marshall recognition among all advocates for more robust Black citizenship and a hallowed place in the African American community. In many ways, he was beyond reproach, even though his integrationist philosophy had been a subject of criticism throughout his career, and even though his unwavering faith in law led him to disapprove of many of the most effective civil disobedience tactics of the civil rights movement.[16]

In awarding "Jurist of the 20th Century" to Justice Marshall, Joyce London Alexander, the first female African American federal magistrate, noted Marshall's "time-honored commitment to equal justice under law" and predicted that his decisions protecting all of humanity would withstand the test of time. Justice Marshall took the podium with a characteristically jocular remark about the standing ovation he received: "Don't keep it up too long or I'll believe it!" Then, he reminded the attendees at the NBA convention of the work to be done. He lamented that racism may be broader and stronger than before and that pleas for patience were falling upon deaf ears, because they were the same pleas that had been offered for generations. In closing, he laid out the vision that had guided his work from the small county courtrooms of the South in the 1930s to his two decades on the Supreme Court of the United States:

We've got to have the one thing in mind. And I'm gonna close with what I've been saying for 50 or 60 years. I don't care about the Constitution alone or the Declaration of Independence or all of the books together. It's not that important. What is important is a goal toward which you're moving, a goal that is a basis of true democracy, which is over and above the law. . . . And that goal is very simple. That goal is that if a child, a Negro child, is born to a Black mother in a state like Mississippi or any other state like that, born to the dumbest, poorest sharecropper, is, by merely drawing its first breath in a democracy, there and without any more, is born with the exact same rights as a similar child born to a white parent of the wealthiest person in the United States. No, it's not true. Of course it's not true. It never will be true. But I challenge anybody to take the position that that is not the goal that we should be shooting for.[17]

This was Marshall's enduring quest: to ensure that neither circumstances nor race would determine the fate of any American. It is a view of citizenship that demands that the nation's most vulnerable are entitled to the same treatment as its most privileged. Given his achievements and veneration, as well as the consistency of his vision, Justice Marshall cast an incredibly long shadow over Black America, particularly the legal community. Thus, when Clarence Thomas awkwardly accepted the attempted-to-be-withdrawn invitation to address the National Bar Association a decade later, he would not be celebrated as the jurist of the century. Given his work to that point, he faced a skeptical audience to say the least. But Justice Thomas took the occasion to assert that he, too, aimed at a similar goal and deserved equal treatment.

AN UNAPOLOGETIC PLEA

The challenge of introducing Justice Thomas to that skeptical audience in June 1998 rested on the capable shoulders of Judge Damon Keith, the chief judge of the Sixth Circuit Court of Appeals who had first been appointed to the federal judiciary by Lyndon Johnson in 1967, the same year President

Johnson appointed Thurgood Marshall to the Supreme Court. "How does one introduce a person that is so well known that virtually every person in this audience has an impression of him, rightly or wrongly?" Judge Keith began. "How does one introduce a person whose views have become so obscured and distorted by those with their own agendas that many have closed their minds to even the thought of engaging in an open dialogue with him?" This was a far different introduction than the celebration of Justice Marshall's decisions protecting all of humanity from a decade earlier. Judge Keith, whose own career to that point in 1998 and extending all the way until his 2019 death earned him a reputation for commitment to racial equality with few equals, rhetorically offered answers to the question of why Justice Thomas's service on the Supreme Court received such great scrutiny: because he has signified a departure from the approach of Justice Marshall; because he has been the fifth vote defining the Court's conservative course; because of a lack of sensitivity to issues of civil rights; because of biased media distortions that sensationalize his views; because his status as a Black American in such a position of power renders him unusually vulnerable to criticism. "Or is it because he has had the courage to pursue his own course without regard to personal popularity?" Judge Keith asked, previewing the argument the justice himself would make. "I hope that today will be the beginning of a process by which you will begin to form your own opinion of Justice Clarence Thomas," Judge Keith added in conclusion.[18]

Justice Thomas approached the podium and began with an acknowledgement of the complexity of the moment: "For those of you with whom I do not share the same opinion, and perhaps that is many, I will take only thirty minutes of your time." Over the course of that half hour, Justice Thomas confronted the "bilious and venomous assaults" against him not by arguing in favor of his way of thinking, but by asserting his right to think for himself. The principal problem, as he defined it, was his rejection of conforming to "the new black stereotype," his refusal to think a certain way simply because he was Black. To him, requiring a "monolithic" viewpoint from African Americans came from the same type of condescension

and notion of Black inferiority that had once allowed the "mythic, disgust-
ing image of the lazy, dumb black." And Thomas was cognizant that, as the
Court's only Black justice, he was being held to a different standard than
his colleagues. Though his

> ideas and opinions themselves [were] not necessarily illegitimate if held
> by non-black individuals, they, and the person enunciating them, [were]
> illegitimate if that person happen[ed] to be black. Thus, there's a subset
> of criticism that must of necessity be reserved for me, even if every non-
> black member of the Court agrees with the idea or the opinion.[19]

As he spoke, Justice Thomas invoked his own biography as well as a
variety of Black thinkers, such as Frederick Douglass, Richard Wright,
Ralph Ellison, and Nina Simone. He recalled his frustration and loss of
faith in institutions following the assassination of Dr. Martin Luther
King Jr. in 1968, the allure of acting upon one's rage, and his own rejection of African Americans who did not take revolutionary postures.
He remembered throwing a copy of Thomas Sowell's 1970 book *Black
Education: Myths and Tragedies* into the trash because he had believed
that no self-respecting Black man could take the positions Sowell had
taken. Looking back, Thomas marveled that Sowell had become a dear
friend and that many of the author's predictions had come to pass, acknowledging the twist of fate that the wrath the young Thomas had
visited upon the author was now being visited upon Thomas himself.
To a smattering of laughter, he quipped, "What goes around does
indeed come around."[20]

But ultimately, recalling a fear that he might be consumed by anger
like Bigger Thomas, the character in Richard Wright's *Native Son*, Thomas
claimed that he had rejected the comforts and security of racial solidarity.
"I am a man, a black man, an American," he asserted, claiming his place of
belonging among a group that seemed to have rejected him:

> It pains me deeply, more deeply than any of you can imagine, to be per-

ceived by so many members of my race as doing them harm. All the sacrifice, all the long hours of preparation were to help, not to hurt.[21]

The NBA speech, delivered to the nation's leading Black lawyers and judges, represented the most direct and substantial effort by Justice Thomas to demand the respect of the Black community. It was not without wanton attacks of its own ("I can't help but wonder if some of my critics can read"), but Thomas soberly delivered what could be described as a plea. He quickly made the case that the focus on efforts for racial uplift should be on individuals rather than racial groups. Though he thought such a strategy in the quest for full Black citizenship would be more effective, less dangerous, and more consistent with the underlying principles of the country and its guarantees of freedom, Justice Thomas acknowledged that he could be wrong. Still, he argued defiantly for the right to think for himself, for the legitimacy of his ideas: "[I] refuse to have my ideas assigned to me as though I was an intellectual slave because I'm black. I come to state that I'm a man, free to think for myself and do as I please."

Black history has always included a diversity of viewpoints, he asserted, and the better course for airing differing and similarly fallible views would be "in an environment of civility" rather than victimizing him for daring to dispute orthodox thinking. "Isn't it time to realize that being angry with me solves no problems?" he asked in conclusion after drawing a long breath. "Isn't it time to acknowledge that the problem of race has defied simple solutions and that not one of us, not a single one of us can lay claim to the solution?" Thomas saw himself as offering a solution, albeit one that had made him rather unpopular among the very people he claimed to aim to help. Looking exhausted, Thomas closed his notes and left the stage, having both made his plea for respect and stood unapologetically by his beliefs. The room responded with prolonged ovation of nearly twenty seconds, but the decades since have demonstrated that Justice Thomas's plea has largely been unanswered.[22]

JUSTICES MISJUDGED

The contrast between Thurgood Marshall's acceptance speech for the National Bar Association's "Jurist of the 20th Century Award" in 1988 and Clarence Thomas's speech to the same group a decade later captures the distance between these two jurists in the popular mind. Justice Marshall was free to reiterate the goal of his life's work, a world in which neither race nor circumstance controlled the treatment of America's children. Justice Thomas was stuck defending his right to hold an opinion counter to his predecessor. In their own ways, both were indicting the worlds they encountered: Marshall saw the persistence of systems of oppression that continued to thwart efforts at equality, while Thomas saw the hypocrisy, particularly among liberals, of celebrating a "freedom" in which African Americans were confined to certain opinions or positions. Each critique thus lamented limitations being imposed on Black Americans, albeit from different sources and with different effects.

Thus, even as the two jurists occupied different places in the minds of many African Americans, they similarly understood the forces lined up against independent Black thought and action. In working from segregated Depression-era Baltimore and mid-century Savannah to reach the Supreme Court, they had encountered so many of those forces. And even as they reached the pinnacle of the legal profession, they faced unique levels of disrespect, binding them together beyond the fact that one succeeded the other on the Court.

No two justices have had their intelligence questioned so directly, a phenomenon reflecting historical stereotypes of African American inferiority that has resulted in the underestimation of both Marshall and Thomas. Most famously, Thomas has been ridiculed for not asking questions during oral arguments before the Court. From 2006 to 2016, Thomas did not ask a single question, and as the decade progressed, this reticence on the bench developed into a regular talking point, even becoming the justice's defining characteristic in the mind of the public (at least those outside of regular Court watchers). His 2016 question generated headlines for an otherwise obscure case. Even an apparent joke by Thomas from the bench amid the cacophony of other justices three years earlier grabbed national media attention and created a scramble to figure out precisely what Thomas said or meant.[23]

Over the years, Thomas had offered various explanations for his silence, ranging from the personal (he had always been self-conscious of his accent from his early childhood in Georgia's low country) to the jurisprudential (he felt that interruptions of lawyers by the justices were unnecessary, even rude, and that the written briefs of the parties were far more useful in adjudicating cases). "Maybe it's the Southerner in me, maybe it's the introvert in me," he said in 2012. "I think when somebody's talking, somebody ought to listen."[24]

In 2020, during the COVID-19 pandemic, the Court moved to telephonic oral arguments with justices asking questions one at a time rather than in the free-for-all that traditionally marked oral arguments. When Thomas used his time to ask questions, just as the other justices did, many news outlets focused on him: the Court's "orderly round of questioning was enough to entice Justice Clarence Thomas, who usually asks none," reported the *Washington Post* in its lead paragraph.[25]

As the Court continued telephonic arguments and Thomas continued to participate, the media continued to gawk. Lurking beneath the "silent Thomas" narrative (which might have developed into a point of pride for an individual with a tendency to stick defiantly to positions in the face of public criticism) was the suggestion that the best explanation was a relative lack of intelligence. Though more serious observers of the Court dismissed such insinuations, the perception of Thomas as an intellectual lightweight persisted.[26] In 2007, only a year into what would be the full decade without publicly asking questions, Justice Thomas gave a televised interview where the interviewer, Steve Kroft, bluntly stated the perception: "The critics will say it's because you're not smart enough or you're too insecure or you're afraid to make a fool out of yourself." Thomas laughed off the question, noting that such critics "make fools of themselves with those comments."[27]

In his own legal practice, Marshall was so conscious of the assumption that the work of African American lawyers was inferior and sloppy that he retyped entire court papers rather than submit briefs with even a single erasure, a practice that gained him a grudging respect from white judges. And while he had been exalted for his unflinching advocacy as a lawyer and trailblazing achievement as the first Black Supreme Court justice, Marshall could not escape ugly insinuations about his competency to serve on the Court.[28]

During his confirmations before the Senate—first as an appellate judge on the Second Circuit, then as solicitor general, and finally as a Supreme Court justice in 1967—there were both blatant and underhanded questions about Marshall's intelligence. Senator Strom Thurmond of South Carolina called him "stupid" on the Senate floor. Even after having achieved his seat at the top of the American legal profession, Marshall was subjected to questions of his fitness for the job. Perhaps most famously, authors Bob Woodward and Scott Armstrong portrayed Marshall as lazy and disengaged in *The Brethren*, their chronicle of the Court's 1969–1975 terms. The book, which seemed to have been drawn from sources within the famously secretive Court, shared stories of Justice Marshall watching television in his office, taking extended lunches, distracting his law clerks from their work through drawn-out off-topic conversations, and relying on his clerks to do his intellectual heavy lifting. The book asserted that some of the clerks of the other justices felt Marshall "unfit for the Court" and "not the intellectual caliber" of the liberal justices with whom he typically voted in agreement.[29]

The Brethren offered another flavor of racist insinuation of Marshall's lack of intelligence by casting him as subservient to a presumably more intelligent (and white) judicial colleague. For Marshall, the pairing was with Justice William Brennan—the authors claimed that clerks even referred to Marshall as "Mr. Justice Brennan-Marshall" due to Marshall's alleged tendency to simply follow the analysis of his liberal ally.[30] Even a generally admiring biography of Marshall noted that Brennan was the "acknowledged master" and "could almost count on Marshall's vote" in most cases.[31] Justice Lewis Powell, with whom Marshall periodically sparred in written opinions, went so far as to say that Marshall was "not ideally suited" to being a judge and simply "voted automatically with Brennan, turning over his writing chores to his clerks while he spent his days telling stories and watching daytime television."[32]

Justice Thomas, too, has been dismissed as a mere "clone" to his longtime conservative ally, Justice Antonin Scalia. As with Marshall and Brennan, Scalia and Thomas *did* often vote together: during Thomas's first thirteen years on the Court, the two voted together 92 percent of the time, the highest correlation of justices during that period. That the justices shared a judicial philosophy of originalism that insisted that the Constitution be interpreted according to the original meaning of the drafters, and a political philosophy that was largely conservative, should have made such agreement unsurprising. However, the impression that it was Scalia who led and Thomas who followed—a portrayal that Scalia himself called a "slur" that was either racist or based on political hatred—was fueled by media early in Thomas's tenure and proved difficult to shake.[33] "You look at Justice Thomas's voting record in his two terms on the Supreme Court," columnist Carl Rowan wrote in 1993, "and you see no reason to even hope that this man who succeeded Thurgood Marshall will ever be anything other than a clone of the most conservative justice, Antonin Scalia."[34] Others referred to Thomas as "Scalia's puppet" or complained that "Thomas and Scalia are one person with two votes."[35] Over time, Thomas periodically publicly bristled at the persisting depiction: "Nino Scalia is my leader and I don't move unless he tells me what to do," he sarcastically told a group in 1997.[36]

That Marshall and Thomas often agreed with their ideological allies on the Court cannot be denied: ideologically aligned justices typically *do* vote together. The alliances of Marshall with Brennan and Thomas with Scalia are marked but not historically unusual. However, uniquely for Justices Marshall and Thomas, such an alliance has been explained by their following of another justice. In both cases, the impression left was that a remarkable white "master" justice was leading an intellectually inferior Black "puppet" justice.

Such an impression overlooked jurisprudential differences that *did* exist. For example, Justice Brennan, one of the most gifted consensus build-ers in the Court's history, was often willing to compromise in cases where Marshall was not. Justice Marshall, particularly on issues of civil rights, grew into an absolutist on the Court to an extent that even frustrated Bren-nan. Similarly, Justice Thomas proved willing to take an originalist reading of the Constitution to an extreme even Justice Scalia would not.[37] Thomas openly called for reconsideration of a wide variety of seemingly established constitutional principles in solitary concurrences or dissents.[38] Even Scalia recognized that Thomas took their originalist interpretive method further, noting that "I'm an originalist and a textualist, not a nut."[39]

In both circumstances, the differences between the alleged puppets and their alleged masters reveal the Black justices to take more princi-pled positions and find greater comfort in ideological isolation than their white allies. Far from exhibiting lack of intelligence, such jurisprudential differences demonstrate contrasting strategies that merit inspection. Yet instead, the work of Justices Marshall and Thomas has been collapsed into the work of Justices Brennan and Scalia (though Justice Thomas has been more fully recognized for his role in shaping the Court's work since Scalia's 2016 death).

The accumulation of these slights on the two jurists' intelligence—Mar-shall as lazy and reliant on his clerks, Thomas as unable to form questions at oral argument, and both as sheep following intellectual masters—im-pacted the public and scholarly perceptions of the two justices. The justices are often deployed as avatars representing simple positions to score points in ideological and political conflicts rather than as serious judicial figures of complex and contrasting jurisprudence. The denigration and oversimpli-fication of Marshall and Thomas has left each vulnerable to caricature by admirers and critics alike.

Marshall was not only the NBA's "Jurist of the 20th Century," but his face graced a postage stamp in 2003, law schools and prestigious awards bear his name, and he was acknowledged as a saint by the General Conven-tion of the Episcopal Church in 2009.[40] Adoration of Thomas has taken place within a narrower community, but among conservatives, he is held up as the model justice. At a meeting of the Federalist Society, the influential conservative legal organization, Vice President Mike Pence (who had chosen Thomas to administer his oath of office) argued for the need to give "Justice Clarence Thomas another colleague on the bench who shares his courage and commitment to our nation's guiding documents."[41] For his unflinching originalism and willingness to reconsider established judicial precedents with which he disagrees, Thomas emerged as the favorite within the Trump administration more broadly, with former Thomas clerks nominated for numerous federal judgeships and other high positions.[42]

As with the contempt though, adulation of the justices can obscure the complexity of their thinking. The elevation of Thomas within the conservative legal community, for example, has tended to overlook the path through which he reached his perspectives. While Thomas has remained a devoted judicial conservative who believes forcefully in limiting the power of government, he has framed his conservatism as rooted in a unique concern about the relationship of government to African Americans. Justice Thomas has often concurred in otherwise conservative results on the basis of the impact on the Black community. For example, his writings in higher education affirmative action cases argue that race-based classifications should be disallowed (the consistent conservative position) because even where they aim to assist African Americans, they do harm (not the consistent conservative justification for that position). From that starting point, Thomas developed a militant opposition to government power that outran even Scalia. This perspective places Thomas within an extended history of Black conservatives, though few have blended their conservatism so thoroughly with a political party or had the power that comes with a seat on the Supreme Court to bring conservative positions to life. Yet, when he is celebrated by the Federalist Society or the Trump administration, this framing of Justice Thomas's conservative philosophy—which is perhaps so militant because of its connection to a professed concern with Black uplift—is deemphasized or disregarded.

Whereas Marshall's staunchest adversaries (like Thomas's) merely dismiss him, adulation can also obscure differences among allies and insulate

Marshall from examination. For example, his unyielding faith in the law in general and courts in particular often rang hollow with more radical civil rights advocates who pressed for demonstrations and boycotts and dismissed racial integration as a desired outcome. In 1961, Marshall spoke on a panel at Fisk University in Nashville that included a young John Lewis, before he became chairman of the Student Nonviolent Coordinating Committee (SNCC) and long before he was elected to Congress. Marshall argued against continuing the Freedom Rides through the South, calling them a waste and insisting that using the courts was the more effective tactic. But Lewis, who acknowledged Marshall's importance in the nation's history, contended that a mass movement, rather than a handful of lawyers in a courtroom, was required for meaningful change. "Thurgood Marshall was a good man," Lewis recalled in his memoir,

> but watching him speak on that April evening in Nashville convinced me more than ever that our revolt was as much against this nation's traditional black leadership structure as it was against racial segregation and discrimination.[43]

In this debate was a rich critique that remained throughout Marshall's career. However, the canonization of Marshall and his integrationist ideals often put the justice beyond reproach and led to a reluctance among admirers to critically engage with his jurisprudence.

The transition from Thurgood Marshall to Clarence Thomas, then, centers two justices whose work has been undervalued and oversimplified. Yet, it also centers two justices who occupy startlingly different places in the African American and American political communities more broadly. They are bound together by race and the trivializing treatment inflicted by racism. But they are also distinguished by jurisprudential and political philosophies that transcend race. To paraphrase Justice Thomas's 1998 speech to the National Bar Association, they are men, Black men, Americans. That they are men, and not women, is a noteworthy fact in itself, highlighting the absence of Black women in comparable positions of influence and impact in the legal profession. The 2022 confirmation of Justice Ketanji Brown Jackson, the Court's first Black female justice, was an important step, though one that took place fifty-five years after Marshall's own confirmation.

In those fifty-five years, Justices Marshall and Thomas have worked within and against the forces that shape the experiences of many Americans. On the Court, they have grappled with the full panoply of topics confronting Supreme Court justices, including the many that define the boundaries of citizenship in a diverse nation. Since the nation's founding, the question of citizenship has proven particularly difficult as the Court has considered the rights of African Americans. Marshall and Thomas's own experiences as citizens would be shaped by the Court's answers, particularly in school cases. Yet, once on the Court, *they* had the opportunity to do the shaping. A generation apart and drawing from their own experiences, each approached the questions of Black citizenship differently, a reality that both reflected their distinct approaches and impacted their perspectives on many other topics. Understanding how the justices came to be the Americans they became is crucial to understanding the 1991 transition that ties them together.

TWO

MR. CIVIL RIGHTS

In 1930, recently married Thurgood Marshall graduated with honors from Lincoln University and, in need of money, returned to a job as a waiter at the Gibson Island Club, a golf and sailing haven for white Protestants nearly twenty miles outside of Baltimore. He told his mother, a teacher whose great ambition for her son had driven Marshall to college, of his plan to attend law school, and Norma Marshall hoped he would attend the University of Maryland. The school, however, was closed to Black students: it had not admitted a Black law student since the 1890s. Understanding this reality, even if seething about it, Marshall never applied to the University of Maryland. Instead, he commuted to law school at Howard University in Washington, DC, and graduated at the top of his class in 1933.[1]

Rejecting an opportunity to study for a year at Harvard, Marshall entered private legal practice determined to find financial stability in the midst of the Great Depression. He also wanted to disprove the lie about the abilities of African Americans that underlay their exclusion from the University of Maryland's law school. He took on more legal work for the NAACP, and, perhaps with the thought of getting even in mind, Marshall brought a potential case to Charles Hamilton Houston, his mentor and the dean of Howard Law. In 1935, Marshall convinced Donald Murray, a Baltimore resident and graduate of Amherst College, to apply to the Maryland law school. When Murray was rejected on account of his race—the same policy that discouraged Marshall from even applying—Marshall, with financial support from the NAACP, served as his lead lawyer.

In *Murray v. Pearson*, the state argued that Murray would get an equal education at Princess Anne Academy or that the state would pay for him to attend school outside of Maryland since there was no law school for Black students within the state. Marshall argued that neither of these options would provide the "equal" education required by the Fourteenth Amendment and the "separate, but equal" obligation imposed by the Supreme Court in *Plessy v. Ferguson* in 1896. Surprisingly, the judge agreed with Marshall and ordered that the University of Maryland law school admit Murray, a historic victory that set the stage for graduate school desegregation suits that would eventually build the foundation for *Brown v. Board of Education* nearly two decades later. That such a trajectory began by defeating the University of Maryland law school was particularly satisfying for Marshall, who later remembered that the first thing he wanted to do after he graduated from Howard was "get even with Maryland for not letting me go to its law school."[2] Here was Thurgood Marshall, in his earliest professional days, previewing what would be his life's work: using his own exclusion as fuel for a fight that would force institutions to confront the chasm between professed ideals and an unequal reality. His vision of Black citizenship demanded equality.

FROM BALTIMORE TO HOWARD

At the turn into the twentieth century, Baltimore sat in that ambiguous space that was neither North nor South. Connected to the metropolises of the Northeast by rail, it served as a common stop during the early waves of the Great Migration of African Americans from the South. But, like the South, Baltimore long had a sizable Black population, including the nation's largest population of free African Americans prior to the Civil War. The size and longevity of the Black population enabled measures of stability, if not prosperity, for Black Baltimoreans that would have been unimaginable in the South. Yet there were regular local reminders of the racism that permeated the nation. In 1899, only three years after the Supreme Court declared racial segregation to be constitutional in *Plessy v. Ferguson*, Democrats gained political control in Baltimore with the slogan, "This Is a White Man's City." In an increasingly oppressive local climate, Blacks in Baltimore were among the first to organize politically to respond to racial hostility, which was often triggered by wealthier African Americans entering historically white neighborhoods. An activist group from Baltimore, the Brotherhood of Liberty, was among those who gathered to form the NAACP in 1909, and the Baltimore branch was the NAACP's second.[3]

Thurgood Marshall had deep roots in the Baltimore area; at the time of the Civil War, all four of his grandparents lived in or near Baltimore, and three were free. His maternal grandfather, Isaiah Williams, served the Union in the war as a captain's steward, and his maternal grandmother, Mary Fossett, was free and literate and taught in a Black private school in the decade after the war. Williams served in the navy until 1869 and married Fossett in 1872. The couple owned a house in a neighborhood with many Black families, but also immigrants from Ireland, Russia, and Germany. Williams operated a successful grocery out of his basement and was well known in the local Republican Party; he even confronted white city officials over police brutality and lobbied for public schools for Black children. The couple's daughter—Norma Arica Williams, Marshall's mother—was born in 1885.[4]

Annie Robinson, Marshall's paternal grandmother, was very light-skinned and was the daughter of a housekeeper for a wealthy white family. Only Marshall's paternal grandfather, from whom he partially inherited a name, Thorney Good Marshall, was enslaved at the time of the Civil War. During the war, however, Thorney Good escaped and lived as a free Black Baltimorean. After the war, Thorney Good enlisted in the army and served on the western frontier of Texas, before becoming ill and returning to Baltimore to wait tables. In 1879, he married Annie Robinson, and the couple had their first son, William Canfield Marshall, Thurgood Marshall's father. Like the Williams family, Thorney Good Marshall also operated a basement grocery in Baltimore, and it is likely that the two men knew each other.[5]

Willie Marshall was a "wild boy" who did not continue formal schooling past elementary school, though he could read. Norma Williams, the daughter of a schoolteacher and the younger sister of one of the first Black teachers in the Black public schools, graduated from "Colored High" in 1904 and enrolled at Coppin State Teachers College. She had yet to graduate when she married Willie Marshall, who worked as a sleeping car porter, in 1905. She gave birth to the couple's first son, William Aubrey Marshall, that same year, but remained in school and graduated. On July 2, 1908, Norma and Willie Marshall had their second child, Thoroughgood. Perhaps already evincing a tendency to alter the world in which he found himself, the child changed his own name to Thurgood before his sixth birthday, later claiming that his given name was simply "too damn long."[6]

Although the shadow of Jim Crow lurked over virtually all elements of African American life through the first half of the twentieth century, young Thurgood Marshall entered elementary school in Baltimore with some relative advantages over Black students elsewhere. As the son, grandson, and nephew of educators, he was surrounded by a family for whom education was central. Willie Marshall, who had not continued past elementary school, likewise encouraged his sons to achieve in school, even threatening them not to bring home poor grades. Because Willie was often away as a railroad porter, the family moved in with Thurgood's uncle, Fearless Mentor. And Uncle Fee, as the boys called him, similarly made education a high priority.[7]

Thurgood also did not grow up as vulnerable as many other African Americans of the same generation. Although his family was by no means wealthy, the adults in his life were regularly employed, and the family enjoyed relative economic stability. Uncle Fee's home on Division Street was situated in a Black, middle-class neighborhood of Old West Baltimore where families had steady work. Further, in Baltimore more broadly, Thurgood was raised in a Black community with at least some modicum of local power; they did not live in constant fear of retribution from all white people. Racism and racial discrimination were ever present, but Marshall experienced non-hostile contact with white Baltimoreans. Uncle Fee's next-door neighbors, the Hales, were Jewish and gave Thurgood his first job delivering groceries alongside Sammy Hale, his white neighbor. On occasion, the Hales joined Thurgood's family at Uncle Fee's home for dinner.[8]

However, Marshall's entire educational experience was a segregated one. He attended elementary school at Public School 103, several blocks from Uncle Fee's home. The school, a two-story red brick structure with twelve classrooms, had been built for white students in 1877, but was converted into a school for Black students in 1911, only a few years before Marshall enrolled. Although Black families took great pride in Public School 103, Baltimore's education leaders did not prioritize Black education. The school year was a month shorter for Black students to accommodate the agricultural calendar, and school commissioner Richard Biggs expressed racist skepticism at the entire enterprise of Black education, arguing that the city should "Stop at once the so-called high education that unfits Negroes for the lives that they are to lead and which makes them desire things they will never be able to reach."[9]

In 1921, Marshall began ninth grade at Colored High, which had opened in 1883 as Baltimore's first public high school for Black students and remained the only such school until the 1930s. The school had no library, cafeteria, or gymnasium when Marshall arrived, and it was the subject of a decades-long push for improvements by local Black community and educational groups. The campaign for a new structure intensified when enrollment doubled between 1920 and 1922, and the principal was forced to hold half-day sessions, each for half the student body, to address the overcrowding. The new facility would be opened in 1925, just after Marshall graduated.[10]

Throughout his schooling in Baltimore, Thurgood Marshall's gregarious, loose personality enabled him to get along with all sorts of people and earned him a reputation as a "cutup and prankster." However, his skill at storytelling also made him an excellent debater, and he led the school's debating team from his first year, being elected captain as a freshman. Marshall seemed to be following his brother Aubrey, a student at Lincoln University, on the path toward college, but Willie Marshall had lost his job in 1924 after falling ill, and it was unclear if the family could afford to have two children enrolled in college. Thurgood graduated a semester early to take up a job as a dining car waiter to earn money for his tuition and in the fall of 1925 enrolled at Lincoln. On his college application, he answered a question about his plans for his life's work with a single word: lawyer.[11]

Lincoln University was opened in rural Pennsylvania by a Presbyterian minister and his Quaker wife in 1854 to provide a higher education opportunity for African American men. Opening prior to the Civil War, it was among the oldest historically Black colleges and universities (HBCUs) in the United States. Renamed Lincoln in 1866 after the slain president, the school was known as the Black Princeton and attracted Black students from across the country. When Thurgood Marshall enrolled, the university served 285 male students. Marshall thrived at Lincoln. As at Colored High, his storytelling and antics made him a popular figure on campus, and he joined Alpha Phi Alpha, providing another arena for his often edgy playfulness. He continued to excel in debating and earned a spot on the university's varsity debating team as a freshman; he went on to be one of the principal debaters for a team that traveled throughout the country.[12]

During his junior year, Marshall found himself in a campus debate with classmate Langston Hughes. Though all of the students at Lincoln were Black, the school's faculty was all white. Hughes pushed for the hiring of Black faculty members and put the question to a campus vote. Marshall, however, opposed integrating the faculty and led the opposition to Hughes's efforts, eventually succeeding when a majority of Lincoln students voted to maintain the all-white faculty. The debate caught the attention of scholar W. E. B. Du Bois, who wrote in the NAACP's newsletter, *The Crisis*, that the vote was a "most astonishing blow." However, Hughes and others continued to push Marshall on the matter as, according to one biographer, Marshall first began to think seriously about Jim Crow practices. After an incident in which Marshall and others refused an order to move to the "colored" balcony at a movie theater, Marshall's thinking began to shift. After Hughes graduated, Marshall led the push for a second referendum, and the result was reversed; the first Black faculty member was hired a year later.[13]

This shift in Marshall was part of a broader maturation: as a senior, he remained sociable but grew increasingly serious. During his senior year, he met Vivian "Buster" Burey, a student at the University of Pennsylvania, and the two were married in 1929, while Marshall was completing his final year at Lincoln. He graduated with honors in January 1930, facing the reality that the University of Maryland would not admit a Black student to its law school. He spent the spring and summer back in Baltimore earning money to pay for law school at Howard University, but Norma Marshall still had to pawn her wedding and engagement rings for her son to afford law school. For Marshall, Howard was relatively close, relatively inexpensive, and open to Black students. But it was unaccredited and had a poor reputation in the broader, majority white, legal community. As Marshall entered Howard's law school in 1930, another individual on campus was working diligently to change that.[14]

CHARLES HAMILTON HOUSTON AND THE ORIGINS OF A MISSION

In 1930, Charles Hamilton Houston was arguably the most highly educated African American lawyer in the United States. He had a law degree from Harvard and had been the first Black student to serve as an editor on the *Harvard Law Review*. He had earned a fellowship to study law at the University of Madrid before moving to Washington, DC, to practice law. There, Houston was recruited by Mordecai Johnson, the first Black president of Howard University, to teach at and eventually transform Howard's law school. At the time, Howard's part-time night program had been a training ground for many Black lawyers who could not afford to be full-time students. Houston's own father graduated from Howard's night program while working as a high school principal, and the law school, established in 1869, had trained nearly three-fourths of the nation's practicing Black lawyers.[15] But Houston joined the faculty with a sense of mission to transform Howard into a fully accredited institution that could overcome the stigma that part-time programs faced. In 1929, he was appointed vice dean of the school's day program, and he quickly sought to infuse his sense that the school should make itself a more efficient training school to fulfill the need for "capable and socially alert Negro lawyers."[16] According to Houston, "Experience has proved that the average white lawyer, especially in the South, cannot be relied upon to wage an uncompromising fight for equal rights for Negroes."[17] Houston pushed Johnson and the university's leadership to move assertively toward accreditation and lobbied for controversial changes, including firing some teachers, raising admission standards, and, most contentiously, eliminating the night program.

Thurgood Marshall and approximately three dozen other students arrived amid Houston's changes and quickly understood that Houston intended there to be great rigor in Howard's law program. Half the students had flunked out by the end of the first year, and by graduation in 1933, only Marshall and five others remained. But Houston's investments were paying dividends; during Marshall's second year, the school won accreditation from both the American Bar Association and Association of American Law Schools.[18]

Thurgood Marshall and Charlie Houston were an unlikely pair. Even the increasingly serious Marshall of his law school years loved to tell stories and laugh. Charles Hamilton Houston's service as an army lieutenant in World War I not only exposed him to the world beyond Washington, DC, but also chiseled a no-nonsense personality that struck fear in Howard's students. Marshall—who lived in Baltimore during law school with his wife Buster, his parents, and his brother and his wife—commuted to Depression-era Washington more aware of poverty than at any other point in his life. His family had been struggling to ensure the funds to pay his tuition at Lincoln and now at Howard, and he was also responsible for providing for Buster. He feared what would happen to him financially if he did not become a lawyer, and he saw in Houston and other Black faculty members a path to challenging work and financial security. This confluence of personal circumstances, an economically reeling nation, and a law school dean hell-bent on molding not only lawyers but "social engineers," transformed Marshall.[19]

Admiring his dean's devotion to excellence and contempt for mediocrity, "in Houston's presence, Marshall sparked like a match touched to flame."[20] By Marshall's third year, Houston added an apprenticeship to the remaining students' education, allowing them to work with him on the murder trial of George Crawford, a Black man accused of killing two white women in Virginia. Seeing Houston do this work up close exposed Marshall to two complementary elements that excited him. First, Marshall for the first time experienced the crucible of a trial, one where an individual's very life was at stake. He found a real-world outlet for the storytelling and argumentation skills that made him such a successful debater. And while trial work may have been compelling to Marshall no matter what the topic, in the Crawford trial Marshall witnessed Houston himself exemplifying the lawyer's responsibility for pushing social change. When a Black man's life was on the line, Marshall must have concluded, it was up to the skill of a lawyer to thwart injustice. George Crawford was ultimately convicted but was spared the death penalty: in 1930s Virginia, Marshall looked back on this outcome as a victory because "normally they [white authorities in Virginia] were hanging them [Black defendants]."[21]

In June 1933, Thurgood Marshall graduated at the top of his class of now six students from Howard University law school, having completed his years of formal schooling during Jim Crow segregation and the depths of the Great Depression. He spurned an opportunity for post-graduate work at Harvard and, after another summer of work as a waiter at Gibson Island, he was prepared to open his law practice and start supporting himself and Buster. Before he began, however, Dean Houston had one final lesson to teach his top pupil. Even while serving as Howard's law school dean, Houston had been providing legal services to the NAACP—indeed, it was this affiliation that had led to his involvement in the George Crawford case. In

1933, he was commissioned to embark on a fact-finding trip through the South, examining the state of schools for Black children, schools that were legally supposed to be "equal" to those for white children. Houston enticed Marshall to join him.

In 1930, the NAACP received a grant to develop a strategy for utilizing litigation to challenge the dual school systems of the South and aimed to document cases of school inequality to provide courts with evidence of the failure of *Plessy's* "separate but equal" mandate. In 1933, Houston and Marshall set out from Washington, DC, to gather that evidence. With the constant threat of harassment—or worse—along the roads of the South and lodging and eating with local families since few motels or restaurants would serve Black clientele, the two men rode through the Carolinas, Georgia, Alabama, and Mississippi, en route to New Orleans. They documented manifest inequality in a lawyerly way, noting the condition of Black school buildings and counting supplies available to Black students—or, more often, the lack thereof. In addition, they took note of the meager pay of Black school employees and the overcrowding experienced by Black students. This was Marshall's first exposure to the racial deprivation of the Deep South and, amid segregation and the oppressive racial hierarchy, coupled with the Depression, he found poverty like he had never seen. He returned to Baltimore with a kernel of an idea of the role he might play fulfilling his mentor's charge of using his law degree to become a social engineer.[22]

By 1934, Charles Houston had taken a leave of absence from Howard to lead the NAACP's legal fight. In his initial report in this new position, he laid out a plan that would remain remarkably consistent over two decades and that would greatly influence the trajectory of Thurgood Marshall. Houston urged that the campaign prioritize segregated education, rather than segregated transportation, because of education's effect on an entire generation. Further, he recognized the limitations of isolated suits: he envisioned a "foundation" of legal work that would include research, cases, and community involvement, a basis that would allow localities to build upon successes elsewhere.

Perhaps most crucially, Houston recommended that the work begin within the existing constitutional command of separate but equal: rather than confronting segregation head on, Houston recommended documenting inequality, as he and Marshall had done, before pushing courts to impose genuine equality. Such a strategy would result in moves toward equalization and could even make segregation intolerably expensive. To further this work, Houston invited Marshall to join him on additional documentation tours through the South; all the while, Houston was impressing upon Marshall his ultimate strategy that only integration could ensure that Black children would receive equal education.[23] "Equality of education is not enough," Houston argued. "No segregation operates fairly on a minority group unless it is a dominant minority. . . . The American Negro is not a dominant minority; therefore he must fight for complete elimination of segregation as his ultimate goal."[24]

Over the next two decades, a growing contingent of lawyers, including Marshall, would put Houston's plan into practice. There were many practical, political, and social impediments, including debate within the Black community and among advocates for civil rights about the most appropriate way to push for equality for African Americans. But the primary constitutional impediment was the 1896 *Plessy v. Ferguson* decision, which had given constitutional license to states to mandate racial segregation, a license southern states were quick to utilize, flagrantly ignoring the "equal" in "separate, but equal." In *Plessy*, Homer Plessy challenged the constitutionality of a Louisiana law requiring racial separation in the state's railcars only to have the Supreme Court, with Justice Henry Brown writing for a 7–1 majority, summarily reject his claims. The Court offered a narrow reading of the reach of the Fourteenth Amendment, noting that "it could not have been intended to abolish distinctions based upon color" or "a commingling of the two races upon terms unsatisfactory to either." Indeed, the Court thought the "underlying fallacy" of Plessy's case to be the assumption that segregation stamped the colored race with a badge of inferiority. "If this be so," the Court wrote, "it is not by reason of anything found in the act, but solely because the colored race chooses to put that construction upon it."[25]

The Court patently rejected the idea that law could have anything to say about social inequality. "Legislation is powerless to eradicate racial instincts or to abolish distinctions based upon physical differences, and the attempt to do so can only result in accentuating the difficulties of the present situation," Justice Brown asserted. "If one race be inferior to the other socially, the Constitution of the United States cannot put them on the same plane."[26]

Charles Hamilton Houston held a different vision of what the Constitution could accomplish, one that he would impart to Thurgood Marshall and that the future justice would hold onto throughout his career. In confronting *Plessy*, Houston faced a choice. He might use *Plessy*'s mandate of equality to push for equalization, reducing the gross disparities facing Black and white citizens. Given the facts available through the first half of the twentieth century, establishing inequality in any individual context would not have been difficult. But this path required a case-by-case approach since a win in one unequal school district did not eliminate the need to prove inequality in others. A second strategy was to confront segregation head-on, to argue, as Homer Plessy had, that the laws themselves caused a situation that could never truly be equal. This strategy held the potential for a broad rejection of state-sponsored segregation but carried a great risk that the Supreme Court might simply affirm the *Plessy* separate-but-equal standard and set the constitutional argument back another generation.

During the two decades between when Charles Hamilton Houston took over as special counsel for the NAACP in 1935 and the Supreme Court's decision in *Brown v. Board of Education* in 1954, the internal debate about the relative merits of these strategies was robust, and Houston sought to pursue them in parallel. Early cases, such as Thurgood Marshall's revenge against the University of Maryland law school, demonstrated that even the equalization strategy—Donald Murray's suit was based on the fact that there was no equivalent law school opportunity for African

Americans in Maryland—could lead to integration. Where states were not providing corresponding options for Black students or where equalization and duplication might prove prohibitively expensive, Black students might simply be admitted to formerly white institutions. The *Murray* case achieved this outcome without establishing a broader legal precedent, but the NAACP team continued to use state university graduate schools as a forum for undoing *Plessy*.

In 1938, two years after *Murray,* the Supreme Court cited and quoted the Maryland decision in holding that the state of Missouri's failure to provide a law school for Black students was unconstitutional. A decade later, with World War II in between, the Court repeated this result in Oklahoma, ordering the state to admit an African American student, Ada Sipuel, because of its failure to provide a law school for Black students. Two years later, the Court confronted the law schools of Texas, where the state, seeing the writing on the wall, had taken steps to establish a law school for Black students. In *Sweatt v. Painter,* however, the Court emphasized that the equality demanded by *Plessy* and the equal protection clause included intangible factors—like reputation of the faculty, experience of the administration, position and influence of the alumni, standing in the community, traditions, and prestige. "It is difficult to believe," the Court concluded, "that one who had a free choice between these law schools would consider the question close."[27]

In the law school cases, Houston and Marshall had convinced the Court to chip away at the denial of full Black citizenship through legalized racial segregation. In a half century since *Plessy*, the nation's tolerance for openly racist legislation had decreased during two world wars in which African Americans fought, the Great Depression in which all Americans suffered, and a massive migration of African Americans fleeing the degradations of the South. Still, the Court took pains to not directly overrule *Plessy*'s separate but equal doctrine in the law school cases.

But the NAACP legal team was bringing cases that were making that avoidance increasingly unsustainable. Marshall's colleague Robert Carter had argued another graduate school case, in which a Black student, George

McLaurin, argued that forcing him to sit in separate rows in his University of Oklahoma classrooms violated the Constitution. *McLaurin v. Regents of the University of Oklahoma* thus presented a Black plaintiff already admitted to the school. The NAACP lawyers were pushing the Court to confront the segregation question without the release valve of equalization, but the Court remained unwilling to overturn *Plessy* even as it sided with *McLaurin*.[28]

Still, the Court signaled a far different understanding of what law might do in terms of social equality. Whereas *Plessy* denied that laws could affect social inequalities, the *McLaurin* Court asserted that state laws prohibiting the intellectual commingling of students provided state sanction to individual prejudices. Removing the restrictions on McLaurin's freedom to sit and eat with other students might not eliminate all of society's prejudices, the Court explained, "But at the very least, the state will not be depriving appellant of the opportunity to secure acceptance by his fellow students on his own merits." The Court offered a new standard—the Fourteenth Amendment required neutrality in treatment based on race—that set the stage for moving the legal fight from graduate schools to the thousands of elementary and secondary schools in the nation. Even as Thurgood Marshall, Robert Carter, and others were pushing *Sweatt* and *McLaurin* toward the Supreme Court, they had simultaneously been laying the foundation for that transition.[29]

THREE

SEPARATE AND UNEQUAL

If Thurgood Marshall's career had ended on May 17, 1954, he would still stand in the annals of American history. That he continued to lead the NAACP Legal Defense Fund through his 1961 appointment to the U.S. Court of Appeals for the Second Circuit—then became the nation's first African American solicitor general, serving as the federal government's top lawyer at the Supreme Court from 1965 to 1967 prior to twenty-four years as a justice himself—only adds additional lines to the biography of one of the nation's most impactful lawyers. But Marshall's legend was confirmed for the role he played in pushing the Supreme Court toward its monumental 1954 decision in *Brown v. Board of Education*.

Few, if any, Supreme Court decisions have had as wide an impact on the nation's social and political fabric as *Brown*. Legally, it corrected a reading of the Constitution's equal protection clause that had permitted legalized racial apartheid under a false pretense of equal treatment. But the legal impact paled in comparison to the broader revolution in the meaning of American citizenship that followed in its wake. In no other context has an institution that had been used to create and protect inequality been transformed into the primary vehicle for overcoming that very same inequality. Yet, this is what *Brown* did to the American school system, an institution deemed vital to creating a citizenry for the nation as far back as the days of Thomas Jefferson.

And *Brown*'s meaning has evolved so that even seventy years later, Americans continue to confront and debate its legacy in the nation's schools, neighborhoods, and everywhere else diverse groups of Americans interact with one another. This is because conversations about *Brown*, including the early work that led to the decision and the decades of effort to implement it, strike to the very core of what it means to be an American. Within the *Brown* story and its still emerging legal, social, and political repercussions is the story of American citizenship. So many of the nation's most pressing questions have been filtered into the story of school segregation, desegregation, and integration—questions that are not limited to education or to race, but often include both.

But while *Brown* and its legacy animate foundational American questions, they also have impacted countless individual American lives. Multiple generations of schoolchildren have learned in an educational landscape molded by *Brown*. The geography of virtually every American city—where people live, where development occurs, where highways are built—has been shaped by *Brown*'s legacy. Political debates about topics as varied as how powerful the federal government ought to be and whether diversity is a goal worth pursuing are built on arguments crafted through *Brown*'s prism. And the persistent struggles over relative social status and power in a multiracial democracy continue to draw on feelings and ideologies forged in *Brown*'s wake.

As a key player in the team that pursued the consolidated cases that became known as *Brown v. Board of Education*, Thurgood Marshall assured that the legacy of his work would generate ripples for generations. And of those consolidated cases, the one Marshall was most directly involved with from its earliest stages all the way to the Supreme Court began in rural Clarendon County, South Carolina.

CONFRONTING SEGREGATION IN SOUTH CAROLINA

According to historian Richard Kluger, "if you had set out to find the place in America in the year 1947 where life among black folk had changed least since the end of slavery, Clarendon County is where you might have come." Clarendon County was cotton country, 600 square miles along the plain of South Carolina between the low country along the Atlantic to the east and the Piedmont to the west. Seventy percent of Clarendon County's 30,000 residents were African American—the largest proportion in the state—though as much as 85 percent of the land was owned by white residents. Black residents typically either rented farmland and worked it or sharecropped, providing the labor on the acres of white-owned farms in exchange for a place to live and a portion of the proceeds. These arrangements resulted in high levels of rural poverty and strong incentives for young African Americans to work in the fields rather than stay in school. Very few Black students attended school beyond the fourth grade.[1]

The relative priority of the education of Black students could also be seen within the county's system of schools, which was governed by an exclusively white administration and board. In 1950, there were 73 schools serving approximately 9,000 Clarendon County students; 61 of those schools served the county's 6,500 Black students, but most were shanties with only one or two teachers. The cumulative value of those 61 schools totaled $194,575, while the value of the 12 schools for the county's 2,375 white students was $673,850. In 1949–50, the county spent more than four times as much per white student as it did for Black students ($179 versus $43), and white teachers were paid two-thirds more than Black teachers. And while these inequalities flagrantly violated the idea of separate but equal endorsed by the Supreme Court, Clarendon County's Black residents did not begin what would become a revolutionary struggle against segregation asking for anything revolutionary. The county had thirty school buses for white students and none for Black students. So it was that in early 1947 Reverend J. A. DeLaine, a teacher at one of the county's schools for African Americans, led the effort to petition for transportation to be provided to enable Black students to better access the schools of Clarendon County.[2]

An initial case, *Pearson v. County Board of Education,* was filed in March 1948. The plaintiff—Levi Pearson, a parent of three Clarendon County students—was represented by Harold Boulware—a lawyer in Columbia, SC, and a 1940 graduate of Howard University's law school who had already argued for pay equalization for Black teachers in South Carolina—and another Howard law graduate, Thurgood Marshall. Boulware was set to handle the case, though Marshall's NAACP offices offered suggestions based on what they had learned in similar cases elsewhere. When the Pearson case was dismissed for lack of standing, Marshall led a meeting in Columbia with national and state NAACP leaders, including Rev. DeLaine, in March 1949. Marshall charged the group with finding twenty plaintiffs and suggested that in a new case, the plaintiffs not merely settle for buses; rather, it was time to demand truly equal treatment.[3]

Given the economic and political vulnerability of Clarendon County's African American residents and the retaliation they would likely face from local white residents, it may have seemed difficult to find potential plaintiffs. But local enthusiasm for fighting inequality had been sparked, and by November 1949, Rev. DeLaine had found the twenty plaintiffs. The first name on the complaint was that of Harry Briggs, a navy veteran with five children who worked pumping gas and repairing tires at a local service station. The named defendant was R. W. Elliott, chairman of the county's board of trustees. And thus, *Briggs v. Elliott* was born.[4]

As initial hearings approached in the *Briggs* case and others, Thurgood Marshall and the NAACP legal team had reached a crossroads. The graduate school cases had not overturned *Plessy,* but they had made clear that equalization required the absolute equality of treatment of students (*McLaurin*) and, where that was not possible, admission of Black students into formerly white institutions (the law school cases). As focus shifted to the public schools, there were many who felt that pursuing further equalization provided the best way to enhance educational opportunities for Black students. Others, such as attorney James Nabrit, who was in the midst of

bringing a school desegregation case in the District of Columbia, advocated for an immediate frontal attack on segregation laws themselves—the
"segregation per se" strategy.

Marshall sought a balance between the two strategies in order to maximize the chances of success, arguing both that schools were demonstrably unequal and that, even if schools were equal, the racial separation of
students violated the Fourteenth Amendment. Still, at the first hearing in
Briggs v. Elliott in November 1950, Marshall hedged. The racial inequalities in the Clarendon County schools were so glaring that winning on
equalization would have been relatively easy. Challenging the state's school
segregation laws would almost ensure defeat, delaying any remedy for the
students of Clarendon County until an appeal to the Supreme Court. And
a victory at the nation's highest court was far from certain. It was a far
safer strategy, and more likely to achieve faster results for the students, to
demand equalization.[5]

Yet, the district court judge in *Briggs*, Judge Waties Waring, urged Marshall to directly challenge South Carolina's school segregation law. Judge
Waring, who had decided in Marshall's favor in previous cases, understood
that the heart of the issue was whether separation of students by race was
consistent with the Fourteenth Amendment. Marshall agreed to amend
his argument to attack segregation head-on, but he still confronted the
problem of how to prove that it was separation—and not just inequality—
that was harming Black students. The lawyers would be forced to disprove
the *Plessy* Court's assertion that nothing in the laws of segregation implied
racial inferiority or stamped African Americans with a badge of servitude.
Marshall had the life experience to know that wasn't true: he had once felt
that Black faculty members were inferior when he initially voted to keep
the Lincoln University faculty all white, and he had felt the stigma of exclusion from the University of Maryland's law school. But knowing would
not be enough. Marshall and the NAACP lawyers would have to prove
that stigma existed.

Marshall's lieutenant Robert Carter took on the job of coming up with
a persuasive way to demonstrate the harm to children that flowed from

racial segregation itself, not just from being provided unequal facilities or supplies. In his search, Carter came across research on Black schoolchildren in Philadelphia by Otto Klineberg that studied many students who had moved to Philadelphia during the Great Migration. The study seemed to indicate that Black students' achievement improved as they escaped the legally segregated South. Klineberg put Carter in touch with an African American social psychologist in New York who, along with his wife, was attempting to demonstrate the psychological impact of racism on young African Americans.[6]

Kenneth and Mamie Clark had developed several techniques for such proof, the most famous of which would become known as the "doll test." Using a pair of brown and a pair of pink dolls, the Clarks asked children a series of questions to demonstrate how segregation caused African American children to feel: give me the doll that is the nice doll; give me the doll that looks bad; give me the doll you like to play with. Carter felt that the Clarks could establish that damage was done by school segregation, though Kenneth Clark told him that it was not possible to isolate the effects of school segregation from the effects of generalized social prejudice. Clark himself was not the only skeptic. As Robert Carter remembered, "The proposed use of social scientists' testimony came under fierce attack from the outset."[7] There was a sense among some within the NAACP camp that the studies were without substance. Even several other psychologists rejected Carter's invitations to testify amid their own doubts about the wisdom or validity of utilizing such testimony. But Marshall concluded that it was a path worth pursuing, and three weeks before the *Briggs* trial was to begin in May 1951, Marshall and Carter rode a train to South Carolina accompanied by Kenneth Clark and his dolls.[8]

In order to make Clark's testimony more convincing, Carter arranged for him to perform the doll study on Black students in Clarendon County. Sixteen children were randomly selected from the Scott's Branch school: all correctly identified the "white" and "colored" doll; ten of the sixteen Black children preferred the pink doll, and eleven said the brown doll looked bad. These responses matched the ratios in the previous studies

Clark had performed with his wife. Speaking generally about the doll research, Clark recalled that "what was surprising was the degree to which the children suffered from self-rejection, with its truncating effect on their personalities, and the earliness of the corrosive awareness of color."[9] Here was evidence from African Americans at a young age of the impact of the cruelty of racism and its impact on young psyches. As Marshall and Carter prepared for the trial—the only one of the four *Brown* cases that Marshall would participate in directly—they felt the social science research might provide the proof they needed to confront segregation head-on.[10]

The white leaders of South Carolina, however, felt that the case should more properly be argued on the question of equalization, and in the months between the initial *Briggs* hearing in November 1950 and the trial in May 1951, the state legislature passed an ambitious school program, including new funds to pay for school construction, bus transportation, and higher teachers' salaries that would be equal for both Black and white teachers. The new governor, James Byrnes, had even said in his inaugural address that "It is our duty to provide for the races substantial equality in school facilities. We should do it because it is right."[11] The first funds were to go to improving the schools for Black students in Clarendon County. Such efforts at equalization were not uncommon when states faced desegregation lawsuits; the strategy was that true equalization would protect the validity of *Plessy* in practice and allay any need for direct constitutional challenges to segregation. While this could also bring short-term improvements for Black students, it did so without rooting out the racist foundations underlying school segregation.

However, while Governor Byrnes was committed to equalization "because it is right," he also made clear that if the issue transformed into a question of ending racial segregation, he would simply ask the state legislature to shut down the state's schools. In part to avoid such a transformation of the *Briggs* case, on the eve of trial, the governor endorsed the strategy of the school district's attorney to simply concede that the schools for Black students in Clarendon County were not equal and emphasize that steps were already being taken to remedy the inequality.[12]

At the trial on May 28, 1951, the courtroom in Charleston was full. Robert Carter remembered that "the trial was of intense interest because of its attack on school segregation and because spectators would have the opportunity to see the legendary Thurgood Marshall in action. He did not disappoint."[13] As he had learned to do in countless other trials in hostile southern courtrooms, Marshall modified the mild upper southern accent of his Baltimore roots to become more pronounced and akin to the drawl of Georgia or Alabama. Regarding the state's admission of inequality, Marshall felt it had "no bearing on this litigation at this stage. I think it is an effort to prevent the plaintiffs in this case from developing their case."[14]

Though Marshall handled the opening and several early witnesses, it was Robert Carter who led the testimony of the social science experts, including Kenneth Clark, bringing to life the strategy he had advocated for to prove that school segregation caused feelings of inferiority in Black students. Clark testified that segregation created "basic feelings of inferiority" in children and that

> these children in Clarendon County, like other human beings who are subjected to an obviously inferior status in the society in which they live, have been definitely harmed in the development of their personalities.[15]

In time, the validity of Clark's methods and conclusions would receive great scrutiny, but at the *Briggs* trial, his testimony and that of the other social scientists on the witness stand created a record of the stigma experienced by African American children.

Marshall rose to summarize the plaintiffs' case and the thrust of the arguments Charles Hamilton Houston had developed all those years before:

> In South Carolina, you have admitted inferiority of Negro schools. All your state officials are white. All your school officials are white. It is admitted. That's not just segregation. It's exclusion from the group that runs everything. The Negro child is made to go to an inferior school; he is branded in his mind as inferior. This sets up a roadblock in his mind

which prevents his ever feeling he is equal. You can teach such a child the Constitution, anthropology, and citizenship, but he knows it isn't true.[16]

Marshall was emphasizing the disconnect between the nation's ideals as embodied in the Constitution and its reality as experienced by Clarendon County's Black children. Like Houston, Marshall had faith that the law, if faithfully applied, could bridge that gap, and he closed his argument with an unambiguous demand: "There is no relief for the Negro children of Clarendon County except to be permitted to attend existing and superior white schools."[17]

Despite Marshall's efforts, the weight of the *Plessy* precedent and the scope of what Marshall was asking the district court to do—to declare an entire battery of racial segregation codes unconstitutional—proved too much to overcome. In a 2–1 decision with Judge Waring dissenting, the district court echoed arguments used to justify segregation and foreshadowed positions Marshall would confront across decades. Writing for the court, Judge John Parker concluded that as long as equality was provided, the question of segregation was best left to state legislatures and "in no field is this right of the several states [of local self-government] more clearly recognized than in that of public education." Local control was necessary, Parker wrote, to ensure that public education would maintain the support of the people. Federal courts, in particular,

> would be going far outside their constitutional function were they to attempt to prescribe educational policies for the states in such matters, however desirable such policies might be in the opinion of some sociologists or educators.[18]

Judge Parker was not persuaded that the testimony of Kenneth Clark and the other social scientists Robert Carter had assembled clearly established that segregation itself denied equal protection of the laws. Indeed, Parker cited the possibility that "mixed schools" might result in racial friction and thus be disadvantageous for African American children. The admitted and undeniable inequality of schools in Clarendon County came from unequal administration by the state rather than any flaw in the law, Parker found, and he issued an injunction requiring the state to promptly provide equal facilities and to report back six months later.[19]

The NAACP appealed the *Briggs* decision to the Supreme Court, but the Court provided the lower court the opportunity to consider additional information about the state's equalization efforts before it would hear the case. In March 1952, Judge Parker issued a follow-up decision noting the state's good faith in its efforts "to equalize conditions as rapidly as was humanly possible." The NAACP again appealed, and the Supreme Court docketed the *Briggs* case for its 1952–53 term. By that time, the Court had also docketed another school desegregation case that would be listed first when the cases were consolidated for hearing in December 1952. That case came from Kansas, and though the lower court in *Brown v. Board of Education of Topeka* had also refused the NAACP's requests to declare segregation itself unconstitutional, it had looked more favorably upon the social science evidence Carter had marshaled. Crucially, that court had made a factual finding that

> Segregation of white and colored children in public schools has a detrimental effect upon the colored children. The impact is greater when it has the sanction of law, for the policy of separating the races is usually interpreted as denoting the inferiority of the negro group.[20]

This was a finding that directly refuted the *Plessy* assertion that segregation did not, in and of itself, present an equal protection problem. Carrying his bruises from his own schooling experiences, Thurgood Marshall began to prepare his team of lawyers for the frontal assault on segregation he had been maneuvering toward since his rides through the South with Charles Hamilton Houston just after law school graduation. That path had led him, ultimately, to rural Clarendon County, South Carolina. And now, what had begun as a simple request for transportation for the county's Black students was headed to the highest court in the land with the constitutionality of segregation laws and the contours of Black citizenship in the balance.

MAY IT PLEASE THE COURT

Thurgood Marshall would stand before the justices of the Supreme Court on three separate occasions to argue his portion of *Brown v. Board of Education*. The litigation from South Carolina, *Briggs v. Elliott*, had been docketed along with the *Brown* case from Kansas and companion school desegregation cases from Virginia, Delaware, and the District of Columbia, and was set for oral argument on December 9, 1952. In his opening comments, Marshall summarized his argument

> that these statutes were unconstitutional in their enforcement because they not only produced these inevitable inequalities in physical facilities, but that evidence would be produced by expert witnesses to show that the governmentally imposed racial segregation in and of itself was also a denial of equality.

Marshall had set out the twin methods of attack: first, that segregation *inevitably* produced inequalities that were detrimental to Black students; and second, that segregation was itself harmful. By the first argument, separate had proven to never actually be equal; by the second, separate was inherently unequal.[21]

Marshall's strategy sought to maximize the cases' chances for success by providing the justices with multiple theories upon which to declare the states' school segregation statutes unconstitutional. At the same time, he was balancing disagreement among his own team of lawyers as to the most appropriate strategy. There remained skepticism at the use of social science evidence as a basis for proving the harm of segregation even as Kenneth Clark prepared an appendix summarizing the growing body of work on the negative effects of segregation on young African Americans. Marshall ultimately chose to utilize all the available evidence in the hopes of providing the justices every reason to rule in his clients' favor. In his oral argument, he highlighted the social science findings, and he argued that leaving decisions to South Carolina "would ultimately relegate the Negro appellants in this case to pleas with the legislature of South Carolina to do what they have never done in the past, to recognize their pleas." And he argued that there was no constitutionally reasonable basis for an education law to distinguish between students based on race. The only possible justification for such a distinction, he argued, would be to "show that Negroes as Negroes—all Negroes—are different from everybody else." Many citizens and government leaders of South Carolina might have believed Negroes to be different from everybody else, but the Constitution could not, Marshall argued. And it was the duty of the Court, not the prerogative of the legislature, to ensure that such prejudices, which had the effect of denying full citizenship, did not make their way into law. "[T]he rights of minorities . . . have been protected by our Constitution, and the ultimate authority for determining that is this Court," he said in closing his rebuttal.[22]

But the justices were not quite ready to decide the case. Six months after the oral arguments, the Court ordered further briefing on a series of five questions and set another round of oral arguments for December 1953. By the time Thurgood Marshall returned to the podium to represent the appellants in *Briggs*, there had been one highly significant change at the Supreme Court. In September 1953, Chief Justice Fred Vinson, who did not seem inclined to overturn *Plessy*, had died of a heart attack. By the end of that month, the governor of California, Earl Warren, had moved to Washington, DC, to begin his service as the fourteenth chief justice of the United States Supreme Court.[23] As the 1991 Court transition would alter the direction of the nation's law, Chief Justice Warren's arrival shifted the dynamics of the Court in a way that reshaped the nation.

In December 1953, Thurgood Marshall again rose to represent the plaintiffs in *Briggs*. As he had a year earlier, Marshall framed the issue as one that would determine whether the segregationist customs of states like South Carolina and Virginia or the intent of the Constitution would prevail. For the segregation statutes to survive, South Carolina would have to show both that there actually were meaningful differences based on race (which science was increasingly disproving) and that such differences related to schooling. The second time around, Marshall was even more direct about the state's purpose in having such statutes: "We charge that they are Black Codes," he claimed, noting that their entire purpose was to maintain a racialized caste system. And in his conclusion, he laid the challenge before the Court:

> The only way that this Court can decide this case in opposition to our position, is that there must be some reason which gives the state the right to make a classification that they can make in regard to nothing else in regard to Negroes. And we submit the only way to arrive at this decision is to find that for some reason Negroes are inferior to all other human beings. . . . The only thing can be is an inherent determination that the people who were formerly in slavery, regardless of anything else, shall be kept as near that stage as is possible, and now is the time, we submit, that this Court should make it clear that that is not what our Constitution stands for. Thank you, sir.

Thurgood Marshall took his seat. In the NAACP's briefs, his team had provided the technical legal analysis, but in his closing rebuttal in *Briggs*, he had narrowed in on the heart of the effort to end legalized segregation: despite what the Court had said in *Plessy*, segregation was established to enforce the subjugation of African Americans and, regardless of the quixotic efforts toward equality, it continued to have that effect. African Americans could never be full citizens as long as laws like that in South Carolina were allowed to persist. And like Houston before him, Marshall believed that the Constitution did indeed have the power to end the practice. Such was his faith in law.[24]

The justices took more than five months before announcing the Court's decision in *Brown* and its companion cases on May 17, 1954. Through Chief Justice Warren's efforts corralling the nine justices toward an opinion each felt comfortable signing on to, they spoke unanimously. After reviewing the Court's half century interpreting the Fourteenth Amendment in segregation cases, from Homer Plessy's suit to ride in a railcar for white passengers through Heman Sweatt's effort to desegregate the University of Texas's law school, the Court accepted that they could no longer avoid the question: "Does segregation of children in public schools solely on the basis of race, even though the physical facilities and other 'tangible' factors may be equal[,] deprive the children of the minority group of equal educational opportunities?" The Court answered definitively: "We believe that it does."[25]

For justification, the court explicitly rejected the finding in *Plessy* that segregation did not denote inferiority. Instead, separation of students "from others of similar age and qualifications solely because of their race generates a feeling of inferiority as to their status in the community that may affect their hearts and minds in a way unlikely ever to be undone." The Court then quoted in full the finding of fact from Kansas about the negative effect of segregation on a student's motivation to learn and asserted that such a finding was "amply supported." At the top of the list of supporting evidence, aggregated in a footnote, was the name of Kenneth Clark.[26]

In conclusion, Chief Justice Warren offered the opinion's most quoted language: "We conclude that in the field of public education the doctrine of 'separate but equal' has no place. Separate educational facilities are inherently unequal." However, the Court did not order any remedy, instead inviting the parties to present still further argument on that difficult question.[27]

And, just like that, the law had changed. That which had been constitutional the week before was unconstitutional. Thurgood Marshall, who was present in the courtroom as Chief Justice Warren read the opinion, began his celebration immediately and continued it into the night once he reached the NAACP offices in New York. "We'd always had parties, drunken parties, after winning, but that was the best," he later recalled. Still, even as he predicted that southerners would fall in line with a ruling of the Supreme Court, a point he had made during the oral arguments as well, he understood that much work remained. After midnight, he pulled some of his close aides nearby and told them, "I don't want any of you to fool yourselves. It's just begun. The fight has just begun."[28]

FOUR

LIVING A POST-'BROWN' REALITY

As Thurgood Marshall set to work in the late 1940s in Clarendon County, urging local African Americans to push the fight for better education, about 130 miles to the south, Clarence Thomas was born in a small town just outside of Savannah, Georgia, a place that matched the rural African American poverty of Clarendon County. As Marshall celebrated the initial victory in *Brown* in 1954, Thomas was set to enter the first grade later that year. Whereas Marshall had completed law school with the urge to tear down the segregation that had kept him out of the University of Maryland's law school, the *Brown* victory offered Thomas and his generation of Black students the promise of something different. Yet as he completed his own schooling, graduating from Yale's law school in 1974, Thomas emerged with scars of his own.

Like Marshall, Thomas sought a well-paying job to support himself and his young wife following his law school graduation. During his final year at Yale, he had been assured by his classmates that he would have no difficulty finding one. After all, Yale was one of the nation's highest-rated schools; unlike Marshall, whose law school options had been explicitly limited due to his race, Thomas had entered the most privileged bastions of American schooling. Yet, Thomas felt that the "high-priced lawyers" he interviewed with for law firm positions in Atlanta, New York, Washington, or Los Angeles treated him dismissively. "Many asked pointed questions, unsubtly suggesting that they doubted I was as smart as my grades indicated," he recalled in his autobiography.[1] By January 1974, only a few months before graduation, he had yet to receive a single job offer, and he felt humiliated and desperate: "Now I knew what a law degree from Yale was worth when it bore the taint of racial preference."[2] Eventually, Thomas met with Missouri Attorney General John Danforth and was hired as an assistant attorney general despite some concerns about the salary and Danforth's being a Republican—at the time, Thomas had yet to become aligned with the GOP. During his time in the attorney general's office and with an eye on future job prospects, Thomas worked to demonstrate what he could do by winning cases rather than relying on his Yale pedigree.[3] Around this time, as a symbol of his disillusionment, Thomas "peeled a fifteen-cent price sticker off a package of cigars and stuck it on the frame of my law degree to remind myself of the mistake I'd made by going to Yale."[4]

Here was Thomas, like Marshall a generation before, evincing in the very first years of his career motivations that would drive his philosophies even as he rose to the highest court in the land. Marshall, steaming about his exclusion from his home state's law school, seeded the earliest successful assault on systemic racial segregation. Thomas, humiliated even after being included in Yale's halls of privilege and power, confronted the bankruptcy of the "integration" he experienced—and that Marshall's work had enabled—with a symbolic 15-cent sticker. The path from *Brown* in 1954 to Thomas's law school graduation in 1974 was one that confirmed the prescience of Marshall's assertion to his colleagues that the fight *Brown* was part of had "just begun." As the nation and courts confronted the repercussions of Marshall's work on the relationships of Americans to one another and to their government, a generation of students that included Clarence Thomas attended the nation's schools amid *Brown*'s ripples. And though doors had been opened, Thomas, for one, still came away bruised.

FINDING STABILITY IN SAVANNAH

With a population under 500, Pinpoint, Georgia, might not have even qualified as a town. Situated in the coastal Georgia low country, Clarence Thomas's birthplace sat wholly isolated, even from Savannah, which was ten miles away. Pinpoint was home to the distinctive culture of a group of people known as Geechees (or Gullahs in the low country of South Carolina), descendants from enslaved West Africans who spoke a Creole-like dialect and were valued during the period before the Civil War for their ability to cultivate rice. Clarence Thomas is the descendant of enslaved people from a rice plantation in Liberty County, Georgia, and his ancestry is filled with the brokenness that has plagued southern Black families from the time of slavery.[5]

Born in 1930, Leola Anderson, Thomas's mother, was the daughter of Emma Jackson and Myers Anderson, though she was not raised by either. Emma Jackson died in childbirth when Leola was only 5, and Leola lived with her maternal grandmother until she died when Leola was 9. Myers Anderson then left his daughter in Pinpoint with Annie Jones, Leola's aunt, so that he could pursue work. Leola began picking crabs to support the family at the age of 9 and left high school after tenth grade. Not long after, she met M. C. Thomas, the son of a sharecropper who had moved with his family to tend the land at an orphanage for white children near Pinpoint, the Bethesda Home for Boys. Thomas did not continue in school past the fifth grade and worked with his family on the grounds of the orphanage. In the isolation of Pinpoint, M. C. Thomas and Leola Anderson met as teenagers, and not long after, Leola was pregnant. At the insistence of Leola's father, the two were married in 1947, and they had three children during their brief marriage: Emma Mae in 1946, Clarence in 1948, and Myers in 1949. The young couple was divorced by 1951, and Clarence recalls only one brief childhood encounter with his father, who left for Philadelphia after the divorce.[6]

In Pinpoint, Thomas was born into a life of rural, southern poverty. He remembered Aunt Annie's (his great-aunt) home as "a shanty with no bathroom and no electricity except for a single light in the living room." He carried water for the home from a nearby faucet or caught rainwater from the roof to wash clothes, and though he and his siblings had only two toys, Thomas recalls skipping oyster shells on the water, playing in the sandy marshes with his cousins, and stringing together empty juice cans to create toy trains.[7]

While Thomas was stringing together juice cans, Thurgood Marshall was arguing the case that had begun a hundred miles north in Clarendon County at the U.S. Supreme Court. The outcome of that work would profoundly alter the lives of millions of other young African American students across the country, students like Clarence Thomas. The Court's most high-minded language was about the importance of education as "the very foundation of good citizenship," but the reversal of what was constitutional in a decree from nine robed white men in Washington, DC, could not immediately change the circumstances young Black students faced.[8]

Clarence Thomas's first-grade year, which began in the fall of 1954, less than six months after the *Brown* decision, did not begin well. Thomas entered school at the Haven Home School, a public school for Black children between Pinpoint and Savannah. Midway through the school year, Thomas returned home to find his aunt's shack burned down after a failed attempt to light the lamps. Thomas's mother Leola, who had been working as a housekeeper in Savannah, took Clarence and his brother Myers with her to a one-room apartment in the city, leaving their sister Emma Mae with an aunt in Pinpoint. In Savannah, Thomas found "the foulest kind of urban squalor," and he slept on a chair that was "too small even for a six-year-old" while his mother and brother shared the bed. He continued first grade at the Florance Street School, which had been built in 1928 during efforts by Savannah's African American community to confront racial inequities in local schools.[9]

But before the next school year began, Thomas experienced one of the most profound transitions of his life. In August 1955, only three months after the Supreme Court had issued a second ruling in the *Brown* cases, Leola sent her sons Clarence and Myers to live with her father, Myers Anderson, and his wife Christine. Although Anderson initially balked at the idea of taking in his grandsons—he had not been involved in Leola's upbringing either—Christine let him know that he ought to pack his bags, because she intended to take the boys in. In the end, Anderson agreed, and the boys moved into a bedroom with twin beds in a gleaming white cinder-block house that Anderson had built himself. Thus, at the very moment Thurgood Marshall had succeeded in the decades-long quest to end segregation in schools, Clarence Thomas was experiencing a far more personal change that would profoundly alter the course of his life.[10]

To that point, Thomas's life had been marked by poverty and the instability that accompanied it. Living with his mother those months in Savannah, he recalled "hunger without the prospect of eating and cold without the prospect of warmth." In his grandfather's home, he found hardwood floors, handsome furniture, and an indoor toilet. He and his brother had their own beds and plenty to eat. But perhaps most importantly, he had a role model in his grandfather, whom he called "Daddy."[11]

Born in 1907, Myers Anderson was in his late 40s when his grandsons arrived to live with him and his wife Christine. Like Thomas, Anderson's early years were marked by poverty and instability; he was born to unmarried parents and lived with his maternal grandmother, who had been enslaved, in Liberty County until she died when he was 12. From there, he went to live with an aunt and uncle who already had thirteen children of their own. By the time he was 17, Anderson had, with different women, fathered two daughters, including Thomas's mother Leola, but he did not play a part in their upbringing. Anderson did not marry either of the two women with whom he had children earlier in his life, but settled down with Christine Hargrove, marrying her in 1933.

"Aunt Tina," as Thomas called her, attended school through sixth grade and could read and write. The couple never had children of their own until Clarence and Myers Thomas arrived in 1955, and Tina served as a full partner in raising the boys. Anderson attended school only through the third grade, and he claimed he received only nine months of actual learning because he spent the majority of his time working in the Liberty

County fields. What Anderson lacked in formal education he made up for with work ethic. By the time the Thomas brothers arrived, Anderson had established himself in Savannah by running a business delivering ice and fuel oil and operating several rental properties in addition to the sixty-acre family farm in nearby Liberty County. He had taught himself plumbing, bricklaying, and carpentry, and upon taking in his grandsons, he set out to provide the type of consistent, stern parenting that he had never provided for his own children. In place of the itinerancy Thomas had known thus far in life, at Daddy and Aunt Tina's he found rules and regulations, swift and stern punishment. As Thomas remembered, "It became clear that he meant to control every aspect of our lives: there would be no more carefree days spent wandering through the marshes hunting for fiddler crabs, no more roaming the streets instead of going to school."[12] The first task for the boys was schooling and Anderson did not listen to any excuses for failure.[13]

In his fierce independence, Myers Anderson had left the Baptist Church practiced by most of his family and converted to Catholicism. Thus, when it was time to enroll Clarence in the second grade in Savannah, Anderson looked to Savannah's local Catholic schools. In September 1955, Thomas enrolled at St. Benedict the Moor, one of three Catholic schools for Black students. This was less than six months after the Supreme Court's second *Brown* decision, and although Savannah's segregated public schools would eventually be impacted by the Court's orders in the desegregation cases, Clarence Thomas's schooling took place in private, segregated schools until high school. These were schools that most Black Savannahians could not afford, but that Anderson's modest success as a local entrepreneur made accessible for Thomas.

Opened in 1915, St. Benedict was run by Missionary Franciscan Sisters of the Immaculate Conception, many of whom were of Irish descent. To some, the nuns were known as the "nigger sisters" for their beliefs in racial equality that ran counter even to the prevailing practices of the local Catholic Church. By third grade, Thomas was the best reader in his household, and by the time he completed eighth grade at St. Benedict, he typically earned all A's. During this period, Thomas served as an altar boy and assisted Anderson with fuel oil delivery around town, but he spent summers at the Liberty County farm in a house that he built along with his brother and grandfather.[14] He also spent many hours at the Carnegie Library, two blocks from home and the only library open to African Americans at the time; being there was like "opening a door to another world."[15]

The nuns of St. Benedict marked the first white people who directly influenced Thomas's life, and he remembered them fondly. He confessed later that "it was not until long afterward that I grasped how profoundly Daddy, Aunt Tina, and the nuns of St. Benedict changed my life."[16] Within the school, however, he recalled being teased for his dark skin and Geechee accent. Still, as Thomas moved on to high school in 1962, the instability and poverty that had marked his first year in school had been replaced with constancy in his grandfather's home and steadiness at St. Benedict. Yet in the broader world of Savannah, the waves of change that had swollen in the wake of the *Brown* decision were rolling to shore.

SEEDS OF RESISTANCE

"I can think of nothing administrative-wise that would take longer than a year," Thurgood Marshall had declared in his oral argument before the Supreme Court in the *Briggs* case. He expressed a faith that if the Court did as he was asking and declared public school segregation unconstitutional, then southern officials would accept the decision and, even if begrudgingly, abide by it. "I, for one, have more confidence in the people of the South, white and colored, than the lawyers on the other side. I am convinced they are just as lawful as anybody else, and once the law is laid down, that is all there is to it."[17] This turned out to be a significant misjudgment, revealing Marshall's overestimation in the power of law to change society.

Almost immediately following *Brown*, state officials signaled an unwillingness to comply. In March 1956, dozens of members of Congress signed the "Southern Manifesto," which referred to *Brown* as "a clear abuse of judicial power" that had destroyed "the amicable relations between the white and Negro races that had been created through ninety years of patient effort." In conclusion, the signatories—nineteen senators and seventy-seven members of the House of Representatives—pledged themselves to "use all lawful means to bring about a reversal of this decision . . . and to prevent the use of force in its implementation."[18]

Such resistance was brought to life, most famously, when school officials in Little Rock set the beginning of the 1957 school year as the date for desegregating Little Rock's Central High School with nine African American students. Arkansas Governor Orval Faubus openly defied the *Brown* mandate to the point that federal troops had to be sent to Little Rock to escort the students into the school past a massive segregationist mob and to guard the students once inside. A year later, the Supreme Court had to intervene with a mandate that the chaos in Little Rock could not be utilized as an excuse to delay efforts to begin desegregation. In *Cooper v. Aaron*, another case argued by Thurgood Marshall, the Court emphasized that "the constitutional rights of [the students] are not to be sacrificed or yielded to the violence and disorder which have followed upon the actions of the Governor and Legislature." Even after such a rebuke—indeed on the very next day—Governor Faubus exploited newly passed laws to simply shut down Little Rock's high schools for the 1958–59 school year, creating a "Lost Year" of school in Little Rock.[19]

The mood in Georgia was no less intransigent. Governor Ernest Vandiver's immediate response to the *Brown* decision was "Come hell or high water, races will not be mixed in Georgia schools." The Georgia legislature passed legislation that would deny funds to integrated schools, and after a federal court ordered Atlanta's schools desegregated in late 1959, Governor Vandiver, like Faubus before him, threatened to close the public schools if necessary.[20]

Meanwhile in Savannah, where Clarence Thomas was working his way through St. Benedict during this period, the push for civil rights and desegregation was similarly intensifying. Only three days after the first *Brown* decision was handed down in 1954, Thurgood Marshall was in Savannah filing a housing discrimination suit, alleging that the local public housing authority enforced a policy of racial segregation. In a community in which

African Americans made up 35 percent of the population by the early 1960s, Savannah saw sit-ins at lunch counters, wade-ins at city pools, and kneel-ins at local churches—activities Myers Anderson supported through membership in the NAACP. Savannah's public schools remained racially segregated through the end of the 1961 school year, prompting the NAACP, led by Constance Baker Motley, one of Marshall's top lieutenants, to file a school desegregation suit, *Stell v. Savannah-Chatham County Board of Education*. The case, which was merely one of scores of others unfolding in communities and in district courts across the South, demonstrated both the ambiguities of the task of desegregation and the varied ways white constituents would seek to avoid it.[21]

While *Brown* made clear that legally mandated racial segregation of students—classifying students by race and assigning them to separate racially identifiable schools—was unconstitutional, it was not at all clear what a school district must do to come into compliance. A year after the initial *Brown* decision, the Court had clarified the charge to school districts to be student assignment "on a racially nondiscriminatory basis." But a policy of non-discrimination might not change much. For example, if a district assigned students based on where they lived rather than the color of their skin, the schools may still have ended up serving exclusively white or Black student populations due to residential segregation. One early interpretation of what might be allowable came from the district court in South Carolina upon rehearing the *Briggs* case after the *Brown* decisions. The court nullified South Carolina's segregation laws but drew a sharp distinction between "nondiscriminatory assignment" and "integration." According to the court,

> Nothing in the Constitution or in the decision of the Supreme Court takes away from the people freedom to choose the schools they attend. The Constitution, in other words, does not require integration. It merely forbids discrimination.[22]

Under such an interpretation, school districts and states that were not openly resisting the Supreme Court's command might conceive more subtle ways of maintaining segregated schools.

In Savannah, where 60 percent of students were white and 40 percent were African American, a group of white parents intervened in *Stell v. Savannah-Chatham County Board of Education,* the local school desegregation case, and utilized social science studies of their own (over the objection of the plaintiffs) to demonstrate that it was *integration*—not segregation—that would cause psychological harm to Black students. Calling upon a series of psychology professors to match the social scientists marshaled a decade earlier in the *Briggs* trial in South Carolina, the white parents introduced evidence of wide disparities in achievement levels of Savannah's white and Black students. The expert witnesses went further to claim that "differences in educability between Negro and white children were inherent" and that differences in abilities were genetically based and could not be overcome through a change in the schools' instructional programs.[23]

Though the Black plaintiffs in Savannah sought to revive the social science arguments of *Brown* to show that racially separated schools were inherently stigmatizing, the Savannah court preferred the new social science evidence and recognized genetically based racial differences that justified continued segregation. Perhaps most cruelly, the court cited Kenneth Clark's own previous writings that Black children in the non-segregated North exhibited greater preferences for white dolls than their southern counterparts. It was *integration*, the court concluded, that threatened harm to Black students because placing students of different abilities in the same classroom would create "serious psychological problems of frustration on the part of the Negro child" and would lead white students to "lose any challenge to further academic accomplishment." This commingling would not eliminate the racial differences in academic achievement and would merely increase interracial prejudices and hostility.[24]

The *Stell* decision demonstrated the extent to which even the most basic premises of *Brown* were being contested, and successfully contested in some cases. The doors to full Black citizenship would not be opened without resistance. The white parents had argued, and the district court agreed, that the school district could constitutionally take race into account as a proxy for allegedly *race-neutral* considerations like academic achievement and schools' physical capacity in making school assignments. The schools in Savannah, the court concluded, were not segregated *solely* based upon racial categories, but based on the reasonable consideration of intellectual differences between Black and white students. This, the school district could constitutionally do, the local court found.

Over time, the Supreme Court would overrule the interpretations offered in the *Briggs* remand in Clarendon County and the *Stell* decision in Savannah, but the cases demonstrated the vulnerability of the *Brown* decision and the avenues available for subverting its mandate that educational opportunity be made available to all on an equal basis. The psychological stigma upon which the Court rested the *Brown* decision was susceptible to counterevidence of other types of stigma. If segregation could not be practiced because it caused psychological harm, then what happened if integration could be demonstrated to cause its own harm? The Supreme Court had left such questions open and vulnerable to the use of evidence of racial capacities for learning, like that presented in Savannah, that reeked of the most pernicious types of racial stereotyping. And for others, including the future Justice Thomas, who held strong views about the limited role of the federal government—and federal courts in particular—the idea that *Brown* may have outlawed segregation without mandating integration was alluring. The Court's mandate in *Brown*, while unanimous, was anything but definitive and would take decades of further litigation to sharpen. And the effort to protect a more robust form of Black citizenship would be contested every step of the way.

The decades that followed would present the Court with opportunities to not only do its work as the judicial branch of American government, but also to confront the many implications of the work embodied in *Brown* of remedying legalized discrimination and ensuring a future that would leave behind the inequities of the past. That work was not merely legal, but social, and the Court would weigh in on some of the social challenges present in a diverse and unequal community. These included not only the questions specific to racial segregation in schools, such as the utility and legality of busing or the constitutionality of affirmative action, but also larger questions of how to define racism or when a government's responsibility to correct past wrongs is fulfilled. Individual justices would connect these questions to broader foundational questions about the role of government, the work of judges, and the appropriate way to reshape society through law.

The question of what school districts should do after *Brown* was further complicated because it was not just white segregationists who questioned the necessity for integration. Throughout the NAACP's campaign against segregation, there had been a steady skepticism among advocates for Black equality and uplift about the imperative of integrating schools. In the immediate aftermath of *Brown*, skepticism about integration from within the Black community existed for a wide range of reasons, such as a concern about employment of Black teachers, a philosophical belief that integration implicitly admitted the inferiority of Black institutions, a desire to maintain the momentum of equalization in schools, and the worry over how Black students would be treated in integrated environments. On the last point, many early examples of desegregation confirmed the trauma Black students would experience in entering schools previously forbidden. Where small numbers of Black students were chosen to desegregate schools as tokens of integration, such as the nine students at Little Rock's Central High School in 1957, the students faced danger both outside the schools and within. In Savannah, nineteen seniors were selected to desegregate two high schools at the beginning of the 1963–64 school year after the Fifth Circuit Court of Appeals reversed the initial result in *Stell*. The Savannah students recalled being taunted and bumped into throughout the year. They felt a constant sense of isolation among their white peers.[25] Though Clarence Thomas would never attend desegregating public schools in Savannah, he too was set to experience new and diverse classrooms and institutions that would profoundly shape his own views about the questions he would one day confront on the Court.

FIVE

PIONEERING AT A PRICE

The 1960s and 70s were a period of disillusionment for many. In the fall of 1964, Clarence Thomas became one of the first two Black students to enroll at St. John Vianney Minor Seminary, a boarding school opened in 1959 in Isle of Hope, just outside Savannah. By the spring of 1974, he was derisively putting a 15-cent price tag on his Yale law degree as he took his first lawyering job working for Missouri's Republican Attorney General John Danforth. The intervening decade was among the most consequential in American history as institutions were challenged by the continuing civil rights movement as well as the Vietnam War and Watergate scandal, all amid an existential cold war that shaped ideas about patriotism and citizenship. The civil rights movement would achieve significant victories, including the appointment of the nation's first Black Supreme Court justice, but would also grow more militant as intransigence with full Black inclusion hardened and coalesced into a broader conservative political movement.[1]

Clarence Thomas, who came of age in this moment, would be touched by both Black nationalism and the emerging conservative movement, as his personal disillusionment with the promises symbolized by *Brown* carried him away from the ideas of integration and the goals and strategies of established civil rights organizations. That disillusionment initiated the decisions that would lead to his rift with much of the Black community and the reflexive disgust many Black leaders have for his work and even for him personally. The distance has only grown more pronounced as Thomas has responded through the decades by asserting his independence from predetermined Black positions by further aligning with a Republican Party that aggressively opposes them. This cycle has been exacerbated even further by revelations of the work by Thomas's second wife Virginia on behalf of extreme conservative causes, including the 2021 insurrection at the U.S. Capitol.[2]

The seeds for Thomas's professional journey can be found during the formative decade he spent between high school and law school. His disillusionment during this period would meld with the sense of individualism he admired so much in his grandfather to shape the jurisprudence Thomas would bring to his work on the Supreme Court.

NAVIGATING A WORLD IN FLUX

In Savannah's Catholic schools, Clarence Thomas's schooling was not directly impacted by *Brown* or the local *Stell* decisions, but he would participate in desegregation nonetheless. Midway through high school, Thomas transferred from St. Pius X, the only Catholic high school for Black students, to the previously all-white St. John Vianney Minor Seminary. Increasingly serious and studious, Thomas chose to transfer to the seminary to pursue a path that might lead him to becoming Savannah's first Black priest, a path of which his grandfather enthusiastically approved. After the 1964–65 school year, the other Black student, Richard Chisholm, returned to St. Pius X, and Thomas continued as the school's only Black student.

At St. John Vianney, Thomas participated in a variety of school activities, including working on the school yearbook, writing for the newspaper, and playing on the basketball team. He worked hard, finding the academic workload heavier, but also struggling with a "constant state of controlled anxiety." As he recalled, "We had always believed that we could do as well as whites if we were only given a fair shake—but what if it turned out that we weren't good enough after all?"[3] Further, as he pushed forward in his education, Thomas began to feel distanced from his extended family and sensed that others resented him for thinking himself better than them. All of this was in addition to the occasional, but painful, racial slights thrust on Thomas from classmates and teachers: being told to lose his accent so as not to be considered inferior, being excluded from a game of pickup basketball, hearing white students use the word "nigger."[4]

In this experience, Thomas's memories reflect those of other African American students who desegregated schools. In his own corner of the educational universe, at a time when Thurgood Marshall, as solicitor general, was pushing the Supreme Court to enforce its school desegregation rulings more assertively, Thomas was paying "the price that my generation of blacks paid for moving out from behind the wall of segregation."[5] And as it would for other pioneering students, the experience would leave lasting scars on Thomas. He felt isolated, both at school and within his family; he struggled with confidence as he internalized doubts about himself that he perceived from others; and he resented the slights, both implicit and subtle, that came from being an extreme minority.

To his credit, Thomas continued to excel academically and survived the social challenges of his trailblazing high school experience. Upon graduating from St. John Vianney in 1967 with strong grades and a sense that he could indeed do as well as his white peers, Thomas looked to continue on his path toward the Catholic priesthood by enrolling at Conception Seminary in northwest Missouri. It was a plan Myers Anderson heartily approved of. This would be Thomas's first experience leaving Savannah, and he would never fully return. At Conception, he again found himself in a historically white institution; there were only a few other Black students within the strictly devout Catholic seminary. Nearing 20 years old, Thomas was increasingly aware of the broader social movements pushing the nation toward change, and he began to find it difficult to reconcile the

Church's conservative positions on civil rights with his growing belief that the inhumane treatment of African Americans demanded condemnation from people of conscience. By the end of his only year at Conception in the late spring of 1968, Thomas had decided that the priesthood was not for him. This conclusion was validated when some of his seminary classmates reacted gleefully to the assassination of Dr. Martin Luther King Jr. in April of that year.[6]

Along with African Americans across the nation, Thomas felt the pull of radicalization of the late 1960s that fed urban rioting and increasing enthusiasm for Black nationalism. In his own recollection, he became "an angry black man" in the aftermath of King's murder. However, leaving the seminary presented Thomas with the problem of breaking the news to his grandfather. Although his initial plan was to return to Savannah, his grandfather's damning reaction to Thomas's departure from seminary convinced him otherwise; the decision created a schism between the two that was never fully reconciled. With Savannah out as an option, Thomas followed the suggestion of a teacher from St. John Vianney and a classmate from St. Pius X and applied to the College of the Holy Cross in Worcester, Massachusetts.[7]

Holy Cross was a Jesuit liberal arts college for men, the oldest Catholic college in New England. When Thomas arrived in the fall of 1968, he was one of six African Americans in the 550-person sophomore class. There were seventeen Black freshmen, two juniors, and a single Black senior. At Holy Cross, Thomas began charting the course of his future. During his sophomore year, he met Kathy Ambush, a Worcester native and freshman at nearby Anna Maria College. The two quickly developed a relationship, attending demonstrations together even as Thomas's faith in mainstream civil rights strategies began to wane. In addition, leery of losing focus at Holy Cross without a concrete goal to work toward, Thomas adopted the goal of attending law school.[8]

Thomas's time at Holy Cross captured his conflicting and evolving impulses on the best strategies for Black empowerment. As Holy Cross admitted increasing numbers of Black students during Thomas's time there, the same spirit of activism that led to the advent of Black student unions on campuses around the country took hold at Holy Cross. Within another predominantly white environment, Thomas found it comforting to be among the small group of African American students and became corresponding secretary of the newly formed Black Student Union. The union achieved a significant victory in the fall of 1969 when it convinced the school's administration to create a separate Black residential space, the "Black Corridor," within one of the dormitories. Thomas, who had not supported the idea, lived in the corridor nonetheless, albeit with his white roommate.[9]

Although Thomas excelled in school and appreciated his involvement with the Black Student Union, he began to sour on some of the ideas held dear by mainstream civil rights leaders. Watching several of his Black class-mates fail or drop out at Holy Cross, he wondered if they might have been better off at historically Black institutions, where they could "grapple with the ordinary challenges of young adulthood without having to simultane-ously face the additional challenge of learning how to live among whites." He questioned the impulse that led institutions like Holy Cross to increase Black enrollment as a "well-intentioned theory that failed to take into ac-count the realities of black life." And he grew increasingly troubled at the limiting role of "enraged victim" being assigned to and adopted by African Americans. Thomas graduated determined to find his own path.[10]

ANOTHER DISENCHANTMENT

After finishing at Holy Cross with an excellent record, Thomas married Kathy Ambush and the young couple moved to New Haven, Connecti-cut, where Thomas would begin at one of the nation's most prestigious law schools, Yale. His enrollment at Yale suggested that Thomas believed that he might overcome the limitations imposed by racism through his educa-tional achievements. This was a widely held belief; indeed, it informed the *Brown* strategy of focusing on schools as a central institution in the pursuit of equal citizenship. But if Thomas entered Yale believing in the promise of education in overcoming racism, he graduated with a different perspective on the issue: he was convinced that efforts to make prestigious institutions like Yale more accessible to African Americans not only were based in their own form of racism, but actually worsened racist beliefs in Black inferiority. Thomas thus condemned advocates for Black inclusion as self-interested and insincere. He claimed to have chosen Yale because it was more liberal than Harvard, but he left law school scarred by "those ostensibly unprejudiced whites who pretended to side with black people while using them to further their own political and social ends, turning against them when it suited their purposes."[11]

But it was not only white liberals who disappointed Thomas during this period. He had entered law school with the goal of returning to practice law in Savannah, using his degree to help his people. During law school, he worked with New Haven Legal Services, the local legal aid bureau, and spent a summer at a firm in Savannah, but these experiences served only to disenchant him. The work at New Haven Legal Services opened his eyes to "bickering and incompetent leadership," while the summer in Savannah— the only extended period he spent in the South after high school—was professionally disappointing and was further complicated by his still strained relations with his grandfather.[12]

Adrift of his initial path toward the priesthood and disappointed at what he encountered in law school and the legal profession, Thomas's stakes in his own future were raised with the birth of his son Jamal during his second year of law school. The addition increased Thomas's urgency to find work that could support his young family, but he did not feel he was being offered the same lucrative prospects as his Yale classmates. He sensed doubts from classmates and potential employers about whether he belonged on the elite campus, concluding that "it was futile for me to suppose that I could escape the stigmatizing effects of racial preference, and I began to fear that it would be used forever after to discount my achievements."[13]

This was not an uncommon sense for non-white students at Yale, though not all took the same lessons as Thomas. A few years after Thomas graduated from Yale, the doubts he perceived about his qualifications were stated directly to another non-white student at a recruitment dinner with a Washington, DC, firm. "Do you think you would have been admitted to Yale Law School if you were not Puerto Rican?" one of the firm's partners asked Sonia Sotomayor, a third-year student who would go on to become the first Latina justice on the Court in 2009. After defending herself at the dinner, Sotomayor filed a formal complaint through the law school, seeking to have the firm's recruiting privileges suspended and ultimately resulting in a full apology from the firm.[14] Whereas Sotomayor had sought relief from an institution she still believed in, Thomas left Yale convinced that his educational accomplishments would forever be devalued and with no faith that the institution could do anything about it.

In the six years since he had left Conception Seminary, disappointed in the failure of the Catholic Church to defend civil rights more aggressively, Thomas had soured on many of the ideas put forth by the 1960s civil rights coalition of Black leaders and white Democrats. At Holy Cross, he began to question the wisdom of affirmative action programs based on race alone, recognizing that not all African Americans were identically disadvantaged. In addition, he took offense at the classism and colorism within the Black community, finding the beliefs of some that their lighter skin made them superior to those with darker skin "not much different from white racism." Given his earliest origins and dark skin color, Thomas had always been sensitive to these concerns, but in college he began to see the consequences African Americans faced when questioning conventional civil rights positions on Holy Cross's "Black Corridor" or the wisdom of affirmative action. At Yale, he concluded that integration was counterproductive, even fraudulent, because it maintained a racial hierarchy while superficially opening doors of opportunity. From Thomas's perspective, mainstream civil rights leaders, university administrators, and Democratic politicians were making things worse and were not truly concerned about genuine equal citizenship in the first place. So disenchanted, Thomas graduated in search of new ideas.[15]

By the time Thomas accepted a position with Missouri Attorney General

John Danforth, it still surprised some of his friends that he would work for a Republican, given that party's reputation in opposition to African American rights. But disenchanted with solutions he saw as failures, Thomas had concluded that the better path to Black empowerment could be found in the foundational lessons of personal responsibility and self-reliance taught to him and personified by his grandfather, Myers Anderson. This was an essentially conservative vision, certainly not unique to Thomas among African Americans. And though some national Republican politicians, including President Richard Nixon, were employing racially coded language to capture white southerners disaffected by the Democrats' pursuit of civil rights legislation, Thomas would find philosophical kinship with the ideas of small government and individual freedom espoused by some Republicans, including Danforth. His reliance on institutions—religious, educational, government—was shattered, but he would rise in reliance on the Republican Party.

Only eight years after graduating from Yale in 1974, he would be nominated by President Ronald Reagan to lead the Equal Employment Opportunity Commission. A decade after that he would stand with President George H. W. Bush in Maine accepting a nomination to the Supreme Court. And in the crucible of his contested confirmation, he would only grow further disenchanted with Democratic politicians and mainstream Black leaders.

Thurgood Marshall's work as lawyer and justice had paved a change in the futures available to Black Americans. For nearly six decades until his 1991 retirement, he had used courts and the law to force the end of legal exclusion and encourage government efforts to open opportunities to a broader swath of citizens than it ever had. Clarence Thomas had come of age in the midst of that revolution, able to access institutions Marshall had been kept out of. Yet Thomas discovered limits in the opportunities Marshall had helped produce and arrived at different conclusions about the roles of courts and law in addressing the enduring challenge of ensuring full citizenship to a group so long excluded.

Over more than half a century, from Marshall's 1967 appointment to the Court through Thomas's decades-long tenure as his successor, their work would reflect a transformation in the Supreme Court's approach to questions central to the nation's legal foundations and essential to its most difficult social and political challenges. At the heart of that work were the questions of *Brown*, questions about how to build a citizenry out of diverse individuals.

PART II

INTEGRATION

SIX

TO ENTER A BURNING HOUSE

In 1944, Thurgood Marshall found a new neighbor amid the offices of the NAACP at 69 Fifth Avenue in New York. For four years, Marshall had been leading the Legal Defense Fund (LDF), a separate organization that had grown out of the NAACP's legal committee and was spearheading the litigation that Charles Hamilton Houston had imagined years earlier. Still just over a decade out of law school, Marshall's work in the office was tireless and loud; he often hosted rousing debates and discussions among the lawyers, filled with jokes (and often liquor as the hours grew late) amid passionate work. The *Brown* cases were still ahead of them, but the LDF had just won an enormous victory at the Supreme Court in *Smith v. Allwright* in which the all-white Democratic primary in Texas was declared unconstitutional.[1]

Marshall's new neighbor found the lawyer next door to be lacking in manners, and he frowned upon the laughter and "barnyard expletives" coming from Marshall's office. W. E. B. Du Bois had helped found the NAACP thirty-five years before, but in 1944 he was returning to the organization after a decade of exile. In early 1934, as a fissure widened between Du Bois and Walter White, the organization's executive secretary, Du Bois had utilized his platform as editor of the organization's newsletter, *The Crisis,* to examine the concept of segregation, including the benefits of racially separate institutions and organizations. In so doing, Du Bois initiated a debate within the NAACP about how African Americans might best confront the social, economic, and legal subjugation they had encountered in the United States since before the nation's founding. What *was* the best strategy for attacking the barriers to full citizenship—barriers used to keep African Americans separated and vulnerable to discrimination? Was it to send individuals across those barriers into prohibited spaces and institutions? Or was it better to take such entrenched barriers as given and work within the African American community to strengthen separated individuals and institutions, thus mitigating the barriers' effects? As Charles Hamilton Houston plotted the organization's litigation plan, these were questions that were front and center. The strategies, of course, were not mutually exclusive, but the relative emphasis of one or the other had generated rivalries among Black advocates for generations.[2]

SEPARATION BY CHOICE OR INTEGRATION BY RIGHT

Du Bois himself had engaged in such rivalries throughout his career. It was, in large part, his disagreement with Booker T. Washington in the first decade of the twentieth century that had led to the creation of the NAACP in 1909. Washington had risen to fame and influence arguing that those who had been enslaved must work to develop and strengthen themselves and their own institutions, a theory he brought to life in his leadership of the Tuskegee Institute in Alabama. By focusing attention more on what African Americans could accomplish separately, Washington's message was eagerly received by white Americans who wanted to maintain racial separation into the twentieth century. In 1895, Washington reached a compromise with white leaders, agreeing to defer advocacy for integration or equality and accommodate the existing white political dominance in the South, in exchange for promises for basic education and due process rights for African Americans. Termed the Atlanta Compromise, Washington's agreement was criticized by Du Bois for submitting to a subjugated status. In response, Du Bois joined several dozen others to form the Niagara Movement, which focused on ending racial segregation and disenfranchisement. As lynchings and race riots revealed the depths of resistance to Black inclusion in American life, the Niagara Movement ultimately gave rise to the NAACP, an organization that wrestled the reins of Black leadership from Washington. Du Bois, one of the NAACP's founders, assumed the post of director of publicity and research, which ultimately included his leadership of the organization's influential newsletter, *The Crisis*.

Years later, Du Bois would find himself challenged by a young activist from Jamaica, Marcus Garvey, who offered a more radical version of Washington's call for Black self-empowerment. In the late 1910s, Garvey founded the Universal Negro Improvement Association and drew support from a segment of the African American population that tended to be younger, angrier, poorer, and of darker complexion than members of the NAACP. Rather than cooperation with the existing American and European power structures, Garvey campaigned for a Black nationalism that appealed to racial pride and empowerment; it included advocacy for separate Black institutions and a pan-Africanist view of a global racial struggle. By the 1920s, a rift between Du Bois and Garvey, and their respective organizations, had widened and exposed internal class dimensions within the movement for Black uplift that the NAACP's status as the leading civil rights organization had obscured. Garvey's movement was ultimately derailed as the leader faced criminal charges of mail fraud, but the ideas of Black nationalism would reverberate throughout the century.[3]

Indeed, it was a form of just that idea that Du Bois himself seized upon in his 1930s spat with the NAACP. His January 1934 *Crisis* editorial, "Segregation," made the distinction between segregation that involved discrimination and segregation that involved "race-conscious black men cooperating together in [their] own institutions and movements." The latter, he argued, had been responsible for most of the advances of African Americans of the prior quarter century and would be the eventual source of broader emancipation. Howard Law School offered a case in point, and Thurgood Marshall, who was graduating as Du Bois was writing, would be a chief example of the ability of those trained in Black institutions to force broader emancipation.[4]

Though Du Bois acknowledged that wider individual contact across lines of race would lead to the "greatest human development," he found it impossible to "wait for the millennium of free and normal intercourse before we unite."[5] For decades, Du Bois had struggled with the potential for self-hatred among African Americans and recognized the danger, articulated by Garvey, that integration represented an elevation of white institutions and norms over Black ones. In his seminal work published in 1903, *The Souls of Black Folk*, Du Bois wrote of an "all-pervading desire to inculcate disdain for everything black."[6] This danger was on his mind, too, when he criticized the students at Lincoln University, including Thurgood Marshall, for voting in 1929 to keep the school's faculty all white. In *The Crisis,* he had wondered how parents of Lincoln students could send their children to an institution only to have them "emerge with no faith in their own parents or in themselves."[7]

Though Du Bois had incorporated Black nationalist ideas into his writing previously, and though his exploration of the benefits of separate institutions could not override his ardent commitment to fighting for integration, in 1934 there were political consequences for a civil rights organization expressing separatist ideas. Indeed, Du Bois's essay endangered efforts to obtain federal support for integrated housing and provided cover for those seeking to ensure continued residential segregation. Undaunted, through the first half of the year, Du Bois continued to explore the idea of separation, even compiling a symposium edition of *The Crisis*. Ultimately, Du Bois pushed the organization to consider the distinction between enforced and voluntary separation, acknowledging the value of "the Negro church, the Negro college, the Negro school, and Negro business and industrial enterprises" while declaring "unyielding opposition to any and every form of enforced segregation."[8] After Du Bois questioned the belief of the NAACP's leadership in the value of Negro history, literature, art, and business, the board voted to disallow criticism of the policy, work, or officers of the NAACP within the pages of *The Crisis*. By July 1934, Du Bois and the NAACP had parted ways.[9]

Although the strategy of pursuing Black equality within current systems through integrating into those systems and the strategy of building Black power by operating apart from such systems could be pursued simultaneously, the competing strategies did create tension. Integrationists feared that the arguments of separatists might inadvertently justify the subjugation-enabling segregation of Black people and exclusion from American institutions. At the same time, separatists warned that the desire to integrate reflected notions of Black inferiority that had stigmatized generations. In due time, Thurgood Marshall and Clarence Thomas would give judicial voice to these perspectives, particularly as they considered the rights of Black students and the role of historically Black schools. Indeed, schools developed into a central forum—perhaps *the* central forum—in which these conversations continued through the second half of the twentieth century and into the twenty-first.

For his part, Du Bois addressed the schooling question in an essay he published during his first year away from the NAACP while at his new post in the sociology department at Atlanta University, one of the nation's preeminent institutions for African Americans. In the essay, published in 1935 in the *Journal of Negro Education,* Du Bois considered a straightforward question: "Does the Negro Need Separate Schools?" In his characteristic scholarly analysis, Du Bois built on the arguments he had developed during his final months at *The Crisis,* concluding that "race prejudice in the United States today is such that most Negroes cannot receive proper education in white institutions." He dismissed efforts to compel integration as futile and pitied Black students who were admitted to white schools only to find life "a living hell." Du Bois rejected objections as evidence of a lack of faith by African Americans in themselves—an inferiority complex. "In the last few years," he wrote, "I have become convinced that until American Negroes believe in their own power and ability, they are going to be helpless before the white world."[10] This was a sentiment that Myers Anderson, Clarence Thomas's grandfather, would have appreciated.

Du Bois also anticipated the misuse of his arguments by those who might claim them as a plea for enforced segregation. Dismissing those who would make such arguments as "illiterate nitwits," Du Bois defended his conclusions as merely a practical response to the world as it was:

> Theoretically, the Negro needs neither segregated schools nor mixed schools. What he needs is Education. What he must remember is that there is no magic, either in mixed schools or in segregated schools. A mixed school with poor and unsympathetic teachers, with hostile public opinion, and no teaching of truth concerning black folk, is bad. A segregated school with ignorant placeholders, inadequate equipment, poor salaries, and wretched housing, is equally bad. Other things being equal, the mixed school is the broader, more natural basis for the education of all youth. It gives wider contacts; it inspires greater self-confidence; and suppresses the inferiority complex. But other things seldom are equal, and in that case, Sympathy, Knowledge, and the Truth, outweigh all that the mixed school can offer.[11]

As Du Bois was exploring the ideas of segregation, even finding benefits in voluntary segregation amid a racist nation, Charles Hamilton Houston was beginning to implement the legal strategy for confronting enforced school segregation as the NAACP's first special counsel. Houston, accompanied by his young colleague, Thurgood Marshall, on fact-finding trips to document inequalities in the schools of the South, was engaging in what would be the NAACP's most impactful period of litigation and was expanding the organization's influence. By the time a 75-year-old Du Bois returned to the NAACP in 1944 to take an office next to Marshall, the work of what he had once known as the "legal committee" had transformed the organization. Not only was the LDF now a separate entity, but its work had also helped the NAACP grow into an organization of 325,000 members in nearly 900 branches across the country. The organization's income had quadrupled, and it had established itself at the forefront of civil rights work, particularly in the courts.[12]

In his essay on separate schools, Du Bois had criticized the NAACP for focusing resources on ending segregation rather than on improving schools serving Black students. In this, he presaged the sentiments of some within Marshall's legal team leading up to the *Brown* litigation who questioned the strategic wisdom and practical utility of pushing to end segregation rather than focusing on inequalities in resources. Such cases were easier to win given the *Plessy* mandate of "separate but equal," and they promised to deliver something tangible to all Black students—increased resources.[13]

As the *Brown* litigation worked its way to the Supreme Court, Du Bois's prediction that his words would be twisted into support for segregation proved correct. Both in the lower court trials and once the case reached the Supreme Court, lawyers arguing to maintain segregation cited Du Bois for the view that separate schools would be preferable—a misreading of his position that conflated voluntary and enforced separation and overlooked the practical nature of Du Bois's argument that separation was necessary primarily because "mixed schools" would not treat African American students decently. In one case, lawyers arguing to uphold the school segregation statutes pointed to Du Bois and others as evidence of the quality of segregated schools, implying that schools that are producing such learned individuals could not be unequal. On this front, they might have cited Marshall as well, given his background in segregated Baltimore schools and his education at Black universities Lincoln and Howard.[14]

A QUESTION OF PRIORITIES

After *Brown,* school district lawyers in Clarendon County, South Carolina, and the Savannah of Clarence Thomas's youth had argued that segregation's unconstitutionality did not necessarily mean that schools had to be racially integrated. In his legal work for the NAACP, Thurgood Marshall had disagreed, arguing that the best evidence of a school district's dismantling of a racially segregated school system would be to see students of different races attending school together: "mixed schools." Dissent from this position may have been unpopular in the initial afterglow of *Brown* as it might be seen as a retreat from a historic victory at the Supreme Court. However, by the time Thurgood Marshall took his seat on the Supreme Court in 1967, some of the sentiments Du Bois had articulated in his exploration of *voluntary* segregation found new expression.

Not only were many school districts resisting any desegregation effort that went beyond mere removal of racial restrictions from school assignments, the decade after *Brown* also demonstrated that the burden for desegregation that did occur would not be borne evenly. Black students would be the ones doing the integrating, often in small numbers. Black teachers would be the ones whose jobs were vulnerable. And, where it was necessary to close schools in the wake of the end of segregation's need for duplication, it would be Black schools that would be closed.

Outside of schools, the decade after *Brown* held many iconic moments of the broader civil rights movement that, like *Brown*, confronted barriers of exclusions. Boycotts and sit-ins, freedom rides and mass marches all worked to end the systematic exclusion of African Americans from American social, political, and economic institutions. By 1967, that effort had secured many legal rights, a process that began with *Brown*'s declaration of segregation's unconstitutionality and culminated in federal civil rights legislation prohibiting discrimination in employment, housing, and voting.

However, just as *Brown* did not magically equalize educational opportunities, legal changes could not immediately deliver liberation for African Americans. Through the 1960s, impatience with the on-the-ground impact of legal changes fueled enthusiasm for a parallel ideology of liberation that focused more on seizing self-determination than on integration. Black Power offered an alternative to the integrationist model that undergirded the NAACP's legal fight and ran counter to the demand for social and economic inclusion within the American system. While both Black Power and integrationist leaders recognized the necessity of ending legalized discrimination and subjugation, they differed on what should follow. Whereas Marshall and Dr. Martin Luther King Jr. fought for inclusion in existing American institutions, Black Power advocates echoed Garvey and built upon Du Bois's claim that such institutions could not be trusted to effectively serve African Americans.

Black Power offered not only an alternative to the integrationist philosophy, but also a critique of integration as buying into systems and institutions, including schools, that were designed to oppress rather than liberate African Americans. In 1963, James Baldwin captured this sentiment best when he asked: "Do I really want to be integrated into a burning house?"[15] After a decade of stalled school desegregation efforts, the same question was being asked about schools. By 1964, Student Nonviolent Coordinating Committee (SNCC) leader Bob Moses was wondering, "Why can't we set up our own schools? Because when you come right down to it, why integrate their schools? What is it that you will learn in their schools?"[16]

While Dr. King continued to imagine a world in which "every vestige of segregation and inferior education becomes a thing of the past and Negroes and whites study side by side in the socially healing context of the classroom,"[17] Malcolm X was articulating Black-controlled institutions as an alternative. Rather than integrating into white institutions with norms, structures, and curricula that perpetuated an inferiority complex in Black students, Malcolm X called for "an all-Black school, that we can control, staff it ourselves with the type of teachers that have our good at heart, with the type of books that have in them many of the missing ingredients that have produced this inferiority complex."[18]

Malcolm X's vision echoed that of Du Bois from three decades earlier and inspired others to bring such "liberation schools" into existence in the late 1960s and early 70s. According to historian Russell Rickford, much of the original impetus for such schools sprang from dissatisfaction with the politics and strategies of integration as leaders sought to develop alternatives to the oppressive social institutions that dominated Black American life. Separate schools had been opened by Marcus Garvey in the 1920s and, later, by the Nation of Islam, the Black nationalist religious group led by Elijah Muhammad of which Malcolm X was a part through the early 1960s. By the end of the decade, "an array of African American activists and educators embraced black independent schools as symbols of a new phase of struggle."[19] Such schools—including Amiri Baraka's African Free School in Newark and New Concept Development Center in Chicago or Greensboro's Malcolm X Liberation University—offered the prospect of self-determination through parallel Black institutions, and civil rights organizations, including SNCC and the Congress of Racial Equality (CORE), shifted their emphasis to the Black Power quest for Black autonomy.[20]

Still, such schools served small numbers of students. Most African American students remained in traditional public schools, and support for integration of such schools remained substantial. According to Rickford, "Pragmatic desegregation as a pathway to social and economic advancement remained as critical to black liberation as did strategic separation. Integrationist and nationalist impulses were never mutually exclusive."[21]

Integration, too, had its enthusiasts. Dr. King had articulated an ideal of coexistence among the nation's diverse population. Even Du Bois had acknowledged that, "Other things being equal, the mixed school is the broader, more natural basis for the education of all youth."[22] In response to the rise of Black Power, others defended integration as an entitlement for a group of Americans who had contributed to the national strength and institutions. The author Ralph Ellison observed that separation was not only an irrational fantasy, but a denial of the role African Americans had played in creating the nation: "Materially, psychologically, and culturally, part of the nation's heritage is Negro American, and whatever it becomes will be shaped in part by the Negro's presence."[23]

Alongside this philosophical argument that justice required integration was a practical one: in a world where power and influence lay disproportionately in the hands of white Americans, the best way to assure access to the nation's resources was by eliminating racially exclusive environments. There may not have been anything inherently magical about schools that were racially diverse, but those favoring integration asserted, with plenty of evidence, that racial identifiability of schools—white schools and Black schools—was the primary way in which resources were unevenly distributed. Eliminating such racial identifiability would have the effect of increasing resources devoted to the education of Black students.[24]

INTEGRATION AND DEMOCRACY

In his continued work as a lawyer on school desegregation following *Brown*, Thurgood Marshall took precisely this position. However, he did not argue merely for the benefits to Black students. To Marshall, there was far more at stake. Four years after he had addressed the justices in the *Brown* arguments, he again stood before the Court in August 1958 under extraordinary circumstances. The justices had gathered for a special session in advance of the October start of their term.

The impetus for the Court's emergency session came from Little Rock. In the aftermath of the dramatic conflicts during the 1957–58 school year—in which nine Black students attended Little Rock's Central High School only after intervention by the 101st Airborne Division of the U.S. Army—the Little Rock school board sought a two-year delay to allow the combustible situation to recede. Concluding that the "chaos, bedlam, and turmoil" was simply too much for the students, teachers, and community to endure, District Court Judge Henry Lemley allowed the delay. The Eighth Circuit Court of Appeals recognized the stakes, noting that "an affirmance of 'temporary delay' in Little Rock would amount to an open invitation to elements in other districts to overtly act out public opposition through violent and unlawful means." The appeals court reversed Judge Lemley's decision, and when the school district appealed, the case arrived at the Supreme Court.[25]

Standing before the justices, several of whom would be his colleagues in a decade's time, Marshall laid out perhaps his clearest and most passionate case for integration. He was protecting the ground that had been gained in the *Brown* decisions but also articulating two distinct points in favor of continuing with integration and rejecting the school board's plea for delay. The first was a normative argument that integration, particularly where it had already begun, provided the better education in a democracy for students of all races. He was mindful of the abuse of Black students in white schools that Du Bois had anticipated and that the pioneering students in Little Rock and elsewhere had experienced. He might even have conceded that the students' education may have been negatively affected. But Marshall argued that education was "teaching of the overall citizenship, to learn, to live together with fellow citizens, and above all, to learn to obey the law." He went on:

> I don't know of any more horrible destruction of principle of citizenship than to tell young children that those of you who withdrew rather than to go to the school with Negroes, those of you who are punished last year ... "Come back, all is forgiven, you win." And therefore, I'm not worried about the Negro children at this stage. I don't believe they're in this case as such. I worry about the white children in Little Rock who are told as young people that the way to get your rights is to violate the law and defy the lawful authorities. I'm worried about their future. I don't worry about the Negro kids' future. They've been struggling with democracy long enough. They know about it.[26]

Acknowledging that the school board faced a difficult task, Marshall flatly rejected the idea that those problems could be resolved by simply excluding Black students.

In these comments, Marshall offered a glimpse into his larger motivations for the pursuit of integration as a remedy. Charles Hamilton Houston had impressed upon him early in his career that the political structure in the United States would never permit schools made up solely of Black students to received equitable resources. But in his *Cooper* argument, Marshall went further. He described integrated schools as essential to democracy and resistance to them through law or violence as a perversion of bedrock American principles. "Democracy is hard!" he thundered before the Court. His aim was not any short-term educational benefit to a small group of African American students ("I don't worry about the Negro kids' future"), but the long-term demand that African Americans have full and equal citizenship within a nation truly governed by the principles it claimed.

This led to Marshall's second point: that part of the necessity for integrating schools could be found in unequivocally rejecting arguments that local school districts and states could simply disregard an order of the Supreme Court. This point struck at deeper constitutional questions that lurked in the aftermath of *Brown*. First and foremost, the *Brown* decisions provided a new interpretation of the equal protection clause of the Fourteenth Amendment. However, the decisions also set up broader questions foundational to the structure of American constitutional governance. The balance of power distributed between the states and the federal government had been at the center of the constitutional convention in 1787 and had been a primary cause of the Civil War. The resistance to *Brown*— whether from the halls of state legislatures, the dithering of school boards, or the unpunished violence of lawless individuals—was rooted in the same idea that the federal government could not force states to do that with which they disagreed. Thus, Marshall's argument for rejecting delay in *Cooper* was consistent with his abiding faith in federal courts to utilize the Constitution to redress wrongs. Were Little Rock allowed to retreat, the Supreme Court—Marshall's primary weapon as an advocate— would be diminished. He almost laughed as he imagined the effect if the Court ruled in the school board's favor: "The *Brown* decision means nothing, except in the areas where the people voluntarily accepted it."[27] That would be a hollow victory indeed.

Marshall's oral argument in *Cooper* was decidedly about *systems* of discrimination and did not emphasize impacts on individuals. The evil to be remedied was a societal one; the impact on individual students of entering hostile environments was lamentable, but unavoidable in the process of tearing down discriminatory systems. That impact would be borne in the generations to come by students like Clarence Thomas, who experienced a system that did not countenance legal exclusion but continued to send more subtle messages of Black inferiority. But from Marshall's perspective, African Americans did not need protection and sympathy ("They've been struggling with democracy long enough"), but rather a strong statement from a branch of government that their rights would not be sacrificed due to popular opposition. To make this point, Marshall appealed to the role of the Supreme Court in protecting citizens.

That strategy worked. The Supreme Court, recognizing the threat to its legitimacy if it allowed opposition to *Brown* to justify indefinite delay in compliance, unanimously agreed with Marshall. In an extraordinary opinion signed by all nine justices, the Court accepted that the "intolerable" situation at Central High School created a condition where the education of all the students suffered, but held that "law and order are not here to be preserved by depriving the Negro children of their constitutional rights." The case presented "questions of the highest order to the maintenance of our federal system of government" that could lead to only one answer if the Constitution were to maintain any relevance: the Constitution, and the Supreme Court's interpretation of it, represented the supreme law of the land, and no state governor or legislature could defy it. In a separate concurrence, Justice Felix Frankfurter echoed Marshall's oral arguments on the threat to democracy in rejecting the school board's request for delay in the face of public pressure. "To yield to such a claim would be to enthrone official lawlessness," Frankfurter wrote, concluding that rewarding the official defiance of Arkansas lawmakers would be condoning behavior that was "profoundly subversive not only of our constitutional system but of the presuppositions of a democratic society."[28] Marshall had emphasized the dangers of acquiescence in the face of obstinacy, and the justices agreed. These were dangers to the nation, not merely to Black students, as these questions about the extent of protection of Black citizenship cut to the heart of the nation's constitutional system.

Whereas advocates like Ellison and Kenneth Clark appealed to justice for Black students, psychologically and materially, Marshall's argument to the Supreme Court was framed around national interests rather than the interests of Black students. At issue were the power of the federal government and the Supreme Court, as well as foundational principles of democracy, law, and order. This framing had much to do with the forum in which Marshall was fighting. The justices of the Supreme Court were guardians of the Court's legitimacy and interpreters of constitutional principles, not advocates for African American students. But the argument was a preview of a tactic Marshall would use repeatedly as a justice with varying success: tying the interests of Black students to broader American interests. Marshall placed great faith in American institutions, the Supreme Court in particular, and he believed those institutions would be strengthened through integration. Integration would, in turn, strengthen individuals.

By the second half of the 1960s, with *enforced* separation having been declared unlawful, advocates for African Americans were questioning whether enforced *integration* remained the best strategy for education or whether separate institutions might better deliver equal education. Black Power advocates might have criticized Marshall for putting American institutions ahead of real people in his embrace of integration. Their appeals to strengthening Black individuals and institutions even to the point of separation were rooted in doubt that those American institutions would ever truly integrate African Americans. Marshall's push for integration may have been correct in principle, but it was doomed in practice, they might have argued.

Amid this contested moment in the civil rights movement, President Lyndon Johnson appointed Thurgood Marshall solicitor general in 1965 and nominated him to the Supreme Court in 1967. King had provided the social movement that pushed Johnson to champion the civil rights legislation of the 1960s, and in nominating Marshall, Johnson had chosen an advocate who was wholly committed to reforming American institutions by making them accessible. He had demonstrated that commitment in his work as a lawyer and would continue to do so upon taking his seat on the Court.[29]

Marshall had built a career arguing for the principle that access was a prerequisite to any sustained improvement for African Americans—access to juries, access to ballots, access to neighborhoods, and access to schools. Separatism, from Marshall's perspective, legitimized exclusion even if it had other practical attractions and thus did more harm than good. To Marshall, a society that permitted exclusion, by law or in practice, was not one in which members of minority groups could ever fully experience justice or full citizenship.

SEVEN

STIGMATIC INJURY

Assisted by a cane, Thurgood Marshall entered the Supreme Court's East Conference Room on June 28, 1991, as he entered many other rooms: to a standing ovation. The day before, only two and a half hours after the Court recessed for the summer and on the heels of his dissent in *Payne v. Tennessee*, the justice announced his retirement after twenty-four years of service in a short letter to President George H. W. Bush. As he entered the East Conference Room, the gathered press paid tribute to the retiring justice, though the feeling did not appear to be mutual as Marshall took his seat and met with the press. For a half hour, Marshall tolerated this perfunctory encounter, but only barely.

As he did with most of the questions that morning, he parried and avoided when asked about the future of school desegregation in the United States. "How can I comment on that?" he asked. "It's obvious I'm not going to have anything to do with it, so why should I be commenting on it?"[1] This was the answer of a jurist resigned to watching an issue that had consumed much of his career slip from his grasp. Justice Marshall's final two decades on the Court were increasingly marked by decisions that diminished the obligation on school authorities to populate schools with diverse student populations. By 1991, the arguments Marshall had made as a lawyer in the Little Rock case about the connection among integration, democracy, and citizenship had been eroded within the halls of the Supreme Court and in much of the nation at large. There was a vast gulf between the Court's treatment of desegregation cases Marshall encountered when he first joined the Court in 1967 and how it viewed such cases as he exited in 1991.

But from Marshall's perspective, the underlying problem remained largely the same. In *Brown*, he had argued that the Constitution could not tolerate outright racial exclusions; in *Cooper*, he had convinced the Court that democracy required protection of Black citizenship. Still, when Marshall joined the Court in 1967, the law might have changed, but the racial makeup of most schools barely had. For most American students, significant (if not total) racial homogeneity in schools was the norm. *De jure* segregation—that imposed by law—was being replaced by *de facto* segregation, the perpetuation of racially identifiable schools despite changes in the law. As a justice, Marshall and his colleagues grappled with whether this reality continued to violate the Constitution. To Marshall, the answer was simple: whether imposed by law or existing as a matter of fact, as long as racially segregated schools reinforced a message of Black inferiority, they ran afoul of the Constitution. Such schools generated and perpetuated a stigma upon any student who attended them: for Black students, that meant the assumption that their education was second rate and the message that their citizenship was second class. As Marshall had argued in *Brown*, this injured Black students' self-esteem and undermined their participation in the nation's social, political, and legal life. On the verge of Marshall's retirement, however, his judicial colleagues seemed no longer to agree that such stigmatic injuries were up to the government to correct. As a result, the eradication of single-race schools was no longer necessary to achieve constitutional compliance.

The sentiments that drove this retreat were rooted in a view of government that required neutrality rather than justice, and while Marshall encountered this view in legal arguments, it also animated broader social and political debates through the 1970s and 80s and has continued since his retirement. For example, the choice to diminish stigmatic injuries suffered by members of minority groups tended to undermine political support for reparative policies by hiding the long-term effects of government discrimination. The mandate of neutrality was easy enough to achieve, and society could move on without having to grapple with how to bring excluded groups into full citizenship. After Marshall's retirement, the argument would be taken even further, so that *reparative efforts themselves* would be critiqued as being insufficiently neutral and thus vulnerable to constitutional challenge. This would mean that not only was actual integration not required, but efforts to secure it could themselves be unconstitutional. The same fate awaited legislative protections, such as the Voting Rights Act. Such an outcome would have been unthinkable to Marshall, who believed strongly that the government not only could but *must* repair stigmatic injuries suffered as a result of the perpetuation of racially separate schools, neighborhoods, and workplaces—all markers of the limitations of Black citizenship. This was a position Marshall consistently promoted from his first school desegregation case until his last.[2]

A MORE ASSERTIVE COURT

The first school desegregation case Thurgood Marshall heard as a justice came from New Kent County, Virginia. Even after Arkansas had been coerced by federal troops and a Supreme Court rebuke in *Cooper* to inch forward with desegregation, Virginia continued a plan of massive resistance to the *Brown* mandate. In the immediate aftermath of *Brown*, the state legislature had passed a battery of laws designed to prevent any meaningful desegregation. Integrated schools were prohibited from receiving state funds and were subject to closure by the governor. In the event of closure, the state would grant school funds directly to students for use at private schools of their choice. The result was a series of private segregation academies, which opened in districts being subjected to desegregation lawsuits. At the most extreme, the entire school system of Prince Edward County, the site of one of the companion cases to the *Brown* litigation, shut down from 1959 through 1964, as white students attended the private Prince Edward Academy, founded in 1959, and Black students moved in with relatives in other counties or learned in makeshift schools, if at all. Some Black students even fled north, as Little Rock students had before them, to attend high school.

This was precisely the type of officially sanctioned resistance that fueled Black nationalists in the integration versus separation discussion within the African American community. Though the Court had rebuked open defiance of *Brown* in the Little Rock case, it had largely avoided school desegregation cases in the years that followed. By the time Marshall was seated, however, the viability of the desegregation project was being called into question. Regardless of what the Court had said, the actual facts in classrooms were largely unchanged: most Black students attended schools with mostly other Black students, while most white students attended schools with mostly other white students. This was young Clarence Thomas's experience in the Catholic schools of Savannah, and he would have found the same racial isolation in the city's public schools as well. Even his experience as the only Black student at his high school came in a racially homogeneous schooling environment, albeit one where he was in the minority. Segregation laws may have been voided, but racial integration was not the result.

In Virginia, courts had succeeded in unwinding open defiance. Faced with the closure of public schools in some communities, the state's highest court declared that the Virginia constitution prohibited the legislature from removing funds from schools simply because they would be integrated.[3] The legislative response, however, was to simply enable less obvious forms of obstinacy. A state Pupil Placement Board undertook all student placements and utilized allegedly race-neutral criteria to determine which students went to which schools. Still, in some districts, segregation remained as fixed in 1964 as it had been in 1954. In rural New Kent County, all of the county's Black students attended the Watkins school, while all of the county's white students attended the New Kent school. Under threat of suit and with the newly enacted Civil Rights Act of 1964 making federal funding for school districts conditional on ending racial discrimination in schooling, the New Kent County school board offered a new plan for beginning the desegregation process. The board adopted a "freedom of choice" plan that required families to choose among the county's two schools; any family could choose to attend either of the district's two schools. Regulations under the Civil Rights Act had explicitly signaled that freedom of choice plans were acceptable, "so long as in operation such a plan proves effective."[4] In Justice Marshall's first school desegregation case, the Supreme Court was charged with determining just what "effective" might mean.

The justices heard arguments in *Green v. New Kent County Board of Education* on April 3, 1968. Though the field of legal legitimacy had firmly turned away from segregation, the still-segregated schools of New Kent County presented a challenge to the Court's legitimacy: the justices and nation might have questioned the value of a decision like *Brown* if racial segregation continued much as before. The Court, in a unanimous opinion written by Justice William Brennan, used *Green* as an opportunity to reassert itself.

According to the Court, there could be no doubt that New Kent County had operated dual school systems. The schools' racial identifiability extended to "every facet of school operations—faculty, staff, transportation, extracurricular activities and facilities."[5] While the school board argued that its freedom of choice plan was non-racial in that a child of any race could choose to attend either school, the Court suggested that opening the doors in this way merely began the inquiry. The school board had an "affirmative duty to take whatever steps might be necessary to convert to a unitary system in which racial discrimination would be eliminated root and branch."[6] A freedom of choice plan was not such a plan, particularly given the school board's decade of delay in taking any action. In its most forceful statement on the matter, the Court declared the time for delay finished: "The burden on a school board today is to come forward with a plan that promises realistically to work, and promises realistically to work now."[7] The Court noted that 85 percent of Black children still attended the all-Black Watkins school, asserting that a district would not be unitary until significant numbers of students of different races were going to schools together. The Court was signaling not only that districts could not segregate, but that districts must integrate.[8]

Though Justice Marshall joined Brennan's unanimous position, his questions at oral argument did not focus on what an effective desegregation plan might look like. Instead, in his questioning of school board attorney Frederick T. Gray, Marshall brought attention to two points that would animate his judicial work on civil rights cases throughout his decades on the bench. First, in the face of Gray's consistent arguments to the contrary, Marshall emphasized that the question of race was never far from the surface of the school board's decisions, despite alleged neutrality. In the coming years, Marshall's pushes for more aggressive action by courts and government actors to overcome racial disparities would be met with the retort, advanced by Gray in *Green*, that the government was bound to behave in a race-neutral manner. Gray was arguing for a colorblindness in government decision making that Justice Thomas would one day promote: the task of government is to treat everyone the same and get out of the way of whatever private decisions people will make, he argued. This empowerment of individuals was the essence of a freedom of choice plan. But Marshall felt that the facially race-neutral freedom of choice plan was designed with race very much in mind. Toward the end of the oral argument, Marshall got Gray to concede that the school board had been aware of the feelings of many of New Kent County's white residents, who preferred to maintain exclusively white schools. This, Marshall concluded, demonstrated that even if race was not evident in the school board's policy, it was very much in the atmosphere as the board made its decision. Indeed, Marshall even suggested that the freedom of choice plan had been adopted "to perpetuate as much segregation as you could."[9]

Where Gray saw free choice, Marshall saw something different. He used his oral argument questions to establish that not all of the citizens in New Kent County truly had a free choice. He asked Gray whether a Black parent who wanted to send his child to the (white) New Kent school and whose employer suggested he not do so would have freedom of choice. Though Gray conceded that this would not be a free choice, he denied that such things had occurred in New Kent County. In Brennan's opinion, the Court cited to a 1966 report of the United States Commission on Civil Rights that had found freedom of choice plans to tend to perpetuate racially identifiable schools because of fear of retaliation against Black parents, violent and economic reprisals, and embarrassments of poverty ("Some Negro parents are embarrassed to permit their children to attend such schools without suitable clothing").[10] Even if the record did not establish that such things had occurred in New Kent County, Marshall brought what he knew to be the realities of desegregation into the courtroom. This, too, would be an argument he would employ repeatedly against mere neutrality in future cases, arguing that it failed to operate evenly in a nation filled with disparities.

Even as the Court in *Green* demanded desegregation plans "that promise realistically to work now," it was evident that reticent states, school boards, and families were going to need assertive interventions to actually change the racial makeup of schools. The Court was careful not to mandate any such interventions in *Green*, but if it was serious about seeing students of different races in schools together, the Court could not avoid such questions much longer.

Three years after *Green*, the Supreme Court got its chance in a school district quite different from the two-school district of New Kent County. The Charlotte-Mecklenburg school system in North Carolina was one of the 50 largest in the United States in 1969–70, serving more than 84,000 students in 107 schools. Approximately 71 percent of the district's students were white, and 29 percent African American, though many schools were racially identifiable. A majority of the district's Black students attended one of 21 schools where the student population was 99 percent African American or higher. Following the Court's ruling in *Green*, African American plaintiffs in Charlotte asked the district court overseeing an existing school desegregation case to take more assertive action in pushing the school district toward unitary status. Using the school district's demographic ratios as a starting point, the court ordered transportation of students so that schools in both the outlying (and mostly white) and inner-city (and mostly Black) areas would approximate the district's 71–29 percent ratio. If the goal was to ensure that students of different races were in school together, this busing plan presented one way to accomplish it.[11]

Green had signaled a Supreme Court more determined to see genuine impact of its decision in *Brown*. The Charlotte case, *Swann v. Charlotte-Mecklenburg Board of Education*, gave the Court an opportunity to offer more specific guidance about the tools that could be used to achieve that impact. By 1971, when the *Swann* case was decided, the more conservative Warren Burger had replaced Earl Warren as chief justice and, as school desegregation began to extend beyond the South, enthusiasm among moderate supporters was beginning to wane. The convergence of interests that had held together civil rights leaders like Marshall with national Democratic lawmakers began to diverge as northern cities began to encounter their own version of desegregation. Still, in *Swann*, the Court spoke unanimously in defining broad discretion for local courts crafting desegregation decrees. On each of the four specific questions posed to the Court, the justices allowed for wide latitude for district courts to order effective desegregation plans, writing that once a constitutional violation had been shown, "the scope of a district court's equitable powers to remedy past wrongs is broad." Of most significance, the Court validated the district court's plan to bus students in order to ensure desegregation: "We find no basis for holding that the local school authorities may not be required to employ bus transportation as one tool of school desegregation. Desegregation plans cannot be limited to the walk-in school."[12]

Though the Court framed *Swann* among other cases where courts were asked to craft effective remedies for successful plaintiffs, the breadth of discretion granted in *Swann* was sweeping. The signal from the Court was clear and was consistent with its statement in *Green*: district courts were to do what needed to be done to get students of different races in schools together. This was as forceful an order to integrate as the Court would issue, and it was the result of Thurgood Marshall's work behind the scenes. Initially, Justice Marshall had withheld support for earlier drafts of *Swann*, and he used the leverage of his vote to push Chief Justice Burger to make changes that expanded the leeway given to district courts. The result was the most significant period of school integration in American history.[13]

However, as district courts began to use tools like busing to ensure integration of schools and as the desegregation moved beyond the South—indeed, as desegregation remedies became substantially more effective than they had been in the first seventeen years following *Brown*—a new wave of resistance arose. Over time, this resistance (which often took the form of white families abandoning desegregating schools and the centers of American cities more broadly) eroded the Court's enthusiasm for desegregation plans that had actually begun succeeding in creating schools where students of different races were in classes together. It would reshape not only the nation's political landscape, but also its physical landscape as it coincided with and contributed to the suburbanization of American metropolitan areas. This resistance was less overt than Virginia shutting down its schools to avoid desegregation in the wake of *Brown*. But the backlash to the changes enabled by *Swann* was no less a rebuke of the efforts toward fuller recognition of Black equality.

By 1991, it was clear that *Swann* had represented a high-water mark in the Court's assertiveness in promoting equal Black citizenship through school integration. In 1971, Justice Marshall had been able to push a unanimous Supreme Court to expand the tools available to achieve actual desegregation in *Swann*. Over the next two decades, transitions on the Court and changes in society led to a retreat from that effort. By the time Justice Marshall was set to retire, the Court was no longer considering how to make desegregation work. Instead, the Court was looking at how to make desegregation—or at least court supervision of it—end.

"ENOUGH" DESEGREGATION

The school desegregation cases that reached the Supreme Court were only a fraction of the hundreds of such cases unfolding in *Brown*'s wake. Each case was animated by its own local circumstances and followed its own trajectory, but the story of Oklahoma City's schools followed a pattern similar to many others. When Oklahoma was admitted to the United States in 1907, its constitution mandated racial segregation in schools. In addition to these laws, school leaders in Oklahoma City were able to rely on residential racial segregation—generated in part through restrictive covenants that prohibited the sale of homes in certain areas to Black buyers—to establish and operate dual school systems. Even after the *Brown* decisions in 1954 and 1955, the Oklahoma City school board maintained policies that ensured that Black attendance in schools formerly reserved for white students would be minimal. This recalcitrance resulted in a lawsuit by Black parents in 1961, *Dowell v. Oklahoma City Board of Education,* a case that would remain open three decades later and occasion Thurgood Marshall's last official statement on school desegregation.[14]

In 1963 and again in 1965, the local district court in Oklahoma found that the schools had been intentionally segregated, were still operating as a dual system, and that race-neutral practices, like zoning all schools by neighborhood rather than race, had failed to remedy the prior segregation. This initial decade of facial compliance (students were no longer being assigned or excluded based on race) with very little change in the racial makeup of schools was consistent with the experience in Charlotte, New Kent County, and elsewhere. White school authorities were testing the Court's will in enforcing the *Brown* decisions.[15]

However, boosted by the Supreme Court's more assertive directives in *Green* and *Swann*, in 1972, the district court in Oklahoma adopted a more aggressive desegregation plan to overcome "the unpardonable recalcitrance of the . . . Board." The so-called Finger Plan paired schools in residentially segregated neighborhoods and bused students to accelerate the prospect of desegregation, much like what had occurred in Charlotte. The school board complied with the plan, but, after only three years, asked that the court order be lifted. In 1977, the district court in Oklahoma acquiesced, noting that the Finger Plan had achieved "substantial compliance with the constitutional requirements" and that the board had "manifested the desire and intent to follow the law." As was occurring elsewhere during the 1970s, the Oklahoma City school desegregation case was transitioning from one where a local court was proactively compelling policies, like busing, that would result in more diverse schools, to a case where schools were incrementally being released from court supervision. In 1977, the Oklahoma court ended its active supervision of the *Dowell* case, concluding that "the Board is entitled to pursue in good faith its legitimate policies without the continuing constitutional supervision of this court."[16] That this occurred only six years after *Swann* demonstrates the speed with which courts backpedaled from the most aggressive efforts toward integration. After decades of legally mandated racial segregation, the local district court ended its supervision after only five years of meaningful desegregation.

This timeline was not unique to Oklahoma City. In the 1980s, multitudes of school boards sought to end court supervision of desegregation even as local groups fought to preserve integration policies only a court could compel. In community after community, the release of court supervision led to reversals of integration gains and to a stalling of the narrowing of racial achievement gaps.

In Oklahoma City, the board sought an adjustment of the Finger Plan in 1984 that would have considerably increased racial imbalance. If approved, more than half of elementary schools would become racially isolated with student populations greater than 90 percent of a single race. In response to this prospective resegregation, the African American plaintiffs sought to reactivate the *Dowell* case and reestablish court supervision; in contrast, the school board sought to have the decree finally dissolved. It was on this question that, after a series of decisions in the lower courts, *Dowell* arrived at the Supreme Court in 1990.[17]

In a 5–3 decision authored by Chief Justice William Rehnquist, the Court considered the appropriate standard for courts to utilize in deciding whether to dissolve desegregation orders. The Court of Appeals (Tenth Circuit) had used a high standard for such a decision, concluding that a decree should remain in effect unless new and unforeseen circumstances caused a "grievous wrong" for the school district or made compliance with desegregation orders the source of "extreme and unexpectedly oppressive hardships." In the absence of such changes in circumstances, the Court of Appeals had allowed the plaintiffs to reopen the case in order to stop the school board from altering its student assignment scheme. Finding the standard of the Court of Appeals too high, the Supreme Court reversed. According to Chief Justice Rehnquist's opinion, a school board could have a desegregation order dissolved as long as it had complied in good faith with the decree and had eliminated the vestiges of past discrimination to the extent practicable. Arguing that desegregation orders were always intended to be temporary and that a goal should be the return of control of education to local authorities (rather than federal courts), the Court found the Oklahoma City school board's thirteen years of good-faith compliance important and signaled a path for school districts across the country to follow to end what had become decades of court supervision.[18]

Thurgood Marshall disagreed. In a blistering dissent lamenting the likely increase in racial isolation for students that would follow removal of court oversight, Justice Marshall dismissively quipped, "The majority today suggests that 13 years of desegregation was enough."[19] He understood that the Court was reducing the likelihood that American students would experience integrated schooling, and his dissent served as a sort of grand tour of his decades of work in the school desegregation arena. He emphasized a beloved theme that government systems had created racial inequality over many years, and that it was the government's responsibility to fix it.

As he tended to do in school desegregation cases, Marshall also provided a history lesson, beginning with mention of the graduate school desegregation cases he had worked on as a lawyer under the tutelage of Charles Hamilton Houston. These cases—including *Sweatt v. Painter* concerning the University of Texas law school and *Sipuel v. Bd. of Regents*, concerning the University of Oklahoma—had laid the immediate foundation for *Brown* and were modeled on his successful suit to obtain admission for Charles Murray into the University of Maryland's law school. Next, Marshall summoned the *Brown* triumph itself, quoting that decision's language about the detrimental effect that segregation caused African American students before referencing the early desegregation cases he heard as a Supreme Court justice, *Green* and *Swann*, to demonstrate that the Court's desegregation jurisprudence had been aimed at "remedying and avoiding the recurrence of this stigmatizing injury." The new diminished standard adopted by the majority, Marshall argued, represented a retreat that threatened to undermine the constitutional rights of Oklahoma City's Black children.[20]

To Marshall, a standard more in keeping with *Brown* would require acknowledgment of the stigmatic injury caused by segregated schools and would not tolerate such schools to persist. Allowing Oklahoma City's proposed plan to proceed would lead to an increase in the number of racially identifiable schools. For Marshall, such a reemergence of racial separation could "revive the message of racial inferiority implicit in the former policy of state-enforced segregation."[21]

According to the Justice Marshall of 1991, the man who had witnessed so much of this story firsthand, it was this message of racial inferiority and the stigma it produced that the government had caused with segregation and that the government remained obligated to eliminate. He offered his final assessment of *Brown*: "Our pointed focus in *Brown I* upon the stigmatic injury caused by segregated schools explains our unflagging insistence that formerly *de jure* segregated school districts extinguish all vestiges of school segregation." Marshall was dismayed that the Court would allow districts to merely remedy the harm "to the extent practicable" rather than forcing them to ensure that no student would experience the psychological and tangible injuries caused by segregated schools. He chided the majority for ignoring that the stigmatic harm identified in *Brown* could continue even after legal segregation ceased. Because racially identifiable schools would perpetuate that stigma, their continued existence stood as a "vestige" of the state-sponsored segregation struck down in *Brown*. Indeed,

Justice Marshall's expansive definition of a vestige as "any condition that is likely to convey the message of inferiority" related back directly to the stigma of segregation. The reemergence of one-race schools, threatened in Oklahoma City absent continued court supervision, would be just such a vestige, in Justice Marshall's mind.[22]

But the harm of segregation was more than merely psychological. Just as *Brown* had initially been motivated by the physical inequalities imposed upon Black schoolchildren—inequalities Marshall had tediously documented on his trips south with Charles Hamilton Houston—in his *Dowell* dissent Marshall reminded his audience that identifiability of schools still tended to perpetuate tangible inequality for Black students. In a footnote, he pointed to high student–faculty ratios, lower quality teachers, inferior facilities, and lower quality course offerings as evidence that only a "radical transformation" could truly eliminate all the vestiges of segregation. In his mind, it was *on government* to push this transformation, and if school boards, local officials, and the elected branches would not do it, then the responsibility fell to the courts. Clearly identifying government as both the source of the problem and the party responsible for its remedy, Justice Marshall summed up his view that "the effects of past discrimination remain chargeable to the school district regardless of its lack of continued enforcement of segregation, and the remedial decree is required until those effects have been finally eliminated."[23] Decades after his own aborted interest in attending law school at the all-white University of Maryland, Marshall still recognized the stigmatizing message sent by racially homogeneous schools. Only access—only actual integration—could refute that message.

He went on to dismiss the various arguments made to justify the majority's more lenient standard for releasing school districts from court supervision, rehashing positions he had taken in nearly two decades of dissents on these topics. But the triumphant lawyer of *Brown* had lost control of the desegregation story. Among the many dissents Justice Marshall penned in his final years on the Court, *Dowell* must have been among the most heartbreaking. He desperately argued for the Court to acknowledge the harm done to Black students by the continued and reemerging racial isolation in schools, to accept that such harm could be directly traced to the government's previous official policy of segregation, and to allow courts to continue pushing school districts to undo that harm. He concluded his nearly sixty years of work in this most central area with resignation:

> Consistent with the mandate of *Brown I*, our cases have imposed on school districts an unconditional duty to eliminate *any* condition that perpetuates the message of racial inferiority inherent in the policy of state-sponsored segregation. The racial identifiability of a district's schools is such a condition. Whether this "vestige" of state-sponsored segregation will persist cannot simply be ignored at the point where a district court is contemplating the dissolution of a desegregation decree. In a district with a history of state-sponsored school segregation, racial separation, in my view *remains* inherently unequal. I dissent.[24]

Although the majority in *Dowell* did not officially release the Oklahoma City school board from court supervision, its lowered standard for such dissolution of desegregation orders signaled the direction of the case. Indeed, when the case was remanded, the lower court in Oklahoma dissolved the decree.

By that time, November 1991, Justice Marshall had retired, having been replaced by an individual whose life experiences led him to a very different perspective on the desirability of racially integrated schools. It would take some time for Justice Clarence Thomas to weigh in on desegregation in elementary schools and high schools, but during his first term on the bench, he encountered a desegregation case from the colleges of Mississippi. Whereas Justice Marshall concluded his tenure on the Court lamenting the stigma of racially identifiable schools, Justice Thomas began his by extolling their benefits.[25]

EIGHT

IN DEFENSE OF BLACK INSTITUTIONS

The Catholic schools of mid-century Savannah were a long way from the public schools of Oklahoma City the Supreme Court considered in *Dowell* in 1991. Yet the legal rejection of segregation in *Brown* was part of a broader societal shift eliminating impenetrable racial barriers even in private institutions. The softening of those barriers enabled new access for African Americans, but it also impacted institutions that had been created to serve the Black community within the constraints of Jim Crow segregation. The first high school Clarence Thomas attended, St. Pius X in Savannah, provides a case in point.

Through the first half of the twentieth century, parents in Savannah's Black Catholic community might send their children to diocese schools through the eighth grade. However, because the diocese schools were racially segregated, and there was no Catholic high school for Black students, schooling for high school would have to continue in Savannah's public schools or other private institutions. After much urging from the local Black Catholic community, the Savannah diocese used five acres of donated land to construct a high school for Black students in the 1950s.

What came to be called St. Pius X opened for the 1952–53 school year and graduated its first class of fourteen students in 1955. However, even as this opportunity was created for African American students, advocates pushed for integration into the diocese's existing white institutions. In 1961, the bishops in Savannah, Atlanta, and Charleston, SC, set in motion policy changes that would allow Black students to enter any Catholic school "as soon as can be done."[1] The first African American students entered formerly white Savannah Catholic schools in 1963. In Savannah, advocates pushed both for the building up of Black institutions (St. Pius X) and for the elimination of racial barriers simultaneously, demonstrating that the two strategies for uplift that had animated debates for centuries were not mutually exclusive.[2]

As elsewhere, desegregation not only brought access for African American students to institutions that had been inaccessible, but also raised questions about the utility of continuing to operate the Black institutions that had been necessary during segregation. In Savannah, the community had worked for years to establish a Black Catholic high school; a decade later, integration threatened St. Pius X's survival. In 1969, a group from the Office of Educational Research at the University of Notre Dame studied enrollment trends and the educational needs within the Savannah diocese, ultimately recommending that St. Pius X be closed in order to accelerate integration. The reaction within the Black community was heartbreak; one woman lamented the closing of St. Pius, highlighting that the school "was so new and meant so much to us." Opponents of the closure cited racism, lack of consultation, and a withdrawal of church support for the Black community, charges the diocese denied, highlighting integration as a primary motivation.[3]

The creation and closing of St. Pius X demonstrated how the tension between the competing strategies for Black empowerment—self-empowerment of Black institutions and removal of barriers to exclusionary white institutions—could play out in the post-*Brown* world. African Americans had worked hard to create an institution to serve the community even as they pushed to gain access to schools that excluded them. Once those schools opened their doors, however narrowly, the existence of the Black institution was threatened. In Savannah, the convergence led to the closing of St. Pius X through "a tragic process" that left lasting scars on the Black Catholic community.[4]

For his part, Clarence Thomas had attended St. Pius at the start of his high school career from 1962 through 1964 before transferring as one of the first Black students to attend seminary and complete high school at St. John Vianney. He thus had experience both with attending a Black institution and with confronting desegregation. These exposures would lead him to a very different position about the continued existence of all-Black institutions than the one Thurgood Marshall had arrived at in 1991. Thomas provided a glimpse of that position during his first year on the Court in a case about the public historically Black colleges and universities (HBCUs) of Mississippi.

At the fulcrum of the most impactful Supreme Court transition in decades were widely different interpretations of the persistence of schools with predominantly African American student populations. Justice Marshall saw on the horizon in Oklahoma City an increase in racial isolation for Black students, the result of the Court's abdication of its role in forcing school systems to fully remedy a decades-long system of oppression, and he lamented the stigma students in such schools would suffer from the implications of separation. Those implications included a belief that Black students were unwanted in predominantly white schools and the historic, racist trope that Black students were unequipped to succeed in them. These were repercussions Marshall knew well even as he sought to—and did—disprove them throughout his life. He had attended HBCUs (Lincoln University and Howard University's law school) and understood their value, but his exclusion from the white institutions that had assumed his inferiority generated a compulsion for Marshall to prove that he was as talented and able as any other lawyer in the country. When he saw schools that served only Black students, he saw the perpetuation of the stigma he experienced onto a new generation.

But Thomas saw something different. In HBCUs, he saw pride and tradition, an opportunity for Black students to learn without the stress and burden of existence in a place where they were not wholly accepted. These were feelings Thomas knew well. As part of the generation that entered schools just as the Supreme Court decided *Brown*, he had experienced those elite, predominantly white institutions to which Marshall was striving to measure up. In his success within those institution, Thomas has proven correct Marshall's assertion that Black students were just as talented as any other students. But while he had done well academically, Thomas suffered a different type of stigma, one also rooted in the feeling that white institutions considered him inferior. Over time, Thomas would attribute that perception of inferiority to the attention that institutions were placing on race in order to increase campus diversity, and he would turn his judicial ire upon it. But in 1992, perhaps recalling his earlier schooling experiences in the all-Black Catholic schools of Savannah, St. Benedict and St. Pius X, he looked longingly at higher education environments that were far different from those he experienced, and he sought to preserve them for the next generation of Black college students.

These different perspectives were partially the result of the generational difference between Marshall and Thomas: each encountered a version of the same problem, racist notions of Black inferiority, that fit the context of their different times. But the differences also stemmed from the paradoxical place of HBCUs and historically Black institutions more broadly during the era of desegregation. These institutions—whether in education, health services, business, and even law—had been forced into existence by segregation. Even Charles Hamilton Houston, the architect of the strategy of integration, had deliberately turned Howard into a training ground for Black lawyers out of a belief that only Black lawyers could do the necessary work.

As legal segregation was delegitimized after *Brown*, the increased access for Black students to formerly forbidden institutions and spaces created a climate where historically Black institutions could be perceived as inconsistent with the push for desegregation. But Thomas pointed out that there was value in preserving and supporting Black institutions, regardless of the push for integration. He hoped to preserve the option for Black students to attend predominantly Black schools, while Marshall wanted to make sure Black students were not forced to do so. Here was the distinction— the difference between enforced and voluntary segregation—W. E. B. Du Bois had contemplated in the pages of the NAACP's *Crisis* decades earlier, and it cut to the contrasting visions Marshall and Thomas brought to the Court.

'BROWN' AND TENSION FOR HBCUS

The forces that led to the creation and ultimate closure of St. Pius X were not unique to the Catholic schools of Savannah. For a group of Americans denied educational opportunity— indeed, punished for taking part in education in parts of the country—the need to create institutions to serve Black students had deep roots. The aftermath of the Civil War brought some of the first formal commitments to schooling for African American students, and in the decade of the 1860s, thousands of young students attended. With the increase in school accessibility for Black children, there arose a new demand: higher education for African Americans. From the Civil War through the 1954 *Brown* decision, that demand was filled primarily in HBCUs. By 1953, 90 percent of African American college attendees were enrolled in HBCUs.[5]

Thurgood Marshall's alma maters, Lincoln University in Pennsylvania and Howard University in Washington, DC, exemplify early efforts. Founded by northern Presbyterians who believed that college-educated African Americans might help spread the religion, Lincoln was established prior to the Civil War, in 1854. Just after the war, also with an eye toward training African American preachers, a group of missionaries envisioned a seminary for Black students in the nation's capital. By 1867, with the support of the Reconstruction Congress and the Freedmen's Bureau, Howard University was established, named for Civil War veteran and commissioner of the Freedmen's Bureau, Oliver Howard. Many of the earliest efforts to create HBCUs were private schools built upon religious motivations and funding, but the federal government also helped enable public HBCUs through two rounds of grants that created seventeen land-grant colleges. The Morrill Land-Grant Acts (1862 and 1890) facilitated a significant growth in American colleges and universities, and the latter act in 1890 mandated that states accepting money through the grant either admit all students or establish separate institutions serving Black students. Amid the legal mandate of segregation, many southern states then established HBCUs under the program. The first land-grant-funded HBCU was Alcorn University (now Alcorn State University), established in 1871 in Claiborne County, Mississippi.[6]

Through the period of Jim Crow segregation, HBCUs provided the primary opportunity for African Americans to enter higher education. Though they had been founded out of necessity resulting from hostility to Black education, many HBCUs thrived, providing the foundation upon which generations of African Americans earned undergraduate and professional degrees and found economic stability. HBCUs would also provide space and training for African American students to engage in discussions about how best to confront the battery of laws and customs that continued to strangle the Black community economically and educationally. This mission of Black empowerment through Black institutions could be seen in Thurgood Marshall's experience at Howard, which provided not only training for Marshall and his colleagues but a sense of mission. HBCUs would remain central to activism through the civil rights movement and beyond.

However, Houston and Marshall's efforts to open the doors of graduate schools (such as the Universities of Maryland, Missouri, and Texas) and the eventual success in *Brown v. Board of Education* would profoundly impact HBCUs. As occurred when the white Catholic leadership in Savannah decided to allow Black students to attend schools from which they had been excluded, the end of legal segregation placed Black institutions in a tenuous position. On one hand, Black institutions provided opportunities for African Americans that were otherwise denied and earned stature and pride. Closing such pillars of the community would have been traumatic, as the closing of St. Pius X had been to Savannah's Black Catholic community. However, with the end of legalized segregation, HBCUs also seemed to represent a vestige of an era that was slowly being discredited. As Black students gained access to previously forbidden spaces, could HBCUs survive?[7]

Survival might have been threatened both as a practical and as a philosophical matter. Practically, as Black students had greater options, sustaining HBCU enrollment and finances might prove challenging. The struggle for survival was nothing new for HBCUs, but the threat after 1954 was (ironically) compounded by the potential inconsistency in advocating both for greater access to previously forbidden institutions and for continued support for institutions whose primary mission remained to serve African American students. Philosophically, HBCUs sat at the center of historic debates about the relative merits of integration and the empowering of Black institutions. Over time, the practical challenge would be diminished in part by a surge in African American college enrollment. The philosophical tension would remain present through the post-*Brown* decades as advocates pushed for desegregation and increased access, while at the same time they fought to preserve HBCUs. Justices Marshall and Thomas would each play a role in working through that tension, within the universities of Mississippi.[8]

RACE AND HIGHER EDUCATION IN MISSISSIPPI

In early 1961, Thurgood Marshall, then executive director of the NAACP's Legal Defense and Education Fund, was contacted by the NAACP's field secretary in Mississippi, Medgar Evers. Evers told of a 29-year-old African American Air Force veteran who owned land and resided outside of Kosciusko, Mississippi, and wished to complete his college education at the University of Mississippi. Three decades before his *Dowell* dissent, Thurgood Marshall was beginning to sense that it was time to move on from the LDF. Marshall had led the organization since 1940, but after two decades filled with extraordinary victories, Marshall was growing weary of the exhausting role as public face, fundraiser, and chief strategist, as well as of the infighting within the organization. By the end of 1961, he would be sworn in as a judge on the U.S. Court of Appeals for the Second Circuit, having been appointed by President John F. Kennedy, an important step on his path to the Supreme Court.

It was Kennedy as well who had inspired the air force veteran from Mississippi. The day after Kennedy's inaugural speech in January 1961, James Meredith had written to the University of Mississippi seeking an application.[9] Upon being rejected, Meredith conferred with Evers, who put the applicant in touch with the LDF. By May, the NAACP lawyers had initiated a case on Meredith's behalf with one of Marshall's ablest deputies, Constance Baker Motley, taking the lead.[10] Along with Alabama, Mississippi was the longest holdout in prohibiting African American students from its flagship university campuses, but by mid-1962, Motley had pushed the Fifth Circuit Court of Appeals to conclude that "from the moment the defendants discovered Meredith was a Negro they engaged in a carefully calculated campaign of delay, harassment, and masterly inactivity."[11] Finding that the university's various excuses for denying Meredith's enrollment—he had missed a deadline, he had too many credits to be admitted as a transfer student, his transfer credits did not count because many came from an unaccredited institution (Jackson State College, one of Mississippi's own public universities), he had no letters of recommendation from alumni—were thinly veiled excuses for excluding an African American applicant, the court ordered the university to let Meredith in for the fall 1962 semester.[12]

Having lost in court, Mississippi governor Ross Barnett mimicked post-*Brown* resistance elsewhere by pledging defiance of the orders. Barnett scored political points among white Mississippians with his rebelliousness and fed into a frenzy of resistance to Meredith's registration. Amid rising tensions, Meredith was secretly brought to campus on September 30, 1962, protected by federal marshals. However, a growing mob of non-students descended upon the campus and initiated a riot of yelling, gunfire, and bottle throwing. Barnett continued to fan the flames of the riot, and by morning there were two people dead and several hundred injured. For his part, James Meredith had remained in an isolated and protected portion of the campus; under protection from an increased presence of federal troops, he filled out his enrollment forms the following morning at the university registrar's office. He spent two semesters at the University of Mississippi and graduated in August 1963 with a degree in political science.[13]

The Ole Miss riot marked the beginning of the desegregation of Mississippi's institutes of higher education. There were eight such institutions, including five that historically had served white students and three that had historically served Black students, and all eight had desegregated to some extent by the end of the 1970s. However, due to slow progress at desegregation and at the urging of the federal Department of Health, Education, and Welfare (HEW), the state and its board of trustees overseeing the eight institutions developed a plan in 1974 aimed at ensuring equal access to all the state's public colleges and universities for members of all races by developing target numbers for both student and faculty of each institution's "opposite race."[14] When that plan was rejected by HEW, a group of Black plaintiffs filed suit in 1975 alleging that Mississippi continued to maintain a racially dual system of public higher education. The parties worked toward an agreement for a dozen years before the case headed to trial in 1987. At that point, the state's universities remained—like the public schools of Oklahoma City—racially identifiable. Student bodies at the state's five formerly white institutions remained between 80 and 91 percent white, while the opposite was true at the HBCUs; there, student populations ranged from 92 to 99 percent Black. Despite these demographics, the state maintained that it had fulfilled its duty to disestablish its state-sponsored segregated system because it maintained "good-faith, nondiscriminatory race-neutral policies and practices in student admission, faculty hiring, and operations."[15] The lower court in Mississippi found this argument persuasive, concluding that the state had ceased its segregative practices and had complied with its constitutional obligations. The appeals court affirmed this decision, and the case landed at the Supreme Court for argument just a month after Clarence Thomas was sworn in.[16]

Though in the context of higher education, the question before the Court was similar to that considered in *Dowell*: the Court was to determine the appropriate standard for continued court supervision of a desegregation order. However, in contrast to *Dowell* where the Court found the lower court's standard too high, the Court in the Mississippi case, *U.S. v. Fordice*, concluded that the lower court had let Mississippi off too easy. In particular, Justice Byron White's opinion for the Court held that "the adoption and implementation of race-neutral policies alone [does not] suffice to demonstrate that the state has completely abandoned its prior dual system." This was a conclusion Thurgood Marshall might have agreed with. For Marshall, good faith and race neutrality were insufficient to justify ending court oversight, a point Justice White echoed in *Fordice*, noting that "even after a state dismantles its segregative admissions policy, there may still be state action that is traceable to the state's prior *de jure* segregation that continues to foster segregation."[17]

In the university system of Mississippi, with its eight institutions readily identifiable by race, the Court found several existing policies with roots in the era of segregation that still seemed to be impacting the racial makeup of the state's public universities. In addition, the Court took issue with the duplication of programs at universities in close proximity to one another, which looked like a continuation of separate but equal. Further, the designation of distinctive missions for each university (three of the formerly white institutions were designated "comprehensive" universities, while the three formerly Black institutions were designated "regional" or "urban" universities) echoed the inequalities of the institutions during the Jim Crow era. Building on the point about duplication, the Court wondered if the continued operation of all eight campuses might itself be a vestige of the segregation era, fostering student choices that perpetuate the racial identifiability of the state's universities. Without taking a position, the Court suggested that on remand, the lower courts consider whether maintenance of each university is educationally justifiable or if any might be practicably closed or merged. It was on this final point that Justice Thomas focused his *Fordice* concurrence.[18]

During his uncertain period at Conception Seminary—when he had determined that he would not be pursuing the priesthood, but he was uncertain what his path would be—Clarence Thomas considered transferring to two of the nation's best-known HBCUs, schools that were producing many of the leaders of the civil rights movement: Fisk University and Morehouse College. However, Thomas never applied. He had heard rumors that the schools used the required photograph with the application to discriminate against darker-skinned students like himself, and so Thomas ended up at Holy Cross. Just as Thurgood Marshall had never bothered to apply to law school at the University of Maryland due to skin color, Thomas perceived that the color of his skin would prevent his admission at these historic Black institutions. However, whereas Marshall dedicated his career to integrating institutions like those that had excluded him, in his *Fordice* concurrence, Thomas lauded the importance of Mississippi's historically Black institutions.[19]

Justice Thomas began his first statement on race and education with a quotation from a 1917 editorial in *The Crisis*, the NAACP's magazine, that he attributed to W. E. B. Du Bois. Du Bois was himself a graduate of Fisk, and he had gone on to become perhaps the most elite African American scholar in the country. But Du Bois was also among the class of Black elites Thomas seemed to have resented in Savannah for thinking themselves better than others. The editorial Justice Thomas quoted from was a repudiation of a forthcoming government report that was expected to recommend closure of many Black institutions and a plea for support of Fisk and other Black schools. "We must rally to the defense of our schools," Du Bois had written and Justice Thomas quoted. As he would in his "Does the Negro Need Separate Schools?" essay, Du Bois recognized the imperative of Black institutions amid a world infected with racism. Based on his own experiences, Justice Thomas had reached a similar conclusion.[20]

In writing separately, Justice Thomas hoped to make clear that mere racial imbalance in Mississippi's universities—schools that had disproportionate numbers of white or Black students—was not a problem. Justice Marshall had claimed that racial identifiability of lower schools caused the same stigmatic injury forbidden after *Brown*, but Justice Thomas argued that the focus in the higher education context must be "on the specific *policies* alleged to produce racial imbalance, rather than on the *imbalance* itself."[21] And he offered his own interpretation of the majority's standard for when those policies should be presumptively unconstitutional: when they began during the period of *de jure* segregation, when they continued to produce racially adverse impacts, and when they persisted without any sound educational justification.

Focusing on the practical flexibility required of courts in evaluating desegregation remedies, Justice Thomas found encouragement in the Court's willingness to consider justifications for policies that might seem unconstitutional at first glance. Specifically, he approvingly referred to *Dowell* for the idea that an otherwise unconstitutional policy may be justified if its elimination were not practicable. Of particular import to Justice Thomas was the idea that sound educational justifications might validate policies that seemed to perpetuate segregation, and he wished to identify one such educational justification: according to Justice Thomas, the majority opinion did not "foreclose the possibility that there exists 'sound educational justification' for maintaining historically black colleges *as such*."[22] While many Black students might wish to attend the state's predominantly white institutions, Thomas understood why not *all* Black students would. He pushed against any presumption that all Black students would want the same thing, a reflection of his own crusade to validate opinions that differed from many other African Americans.

The final two paragraphs of Justice Thomas's short concurrence served to enthusiastically summarize the benefits of HBCUs for Black students. The schools had survived and flourished even as opportunities for African Americans had expanded. They were a source of pride and hope, and they provided leadership in developing educational opportunities for Black students at all levels. To Justice Thomas, who had opted against attending HBCUs from high school on, this success was due in part to the institutions' "distinctive histories and traditions." He sought to make sure that no one confuse the majority's skepticism of program duplication, designed to "separate the races for the sake of separating the races," with the institutional diversity involved in operating some schools with distinctive histories.[23] Such diversity was based upon sound educational justifications, Thomas argued, since universities are not fungible.

Then, in his final sentence, Justice Thomas perhaps had in mind his old school, St. Pius X, the Catholic high school for African Americans in Savannah. When the Catholic schools began to desegregate in the early 1970s, St. Pius X was closed, and Black students were sent to the existing schools for white students. The closure of Black institutions was a legacy of the larger effort of desegregation, as burdens fell disproportionately on African Americans. Justice Thomas wished to avoid such a fate for the HBCUs of Mississippi. "It would be ironic, to say the least," Justice Thomas wrote, "if the institutions that sustained blacks during segregation were themselves destroyed in an effort to combat its vestiges."[24]

Implicit in Thomas's opinion is the beginning of what would become his broader critique of the post-*Brown* narrative. In this, he echoed Du Bois's 1935 argument that the circumstances of the United States are not conducive in most places to effective education for African Americans in predominantly white institutions. This was a criticism that would grow as the decades after *Brown* revealed the extent to which resistance to meaningful integration of schools would undermine courts' ability to deliver on the vision of integrated schools providing equal educational opportunities for Black students. That resistance began in governors' offices and state legislatures in the immediate aftermath of *Brown* and could be seen in the popular white resistance—first to desegregation of any sort and then to more aggressive remedies like busing. It began as open hostility to Black students when they dared enter formerly white institutions and morphed into widespread abandonment of entire systems of schools by white families, a phenomenon known as white flight.

By the time of *Dowell* in 1991 and the sunset of Justice Marshall's tenure on the Court, the Supreme Court had already given in to the forces that made integration of schools so difficult. But the transition from Marshall to Thomas brought not only the further cementing of this judicial reality, but also an entirely different way of thinking about the strategy of integration for confronting inequality. Whereas Marshall had seen the continued racial isolation in the schools of Oklahoma City as a cause of ongoing stigmatic harm and a perpetuation of systemic discrimination against African American students, Justice Thomas saw something very different. Four years after *Fordice*, he would expand his critique of integration, offering a different take from his predecessor on *Brown* itself. In so doing, he echoed the sentiments of Black nationalism that had animated Marcus Garvey and Malcolm X and that had led to the creation of schools specially concerned with the development of African American students.

"It never ceases to amaze me that the courts are so willing to assume that anything that is predominantly black must be inferior," Justice Thomas began in his concurrence in *Missouri v. Jenkins* in 1995. More than in *Fordice*, the *Jenkins* case would provide Justice Thomas an opportunity to fully develop his critique of not only the integration strategy, but also Justice Marshall's interpretation of the Constitution's equal protection clause. Ever skeptical of the value of integration, Justice Thomas observed that desegregation had not produced leaps forward in educational achievement, and he built upon his *Fordice* concurrence:

> [I]t may very well be that what has been true for historically black colleges is true for black middle and high schools. . . . Because of their distinctive histories and traditions, black schools can function as the center and symbol of black communities, and provide examples of independent black leadership, success, and achievement.[25]

Justice Thomas saw something else at work in Marshall's belief that racially isolated schools continued to cause psychological harm to Black students even after *enforced* segregation had ended. Marshall had written in *Dowell* that the same harm the Court had confronted in *Brown* was at stake if racially neutral policies continued to produce racially isolated schools. Justice Thomas rejected that reading of *Brown*, opining that the harm in *Brown* was tied purely to *de jure* segregation and that psychological harm was "irrelevant to the question." Perhaps with memories of his dabbling in the Black nationalist politics of the 1970s, he wrote,

> [I]f separation itself is a harm, and if integration therefore is the only way that blacks can receive a proper education, then there must be something inferior about blacks. Under this theory, segregation injures blacks because blacks, when left on their own, cannot achieve. To my way of thinking, that conclusion is the result of a jurisprudence based upon a theory of black inferiority.[26]

A starker contrast to Justice Marshall is difficult to imagine, and no other justice could have made such a point.

Justice Marshall may have even conceded some shortcomings to the integration strategy, but he also understood that the history of American education demonstrated that when African American students were able to be separated from white students, they would not be treated equally. That had been true during his visits through the South in the 1930s; it remained true in 1991, and it would still be true into the twenty-first century. There was thus a pragmatism to the strategy of integration independent of any principled objection to racial identifiability of elementary and secondary schools: integration may have been the only viable path to sustainable and widespread improvement in educational opportunities for Black students.

The root of this disagreement upon tactics (as it is not a disagreement upon goals) is the broader conversation among advocates for African American uplift across centuries about the relative advantages of integration into the mainstream American fabric versus the separate development of Black institutions. In their judicial writings on race and education, Justices Marshall and Thomas infused this conversation with their contrasting legal philosophies. For Marshall, the best evidence that government had sufficiently righted the wrongs caused by state-sponsored subjugation of African Americans could be seen in meaningful integration in which individuals of every race would be empowered with equal opportunities. For

Thomas, the better path to Black empowerment would come from the individual's achievement of skills that would enable success, regardless of the environment in which those skills were attained. Though evident in their writings on either side of the 1991 transition from Justice Marshall to Justice Thomas, the implications of their contrasting philosophies would become clearer over time as Thomas had the opportunity to confront cases and topics akin to those Marshall once faced. The transition would cement the Court's shift from focusing on systems to focusing on impact to individuals. Thomas's restrictive vision of what the Constitution could accomplish would slowly replace Marshall's expansive view of the federal government's obligation and ability to right historic wrongs. And though these contrasts were born of distinctions in how best to ensure full citizenship and schooling for African Americans, they would have more far-reaching effects in the work of the Supreme Court and its interpretation of the Constitution.

PART III

INDIVIDUALS AND GOVERNMENT

NINE

CYCLES OF EXPANSION AND BACKLASH

In 1912, a 4-year-old boy entered a one-room schoolhouse built two years earlier just north of the Pedernales River in Gillespie County, Texas. The student would only spend four months at the Junction School due to an outbreak of whooping cough, but he would return more than a half century later, its most famous pupil. Seated next to his Junction School teacher, Katie Deadrich, at a table on the lawn outside the schoolhouse, President Lyndon Johnson signed the Elementary and Secondary Education Act (ESEA) into law on April 11, 1965.[1]

"No law I have signed or will ever sign means more to the future of America," the president boasted. The law, which Johnson had been pursuing as a cornerstone of his war on poverty within his vision of a Great Society, represented a "major new commitment of the federal government to quality—and equality—in the schooling that we offer our young people." As a former teacher, Johnson understood the impact education could have in shaping lives, declaring, "Education is the only valid passport from poverty."[2]

Johnson's triumph in passing the ESEA represented a seismic shift in the role of the federal government in American education and required overcoming a thorny obstacle that had both legal and psychological dimensions. There was perhaps no greater symbol of local democratic governance than the one-room schoolhouse, like the Junction School that served as the president's backdrop. Such schools represented a small community's effort to serve its children, controlling everything from the construction of the building to the selection of the teacher to the curriculum to be taught. Of course, by mid-century, most American students learned in more contemporary settings, though the ideal of a locally controlled school remained powerful in the American mind. The school was the site of a citizen's most direct interaction with government, so the pull for local control and governance at the smallest unit remained strong.

Yet this localism helped contribute to vast disparities in educational quality. Beyond the inequalities imposed along racial lines, schools in neighboring districts and even schools within the same district exhibited wide variations in resources and quality. Localism could be inefficient, too, a reality many states and school districts increasingly appreciated throughout the twentieth century. With the widespread adoption of compulsory education came a trend of school district consolidation: between 1930 and 1970, 90 percent of American school districts were eliminated through consolidation. Such mergers could solve inefficiencies, but they did not address the resource disparities plaguing American schools. Johnson's vision sought to cast the federal government as an equalizing force. Title I of the ESEA provided funds to states and school districts across the country, targeting students in poverty and carving a new and more substantial role for the federal government in education policy. Prior to 1950, the federal role in education was virtually nonexistent as opponents skeptical of federal involvement had blocked legislation. But forces of social change in the mid-1960s had led to a landslide election in 1964 that gave Johnson the necessary support in Congress to make ESEA happen.[3]

The federal *judiciary*, at the persistent prodding of Thurgood Marshall and colleagues, had already been intervening in local education for more than a decade. The post-*Brown* desegregation lawsuits happening throughout the South were involving federal judges in the intricacies of school attendance zones and student assignment policies. ESEA, combined with Title VI of the Civil Rights Act of 1964's prohibition on discrimination by entities receiving federal funds, accelerated federal involvement in desegregation beyond the courts. Indeed, it had been a fear of increased federal intervention undermining segregation that had long animated some of the opposition to aid programs like ESEA. After passage of the bill, increased involvement *did* lead to the desegregation cases from Virginia (*Green*) and North Carolina (*Swann*) that Marshall encountered during his early years on the Supreme Court, cases that seemed to expand the discretion of federal judges and further the role of the federal government more broadly.

But those results had consequences in the ongoing debate about the appropriate balance between national and local power. *Swann*, in particular, provided a new symbol for those hostile to federal involvement to rally against—busing. At the same time, the 1960s legislation was helping advocates push desegregation beyond the South and into places yet to be touched directly by *Brown*.

All of this meant that by the early 1970s, schools were a primary arena for the perpetual American debate about the proper boundary between national and local power. Johnson had placed the weight of the federal government on the side of greater involvement, making the case that it was the government's responsibility to ensure greater equity for American children. Through ESEA, the government was committed to providing resources for students in poverty. Still, the vast majority of funding for schools came from state or local taxes, and school boards had wide discretion in operations outside of the few areas where the federal government was involved.

To Marshall and Johnson, the federal government's increasing effort to address disparities in educational opportunities based on race and poverty was a welcome development. But these federal interventions spawned forceful resistance as well. The authority the federal government was asserting through legislation and court decisions came at the expense of the autonomy of local school boards and citizens. They upset the balance of power between federal and state governments, a balance that had been the subject of intense disagreement since before the nation's founding and that frequently implicated the rights of African Americans.

DUAL SOVEREIGNTY IN THE CONSTITUTION

Even before the ratification of the Constitution, some Americans worried that it would create a strong central government with control over individual lives, similar to the British monarchy the fledgling nation had just shed. Indeed, had those who orchestrated the Constitutional Convention in Philadelphia in 1787 revealed an intent to not merely revise the Articles of Confederation but replace them with a new constitution and a stronger national government, states would never have sent delegates. Once in Philadelphia, the central problem facing the document's principal author, James Madison, was how to craft a national government that the states would accept, but not simply ignore. The Constitution, with its dual sovereign model—a federal government alongside state governments, each sovereign in its own sphere, and protection of state influence even within the national government, through the Senate and the electoral college—represented a compromise that would be regularly revisited. Too much federal power risked nullifying the principle of self-government within the states, but too much state power threatened to undermine the ability of the nation to exist as anything but a patchwork of confederated states. The national government that emerged from the Constitutional Convention was more restrained than Madison had imagined would be necessary, but the states had given up a great deal in order to strengthen their union.[4]

The question of the appropriate balance of power between federal and state governments opened the schism that birthed the nation's first political parties: Hamilton's Federalists and the Republican Party of James Madison and his fellow Virginian Thomas Jefferson. In the nation's earliest decades, Republicans would invoke "liberty" and "democracy," while pushing to protect state power and promote individualized agriculture within the nation's economy, while Federalists embraced a strong central government and policies that promoted manufacturing and industry.[5] The question of whether states could be bound by federal laws was an open one. Jefferson, while serving as vice president of the federal government in the late 1790s, drafted (secretly) resolutions for Kentucky and Virginia that would embrace the right of states to simply nullify federal laws the states felt were inconsistent with the Constitution. This idea, "interposition," would reemerge in the long buildup to the Civil War, with politicians like South Carolina Senator John Calhoun arguing that the fears of Madison and Jefferson that the central government would subvert states' rights were finally being realized.[6]

The question of slavery was never far from the surface in these debates. The fear that a powerful federal government would be used to prohibit slavery was at the heart of the distrust that drove opposition to ratification of the Constitution. In Virginia, Patrick Henry opposed ratification, claiming that the proposed national government with its allocated powers, such as the power to tax, was a threat to state autonomy and individual freedom: "Here is a revolution as radical as that which separated us from Great Britain. . . . Our rights and privileges are endangered, and the sovereignty of the states will be relinquished."[7] In the end, the price for ratification would be a Bill of Rights, authored and proposed by Madison during the first session of the new American Congress, that specifically enshrined individual freedoms and explicitly noted that powers not granted to the federal government would remain with the states.[8]

For the first half of the nineteenth century, the states maintained a delicate balance that would ensure the federal government's neutrality on the slavery question—a neutrality that would permit states to continue the peculiar institution without federal interference. However, the balance was regularly revisited each time the nation expanded its territory and admitted additional states. The Ohio River served as a *de facto* boundary between free and slave territories as nine states joined the union through 1819—four prohibited slavery, while five permitted the institution. In 1820, the Missouri Compromise momentarily solved the crisis as the nation's territory expanded further west by admitting one slave state (Missouri) and one free state (Maine) and sought to foreclose future iterations of the predicament by extending a line westward at the latitude of 36 degrees 30 minutes, north of which slavery would not be permitted and south of which states could determine the question for themselves. Kentucky Senator Henry Clay, the architect of the compromise, hoped, ultimately in vain, that time would enable the slavery question to be answered without disunion.[9]

The questions of federal and state power were thus intimately tied up with the citizenship status of the nation's Black residents. On the question of Black citizenship, the Constitution's framers had attempted to cleanse the document of any direct reference to legalized ownership of human property—after all, the revolution that birthed the new nation had been built on ideas of freedom and liberty. Still, provisions, including the "three-fifths clause," acknowledged the presence of people in the nation who were denied basic rights. Apportionment of members of the House of Representatives would be made "by adding to the whole Number of free Persons, including those bound to Service for a Term of Years, and excluding Indians not taxed, three fifths of all other Persons." The "all other Persons" referred to the enslaved Black residents, most of whom resided in southern states. The irony of the three-fifths clause was that counting enslaved individuals at all, even at three-fifths, artificially inflated the relative political strength of states with legalized slavery within the new national government.[10]

The three-fifths clause was only the first compromise that would devalue Black citizenship in exchange for national unity, but by the middle of the 1800s, compromise was becoming increasingly untenable. Three decades after the Missouri Compromise, the Mexican-American War upset the nation's balance again with the acquisition of new territory. The Compromise of 1850 admitted California as a free state but also included the Fugitive Slave Act that deemed the rights of owners of human property absolute, even in states and territories where slavery was forbidden. Aiding or even simply not arresting individuals accused of having escaped became a federal crime, thus expanding the reach of slavery into free states, jeopardizing the freedom of every African American in the nation and amplifying the rancor among Americans with competing ideas about the nation's destiny.

It was in this moment that an African American named Dred Scott brought suit for his and his family's freedom. Scott had been brought in bondage to Missouri in 1830 from Alabama, and in the years since, had been sold and inherited, his rights passing from one owner to another as permitted by law, until the rights to his labor came to be owned by Eliza Sanford in 1843. During that journey, Scott had traveled to places like Illinois and the Wisconsin territory, where his enslavement was not permitted. In addition, he had married and started a family, and after his efforts to purchase his own and his family's freedom were denied, Dred Scott sued. His case, *Dred Scott v. Sandford*, would force the Supreme Court to confront several questions that political leaders had been reluctant to directly address since the ratification of the Constitution.[11]

Specifically, the Court considered two distinct questions that would define the relationship between the nation's government and the Black people living within its borders: Were African Americans entitled to the protections of the Constitution? And could the federal government prohibit states from coming to their own answer on the question of slavery? The Court's answers to these questions of citizenship and government authority would propel the nation on its path toward civil war.

Dred Scott's case arrived at a Supreme Court led by Chief Justice Roger Taney, a former attorney general of Maryland who had served in various roles in the administration of Andrew Jackson before being confirmed as the nation's fifth chief justice in 1836. Taney authored a decision that has grown infamous for its demeaning dismissal of Scott's rights and of the prospect of Black citizenship in the United States. The Court concluded that African Americans were "not included, and were not intended to be included, under the word 'citizen' in the Constitution."[12] African Americans were not among the "people" in a document put forth by "We, the people."

But the Court was not dismissive of all individual rights. For owners of human property, the Court noted that "the right of property in a slave is distinctly and expressly affirmed in the Constitution."[13] Indeed, according to Taney's opinion for the Court, the federal government had a duty to protect the *ownership rights* of enslavers. The Missouri Compromise, which had set a boundary on slavery's expansion, was inconsistent with this duty, according to the Court, since it did not sufficiently protect the rights of enslavers. The Court elevated the rights of states to determine the slavery question for themselves over the federal government's ability to draw compromises to preserve the union.

In the name of protecting the rights of enslavers, the *Dred Scott* Court tilted the balance of power toward state sovereignty and self-governance, weakening the ability of the federal government to protect even the most basic rights of individuals within the states. Combined with the Fugitive Slave Act, the decision reduced the rights of African Americans to perhaps their lowest point in the nation's history. It would take a civil war and amendments to the Constitution to undo what the *Dred Scott* opinion had done. It would take another century, and the work of another lawyer from Maryland, to push the Supreme Court to recognize that the rights created in those amendments precluded the separation of Americans from one another based on race.

FEDERALISM AND BLACK CITIZENSHIP

For African Americans, the stakes of the tussle between federal and state governments could not have been more significant. The legal, social, and political vulnerability of African Americans increased the stakes of their relationship with governments operated exclusively by white men to the point that the freedom of 4 million people depended on whether states could continue legalized human bondage or whether the federal government could prohibit it. While this might lead to an embrace of federal power in the moment, African Americans had good reason for suspicion of *any* sort of government—after all, law and government, including federal law and government, had played a decisive role in subjugating the race since before the nation's founding. There was no group more invested in the idea of individual freedom. Thus, there was at once a paradoxical reliance on government to eliminate the legality of slavery and a strong desire for freedom *from* government.

During the war, Frederick Douglass expressed each of these potentially conflicting ideas. "Let them alone," he argued on the topic of what should be done with individuals once emancipated. "Your doing with them is their great misfortune." In words that Clarence Thomas would quote into the annals of the Supreme Court reports, Douglass added to his plea for freedom from government: "If the Negro cannot stand on his own legs, let him fall. . . . Your interference is doing him positive injury."[14]

But unlike Thomas, Douglass added to this call for self-help a demand for government intervention to uplift those it had disenfranchised for so long. Self-help might assist emancipated individuals with dignity and self-respect, but most also faced material needs for shelter and food, as well as protection from hostile white neighbors. Douglass would applaud and defend the Freedmen's Bureau, the federal agency chartered in 1865 to provide food, shelter, clothing, medical services, land, and eventually education to newly emancipated Americans.[15] According to Douglass biographer David Blight, Douglass

> never stopped arguing that the legacy of slavery would require federal aid to the freepeople, but he also never surrendered his commitment to a fierce individualism. . . . While demanding a rugged self-reliance from his people, so many of whom emerged from slavery with little or no human or physical capital, he also demanded justice and fairness from the nation.[16]

This paradox—holding government accountable for historic oppression while freeing African Americans from government interference—would echo across centuries of debate about the best strategies to achieve justice for African Americans.

The Freedmen's Bureau itself was a new step for the national government as it took a more active role in providing services to citizens during Reconstruction that presaged the efforts of Johnson's Great Society a century later. Indeed, the entire federal government would be transformed in the aftermath of the war, expanding to become the nation's largest employer and impacting individual lives in new ways through economic and social policies.

In contrast to the *Dred Scott* decision's protection of the individual freedom of enslavers through restraining the government, the Reconstruction period witnessed the federal government protecting and promoting a different type of individual freedom that saw government taking responsibility for ensuring the well-being of its most vulnerable citizens.[17]

Legislatively, this took the form of three constitutional amendments expanding protections, particularly for African Americans, as well as a series of civil rights statutes aimed at enforcing those protections. The Thirteenth Amendment officially abolished slavery in the United States, ending the legalized subordination that had tainted the Constitution since its drafting, and the Fifteenth Amendment prohibited the denial of voting rights on account of "race, color, or previous condition of servitude." The Fourteenth Amendment would become the most significant in the ongoing debates about the relationships of governments and people. The amendment overruled the *Dred Scott* conclusion by declaring that "all persons born or naturalized in the United States . . . are citizens of the United States and of the State wherein they reside." It went further to prohibit states from depriving people of life, liberty, or property without due process and denying "any person within its jurisdiction the equal protection of the laws," giving Congress the authority to enforce the provisions of the amendment.[18]

Though the war was over and the Constitution transformed, the debate about the proper role of government in American society was not. Resentment about the expanding federal power and the protection of African American rights in particular eroded the Reconstruction effort. White terrorism challenged the authority and will of the federal government, and by 1876 Reconstruction was abandoned. The federal government would not take such assertive action to promote the welfare of citizens until the nation faced the economic crisis of the Great Depression, more than a half century later.[19]

The Supreme Court would do its part in undermining the authority of the federal government to intervene in individual and local matters. In 1883, the Court decided a series of cases challenging the last of the Reconstruction-era civil rights laws, which had prohibited racial discrimination by public accommodations, such as hotels and railroads. Among the cases was one from Missouri, where an innkeeper had refused service to an African American customer. An 8–1 Court declared that discrimination by private citizens, such as innkeepers, was beyond the reach of the Fourteenth Amendment. "Individual invasion of individual rights is not the subject matter of the amendment." Explaining its conclusion, the Court went on to express its skepticism of government's responsibility toward emancipated African Americans:

> When a man has emerged from slavery, and, by the aid of beneficent legislation, has shaken off the inseparable concomitants of that state, there must be some stage in the progress of his elevation when he takes the rank of a mere citizen and ceases to be the special favorite of the laws, and when his rights as a citizen or a man are to be protected in the ordinary modes by which other men's rights are protected.

The Court thus protected the individual freedom to discriminate—to be free from government interference—and rejected government efforts to promote individual freedom through "beneficent legislation" on the basis that individuals could not "be the special favorite of the laws." As it would in the aftermath of *Brown* decades later, the Court quickly backtracked in its enthusiasm for protecting Black citizenship: after a century of constitutionally protected slavery, the Court shackled the power of the Fourteenth Amendment within fifteen years of its ratification.[20]

Twelve years later, the Court went a step further, holding in another 8–1 decision that states could classify and segregate citizens based on race. In *Plessy v. Ferguson*, the Court upheld Louisiana's segregation statutes and offered a narrow vision of the power of government to remedy inequality: "If one race be inferior to the other socially, the Constitution of the United States cannot put them upon the same plane."[21]

FROM NEW DEAL TO GREAT SOCIETY

The schisms over government authority that could be traced to the debates
about ratification of the Constitution continued throughout the twentieth
century. Supremacy waxed and waned across the decades, but competing
visions of the role of government in American life fueled the century's political struggles and animated the perspectives of both Thurgood Marshall
and Clarence Thomas. Marshall would graduate law school in the midst
of the Great Depression, a pivot point that led to a vision of the federal
government as an essential provider of rights and services. Decades later,
Thomas would graduate as a more conservative vision that prized government restraint was emerging. Ultimately, Marshall and Thomas would provide judicial voice to these contrasting visions, each forcefully promoting
his distinct view about the appropriate relationship between individuals
and government.

As the Civil War had before it, the Great Depression radically shifted
the role of the federal government in American life. The crash of 1929 dev-
astated the finances of individuals, businesses, and state and local governments. Roosevelt's predecessor, Herbert Hoover had taken an ideological
stand favoring small government and against active federal intervention,
resisting government aid to individuals through employment programs or
direct payments. During the Depression, Roosevelt would utilize his New
Deal as the primary engine for recovery, vastly expanding the role of the
federal government. By 1945, the number of federal employees had grown
from 500,000 to more than 6 million, and federal revenue had climbed to
nearly 20 percent of gross domestic product from 3 percent during Hoover's
administration.[22]

Though Roosevelt's vision would prevail, it was not without critics. The
roots of the conservative movement of the second half of the twentieth
century were planted in opposition to the New Deal. As it had in the aftermath of Reconstruction, the Supreme Court took a skeptical approach to
such an expanding federal government. During the first half of the 1930s,
the Court deemed several New Deal programs to have overstepped the au-

thority of the federal government under the Constitution. However, amid pressure from Roosevelt and a threat to expand the number of justices, the Court eventually relented in striking down such programs and began a half century in which the Court tilted toward deferring to the expansion of the federal government.[23]

In addition to economic policies, Roosevelt put forth a vision of government as a provider of rights rather than merely a protector of them, which would echo in Johnson's Great Society. Toward the end of his historically long tenure, with the country having pushed through the Depression and engaged in World War II, he proposed an "economic bill of rights" that imagined programs that would have government guarantee employment, food, clothing, fair incomes, housing, medical care, and education. Social Security would become the most visible and lasting such program.

Though African Americans had much to gain from these social programs given continued economic and social discrimination, many New Deal programs maintained racially discriminatory policies in their implementation. Still, advocates for African American justice would push and utilize a strengthened federal government to deliver on the promises of Roosevelt's vision. During the New Deal and into the 1950s, Thurgood Marshall's generation of lawyers used the federal courts to undermine racially discriminatory practices in the states. Whereas the Court had historically deferred to state autonomy, the Court of this era increasingly began to recognize that segregation and even private discrimination ran afoul of the mission of the Fourteenth Amendment.[24]

In 1954, *Brown* would free the equal protection clause from the separate-but-equal reading of *Plessy*. The Court prioritized the rights of Black students to be free from discrimination over the right of state legislatures to enact segregation laws. While it established federal supremacy over state autonomy on the question of segregation, *Brown* would also trigger a renewed spirit of states' rights as an ideology of restrained government would again merge with an ideology of white supremacy as it had during Reconstruction. As Jefferson had 150 years earlier and as Calhoun had encouraged in the buildup to the Civil War, leaders invoked the ideas of nullification and interposition in their claims for state freedom. These ideas forced a federal response: when President Eisenhower sent troops to Central High School in Little Rock in 1957, it was more a defense of the authority of the federal government than of the rights of the nine African American students.

Following *Brown*, the energy of the civil rights movement would turn to Congress and the president, an effort that culminated in the civil rights legislation of Lyndon Johnson's administration. Johnson's Great Society, which established more robust spending in education and health care and sought to confront poverty more directly, was a further expansion of Roosevelt's New Deal vision of the federal government. It saw government as a force for promoting equality. Johnson most famously distilled his ideas in the 1965 commencement address at Howard, in which he declared it insufficient to merely open the gates of opportunity:

> You do not take a person who, for years, has been hobbled by chains and liberate him, bring him up to the starting line of a race and then say, "you are free to compete with all the others," and still justly believe that you have been completely fair.[25]

Johnson called for government to work to provide African Americans the same chance to succeed as other Americans. This was a view that recognized the responsibility of government to address the continuing legacy of past discrimination in order to promote more comprehensive freedom, and it would be reflected in his final appointment to the Supreme Court.

By the end of Johnson's term, however, the lingering war in Vietnam and social unrest at home dampened enthusiasm for further expansion of his vision. Richard Nixon would successfully unite those opposed to the decades of federal action that began with the New Deal and included the Supreme Court's more robust protection of minority rights. During Nixon's term, he would continue to draw on this alliance of small government advocates and opponents of Black progress, turning the continuing implementation of the *Brown* decision into a rallying cry and initiating a conservative revolution in the prevailing vision of government that would appeal to Clarence Thomas as he emerged from law school.

LIMITED GOVERNMENT

When Clarence Thomas left Missouri and Conception Seminary in 1968, he did so carrying a disillusionment about the commitment of the Catholic Church to the rights of African Americans. When he returned to Missouri in 1974 to work for Attorney General John Danforth after his time at Holy Cross and Yale, he was disillusioned in a new way. During those years, Thomas had participated in his corner of the late civil rights movement and had entered institutions once forbidden to African Americans, but he found emptiness rather than empowerment. In his disenchantment with both mainstream civil rights ideas and elite institutions, Thomas was building toward a worldview protective of individualism and skeptical of government and institutional efforts to better society, including African Americans.

Among the ideas that the conservative movement was coalescing around was a belief that the major aim of the American constitutional system should be to protect a certain type of individual freedom: freedom from government. Born in opposition to decades of government expansion and social assistance from the New Deal through the Great Society—the period in which Thurgood Marshall matured from boisterous student to Supreme Court justice—the emerging conservative movement applied this idea to any number of contexts. It saw the decentralization of the American system as a crucial structural safeguard and rhetorically insisted on strictly maintaining the separations of powers built into the Constitution. Thus, in navigating spheres of power between the federal government and those of the states, conservatives insisted on protecting the autonomy of states. Many would take this a step further to promote the will of local governments, again protecting the autonomy of self-governance down to the town council or school board.[26]

Within governments as well, this philosophy demanded strict separation among the branches of government. Policymaking should be the exclusive province of the political branches—the executive and legislative—while judges must refrain from interfering unless specifically identified personal freedoms were at stake. Though Alexander Hamilton had declared the judiciary to be the "least dangerous" branch in the nation's earliest days, judges (particularly federal judges) were seen to be particularly dangerous to the emerging conservatives because of their insulation from democratic accountability (they were not elected) and the power they had to define the boundaries of the Constitution.[27] Indeed, these characteristics were precisely what made federal courts the preferred venue of Thurgood Marshall in his quest to push African Americans into full American citizenship.

Though rooted philosophically in individual freedom from government, a common feature of this movement was resistance to African American empowerment. The ire for government seemed particularly potent when government seemed to be providing practical assistance or elevating the citizenship status of disempowered groups, as the New Deal and Great Society programs sought to do. The *Brown* decision—a federal judicial decree overturning a locally enacted policy—incited particular vitriol. In the early pages of the *National Review*, the magazine that provided the ideological lifeblood of the movement, the decision was criticized as "one of the most brazen acts of judicial usurpation in our history."[28] Over time, the implementation of *Brown* would cement this two-headed condemnation of judges, and the combination of white supremacists and ideological conservatism would bear fruit as Richard Nixon succeeded in bringing disenchanted Southern Democrats into the Republican Party through his Southern Strategy.

Before Nixon took the presidency, however, the future direction of the Republican Party could be glimpsed through the nomination of Barry Goldwater for president in 1964. Though Goldwater would lose to incumbent Lyndon Johnson, who would use his term to expand his Great Society ideas (and appoint Justice Thurgood Marshall), the campaign also launched the national career of Ronald Reagan (who would appoint Clarence Thomas director of the EEOC), whose "Time for Choosing" speech on the Goldwater campaign trail distilled the movement's ideology:

> The Founding Fathers knew a government can't control the economy without controlling people. You and I are told that we must choose between a left or right, but I suggest there is no such thing as a left or right. There is only an up or down. Up to man's age-old dream—the maximum of individual freedom consistent with law and order—or down to the ant heap of totalitarianism.[29]

From this viewpoint, maximum individual freedom was pitted against government control. Rather than a tool for promoting social good, government was a tool toward totalitarianism.

Such institutional distrust must have felt familiar to Clarence Thomas as he arrived to take his new post as an assistant attorney general in Missouri. Through the example of his grandfather, he had seen what individual effort could produce if only individuals could be left alone. Through the example of his own experiences in New England, he had seen that even well-intentioned interventions could not eliminate the disadvantages and disrespect African Americans faced—and might even make them more pernicious.

So disillusioned, Thomas would find kinship with the conservative movement that was emerging. It was a movement that rhetorically favored small government over large, local solutions over national ones, the will of the majority over the whim of the judiciary, and, above all else, the individual over all forms of government. These ideas may have been emerging, but they were not new. They were at the heart of the longest-running constitutional dispute in American history. And in the early 1970s, Republican politicians were beginning to transform the Supreme Court to promote these ideas more forcefully in the cases it encountered, an effort that would profoundly impact the experience on the Court of Justice Thurgood Marshall.

A TRANSFORMING COURT

The Supreme Court transition from Thurgood Marshall to Clarence Thomas in 1991 was impactful, in part, because it was the culmination of a process that began very early in Marshall's tenure on the Court decades earlier. Marshall arrived at a Supreme Court with a progressive majority that reflected the New Deal–Great Society vision of the responsibility of government to address social problems. Dwight Eisenhower was the only Republican president to nominate justices between 1932 and 1968, and two of his nominees (Earl Warren and William Brennan) turned out to be among the Court's most progressive voices. Though it could not have been known at the time, Thurgood Marshall, confirmed in 1967, was the final justice in this line. The next justice appointed by a Democrat president would not be until 1993, after Marshall had retired. The transitions that would transform the Court, and culminate when Justice Marshall himself was replaced, began in June 1968 when Chief Justice Earl Warren approached President Lyndon Johnson with a plan to preserve their legacies.

Johnson's ambitious Great Society programs had extended the role of the federal government in creating opportunity (through the ESEA, for example) and ensuring a social safety net, while Warren's stewardship of the Court had led to the end of legalized racial segregation. However laudable to some, these extensions of the work of the federal government also led to backlash; those skeptical of expansive government coalesced in an effort to restrain this expansion.

Chief Justice Warren, ever a politician, understood the landscape, and a week after the leading Democratic presidential candidate Robert F. Kennedy was assassinated, he approached Johnson with a plan. Facing the potential of a Richard Nixon presidency, Warren proposed that he retire during the Court's summer 1968 recess to enable Johnson to appoint his replacement before his term ended. However sound the plan, it backfired spectacularly. Johnson quickly nominated Associate Justice Abe Fortas to take over as chief justice, but in a preview of the alliance that would win Richard Nixon the presidency months later, northern Republicans and

Southern Democrats in the Senate filibustered the nomination. Without a replacement, Warren stayed on for the 1968–69 term before retiring.[30]

By the conclusion of the 1968–69 term, the situation at the Court was very different. Richard Nixon was president, having ridden the backlash against Johnson into the White House. Among his campaign promises was a pledge to appoint a "strict constructionist" to the Court as Warren's replacement: by this, Nixon meant a jurist who would not find constitutional justification for expansion of the federal government. In addition, Nixon spent his earliest months pushing an already-weakened Justice Fortas toward resignation in May 1969, leaving two vacancies on the Court in the first months of the Nixon administration.[31]

For chief justice, Nixon nominated Warren Burger, one of the most conservative judges on the Court of Appeals for the DC Circuit and a person who, like Nixon, despised the work of the Warren Court. Replacing Fortas proved more complicated as Nixon's first two nominees, both southerners, were rejected by the Senate, due in part to their recalcitrant views on civil rights issues. Nixon next turned to Harry Blackmun, a friend of Burger's who sat on the Eighth Circuit Court of Appeals, and Blackmun was confirmed unanimously in April 1970. Only four presidents had ever before had two Court appointments confirmed so quickly.[32]

While the replacement of Warren and Fortas with Burger and Blackmun shifted the ideological landscape of the Court, it did not create a conservative majority. However, during a week in September 1971, Nixon was given another opportunity for a pair of appointments after two justices in poor health (Hugo Black and John Marshall Harlan) resigned within days of one another just weeks before the Court's 1971 term was to begin. Nixon nominated Lewis Powell, an attorney who had chaired the Richmond school board during the early years of desegregation. During his tenure on the school board, only 2 of the city's 23,000 African American students were enrolled in desegregated schools. To fill the second vacancy, Nixon nominated William Rehnquist, who was only 47 years old and thus had the potential for a lengthy career on the Court (he would ultimately serve thirty-five years, including nearly two decades as chief justice). Rehnquist was not only young but staunchly conservative: Barry Goldwater, on whose 1964 presidential campaign Rehnquist had worked, called him the most conservative lawyer he had ever met.[33]

Though Rehnquist would ultimately be confirmed comfortably (68–26), his nomination ran into difficulty when a memo bearing his initials from his year as a clerk for Justice Robert Jackson in 1952–53 surfaced. During that term, the Court had heard the initial round of oral arguments in the *Brown* cases, and Rehnquist submitted a memo to his boss noting that it would be inappropriate for the Court to overturn *Plessy v. Ferguson*'s separate-but-equal interpretation of the Fourteenth Amendment simply because a majority of the justices disliked segregation: this would "differ from the [*Plessy*] court only in the kinds of litigants it favors and the kinds of special claims it protects." The memo went on to conclude: "I realize that it is an unpopular and unhumanitarian position, for which I have been excoriated by 'liberal' colleagues, but I think *Plessy v. Ferguson* was right and should be re-affirmed."[34] During his confirmation process, Rehnquist denied that the memo represented his personal views, but given his ideological opposition to federal power and an interpretation of the Constitution that disclaimed special protections for African Americans, it was clear that Rehnquist and Marshall would approach future cases very differently. This was an outcome Nixon encouraged. He told the newly appointed justice to "be as mean and rough as they said you were."[35]

Powell and Rehnquist were sworn in on the Court in January 1972, making it four appointments for Nixon during his three years in office. Cumulatively, these transitions began to push the Court away from its embrace of broad federal power and judicial discretion, elevating freedom *from* government as an animating principle. This stood in sharp contrast to the view of Justice Marshall but represented yet another swing in the centuries-long debate over the proper role of the federal government. And as had been the case throughout the nation's history, the consequences of this shift would be acutely felt by African Americans.

TEN

STEPPING BACKWARDS

As the nation's political winds began to replace enthusiasm for robust federal government programs with a resurgence of small government conservatism, groups of students 1,500 miles apart demanded more from their schools. In April 1966, a group of Black students at Detroit's Northern High School walked out of their school in protest of deteriorating conditions and their principal's refusal to publish a student editorial decrying low academic standards and contrasting the school's offerings with those at a nearby predominantly white high school. Before the year was out, the principal had been reassigned, and the Detroit school board agreed to establish a committee to study conditions in the city's high schools. The walkout was an early event in a series of late-60s efforts among school advocates to confront the increasing racial segregation and disparate opportunities in Detroit schools.[1]

Two years later, the spirit of 60s protest led another group of four hundred students at Edgewood High School in San Antonio to walk out of *their* school, complaining of deteriorating facilities and a glut of classes taught by uncertified teachers. In support of their children, a group of parents formed the Edgewood District Concerned Parents Association, and though they did not know it from the outset, they were about to learn a great deal about how schools in Texas were funded.[2]

These two student-led protests, condemning what students knew to be disparate educational opportunities within their communities, led inexorably toward federal courtrooms and, ultimately, the Supreme Court. In Detroit, plaintiffs pulled together by the nation's largest branch of the NAACP sued the school district, the state of Michigan, and others, claiming that the Detroit schools were unconstitutionally segregated by race. In San Antonio, having compiled evidence of widespread disparities in funding among adjacent school districts, plaintiffs sued for a declaration that Texas's methods for funding schools was unconstitutional. In both cases, plaintiffs saw in the federal equal protection clause and federal courts an opportunity to confront disparities at the local level. But in both cases, the plaintiffs lost. Between the protests of the late 1960s and the moments the cases would reach the Supreme Court in the 1970s, there had been a significant shift in the nation and on the Court about the proper role of government. In the two cases, the newly constituted Court imposed limits on the power of the equal protection clause to confront educational disparities, limits that both reflected and amplified a more limited view of government's responsibility for addressing social problems. The tool that Thurgood Marshall had used—from the earliest days of his career through his advocacy among fellow justices only two years earlier in *Swann*—was being constrained.

A SHIFTING EDUCATIONAL LANDSCAPE

Thurgood Marshall had a deep understanding of the racial dynamics in Detroit. In 1943, as an NAACP lawyer, he had been sent to report on a deadly riot in which frustrated Black residents had targeted white-owned businesses in Belle Isle. Frustrations were high as thousands of African Americans had come to northern cities to escape the oppression of southern segregation only to find new forms of exclusion. Detroit's Black population increased by 40 percent between 1910 and 1930, but opportunities remained unequal.[3]

Another migration, not unrelated to the Great Migration of African Americans from the South, was simultaneously reshaping the nation's urban centers in the middle of the twentieth century. New roads and more affordable cars made it possible for many Americans to migrate from inner cities to suburbs, where they found attractive green lawns and open spaces, not to mention distance from the changing city. But suburbanization was not available to all. Developers wishing to build new housing in suburbs needed insurance from the Federal Housing Authority to begin construction, but the FHA would not provide that insurance unless developments would remain racially segregated. For example, a Detroit builder had been denied insurance for a development near an African American neighborhood until he constructed a half-mile concrete wall to separate the neighborhood from the development. In addition, the government kept maps to determine which neighborhoods would be appropriate risks in which to lend money to aspiring homeowners; a neighborhood with African American residents would be coded "red" as too risky, giving birth to the term "redlining."[4] These were the types of government actions that might have led Frederick Douglass to demand that government simply leave African Americans alone, as these acts demonstrated that even when the federal government intervened, it held the capacity to cause harm to Black communities.

Such residential segregation was also perpetuated through private agreements known as restrictive covenants—often enforced by a burgeoning number of private homeowners' associations—that prohibited the sale of property to African Americans. In 1948, Marshall had won a landmark victory representing a Black plaintiff from Detroit and convincing the Supreme Court to declare such covenants unenforceable.[5] But the covenants remained in the land records as messages of exclusion, and their effect would be perpetuated if residents adhered to them voluntarily, a practice the federal government encouraged. White residents had other ways of excluding African Americans from these newly forming havens, including outright violence toward Black residents willing to attempt to integrate all-white neighborhoods. In Detroit, this resulted in over two hundred incidents, ranging from harassment and window breaking to arson and effigy burning.[6]

The rise of suburbs also meant that municipal boundaries between cities and suburbs increasingly symbolized a racialized divide within a metropolitan area. Suburbs utilized the independence championed in the localist ideal of small democratic units making local decisions that reflected local values to maintain existing racial demographics. In Dearborn, Michigan, for example, the mayor bragged to an Alabama newspaper that "Every time we hear of a Negro moving in, we respond quicker than you do to a fire."[7] The results spoke for themselves: of the 2.7 million residents of Detroit suburbs in 1970, only 3 percent were African American. In three of the largest suburbs, home to 400,000 people, there were only 186 Black residents. Meanwhile, the city of Detroit lost population between 1950 and 1970 (from 1.85 million to 1.51 million), though its number of Black residents more than doubled. This meant that a city that had been 16.2 percent African American in 1950 was 44.5 percent African American in 1970.[8]

Within the increasingly segregated city, Black residents complained of overpolicing and police brutality, and in July 1967, the fuel ignited into a massive riot that gave rise to what became known as a "long, hot summer" of riot and protest across the nation. The Detroit riot occurred after the fourth day of Thurgood Marshall's Supreme Court confirmation hearings, and when Marshall returned to the Senate Judiciary Committee for what would end up totaling the most hours of questioning of any Supreme Court nominee to that point, southern senators sought to tie him to the perceived lawlessness in Detroit.[9]

The effort failed, and Marshall was confirmed by the full Senate, 68–11, in August 1967, but President Johnson was sufficiently troubled by the riots that he established the National Advisory Commission on Civil Disorders, a group that would come to be known as the Kerner Commission after its chair Otto Kerner. The Kerner Commission reported what the protesting students in Detroit and San Antonio were trying to express. According to the report, many grievances in the Black community "result from the severely disadvantaged social and economic conditions of many Negroes as compared with those of whites in the same city and, more particularly, in the predominantly white suburbs." The commission came to this conclusion: "Our Nation is moving toward two societies, one black, one white— separate and unequal."[10]

The Kerner Commission had made a diagnosis. The protesting students of Detroit and San Antonio had set in motion events that would cause the Supreme Court to consider what role the federal government would have in crafting a treatment.

'RODRIGUEZ' AND 'MILLIKEN'

Edgewood ISD (independent school district) was one of seven districts within the San Antonio area. Each district operated with autonomy, raising local taxes from within its own boundaries and making hiring and student assignment decisions, though each district also received guidance and funding from the state. The same uneven growth that characterized Detroit had occurred in San Antonio, such that each independent district served student populations that were ethnically and socioeconomically homogeneous. In Edgewood, that meant that the school district served a student population that was 90 percent Mexican American and 6 percent African American; meanwhile, the median family income within Edgewood ISD ($4,686) was the lowest among districts in the area. The plaintiffs, however, did not argue that the districts in San Antonio were unconstitutionally segregated; rather, they focused on the funding disparities among the districts.[11]

Edgewood ISD not only had the poorest residents among districts in the area; it also had the highest taxes. However, because property values were low, these high taxes did not result in substantial funds coming into the school district; in 1967–68, the district only raised $26 per pupil from local sources, with the balance of its $356 per pupil spending coming from the state or from federal programs like the ESEA, the federal education bill

President Johnson had signed in front of a schoolhouse sixty-five miles to the north. Throughout the litigation, Edgewood would be compared with the adjacent Alamo Heights ISD, which was roughly the same geographic size. In contrast to Edgewood, Alamo Heights had lower taxes but yielded more than ten times the amount of local funding per student: $333. With its state and federal funding, the per pupil spending of Alamo Heights was $594. Meanwhile, more than 80 percent of Alamo Heights students were white. The plaintiffs argued that this system of financing—where local tax efforts resulted in unequal outcomes in different communities—was unconstitutional, claiming that though residents in Edgewood ISD were committed to education as evidenced by their willingness to pay taxes to support local schools, they were trapped by the funding scheme with schools that were underfunded, deteriorating, and without the same op-portunities available in other districts.[12]

While acknowledging the undeniable disparities, Texas argued that the scheme preserved decision-making power for local districts and parents, claiming that the equal protection clause did not mandate equal spending across school districts. After losing in the lower court, the state appealed the case, *Rodriguez v. San Antonio ISD*, to the Supreme Court.[13]

Meanwhile, in Detroit, the walkout at Northern High School was part of an ongoing struggle for power in a school system that was serving an increasingly African American student population. In the late 1960s, Black leaders offered competing plans, with some pushing for increased community control—Black control for Black schools—and others, noting that Detroit residents had rejected tax increases for its segregated schools, pushing for greater integration. When the city's school board adopted a plan that would prioritize integration, the reaction was swift both from individuals and the state government. At one board meeting, both Black and white speakers expressed disapproval at the push for integration, and a white parent declared ominously, "I will move out in the suburbs" rather than send his child to a predominantly Black school. The Michigan legisla-ture quickly overrode the local plan and mandated neighborhood schools, a plan that would maintain and possibly worsen racial school segregation given the city's residential segregation. The governor signed the bill in July 1970; plaintiffs brought suit a month later.[14]

Desegregation suits outside the South were more complicated than the early post-*Brown* cases. Whereas proof of unconstitutional racial segregation was easy to produce in a place like Charlotte, North Carolina—where state law and official policy had mandated segregation—proving racial segregation in the absence of an explicit policy was more difficult. Cases had failed because school districts were able to claim that segregation was a result of private choices by private individuals about where to live (*de facto* segregation) and not due to any official government action (*de jure* segregation). But the events in Detroit, including the intervention by the state, allowed the plaintiffs to provide a comprehensive theory that the state, and not merely the Detroit school district, was responsible for the racial segregation in Detroit schools.

In a forty-one-day trial in the case, *Bradley v. Milliken*, the plaintiffs presented voluminous evidence of intentional acts that had worsened segregation. Banks and federal agencies had combined with racially restrictive private agreements to ensure residential segregation. The school district had created attendance zones, made school construction decisions, transported students, and allowed optional transfers that perpetuated school segregation. And when the Detroit school board waded into an integration plan, the state had intervened to forbid it. The cumulative effect could be seen in schools and a district that were increasingly made up of African American students: between 1960 and 1970, the white population in the schools decreased from 53.6 percent to 34.8 percent; the number of schools with no white students increased from eight to thirty. "There is enough blame for everyone to share," wrote district Judge Roth in finding for the plaintiffs.[15]

Although it was significant that the Court concluded that a school district that had not explicitly segregated had nonetheless violated the Constitution, Judge Roth recognized that the challenge would be in crafting an effective remedy. Citing the demographic trends in the Detroit metropolitan area, he concluded that the district would be entirely African

American by 1992 if those trends continued. Desegregation in a single-race district was not possible. Meanwhile, Detroit's share of the metropolitan population continued to decline, and surrounding the increasingly African American Detroit schools were scores of suburban school districts serving the area's white students and enjoying the same financial advantages of being able to tax low and spend high as was evident in the San Antonio case. Concluding that ordering desegregation in Detroit alone would be futile, Judge Roth ordered a plan that would incorporate fifty-three adjacent suburban districts into a metropolitan-wide desegregation plan.[16]

The district court decisions in both *Rodriguez* and *Milliken* demonstrated an expansive view of the power of the federal Constitution and of federal courts to override state and local policies. In *Rodriguez*, a federal court had demanded changes to a state's school funding scheme; in *Milliken*, a federal court was mandating a desegregation plan that crossed district and municipal boundaries. When these cases reached the Supreme Court, however, the plaintiffs found a contingency of newly appointed justices duly skeptical of such expansive federal power.

Both *Rodriguez* (1973) and *Milliken* (1974) were decided 5–4 at the Supreme Court, with Nixon's four justices siding with Justice Potter Stewart to overturn the lower court opinions. In the annals of constitutional law, *Rodriguez* and *Milliken* stand for specific principles: *Rodriguez* rejected education as a fundamental right under the equal protection clause, while *Milliken* defined a limit on judicial discretion in crafting constitutional remedies. But at the core of both decisions was the principle of localism wielded by generations of Americans skeptical of the power of the federal government. If Nixon rode into the presidency exploiting the backlash against expansive government from the New Deal to the Great Society, the four justices he appointed delivered in putting the brakes on federal intervention in schools, particular from federal courts. Both decisions highlighted the hallmarks of the criticism leveled at federal judicial intervention: the federalism argument that decision making should be left to local authorities and the separation of powers argument that policy decisions should be left to elected officials rather than to judges. Though cases would continue for decades, the tide Thurgood Marshall had built from before *Brown* and through *Swann* inalterably shifted after *Rodriguez* and *Milliken*.

Those arguing for limiting centralized federal power in the perpetual American struggle over the appropriate balance between state and federal governments often pointed to the opportunities for decentralized states or localities to serve as "laboratories of democracy."[17] In the schooling context, the idea was that local control of schooling allowed local communities the freedom to determine how much money to spend, what programs to prioritize, and how best to educate the next generation of their community. This was a theme reflected in both cases. Writing for the majority in *Rodriguez*, the former Richmond school board chair Justice Powell pointed out that smaller school districts would be "free to tailor local programs to local needs" and could take advantage of the "opportunity for experimentation, innovation, and a healthy competition for educational excellence."[18] In *Milliken*, Chief Justice Burger authored the majority opinion and elevated local control among other constitutional considerations:

> No single tradition in public education is more deeply rooted than local control over the operation of schools; local autonomy has long been thought essential both to the maintenance of community concern and support for public schools and to quality of the educational process.[19]

The Court thus identified that school funding ("community concern") might be contingent on strong local autonomy for a school district and prioritized placing decision-making power at the smallest level of government over the district court's efforts to remedy metropolitan segregation.

The decisions were less flattering regarding the federal judges involved in the administration of schools due to the desegregation cases, noting that judges lacked familiarity with local circumstances as well as expertise in public administration. In *Rodriguez*, Powell, the former school board member, wrote that judges should avoid imposing "inflexible constitutional restraints that could circumscribe or handicap the continued research and experimentation so vital to finding even partial solutions to educational problems."[20] In *Milliken*, the Court warned that allowing a district court widespread discretion in crafting remedies to educational problems would turn judges into *de facto* school superintendents for the entire metropolitan area. This was a task "few, if any judges [were] qualified to perform, and one which would deprive people of control of schools through their elected representatives."[21]

Undergirding these decisions was a skepticism that the proper role of government, the federal government in particular, included solving social problems. In *Rodriguez*, the Court found that massive funding disparities did not run afoul of the Constitution, while in *Milliken*, it held that district lines could not be casually ignored even though the urban–suburban segregation of metropolitan Detroit looked eerily similar to the segregation declared unconstitutional in *Brown*. But the 5–4 majority did not share *Brown*'s faith in law, instead offering a constricted view of the power of the Constitution in language that harkened back to *Plessy*: "[T]he Constitution does not provide judicial remedies for every social and economic ill."[22] For decades, Thurgood Marshall had been using the Constitution as his weapon for curing the nation's ills, stretching the equal protection clause beyond earlier interpretations. Now he was left to vent his dissent.

FIGHTING FOR AN EQUAL START IN LIFE

"I cannot subscribe to this emasculation of our constitutional guarantee of equal protection of the laws," Justice Marshall wrote in his *Milliken* dissent. The interpretation of the equal protection clause that Justice Marshall mourned was one that he helped build, one that would not tolerate gross disparities in school spending across district lines or allow those district lines to serve as fences stopping effective solutions to unconstitutional behavior. Where the majority had warned of judicial overreach due to a lack of authority or expertise, Marshall saw a duty for federal courts to deliver on "the right of every American to an equal start in life." This difference reflected the gulf between Marshall and his colleagues in the majority on the question of the power of federal courts to remedy social disparities—between rich and poor in Texas, and between Black and white in metropolitan Detroit. This was a judicial incarnation of the long American struggle between federal power (statism) and local liberty (localism), the persistent redefinition of the appropriate line between individuals and their government. Local liberty often led to disparities, and Justice Marshall, like the president who appointed him, felt not only that the government and its courts could intervene, but that it *must*. Disdainful of the result in *Milliken* restricting judicial power, he lamented that the Court's retreat was "giant step backwards."[23]

Marshall's dissents in *Rodriguez* and *Milliken* offered characteristically careful and specific rebuttals of the majority opinions, but they rested upon fundamental disagreements about both the causes of the problems present in the cases and the ability and responsibility of government to confront them. Funding disparities in Texas and differing racial makeups among the school districts of metropolitan Detroit could not simply be regarded as the result of "unknown and perhaps unknowable" causes, as Justice Potter Stewart argued in a concurring opinion in *Milliken*. Marshall had little difficulty identifying the lingering impacts of discriminatory government policies and noted that "the rippling effects on residential patterns caused by purposeful acts of segregation do not automatically subside at the school district border." Indeed, by perpetuating and protecting segregation in neighborhoods and schools, government policy had even distorted private attitudes—having failed to enable individuals of different races to learn together, "the State is responsible for the fact that many whites will react to the dismantling of that segregated system by attempting to flee to the suburbs."[24]

This expansive view of government causation, including its influence on the attitudes of citizens, was classic Marshall. He fully understood the allure of local control and the separation of powers that the majority championed, but he had seen enough to doubt that these offered any meaningful redress for the vulnerable students in San Antonio or Detroit. In the Texas funding scheme, which the majority justified because it allegedly preserved local control, Marshall saw a system that *restricted* the options for local districts like Edgewood. The disparities in available resources across school districts would manifest themselves in less flexibility for poorer districts, making it more difficult to attract and pay teachers, build and maintain facilities, and develop courses and special programs. The stakes were too high, in Marshall's opinion, for the educational opportunity afforded to Texas schoolchildren to depend on the amount of property wealth in the school district in which they happened to reside. "That a child forced to attend an under-funded school with poorer physical facilities, less experienced teachers, larger classes, and a narrower range of courses . . . may nevertheless excel is to the credit of the child, not the State." With sorrow, Marshall went on: "Indeed, who can ever measure for such a child the opportunities lost and the talents wasted for want of a broader, more enriched education?"[25]

Meanwhile, Marshall saw the result in *Milliken* as making a "solemn mockery" of *Brown*. The Court seemed to countenance the perpetuation of segregation, a result that would send an inescapable message to African American students in Detroit:

> It will be of scant significance to Negro children who have for years been confined by *de jure* acts of segregation to a growing core of all-Negro schools surrounded by a ring of all-white schools that the new dividing line between the races is the school district boundary.[26]

As he had in *Brown* and as he would in *Dowell*, Marshall brought attention to the psychological injury segregation caused Black students.

But Marshall saved his most biting rebuke for the idea that students were better off relying on elected local officials rather than federal courts:

> The Court's suggestions of legislative redress and experimentation will doubtless be of great comfort to the schoolchildren of Texas' disadvantaged districts, but considering the vested interests of wealthy school districts in the preservation of the status quo, they are worth little more.[27]

In Marshall's view, judges may not be experts in educational policy, but when it came to addressing the needs of students disadvantaged by existing systems, local districts and state legislatures were worse. They had proven themselves "singularly unsuited"[28] to the task of protecting the "right of all children, whatever their race, to an equal start in life and to an equal opportunity to reach their full potential as citizens."[29]

For solutions, Marshall put his faith in federal courts. He preferred the federal system since he had seen states abuse their sovereignty to legalize racial oppression. The federal government's racial record was far from perfect, but Marshall had seen leaders like Lyndon Johnson put the weight of the federal government into the task of uplifting that nation's most vulnerable. Marshall's view aligned not only with Johnson and Roosevelt, but also Hamilton and Madison (at least prior to ratification)— the architects of the federal government.

Marshall's preference for courts (as opposed to legislative bodies) was born of his professional experience using the judiciary to pursue justice. Marshall had convinced courts to push states and localities to live up to principles of equality in virtually every area, from criminal justice to housing, voting to education. Marshall saw policies having the predictable (perhaps intended) effect of restricting the choices and opportunities of disadvantaged individuals, and he wished to give courts the power to level the playing field. In his dissents, he called for greater judicial scrutiny of government policies, even those, like Texas's funding scheme, that did not explicitly discriminate based on race or wealth, but still caused disparities. He also embraced greater judicial discretion in utilizing whatever tools were necessary to craft constitutional remedies that would actually be effective. Seeing his colleagues on the Court turn away from the schoolchildren of Texas and Detroit in the name of preserving local control and deference to local elected officials must have been a sour defeat.

Even as others doubted the capacity of government and courts to meaningfully redress harms it had caused, calling for freedom from even ameliorative government action, Marshall's faith in law never wavered.

Surveying the nation from which he emerged, he saw government as a cause of persistent disparities. Rather than demanding independence from government, he was willing to charge government with the responsibility of eliminating those disparities. They were not going to fix themselves.

Some would criticize Marshall's faith in law as misplaced, even irresponsible, given the nation's history of legal subjugation. Liberty and freedom were better pursued by less, rather than more government, these critics would argue. But Marshall might be excused for his brash optimism since more than perhaps any other American, he had pushed the law to vindicate the rights of individuals through sheer force of will. Decisions like *Rodriguez* and *Milliken* prevented Marshall's vision from truly being tested, however. They signaled an end to the expansion of federal power as ideas of more limited government, often welded as they were with opposition to Black empowerment, began to push the Supreme Court in the opposite direction. Few argued as forcefully for independence from government as did Justice Marshall's successor.

ELEVEN

PUTTING THE GENIE BACK IN THE BOTTLE

In Kansas City, Missouri, residents would have readily related to Justice Marshall's admonition in *Milliken* about administrative "fences to separate the races." Troost Avenue was just such a fence. A boulevard stretching south from the city's central business district, Troost served as the *de facto* barrier between Black and white students in Kansas City. Echoing Marshall's language, the road became known locally as the Troost Wall.[1]

Troost was one of a variety of walls dividing metropolitan Kansas City. In addition to the avenue within the city limits, the metropolitan area—like Detroit—had many growing suburban municipalities as well as the state border between Kansas and Missouri. Discriminatory housing practices and school assignment policies organized around each of these fences ensured the perpetuation of racially identifiable neighborhoods and schools. In the two decades after *Brown*, over a dozen elementary schools east of Troost transitioned from entirely serving white students to serving a student population that was more than 90 percent Black; meanwhile, in a school district that had become nearly two-thirds African American, all but one of the elementary schools west of Troost served student populations that were less than one-quarter Black. As in Detroit, the increasing racial identifiability of the entire district—the schools had been 16 percent African American in 1954—reflected a racialized sorting within the broader metropolitan area.[2]

After being pushed by a growing coalition of African Americans within the city, the Kansas City Missouri School District (KCMSD) sued just about every governmental entity it could in May 1977 to seek assistance in breaking up the district's increasing segregation. Among the defendants were the federal government, the states of Kansas and Missouri, and eighteen suburban school districts in both states. The case, *Missouri v. Jenkins*, would reach the Supreme Court on multiple occasions, including on either side of the 1991 transition from Justice Marshall to Justice Thomas. When the case reached the Court in 1995, Justice Thomas authored a concurrence that articulated his deep skepticism of government interventions, a philosophy born, like the case itself, during Thomas's time in Missouri in the 1970s. In so doing, Thomas, who was sitting for the Missouri bar in 1974 while Marshall was dissenting in *Milliken*, would help complete the work (begun by Nixon's appointees in *Milliken*) of reining in the power of federal judges in desegregation cases.[3]

ACCEPTING CONSERVATISM

While Clarence Thomas was a law student at Yale, someone gave him a copy of the book *Black Education: Myths and Tragedies* by Thomas Sowell. Thomas "skimmed it angrily and threw it in the trash."[4] Like Thomas, Sowell was born into a rural southern family and had worked to earn admission into the most elite of American institutions. His family had left sharecropping in North Carolina when he was 8 as part of the Great Migration, and after a stint in the military, Sowell enrolled at Howard University before transferring to Harvard. From there, he went on to earn a PhD in economics from the University of Chicago, studying with the conservative economist Milton Friedman. *Black Education* was a "courageous indictment" of higher education admission practices that reached out to Black students.[5] Thomas, a Yale student struggling with his own place within an elite institution was "furious that any black man could think like that."[6]

However, upon graduating from Yale and moving to his new position as an assistant attorney general in Missouri with John Danforth, Thomas was beginning to find others leveling the same charge at him. On the topic of busing, for example, Thomas was a skeptic. Following *Swann* and as school desegregation moved north and west, busing of students became a central tool for judges to employ to achieve desegregation and a most abhorrent symbol for those resisting it. Busing touched a nerve because it allowed federal courts to override the personal residential choices of families, particularly white families, in determining which students attended which schools. Thurgood Marshall might have said that those residential choices had never been equally available to all Americans, making judicial intervention necessary to undo a more complex system of segregation. But to those in neighborhoods and growing suburban communities populated almost exclusively by white residents, busing represented a flagrant overreach by the federal government into the decisions of individuals and the powers of local self-government. Indeed, busing was a poignant symbol for the conservative revolution of the 1970s.

Yet busing was not unanimously supported by African Americans either. Clarence Thomas recalled that busing was a rare topic that he and his grandfather continued to agree upon by the mid-1970s: "We both saw busing as a tragic digression from the quest for real equality." Though Thomas lamented the hypocrisy of white busing opponents who had not minded sending Black students past white schools to maintain segregation, he believed that "what mattered most was the quality of the education that black children received, not the color of the students sitting next to them." Yet when he expressed his skepticism of the efficacy of busing, he recalled the rebuttal from Black colleagues being "that no black person had a right to think the way I did."[7]

The frequency of this response caused Thomas to question his connection with his African American roots, so it was a revelation when Thomas encountered Thomas Sowell again. Steered by a colleague toward Sowell's

1975 book *Race and Economics*, Thomas found sustenance. Whereas Black nationalists had opposed integration with principled and strategic arguments, Sowell offered a scholarly critique of liberal policies from a Black perspective. However, the foundation of both was a principle central to Thomas's own philosophy: self-reliance. In his autobiography, Thomas quoted from the last paragraph of Sowell's book:

> Perhaps the greatest dilemma in the attempts to raise ethnic minority income is that those methods which have historically proved successful—self-reliance, work skills, education, business experience—are all slow developing, while those methods which are more direct and immediate—job quotas, charity, subsidies, preferential treatment—tend to undermine self-reliance and pride of achievement in the long run. If the history of American ethnic groups shows anything, it is how large a role has been played by attitudes—and particularly attitudes of self-reliance.[8]

Thomas immediately identified with the substance of the argument: "It was as though he were talking directly to me."[9] But he also recognized that the outright rejection of it by other African Americans—including himself a few years earlier—was part of a mandated dogma of acceptable Black thought that he would spend his career refuting.

Neither John Danforth nor Thomas Sowell turned Clarence Thomas into a conservative, but both played an important role in revealing to Thomas the ways conservative philosophies of limited government and self-reliance fit with Thomas's own beliefs. Thomas was aware of the consequences of publicly embracing such ideas and criticizing positions held by the most visible African American leaders, but he knew that he would have to confront that fear eventually. After John Danforth was elected to the U.S. Senate, Thomas left the attorney general's office for private practice at Monsanto, the agricultural corporation, before moving to Washington to again work for Danforth as a legislative aide in 1979. Thomas arrived in Washington on the cusp of the Reagan revolution, in which small government ideas that had been incubating in opposition to the New Deal and the Great Society would have their moment. Danforth had invited him into this movement, but it was Sowell who would prompt Thomas to go further.[10]

After Reagan's 1980 election, Sowell invited Thomas to sit on a panel at a conference on race in America. There, listening to Reagan's advisor Ed Meese at lunch, Thomas struck up a conversation with Juan Williams, a journalist with the *Washington Post*, who turned their exchange into the basis of a column featuring the 32-year-old Thomas as the face and future of Black conservatism.[11] "You've heard about Clarence Thomas, but not by name," the column began. "He is a Republican, a long-time supporter of Ronald Reagan, opposed to the minimum wage law, rent control, busing, and affirmative action." Thomas, who spoke at the conference on issues of education, was cited as a supporter of school vouchers that would allow parents to send their children to any school they chose. Williams noted that Thomas sent his own son to private school because, Thomas claimed, public schools teach children they can get by without working.[12]

The *Post* column propelled Thomas's profile, and though he knew his life would not be the same since being "honest about race meant that I would be subjected to punishing personal attacks from all sides," he felt he had to choose between speaking his beliefs and becoming an outcast within the larger Black community or being dishonest. He accepted the role of outcast. Early the following year, he would have another new role, within the administration of President Ronald Reagan.[13]

RESTRAINING GOVERNMENT

During the 1970s, Ronald Reagan had set himself apart from even other conservatives with the vehemence of his rejection of the federal role in education. Though Richard Nixon had taken advantage of the growing sense that the power and influence of the federal government had expanded too far, his administration had not been able to limit spending under ESEA—in fact, education spending had expanded. Reagan, however, took particular umbrage at federal involvement in education, warning that the end goal

would be "federalizing education in this land." Reagan often cited the need
to halt this process during his 1980 campaign and ensured that the Republican Party's platform included a commitment to abolish the Department
of Education, which had been created in 1979.[14]

Once elected, Reagan's transition team, including Thomas Sowell, developed a plan to reduce the federal role in education through reductions
in funding, consolidation of department programs, and deregulation on
the way toward eventual abolition of the department. This agenda was consistent with Reagan's broader push toward limited government power and
maximum individual freedom, a vision he had articulated over a decade
before in his "Time for Choosing" speech during the Goldwater campaign.
To put this vision into practice, he appointed anti-statist conservatives to
key positions, including within the Department of Education. Among the
president's political appointments within the department was Clarence
Thomas as assistant secretary within the department's Office for Civil
Rights (OCR) in March 1981.[15]

While intellectually aligned on skepticism about government, Thomas
had reached his position differently than white Reaganites, some number
of whom had, like localists before them, married a vision of restricted government authority to resistance to government efforts to promote Black
progress. For his part, Thomas had come to the belief that restricting government authority was crucial to the goal of promoting Black progress.
This disconnect left Thomas and others within the administration concerned about issues affecting the Black community in a "no-man's land"
with a sense that African Americans "never quite seemed to fit into the
Reagan administration."[16] Since African American voters had not supported Reagan, priority was given to other constituent groups, such as
evangelical Christians. Thomas claimed to have nearly resigned in 1982
when the administration chose not to defend an IRS decision to revoke
tax exempt status for the Christian college Bob Jones University on account of its racially discriminatory policies, including its prohibition on
interracial dating.[17] Even as he rose in prominence within the Reagan
administration throughout the 1980s and endured accusations of selling

out his race by working for an administration eager to erode hard-earned civil rights protections, Thomas would regularly clash with others who had reached their positions in a different way. During his time at the EEOC, he asked a colleague, "Is there some way to be a conservative without being a Confederate?"[18]

As Reagan arrived in the presidency, policies were driven by those in the administration keen on proving their conservative ideological credentials, including on the topic of shrinking and eventually eliminating the Department of Education. However, while Reagan had tapped into the backlash against growing federal influence, pragmatic conservatives were coming "to accept the basic principle that the federal government had a legitimate role to play in helping school districts meet their responsibilities, especially in meeting the needs of disadvantaged children," according to Gareth Davies, an historian of federal education policy. Ironically, for all of its language about local control, *Rodriguez* may have contributed to this need by preserving the wide disparities in funding across school districts. By the time of Reagan's reelection in 1984, the department had survived, and confirmation of the incoming Secretary of Education, William Bennett, was made contingent on setting the quest for abolition aside. The tug over the proper balance between government power and individual liberty was again finding an equilibrium.[19]

NEW REMEDIES FOR OLD PROBLEMS

Meanwhile, communities and federal courts were grappling with the effects of *Milliken* and *Rodriguez*. Wide gaps in funding continued to exist among school districts, a phenomenon particularly glaring between inner-city districts and adjacent suburban ones. Those districts were also growing increasingly identifiable by race as white students exited city schools. The *Rodriguez* and *Milliken* decisions restrained federal courts' abilities to confront either of these issues.

In 1977, the *Milliken* case returned to the Supreme Court. Having been prohibited from ordering a metropolitan desegregation remedy, the lower court had responded with a Detroit-only order that called for implementation of "educational components," such as magnet and specialized schools, remedial reading skills programs, and other programming designed to increase educational quality within Detroit. To pay for this, the court ordered costs to be equally borne by the Detroit school district and the state of Michigan, an outcome the Supreme Court unanimously affirmed. In a brief concurrence, Justice Marshall emphasized that what had occurred in Detroit was happening elsewhere: "What is, to me, most tragic about this case is that in all relevant respects it is in no way unique."[20] One place where a metropolitan area was similarly racially divided and Black students left with fewer resources in a central city district was Kansas City.

Taken together, the two *Milliken* cases set the framework for the coming era of remedying school segregation. In the first case, the Court had ensured that districts would remain sovereign and separate; given residential patterns and discrimination accompanying suburbanization, this meant that districts were likely to remain racially identifiable. The appropriate remedy then, endorsed in the second *Milliken* decision, would be to focus on improving the educational quality within districts and enlist the financial support of the state in paying for it. In a way, this was a return to the idea of separate but equal.[21]

The Kansas City suit was initiated in 1977, the same year as the Court's second *Milliken* decision. The lower court found the KCMSD guilty of unconstitutional segregation for, among other things, utilizing Troost Avenue as a *de facto* racial dividing line. To remedy this, the court ordered a series of remedies during the 1980s that tracked those endorsed in *Milliken II*. The district was ordered to undertake extensive capital improvements to school facilities, reduce teaching loads and class sizes, and improve the quality of the curriculum. Later, the court approved the operation of magnet schools—schools with targeted resources meant to attract students from throughout the area. The long-term goal was "to make available to all KCMSD students educational opportunities equal to or greater than those presently available in the average Kansas City, Missouri, metropolitan suburban school district."[22]

The problem with this ambitious remedy, however, was funding. The total cost of the original remedy was to be almost $88 million, to be apportioned between the district and state. Kansas City voters rejected tax increases to pay for it, and neither the city council nor the state legislature stepped in to fill the gap. This reluctance put the district court in a difficult position between the constitutional command to remedy the effects of Kansas City's prior system of segregation—the Supreme Court's embrace of educational remedies within a district in *Milliken II*—and the unwillingness of anyone to pay for them. This was a clash of federal judicial authority with local governance of a different sort than what had occurred in *Milliken*: rather than confronting individual parental rights to determine where children attended school, the court was confronting individual taxpayers' rights to control local funding and tax rates through self-government. Eventually finding itself with no other choice, the district court ordered a tax increase and an issuance of $150 million in capital improvement bonds. In 1990, the case reached the Supreme Court.[23]

On the question of tax increases, even Justice Marshall agreed that the lower court had gone too far. The Court split, however, on the question of whether the educational remedies ordered were appropriate. Missouri argued that the funding gap—and therefore the district court's overreach in levying a tax—would not have been necessary but for the excessive scope of the remedy the court had ordered, with its magnet schools and capital improvement projects. Here, Justice Marshall joined a 5–4 majority asserting that the scope of the remedy was not properly before the Supreme Court. Rejecting the argument that federal courts could not mandate educational programs, the majority concluded that the constitutional violations of the state and school district enabled lower courts some freedom to override local policies, such as limits on taxing, that interfered with necessary remedies. The question of whether the court's efforts to do so in Kansas City was saved for another day. The 5–4 outcome served as a reminder that though Justice Marshall had found himself often in dissent, he was not always on the losing side of school desegregation cases in the years immediately preceding his retirement.[24]

The Kansas City case was remanded to the lower court but would work its way back to the Supreme Court by 1995. Upon its return, the question of whether the expansive educational remedies were within the power of the district court—the question that had split the Court in 199—was directly presented. In the interim, just as there had been a flurry of new Supreme Court justices in the first years of Richard Nixon's presidency, four new justices were appointed between the 1990 and 1995 hearings in *Missouri v. Jenkins*. When the case returned, three of the new justices voted the same as their predecessors had. One did not, and that was enough to swing the case.

The majority opinion in the 1995 *Jenkins* case was written by Chief Justice William Rehnquist, who had patiently worked from early in his tenure in the early 1970s when he was the lone dissenter on desegregation to writing for a Court majority in *Jenkins* two decades later. Signals from the 1990 case had suggested that though the district court could not tax Kansas City residents directly, it could continue to order expensive educational remedies that would force the district to raise funds, even in contravention of state law. So emboldened, the district court continued its effort to improve student achievement in KCMSD during the early 1990s, including ordering increases in teacher salaries and continuation of educational programs under the desegregation decree. The state of Missouri pleaded that it had done enough to earn at least a partial release from judicial oversight and, as it had argued in 1990, that the court had overstepped its authority. This time, the state won.[25]

In the majority opinion, Rehnquist described the extraordinary features of the Kansas City district, highlighting a planetarium, a twenty-five-acre farm, and a model United Nations wired for language translation. The district court had implemented "the most ambitious and expensive remedial program in the history of school desegregation," with costs approaching $200 million annually. This, the Court said, was unsustainable. It exceeded the proper role of courts, ignored the need for articulable limits on desegregation remedies, and disregarded the goal of returning control of schooling to local school districts. In 1990, four justices (Rehnquist, Sandra Day O'Connor, Anthony Kennedy, and Antonin Scalia) had offered the same conclusion, but without a majority. In 1995, these four justices found an additional vote from Justice Clarence Thomas.[26] The shift from Justice Marshall to Justice Thomas provided the decisive vote, in *Jenkins* and elsewhere, that shifted the Court—and federal courts more broadly—definitively away from the use of federal power to remedy social ills. Within the judicial arena, this was a triumph of Reagan's vision over Johnson's.

CURBING THE POWER OF COURTS

"The time has come for us to put the genie back in the bottle," Clarence Thomas wrote in his 1995 concurrence in *Missouri v. Jenkins*. The genie Justice Thomas spoke of had been coaxed out decades earlier by Thurgood Marshall, the lawyer. Yet, so many decades later, Clarence Thomas looked to the state of education and concluded that "desegregation has not produced the predicted leaps forward in black educational achievement."[27] His *Jenkins* concurrence provided him an opportunity to provide a thorough distillation of his jurisprudence on a number of topics. Its two foundations were the pillars of his worldview: a skepticism at the efficacy of integration as a strategy for Black uplift and a belief in self-reliance in the form of independence from government intervention. On the latter point, his vote with the Court's majority signaled the triumph of the restraint on federal judges in desegregation that had begun two decades earlier in *Milliken I* and had been fervently contested in many other cases through the years, including the second *Milliken* and first *Jenkins* cases. The replacement of Justice Marshall with Justice Thomas had sealed the fate of the dispute.

Justice Thomas recognized that the debate about judicial discretion to craft desegregation remedies was a version of one that went back to the nation's founding. With vim, he criticized the unleashing of such boundless discretion—even for worthy goals—as being at odds with the design of the Constitution's framers. To Thomas, such an expansive reading of judicial power—*federal* judicial power, no less—undermined constitutional principles of federalism between state and federal governments and the separation of powers. For decades, these had been the consistent critiques of conservative opponents in the civil rights cases from the Warren Court to more contemporary critics of Justice Marshall.[28]

To support his reading of the directives of the Constitution, Thomas cited Thomas Jefferson, author of the theory of interposition of states' rights to nullify federal laws, for the principle that judges must be bound strictly by text. He drew from the writings of Anti-Federalists during the ratification struggle, arguing that even before there were federal judges, there were Americans who feared the ability of federal judges to interpret a flexible constitution in a way that would result in a growth of federal power and subversion of the autonomy of states. Ratification in the face of such critiques, Thomas asserted, revealed a compromised understanding of the breadth of federal judicial powers.[29]

Looking at the record since *Brown*, Thomas observed an extreme departure from that understanding. He considered the initial expansion "understandable" in the face of the lack of good faith effort from local officials after *Brown*, but he felt "such powers should have been temporary and used only to overcome the widespread resistance to the dictates of the Constitution." Instead, as Thomas saw it, the Court had enabled federal courts to craft perpetual remedies with shifting goals and to override the decisions of even elected local and state governments acting in good faith. Not only was this contrary to the proper constitutional role of federal judges, but it ultimately detracted from the dignity and independence of federal courts by allowing judges to "intrude into areas in which they have little expertise." The end result was that the federal judiciary was transformed from "the least dangerous branch into the most dangerous one."[30]

This was a fundamentally different view than that offered by Justice Marshall. In *Milliken*, Marshall lamented a "giant step backwards" when the majority had limited the lower court's power to remedy a constitutional violation, calling it an "emasculation" of the guarantee of equal protection. Federal courts had the "responsibility" to see to it that dual systems of schooling were terminated. And where Thomas wished to reward what he perceived as the good faith of local school districts, Marshall lamented local officials who had never demonstrated any interest in protecting the most vulnerable students.[31]

Twenty years later, Justice Thomas argued that boundless judicial power was the greater threat to liberty. Where Marshall had seen the lingering and unremedied effects of prior discrimination, Thomas felt that the educational disparities were better explained by "voluntary housing choices or other private decisions." Indeed, he declared that the "white flight" in Kansas City had been caused more by *de*segregation than prior state-enforced segregation. "As state-enforced segregation recedes further into the past," Thomas wrote in *Jenkins*, "it is more likely that [continuous and massive demographic shifts] will be the real source of racial imbalance or of poor educational performance in a school district."[32]

CONTRASTING VISIONS FOR SOLVING PROBLEMS

These contrasting perspectives of judicial power that were most evident in this area—the schooling of African American students—and that had shaped both justices' lives revealed the core differences between these two individuals and reflected one of the great divides in American constitutional interpretation. They disagreed about the proper aim of Black education, the wrong to be remedied. They disagreed about the causes of racial segregation and therefore disagreed about how much responsibility government should take in addressing it. They disagreed about the power and skill of the government in intervening. And because of these disagreements, they disagreed about how much power federal courts should have.

To Marshall, desegregation was about ensuring that Black and white children in fact attended schools together. In *Milliken*, he decried the rejection of the metropolitan desegregation plan because it would perpetuate the racial identifiability of schools and continue to send the message of inferiority to Black children. Thomas, however, felt that the psychological harm was irrelevant: "Segregation was not unconstitutional because it might have caused psychological feelings of inferiority." Thomas disparaged the "unnecessary and misleading" reliance on social science studies in favor of the simple principle that "government must treat citizens as individuals, and not as members of racial, ethnic, or religious groups."[33] To Thomas, racial isolation was not a constitutional harm; only state-enforced segregation required court intervention. Marshall saw a state-sanctioned message of Black inferiority in the continued segregation of students; Thomas found the same message in efforts to integrate them. That Marshall had experienced only segregated schools while Thomas attended schools alongside mostly white peers surely informed such contrasting conclusions. From these differing lessons from their own schooling experiences, the work of the Supreme Court would be transformed.

Given his work over the course of his career, there could be no doubt about Thurgood Marshall's desire to uplift Black students, even if there was room to critique his strategies. But many in the Black community questioned Clarence Thomas's sincerity in that effort. In *Jenkins*, he referred to the desire to aid Kansas City's Black students as a "worthy task" and a "deserving end" but nonetheless cast the deciding vote for discontinuing the school district's efforts.[34] The equal protection clause that Justice Marshall saw as requiring government to provide all an opportunity to an equal start in life, Justice Thomas saw as a far more limited tool: the government did not need to be solving problems beyond its authority and capacity; rather, it needed to stop interfering with the efforts of individuals to solve problems themselves. In 2002, Thomas offered his perspective on the better strategy for serving Black students, one more in line with his antigovernment worldview.

The schools of Cleveland, Ohio, had followed a pattern similar to those in Detroit and Kansas City, with the city's central district serving a majority African American student population while surrounding suburban districts served most of the region's white students. Further, by the 1990s, the forces straining the efforts of urban districts across the country had led the state to take over Cleveland's schools to address poor performance. Like Cleveland, Detroit had seen its schools taken over by the state in 1999, and in 2000, Kansas City became the first district in the nation to lose its state accreditation; these were results Thurgood Marshall might have anticipated from the Court's retreats in *Rodriguez* and *Milliken*, though they were certainly results he would have bemoaned. Among the strategies to address this educational crisis was Ohio's Pilot Project Scholarship Program, through which the state provided vouchers to families to pay up to 90 percent of tuition at private schools. When the program reached the Supreme Court on the question of whether it might violate the separate of church and state, the Court (with the same 5–4 lineup as in *Jenkins*) concluded that it did not. And Thomas took the opportunity to offer a full-throated indictment of government schooling.[35]

Justice Thomas's concurrence in the case, *Zelman v. Simmons-Harris*, opened and closed with quotes from Frederick Douglass about the importance of education, thus including in the Supreme Court annals a voice not often present. Indeed, over his tenure, Justice Thomas introduced a greater number of African American thinkers into Supreme Court cases than any other justice, including Justice Marshall. Douglass had said that education "means emancipation," and looking at the state of schooling for African American children, Thomas observed that "many of our inner-city public schools deny emancipation to urban minority students" who are "forced into a system that continually fails them."[36] This was an indictment Marshall might have predicted to be the result of the Court's elevation of local control over equal educational opportunity in *Rodriguez, Milliken,* and later in *Dowell*—he had warned that there would be consequences for Black students of such disengagement of judicial oversight.

Rather than being "condemned to failing public schools," Thomas applauded that poor students in Cleveland were provided a choice through the voucher program "that those with greater means have routinely exercised."[37] It was a choice, Thomas asserted, that many African Americans supported as providing the greatest educational opportunities for their children. Here was Thomas, arriving at a conservative position, but justifying it for its impact on African Americans.

Though public education represented a "romanticized ideal" that "resonate[d] with the cognoscenti," Thomas cited Thomas Sowell for the conclusion that African Americans faced too many real-world problems to be romantics. In the real world, "the quality of public schools varie[d] significantly across districts," and "the promise of public school education has failed poor inner-city blacks." Such failure contributed to the "cycle of poverty, dependence, criminality, and alienation" plaguing African Americans. Rather than awaiting the government's solution to failing schools— or worse, from Justice Thomas's perspective, forcing integration and its underlying belief in Black inferiority—Thomas found vouchers to be not only constitutional, but the better solution for Black students. Thomas did not believe that society could end discrimination, and he certainly did not believe that the government could: "If society cannot end racial discrimination, at least it can arm minorities with the education to defend themselves from some of discrimination's effects."[38]

In *Rodriguez*, Justice Marshall had disparaged an unequal *system*. Marshall, who had spent most of his career as a lawyer fighting against the government, held a conviction that the government had the responsibility to remedy that system. He was no less a lover of liberty, but he felt that liberty must begin with "an equal start in life."[39] And since the government had taken it upon itself to mandate education, government must provide that equal start. To Marshall, enabling government to avoid its obligation to remedy inequality was perpetuating the systemic oppression.

To Thomas, in contrast, relying on government was a form of dependence, the antithesis of self-reliance and, ultimately, a restriction on individual liberty. In the past, Thomas had criticized his own sister for her reliance on government support, and in *Zelman* he argued that the best the government could do for the problem of unequal schools was to provide students the choice to escape.[40] This was an extremely narrow view of the role of government taken by an individual whose entire working career aside from his stint at Monsanto had been as a government employee. From skepticism in government came skepticism about public schools.

The two justices had found philosophical kinship with presidents who took decidedly different sides in the centuries-long American discussion of the appropriate role of government: Johnson, the pursuer of the Great

Society of government safety nets and support, and Reagan, the advocate of a small and limited government that allowed individuals to thrive. Their philosophies represented two sides of an American debate that traced all the way to the nation's founding. On the Court, each most thoroughly articulated their philosophies when the education of vulnerable, mostly African American students was at stake. And the replacement of Marshall with Thomas had tipped the balance on the Court away from the idea of government solutions, a transformation that would impact the Court's work in virtually every sphere.

In the years to come, the Court would continue to scale back federal interventions from the federal Voting Rights Act to the federal judicial protection of reproductive choice, results that became achievable with the Marshall-to-Thomas transition but that needed additional changes on the Court to fully realize. Still, the 1991 transition itself would force the nation to confront another of its enduring questions: how to appropriately account for equal opportunities in a nation of diverse citizens.

PART IV

DIVERSITY

TWELVE

QUOTAS

When constructing the Constitution, James Madison surveyed his new nation and came to a somewhat counterintuitive observation. His study of confederations of the past suggested that they lasted only so long as they shared a common enemy or were loyal to a strong leader. Diverse confederations, it seemed, were not sustainable. In a country with the potential vastness of the United States, diversity could prove destructive.

Yet Madison saw diversity not as a weakness, but as a potential solution to a separate and more vexing problem that had doomed representative democracies of the past: the tyranny of the majority. Given the principles of democracy, such as majority rule, there was little to prevent a majority from imposing its will on minorities with the same force as a tyrant. What Madison saw, however, was that more diversity would make it more difficult for there to be such a tyrannical majority. With greater heterogeneity, greater diversity, no single factions could dominate independently, and all would have to cooperate in order to accomplish any of their aims. Alliances and common interests might shift depending on context, creating a dynamic patchwork without permanent winners or losers.[1]

Madison sought to build diversity into the constitutional structure. The diffusion of power between state and federal governments, between legislative houses within the federal government, between branches of government, and between government institutions and the people sought a balance that would prevent tyranny from any single source.

The nation was already populated by as eclectic a group of human beings ever to attempt to found a nation. With the exception of Native Americans, who were being cruelly displaced, it would be a nation of immigrants, from diverse corners of the globe. By the time Madison and the other drafters of the Constitution gathered in Philadelphia in 1787, the nation already had religious and ethnic diversity, as well as regional differences. By contemporary standards, the founders were not a particularly diverse group—all were white, all were male, all were Christian in some form—yet they came from different places with different climates, economies, and local values. No individual or state held enough power to dictate the terms of the Constitution, and so the document represented a compromise among the diversity in the room. But, of course, there was a great deal of diversity in the United States that was not in the room. Over the centuries, the nation repeatedly faced the challenge of applying the principles in the Constitution to an expanding concept of the American citizenry that continued to grow ever more diverse.[2]

The original Constitution did not deal with the diversity of individuals present in the United States, but rather concerned itself more with the institutional diversity—the checks and balances—Madison thought could create a sustainable republic. However, the document was quickly amended to protect minority rights from the tyranny of the majority. In the First Amendment, religious diversity and a diversity of viewpoints were protected by its guarantees of free speech and freedom of religion. No matter how unpopular an opinion or how unorthodox a religion, the Bill of Rights aimed to protect individuals from the whims of democratic oversight.[3]

These principles were stated in absolute terms—"Congress shall make *no law* . . ."—but their meaning has been subject to interpretation across the centuries. Writing in the context of World War I, Justice Oliver Wendell Holmes articulated the importance of protecting even speech that was critical of the government's war efforts. According to Holmes, the theory of the American Constitution was that "the best test of truth is the power of the thought to get itself accepted in the competition of the market." As such, "we should be eternally vigilant against attempts to check the expression of opinions that we loathe and believe to be fraught with death."[4] In a nation with diverse viewpoints, unless the country's very existence was at stake, Holmes suggested that individuals must be free to express them if the country was to grow. Combined with Madison's institutional diversity in the constitutional structure, the protection of a diversity of ideas would nurture a sustainable democracy.

But that democracy had been sustained with very little protection for the diversity among *individuals*. As Thurgood Marshall observed in a 1987 speech commemorating the bicentennial of the Constitution, "When the Founding Fathers used [the phrase 'We the People'] in 1787, they did not have in mind the majority of America's citizens."[5] Rather than a strength that would enable diffusion of power or a quest for truth, the diversity of individuals in the United States has proven a fertile source of conflict between the nation's expressed ideals and its actual practice. Rather than tolerance for diversity as embodied in the Constitution, American laws and social customs often exhibited *intolerance* of difference. The erasure and displacement of Native Americans, legalized subjugation of African Americans, and systematic exclusion of women sit alongside discrimination against immigrants, individuals with disabilities, or those who do not conform to majority norms of sexuality or gender as examples where individuals who are members of groups without power have been subjected to oppressive laws. Meanwhile, socially, there has been pressure for diverse Americans to assimilate into a traditional hierarchy with white, Christian males and their norms at the top.

Whereas the First Amendment promoted legal tolerance of minority religions or viewpoints, the Constitution did not promote legal equality of all citizens until the adoption of the Fourteenth Amendment in 1868. Still, when it came to interpreting that amendment, the Supreme Court tended to defer to democratic majorities passing laws, like the one mandating racial segregation in railcars challenged in *Plessy v. Ferguson* in 1896. Such deference left diverse individuals vulnerable to decades of oppressive laws.

A hint of change came in an unlikely case in 1938, only a few years before the nation went to war with a historically intolerant regime in Germany. In a footnote of a case about a federal law prohibiting filled milk from being shipped in interstate commerce, Justice Harlan Stone commented that though courts should tend to defer to the democratically elected branches of government, there may be some situations where such deference would be less appropriate. In particular, Stone seemed concerned about situations in which democracy might not be trusted. Laws that restricted the right to vote or interfered with political organizations might be "subjected to more exacting judicial scrutiny." Similar scrutiny might be appropriate for statutes directed at religious, national, or racial minorities because

> prejudice against discrete and insular minorities may be a special condition, which tends seriously to curtail the operation of those political processes ordinarily to be relied upon to protect minorities.[6]

This footnote in *U.S. v. Carolene Products* opened the door to members of minority groups to challenge oppressive laws. It was through this opening that Thurgood Marshall, the lawyer, was able to push the Court to reconsider the constitutionality of racial segregation. Marshall's work was part of a revolution of individuals demanding that the nation adhere to its professed ideals for *all* of "the people" in all of their diversity. Over time, this revolution led the nation to enact policies designed to affirmatively undo its prior oppressions, policies that would ultimately be tested at the Supreme Court. These cases would force a reckoning about how the nation ought to face the effects of its treatment of minority groups and deal with the diversity of its people. But they would also force a collision among ideals that had driven Marshall and others to push for change. Specifically, affirmative action revealed a tension between the desire for laws to treat all citizens equally and the need for laws to be attentive to the different circumstances faced by the nation's diverse citizenry.

This tension animated the 1991 transition from the nation's first Black Supreme Court justice to its second, and the word "quotas" was at its center.

WHAT ROLE FOR RACE?

As mentioned in Chapter 7, at his farewell press conference in the Supreme Court's East Conference Room, Thurgood Marshall proved a consistently hostile witness. Marshall parried virtually every invitation to ponder a wide range of topics: his legacy, the future of the Court, the reasons for his retirement, the progress of civil rights, the future of school desegregation. To a press eager for reflection, Marshall was not forthcoming. On his mentor Charles Hamilton Houston: "You know my memory never was too good." On his legacy: "I don't know what legacy I left. It's up to the people." On that morning's reporting in the *New York Times* that he was retiring out of frustration with an "ascendant conservative majority" on the Court: "Who said that? . . . That's a bald-faced lie." On the varied reactions to his retirement: "President Roosevelt and Winston Churchill both died, and the world went right along." On his plans for retirement: "Sit on my rear end." To a (white) reporter who asked whether "black people" were better off than when he joined the Court, he lectured, "I am not a 'black people.' I am an Afro- American." When the question was rephrased, he sloughed it off: "That is a question that has no relationship whatsoever. So are the white people better off since I sat on the Court."[7]

Marshall had never been afraid to ruffle feathers or speak his mind; his fearlessness was certainly a part of what enabled him to succeed as he did. In his early career, he had mixed a kind of raunchy charm into his sarcastic and cutting style that garnered him respect from (and sometimes camaraderie with) opponents, even as it fueled rivalries among allies. But as he neared the end of his career, the justice had grown increasingly cantankerous. While he had long aired disappointments in his dissents, in the 1980s he increasingly vented beyond the confines of judicial opinions. In speeches, interviews, and even during oral arguments and the justices-only conferences at the Court, Marshall's caustic tone permeated his persona. He filled the thirty minutes of his press conference with flippant responses and outright refusals to address any business of the Court or its cases, squinting with his nose scrunched as he deflected question after question.

The question most reporters were focused on was more forward-looking: What role should race play in the nomination of Justice Marshall's replacement? Here, Marshall revealed concern that a focus on the race of a nominee would obscure investigation into whether the nominee's positions were favorable to African Americans. Marshall emphasized that he did not think race should be an "excuse" for nominating "the wrong Negro." He highlighted that he had recommended a white replacement when he left his position as solicitor general in 1967. He was no Pollyanna about race's relevance as a factor ("You can't ignore it"), but he was wary of making it the most important one: "I think the most important factor is to pick the best person for the job, not on the basis of race one way or the other." Marshall was keenly aware of how race could be misused to undercut African Americans, and he was deeply suspicious of the conservatives in power, on the Court and in the White House. "My dad told me way back that you can't use race. For example, there's no difference between a white snake and a black snake. They'll both bite."[8]

Perhaps Marshall knew the conservative Clarence Thomas would be a tempting candidate for the president to solve the complex ideological and racial puzzle presented by Marshall's retirement. But when Marshall was asked specifically about the possibility of Thomas—who had been a candidate when President Bush had nominated David Souter to replace Justice William Brennan the year before—he did not engage: "I think the President knows what he's doing and he's going to do it."[9]

Once the retiring justice had had enough, he announced his intention to terminate the press conference by simply pushing himself up from his chair with his cane and leaving the room. It was now up to the president to do what he was going to do.

While Marshall, who had spent his entire life advocating for Black access to forbidden spaces, was reduced to warning against appointing "the wrong Negro" to replace him, Marshall's retirement would also force President George H. W. Bush to twist ideologically in order to justify his decisions. Less than nine months earlier, President Bush had vetoed the Civil Rights Act of 1990 on the grounds that it promoted the use of quotas in employment. According to the president, economic, employment, or education policies that explicitly encouraged Black participation or inclusion violated the principle of neutrality and non-discrimination that ought to guide the laws of a diverse nation. Yet he would have a difficult time convincing others that the choice of Clarence Thomas was made independently of race. The president was caught between contrasting ways of dealing with the diversity of citizens. On one hand, under professed American ideals of equality and individual merit, race ought not matter; yet, within the United States as it actually existed, race often did.

The extent to which race played a role—and ought to have played a role—in selecting Thurgood Marshall's replacement would haunt not only the weekend between Marshall's retirement and Bush's announcement of Clarence Thomas as nominee, but also the Supreme Court career of Justice Thomas. On the Court, Justice Marshall had never denied the relevance of race in American life: he judged the world in the context in which he encountered it and advocated outcomes that accepted that reality. Yet Thomas would be drawn more to principles of neutrality, applying principles for a world as it ought to be.

ON THE MERITS

Three days after Marshall's retirement press conference, President Bush stood in the open air outside his retreat in Kennebunkport, Maine, announcing Clarence Thomas as his nominee to the Supreme Court. "Judge Thomas's life is a model for all Americans," the president declared, emphasizing the trajectory of Thomas's life from humble beginnings in Georgia and the personal characteristics that had drawn the president to him ("delightful, warm, intelligent," "great empathy," "wonderful sense of humor," "fiercely independent").[10]

In his remarks, Thomas, who was serving as a judge on the Court of Appeals of the District of Columbia at the time, fought back tears. "As a child, I could not dare dream that I would ever *see* the Supreme Court, not to mention be nominated to it," he began.

> Indeed my most vivid childhood memory of the Supreme Court was the "Impeach Earl Warren" signs which lined Highway 17 near Savannah. I didn't quite understand who this Earl Warren fellow was, but I knew he was in some kind of trouble.

Thomas thanked his grandparents and expressed his belief that "only in America" could his journey have occurred. He closed with a pledge "to be an example to those who are where I was and to show them that indeed, there is hope."[11]

However, just as members of the press had done at Justice Marshall's retirement press conference the Friday before, reporters wanted to know the role race had played in President Bush's selection. Lingering just beneath the surface of these questions was the unstated assertion that but for his race, Clarence Thomas would not have been the nominee. This was a suggestion at which President Bush visibly bristled. Among the first questions to the president was one that connected the Thomas nomination to the veto of the Civil Rights Act of 1990, asking whether there was any inconsistency in the president's positions against employment quotas. The typically mild-mannered president showed a flash of anger as he answered:

> I don't even see an appearance of inconsistency because what I did was look for the best man and Clarence Thomas's name was high on the list. And the fact that he is black and a minority has nothing to do with this.[12]

Echoing the words of President Johnson twenty-four years earlier announcing the nomination of Thurgood Marshall, Bush called Thomas "the best man at the right time." Speaking of his own court nominee, Johnson had said

I believe he earned his appointment; he deserves this appointment; he's the best qualified by training and by very valuable service to the country. I believe it's the right thing to do, the right time to do it, the right man, the right place.[13]

The invocation of qualifications, however, served a different purpose in 1991 than it had in 1967. President Johnson was confronting a racist notion that no African American could be qualified to serve as a Supreme Court justice, arguing that race should not be relevant in determining a nominee's ability to do the job. In contrast, President Bush's comment was uttered in an environment in which there was high resentment of policies aimed at advancing the interests of African Americans, which had led to a shift among white southern voters to Bush's Republican predecessors, Richard Nixon and Ronald Reagan. In this atmosphere, the impulse to describe Clarence Thomas as "best qualified" was meant to rebut any feeling that less-qualified African Americans were being given opportunities that were not deserved. Though distanced from open bigotry, this feeling also rested on a racist notion that many African Americans were not qualified for the positions they had.

Members of the press were skeptical, but the president did not relent:

I . . . strongly resent any charge that might be forthcoming on quotas. . . . I don't feel that I had to appoint, nominate, a Black American at this time for the Court. I express my respect for the ground that Mr. Justice Marshall plowed, but I don't feel there should be a black seat on the Court or an ethnic seat on the Court.[14]

The president then echoed Justice Marshall's sentiment from his own press conference the week earlier that race should not be determinative. Marshall, who had warned of snakes who bite regardless of their color, had identified the most important factor as "to pick the best person for the job, not on the basis of race, one way or the other." Bush, who had nominated a Black judge to fill Marshall's seat, claimed, "I kept my word to the American people and to the Senate by picking the best man for the job on the merits." Still, Bush did acknowledge that race was not wholly irrelevant: "the fact that he is minority, so much the better."[15]

The president's nominee was asked outright how he would respond to critics who said he was only being picked because he was Black. "I think a lot worse things have been said," Thomas quipped. "I disagree with that, but I'll have to live with it."[16]

INCREASING ACCESS IN A DIVERSE SOCIETY

In 1991, "quota" had become shorthand for opponents of affirmative action policies that encouraged, even required, consideration of race in decision making. Opponents asserted that such policies replaced considerations of merit with the naked use of race for "preferential treatment." In this telling, a quota was a target of minority inclusion being mandated by law at the expense of more proper considerations of quality. Worse, quotas violated a principle that the government should never consider race among its diversity of citizens; the government, these opponents implored, must be colorblind.

Colorblindness had first entered the lexicon of American constitutional interpretation as a way of rejecting race-based laws. In *Plessy v. Ferguson*, Justice John Marshall Harlan had dissented from the Court's 8–1 decision and embraced a vision of a country without any superior, dominant ruling class:

> There is no caste here. Our constitution is color-blind, and neither knows nor tolerates classes among citizens. In respect of civil rights, all citizens are equal before the law. The humblest is the peer of the most powerful. The law regards man as man, and takes no account of his surroundings or of his color when his civil rights as guaranteed by the supreme law of the land are involved.

In the context of segregation, Harlan imagined the Constitution as mandating neutrality, colorblindness. Only in such an environment could the humblest and the most powerful be peers. Harlan foresaw that if similar segregation laws were adopted more broadly, the result would be the perpetuation of the oppression of a class of the nation's diverse citizens. Such a result interfered not only with Harlan's reading of the Constitution, but with a professed ideal that Americans ought to be judged based on merit, rather than skin color.[17]

When President Bush criticized quotas a century later, he invoked a similar idea. Where Harlan had lamented that utilizing a characteristic like race to *restrict* opportunities would improperly interfere with merit, Bush felt that utilizing race to *expand* opportunities violated the same principle of colorblindness.

However, affirmatively reserving a certain number of benefits for a previously excluded group and openly restricting opportunities for members of that group may have both considered race, but they were not the same thing. Quotas that aimed to include formerly excluded Americans sought to uplift those whose full citizenship had been denied, not further oppress them. Where President Bush saw equivalency in these two interferences with the ideal of colorblindness, others made distinctions they felt merited different ways of thinking.

The national history with quotas evinced more examples of maintaining the nation's hierarchy among its diverse constituents (quotas of exclusion) than of increasing access for a more diverse group of individuals to the nation's institutions and workplaces (quotas of inclusion). For example, in the 1920s, quotas were utilized to limit immigration from Asia and southern and eastern Europe in a naked attempt to maintain the existing white, Protestant preeminence within the United States. Similarly, quotas were utilized to control enrollment at prestigious universities, an effort aimed principally at limiting the numbers of Jewish students. These quotas were artificial limits aimed at preserving a status quo. The education quotas in particular interfered with the model of an objective, merit-based system of admission that better aligned with the individualistic ideal—each American achieving based on his or her own talents and work ethic. Inclusion of any other characteristic—such as religion, national origin, or race—that did not reflect an individual's ability could only be an unwelcomed glitch in the meritocracy.

But American history was littered with such glitches, particularly with regard to race, where an individual's race—and not his or her merit—was often *the* characteristic that determined a life's trajectory. Public and private racial discrimination had been a defining feature of the American system from the outset, and generations of advocates for African American freedom and equality had argued the injustice of allowing race to override individual merit. Perhaps the most powerful expression of this ideal came in the throes of the American civil rights movement when Dr. Martin Luther King Jr. declared his dream to live in a country where his children would be judged "not by the color of their skin, but by the content of their character." By invoking this ideal, President Bush found a potent tool in the fight against affirmative action, but one that he was implicitly accused of violating in nominating a Black judge to replace Thurgood Marshall.

The conflict surrounding quotas was ultimately a question about diversity and the central American challenge of building a nation among diverse citizens. Through the 1980s, both Thurgood Marshall and Clarence Thomas held positions of significant influence that forced them to confront the question in the context of employment.

CONSTITUTIONALLY GERMANE AND DISMAYINGLY RELEVANT

Among the achievements of the civil rights revolution Thurgood Marshall helped ignite was the Civil Rights Act of 1964. Pushed through by President Johnson in the months following the assassination of John F. Kennedy (and opposed by 1964 Texas Senate candidate George H. W. Bush), the statute included extensive antidiscrimination provisions in areas from education to employment. The legislation had been a significant goal of the civil rights movement, and its most wide-ranging protections confronted the scourge of racial discrimination in employment. In its most direct clause, Title VII of the act made it unlawful for an employer to fail or refuse to hire or to discharge any individual, or otherwise to discriminate against any individual with respect to his compensation, conditions, or privileges of employment, because of such individual's race, color, religion, sex, or national origin.

The act also created the Equal Employment Opportunity Commission (EEOC) to enforce the law, an agency Clarence Thomas would lead from 1982–1990.[18]

While Title VII obviously outlawed intentional discrimination in employment, it was less clear how the law would apply to race-neutral (i.e., colorblind) policies that still had racially disparate impacts. The question arrived at the Supreme Court in 1971 in a case where Black plaintiffs challenged a company's requirement of a high school diploma for its higher paying jobs. The requirement was race neutral—*all* applicants were required to have a high school diploma for the higher paying jobs, regardless of race—but had the effect of keeping African American employees, who had substantially lower high school graduation rates, from better opportunities. Indeed, the diploma requirement had only been adopted in 1955 after the company had eliminated a prior explicit exclusion of Black employees from such jobs. The Court (including Justice Marshall) unanimously concluded that such race-neutral policies could indeed violate Title VII, with Chief Justice Burger writing that "practices, procedures, and tests neutral on their face, and even neutral in terms of intent, cannot be maintained if they operate to 'freeze' the status quo of prior discriminatory employment practices."[19]

This expansion of discrimination beyond *intentional* discrimination and the shifting of the burden to employers to justify the "business necessity" of neutral practices was controversial from the start, and the Court incrementally narrowed it. Part of the justification for such a narrowing was that maintaining a high burden on employers to establish the "business necessity" of neutral practices would lead to employers simply establishing employment quotas to avoid disparate impact lawsuits altogether. Justices described the dilemma employers faced as a "Hobson's choice": employers could maintain their existing practices and risk a lawsuit if those practices had a disparate impact, or they could adopt new expensive procedures that would be perfectly tailored to the needs of each job and thus could survive the scrutiny of a lawsuit. "If quotas and preferential treatment become the only cost-effective means of avoiding expensive litigation and potentially catastrophic liability, such measures will be widely adopted," Justice O'Connor wrote in a 1988 plurality opinion. "The prudent employer will be careful to ensure that its programs are discussed in euphemistic terms, but will be equally careful to ensure that the quotas are met."[20] By the end of the 1980s, the Court had relaxed the standard on employers and thus undermined the claims of employees arguing that race-neutral practices were having racially disparate effects. The outcome came in a 5–4 decision, with Justice Marshall joining the dissent.[21]

It was against this backdrop that members of Congress developed the Civil Rights Act of 1990 that President Bush had vetoed. The president argued that despite using the term "civil rights," the legislation would "introduce the destructive force of quotas" by placing the burden on employers to scrupulously justify race-neutral practices with racially disparate effects. But Justice Marshall argued that such framing of quotas seemed deliberately ignorant of context. In his dissent in *City of Richmond v. J.A. Croson, Co.* in 1989, Marshall wrote:

> A profound difference separates governmental actions that themselves are racist, and governmental actions that seek to remedy the effects of prior racism or to prevent neutral governmental activity from perpetuating the effects of such racism.

The case was about the constitutionality of Richmond's "set-aside" program that required at least 30 percent of the city's construction contracts to be awarded to minority-owned businesses. The *Croson* case actually presented a more direct example of race-conscious quotas than anything that had been discussed in the Civil Rights Act of 1990: here, the government was requiring consideration of race and imposing a specific target within an industry with a history of race discrimination. Though in dissent, Justice Marshall found the program laudable: "It is a welcome symbol of racial progress when the former capital of the Confederacy acts forthrightly to confront the effects of racial discrimination in its midst."[22]

Marshall's dissent sounded themes that animated his consistent recognition of the vestiges of racial discrimination and his belief that government should be allowed the leeway to remedy them effectively, even through use of race-conscious policies like the set-aside program. Marshall criticized the Court's majority for "wishful thinking" about racial progress:

> [A] majority of this Court signals that it regards racial discrimination as largely a phenomenon of the past, and that government bodies need no longer preoccupy themselves with rectifying racial injustice. I, however, do not believe this Nation is anywhere close to eradicating racial discrimination or its vestiges.

Marshall understood that government neutrality would not undo racial disparities, a belief he shared with the Richmond leadership who had adopted the set-aside program, leaders Marshall noted were "deeply familiar" with what racial discrimination was. The city had tried race-neutral policies, barring all racial discrimination by public contractors for over a decade, but minority-owned businesses still received less than 1 percent of public contracting dollars. "Race is constitutionally germane," he wrote, "precisely because race remains dismayingly relevant in American life."[23]

Thus, whereas the opponents of quotas, set-asides, and preferential treatment portrayed those race-conscious policies as making the outcomes of employment and other economic decisions unjust, Justice Marshall found just the opposite. But for the race-conscious interventions, he argued, the effects of the unjust past would continue to produce unjust outcomes in the present. But Marshall wrote as a dissenter in *Croson*. According to the 5–4 majority, the problem with Richmond's plan was that it "denies certain citizens the opportunity to compete for a fixed percentage of public contracts based solely upon their race."[24] The majority wanted the contracts to be awarded not based on the color of skin, but on the content of a contractor's proposal. For Justice Marshall, it must have seemed that the sharp tools he had once wielded to advance the interests of disadvantaged minorities were being turned against him.

Coming less than nine months after President Bush's veto of the Civil Rights Act of 1990 and amid consideration of a new civil rights bill, the nomination of Clarence Thomas to fill Thurgood Marshall's Supreme Court seat tested the principles that had been expressed in the employment cases. Justice Marshall, who had found set-asides justified in *Croson* based on the history of racial discrimination, was cautioning that race should not be an "excuse" for appointing "the wrong Negro." And while Marshall would largely leave the civil rights stage following his retirement press conference, the nomination of Thomas, a conservative African American judge, placed other civil rights leaders in the uncomfortable position of either supporting a nominee whose positions appeared to be out of alignment with the majority of civil rights leaders (and also with the majority of African Americans) or opposing only the second African American to be nominated to the Supreme Court.

But the Thomas nomination also laid bare the interests of the President and his allies. Though they had argued forcefully that merit and not race should dictate hiring decisions, that set-asides denied citizens the opportunity to compete in a colorblind meritocracy, nominating an African American to fill Marshall's seat implicitly conceded that race was not wholly irrelevant. For the president and his supporters, nominating Clarence Thomas must have seemed a tempting opportunity to both appoint a conservative justice and expose the hypocrisy of civil rights leaders who argued for workplace diversity but were now claiming that there were "right" and "wrong" Negroes for the job, even if it meant sacrificing colorblindness and engaging in some hypocrisy of their own.

SUPPOSED BENEFICIARIES

For his part, Clarence Thomas spent the 1980s as head of the EEOC, the body charged with enforcing Title VII's prohibitions on employment discrimination. Thus, at the same time Justice Marshall was interpreting the statute's application in disparate impact cases, Thomas led the agency enforcing the law. It was Thomas's performance at the EEOC and his positions on these topics—quotas, set-asides, affirmative action, and other race-conscious remedies—that initially raised the ire of civil rights groups opposing his Supreme Court nomination. Just as it was Marshall's record tearing down Jim Crow that made southern opposition to him so adamant, it was Thomas's alliance with conservatives on the racial issues of his day that made him anathema to mainstream civil rights leaders.

Though Thomas reached the same conclusion as the conservatives on the Court who had undercut race-conscious remedies in employment, Thomas's starting point differed. Observing the field of discrimination in the 1980s as head of the EEOC, Thomas concluded that race-conscious remedies like quotas or set-asides were not only legally questionable but also counterproductive to the cause of racial equality.

In a 1987 article in the *Yale Law & Policy Review*, Thomas made the case against using racial goals to confront discrimination that directly countered Marshall's arguments in his *Croson* dissent. His title "Not Tough Enough!" declared that numerical goals should be opposed, and Thomas opened with a detailed explanation of his own disagreement with numerical remedies in an extraordinary footnote:

> I continue to believe that distributing opportunities on the basis of race or gender, whoever the beneficiaries, turns the law against employment discrimination on its head. Class preferences are an affront to the rights and dignity of individuals—both those individuals who are directly disadvantaged by them, and those who are their supposed beneficiaries. I think that preferential hiring on the basis of race or gender will increase racial divisiveness, disempower women and minorities by fostering the

notion that they are permanently disabled and in need of handouts, and delay the day when skin color and gender are truly the least important things about a person in the employment context.[25]

Here was an articulation of opposition to "preferential hiring" rooted not in technical arguments about burdens of proof, but in a belief that such practices would perpetuate the relevance of race. Thomas concerned himself with individuals, noting that preferences based on class membership harmed both whites and men ("those individuals who are directly disadvantaged") and minorities and women ("those who are . . . supposed beneficiaries"). Thomas spoke of a stigma that would attach itself to these "supposed" beneficiaries: the assumption that but for the "handouts," Black or female applicants were not qualified.

In the remainder of the article, Thomas built the case against the use of race-conscious goals from his articulated goal of focusing attention on what he saw as the real issues in the battle against employment discrimination. In his tenure, Thomas had sought to transform the EEOC from an agency focusing on class action, group-based cases to one where it could "fight to vindicate the Title VII rights of every individual victim of discrimination." He was skeptical of numerical goals (i.e., quotas) because he found that it was often *employers* pushing for them. Thomas saw this as a self-interested quest for administrative simplicity, not a viable strategy to end discrimination. It was in an employer's interest to settle a case by agreeing to strive toward a numerical hiring goal because the other alternative would involve identifying actual applicants who had been discriminated against and paying them damages; it was far cheaper to agree to do better in the future than to pay for unlawful behavior of the past. Through such hiring goals, employers would

> shift the cost of the remedy from themselves to the actual victims of their past discrimination, who never receive the back pay and jobs to which they are entitled, and to the qualified persons who will be deprived of an employment opportunity because someone else was given a preference under the remedial plan.

The race-conscious goals provided no end to discrimination, but rather merely a "numerical smokescreen" behind which employers might hide continued racial harassment or other discrimination.[26]

Rather than focus on numerical goals (quotas) that were ineffective at ending discrimination and carried with them the side effect of stigmatizing Black employees as unqualified, Thomas advocated tougher remedies, including heavy fines, jail sentences, detailed reporting requirements, and extended court oversight of discriminatory employers. Recognizing the disadvantages that minorities face—such as unfair deprivations of education or training and the increasing importance of proper skills in a service-based economy—Thomas called for providing individuals "with the tools that may allow them to help themselves" rather than "pity or handouts." Chairperson Thomas was not opposed to *any* preferences: he felt that preferences "should be directly related to the obstacles that have been unfairly placed in . . . individuals' paths, rather than on the basis of race or gender, or on other characteristics that are often poor proxies for true disadvantage." This would be a "tougher course," Thomas acknowledged, but it "promises to yield genuine and lasting equal opportunities."[27]

The EEOC's transition away from large class-action suits that led to the use of numerical goals and timetables and toward enforcement of individual cases of discrimination was hotly debated within the EEOC, and despite Thomas's avowed motivations, his position was unpopular with traditional civil rights groups. For example, Herbert Hill, a former labor director for the NAACP, charged that Thomas had transformed the EEOC into a "claims adjustment bureau" by focusing on individual random acts of bigotry while ignoring systemic patterns of discrimination.[28] The focus on individual cases resulted in a big backlog, particularly age discrimination cases, that had lapsed because the EEOC had failed to act within time limits. In addition, there were charges that regional EEOC offices were dismissing cases without fully investigating, a claim that fed the sense that enforcement deteriorated during Thomas's tenure as chair.

According to one study, when Thomas began at the EEOC, nearly one third of cases were settled satisfactorily, and less than one third of complainants were told they had no case; in contrast, by the time Thomas left, fewer than 14 percent of cases were settled satisfactorily, and over half of complainants were told they had no case. Regardless of the sincerity of Thomas's philosophical objections to race-conscious remedies, his critics charged, his record seemed to have produced outcomes counter to the interests of individuals who were members of disadvantaged groups. Not only that, but by framing his positions as motivated by a desire to confront the "true" challenges of racial discrimination, Thomas sought to blunt charges that conservatives were hostile to Black citizenship. In this way, Thomas was a particularly valuable public figure within the conservative movement: white leaders who took the same positions might be criticized as racist, but Thomas's framing sought to rebut that critique.[29]

Of course, this came at a cost to Thomas, whose tenure at the EEOC and on the Court would produce an ever-widening rift with the majority of African Americans. Even before the revelations of sexual harassment raised by Anita Hill, Thomas's confirmation would spark controversy based on the criticisms of his leadership of the EEOC. Combined with the obvious stakes of replacing Justice Marshall with a conservative justice, these criticisms fueled opposition to his nomination despite President Bush's words of high praise. Yet Thomas would win confirmation by a vote of 52–48; no Supreme Court justice had ever been seated with more "no" votes.[30]

From the Supreme Court, Thurgood Marshall looked at the landscape of the 1980s and saw vestiges of public and private discrimination continuing to infect the economy. He concluded his *Croson* dissent with the declaration, "The battle against pernicious racial discrimination or its effects is nowhere near won."[31] From his own vantage point as chair of the EEOC, Clarence Thomas looked upon that same landscape and found the emphasis on "systemic" suits and "societal discrimination" to be misguided. Contemporary discrimination, in Thomas's view, was caused by "individual bigots in positions of authority." Thus, he concluded that "the discrimination we find today more often has a narrow impact, perhaps influencing only a few hiring decisions, and does not warrant the use of a goal that will affect a great number of subsequent hires or promotions."[32]

These distinctions would be translated into narrow legal questions as each justice encountered affirmative action cases: What is the appropriate degree of scrutiny a court should give to policies that use racial classifications to *advantage* African Americans, and ought it be the same as for policies that disadvantage? And how compelling is the public interest in promoting greater access for individuals who are members of previously excluded or disadvantaged groups?

But the cases also illustrated the justices' perspectives on how African Americans and members of other subjugated groups might transcend discrimination of the past and disparities of the present to claim full citizenship. Could they do so as members of groups who had suffered systemically, as Marshall argued, or must they rise as individuals, as Thomas insisted? These were challenges inherent in a diverse nation, a version of the very question reporters were asking during the 1991 transition: How much should race matter?

THIRTEEN

GETTING SOMEBODY IN,
KEEPING SOMEBODY OUT

Chief Justice Warren Burger retired from the Supreme Court at the end of the 1985–86 term, having served longer than any other chief justice of the twentieth century. But upon leaving the Court, Burger continued in public service in a role he had taken on a few years earlier. In September 1983, Congress had established the Commission on the Bicentennial of the United States Constitution to plan and develop activities commemorating the 200th anniversary of the signing of the Constitution: September 17, 1987. The chief justice was appointed the commission's chair, and he continued in this role into his retirement.

Looking back on his service and the commission's work, Burger recalled that the aim was less about parades and fireworks—though there would be a tremendous celebration attended by President Reagan in Philadelphia on the date of the bicentennial—and more about "long-term programs designed to improve Americans' understanding and appreciation of our heritage and to make the 'informed electorate' the Founding Fathers thought imperative to the preservation of democracy." The commission's twenty-three members felt that a national civics lesson was in order. Burger cited a Hearst Foundation study that found that most respondents had incorrectly cited the Constitution as the source of the Karl Marx statement "from each according to his abilities and to each according to his needs." Over seven years, the commission oversaw grant programs and essay contests, developed educational materials and public exhibits, and disseminated over 55 million pocket Constitutions, with the aim of remembering the nation's past upon moving into an exciting, though uncertain future.[1]

But in May 1987, Burger's former colleague, Justice Thurgood Marshall, offered a somewhat different lesson. Addressing an audience in Hawaii, Marshall lamented the tendency to oversimplify and regretted that the bicentennial celebration invited "a complacent belief that the vision of those who debated and compromised in Philadelphia yielded the 'more perfect union' it is said we now enjoy." Marshall rejected the invitation to celebrate, noting that the wisdom, foresight, and sense of justice exhibited by the Constitution's framers was not particularly profound: "When contemporary Americans cite 'The Constitution,' they invoke a concept that is vastly different from what the Framers barely began to construct two centuries ago."[2]

To Marshall, it was not the Constitution's drafting and ratification but the two centuries of effort to expand on the framers' compromised and limited notions of liberty, justice, and equality that deserved commemoration. He traced the flaws in the document—from the exclusion of African Americans and women from the guarantees given to "We the People"; through the forced reshaping of the Constitution less than seventy-five years after ratification in the aftermath of the Civil War; to the additional century before Black Americans were able to share equally in education, housing, employment, and voting, despite having served in the nation's military, worked in its factories and farms, and helped expand its prosperity. Those who gathered in Philadelphia in 1787, Marshall asserted, could not have envisioned the changes over the centuries, including that the document they drafted "would one day be construed by a Supreme Court to which had been appointed a woman and the descendent of an

African slave." There had been progress, but "credit does not belong to the Framers," Marshall claimed. "It belongs to those who refused to acquiesce in outdated notions of 'liberty,' 'justice,' and 'equality,' and who strived to better them."[3] He did not say it, but by almost any measure, Thurgood Marshall would sit near the top of such a group.

Marshall did plan to celebrate, just not the birth of the Constitution. Instead, he wished to commemorate the "suffering, struggle, and sacrifice that has triumphed over much of what was wrong with the original document." After all, the effects of the Constitution's compromise and its contradiction in "guaranteeing liberty and justice to all, and denying both to Negroes" have remained for generations, Marshall observed. What he found worth commemorating was a "living document" that had been and continued to be evolving to close the chasm of those compromises and contradictions: "The true miracle was not the birth of the Constitution, but its life, a life nurtured through two turbulent centuries of our own making."[4]

Coverage of Marshall's speech made the front page of the *New York Times*, which commented that Marshall's address "struck the most negative note yet sounded" on the bicentennial and contrasted sharply with the adulation heaped on the framers by Burger and President Reagan.[5] In his 1987 State of the Union, Reagan had praised the framers as "giants, men whose words and deeds put wind in the sails of freedom," but did not mention slavery.[6] Marshall's effort to make the bicentennial more than a mere "blind pilgrimage" was portrayed as a counterpoint to the president, but there was little in what Justice Marshall said in 1987 that he had not said before. Indeed, nearly a decade earlier, he had offered a similar history lesson, along with an admonishment that the Constitution must be interpreted in context rather than with fixed understandings frozen in time. These points were articulated in Marshall's dissent in the case of Allan Bakke.

ACCESS AND ADMISSIONS

Had they met in another context, Allan Bakke and Thurgood Marshall might never have known the perspective they shared. Bakke, who had attended college on an ROTC scholarship and served a four-year term in the Marines during the Vietnam War, was working as a NASA engineer in California in the early 1970s when he decided he wanted to go to medical school. In 1973 and 1974, he applied to twelve medical schools and was rejected by all. His credentials were strong, though not exceptional; it seemed that the main factor working against him was his age. At least two schools explicitly told him that at 32, he was simply too old to start medical school. Undeterred, Bakke targeted the medical school at the University of California at Davis in 1974 since it was relatively new and seemed to provide the strongest opportunity for admission. In the process, Bakke learned of a special admissions program at the school, which set aside sixteen of the school's one hundred spaces for admission for students classified as disadvantaged. Although the school did not specifically define "economically and/or educationally disadvantaged," all students admitted under the program were members of minority groups. Despite his hopes, Bakke, who was white, was denied admission.[7]

In the 1930s, aware of its policy of excluding African Americans, Thurgood Marshall had not bothered applying to law school at the University of Maryland. Instead, he went to Howard, graduated top of his class, and eventually found Donald Murray to apply to Maryland's law school so that Marshall could challenge the school's discrimination in court. When Allan Bakke received his rejection from UC Davis's medical school in 1974, he felt that he—like Donald Murray—had been denied admission because of his race due to the sixteen seats reserved for disadvantaged students. He filed suit in California, framing his exclusion as one of unconstitutional discrimination and wading into a contentious national discussion about affirmative action. In 1978, the *Bakke* case reached the U.S. Supreme Court, where Thurgood Marshall was among those who felt that the exclusions of Donald Murray and Allan Bakke were quite different indeed.

The UC Davis program was one example of a far broader effort by colleges and universities to address the persistent underrepresentation of female and non-white students on campus in the 1970s. Despite the delegitimization of legalized racial exclusion in *Brown* and federal legislation such as the civil rights statutes of the 1960s, it soon became clear that merely ending restrictions would not substantially affect the status quo. As had been the case in elementary schools and high schools, colleges and universities that had previously served an exclusively white student body would continue to do so unless they altered the ways in which students were admitted. Given the history of discrimination, use of traditional criteria would continue to systematically hinder students from disadvantaged high schools or challenging economic circumstances. For example, in California, Black and Spanish-surnamed students were underrepresented in higher education, and the rates of eligibility to enter either the state's UC or state university system were three times greater for graduates of high-income high schools than for graduates of low-income schools. To remedy this, schools adopted affirmative action programs to recruit students from underrepresented groups and began to consider characteristics of disadvantage, including race, in the admissions process.[8]

Within the medical profession, the problem of underrepresentation was particularly egregious. In 1974, African Americans comprised 2 percent of the nation's doctors and 2.8 percent of medical students, but 11 percent of all citizens. In the late 1960s, the American Medical Association had endorsed the goal of increasing the number of Black medical students to address such disparities, a charge with which the UC Davis program was consistent.[9]

The problem, at least as Allan Bakke saw it, was that the traditional credentials of those admitted under the special program were demonstrably worse than Allan Bakke's. The school noted that every student accepted under the special program was expected to succeed in medical school and argued that such programs were "clearly the most effective way of improving minority access to graduate and professional instruction."[10] But to Bakke, the fact that some students admitted through the program had lower GPAs or admissions indexes than he did demonstrated that he was being discriminated against based on his race. This, he argued, was unconstitutional.[11]

As summarized in Table 1, the Supreme Court had built an outline for discrimination analysis under the Fourteenth Amendment's equal protection clause that declared that "legal restrictions that curtail the civil rights of a single racial group are immediately suspect" and should be subjected to the "most rigid scrutiny."[12] This outline had been sharpened into a framework in which the initial question for a reviewing court was whether the government was utilizing any sort of racial classification that would demand that "most rigid scrutiny," or "strict scrutiny" as it came to be known. If the government was not using such a suspect classification, then it had a lower bar to meet: the government need only justify a challenged policy as having a rational basis, a minimal connection to a legitimate goal that was not arbitrary or capricious. But if the government *was* making a suspect racial classification, then the challenged policy could only survive if it furthered a "compelling" interest and was narrowly tailored to further that interest.

In most cases before *Bakke*, the claims of unconstitutional behavior arose from members of groups that had historically been discriminated against, and the government's discrimination was explicit. The segregation cases, for example, were brought by Black plaintiffs demanding protection of the constitutional rights governments had long denied. But in the late 1970s, the Court encountered two types of cases that forced it to go beyond this archetype.

The first type of case foreshadowed the discussion about quotas that would haunt Clarence Thomas's tenure as head of the EEOC. In *Washington v. Davis*, the Court concluded (over Justice Marshall's dissent) that race-neutral policies that had racially disparate effects did not in and of themselves violate the Fourteenth Amendment. Thus, the Court allowed a police department to continue to use neutral criteria that disproportionately excluded African Americans from higher paying jobs. Constitutional discrimination claims were limited to situations where plaintiffs could show an *intent* to exclude based on race.[13]

Category of constitutional analysis	How much judicial deference to government action?	Standard for a challenged provision to survive
Strict scrutiny	Little to none	Challenged provision will only survive if it serves a compelling government interest and is narrowly tailored to serve that interest
Intermediate or heightened scrutiny	Moderate	Challenged provision can survive if it is substantially related to an important interest
Rational basis	Substantial	Challenged provision will survive if there is any rational basis for the government to take such action

TABLE 1. Degrees of constitutional scrutiny that might be applied to claims of racial discrimination. Made by author.

The second type of case was Allan Bakke's. *Bakke* was asking the Court to apply the equal protection clause with equal force to policies that *favored* disadvantaged groups as it had been applying to policies that disfavored those groups. He was arguing for a colorblindness in interpretation that evaluated the consideration of race in Donald Murray's exclusion from the University of Maryland law school in the 1930s as strictly as his own exclusion from UC Davis medical school. Though the contexts differed, the principle of non-discrimination ought tolerate *no* consideration of a characteristic like race, Bakke argued.

This argument forced judges to consider whether constitutional principles, such as non-discrimination, were fixed or whether they instead should be evaluated in context. This dispute would be echoed in the predominant methods of constitutional interpretation as the twentieth century turned into the twenty-first.

NEW QUESTIONS, MUDDLED ANSWERS

The *Bakke* case arrived at a still uncertain moment in this contested space, and it generated enormous interest when it reached the Supreme Court. At the time, the case established the record for the most *amicus* ("friend of the court") briefs filed with the Court by individuals and organizations interested in the issue, but not directly involved as parties. This was also a reflection of affirmative action programs hitting a nerve in the nation. While the legal arguments were well covered in this litany of briefs, one scholar has observed that "the most striking and lasting impression is how much of the discussion [in the briefs] was overtly political or sociological in nature."[14] That the case was pushing the Court into new territory was also evinced by how long it took to decide. Though it was argued in the opening weeks of the Court's 1977 term—October 12, 1977—it was one of the last decisions announced, during the term's final weeks on June 26, 1978.

In his opening remarks at the October 1977 oral argument, Bakke's lawyer Reynold Colvin argued that Bakke had been "excluded . . . because that school had adopted a racial quota which deprived him of the opportunity for admission" and that "Allan Bakke's position is that he has a right . . . not to be discriminated against by reason of his race."[15] But before he got much further, Colvin was interrupted by a skeptical Thurgood Marshall. Initially, Marshall pressed Colvin on holes in the record, such as the details of how the admissions policy was developed and for what purpose. Marshall dismissed most of what was in the record as mere "hearsay," implying to his colleagues that such a poorly developed record provided an inappropriate vehicle for such an important decision.

Another uncertainty from the record as it existed was whether Bakke would have been admitted even had there been no special admissions program for disadvantaged applicants. Nearly fifty white applicants with numerical indicators superior to Bakke had also been rejected, while several candidates who had scored lower than Bakke were accepted. Still, Colvin went on to develop his argument that Bakke had been rejected on account of his race because white applicants were only eligible to compete for eighty-four of the school's one hundred seats. This prompted another question from Justice Marshall, who wondered if Colvin would make the same argument if the school had only set aside one seat for disadvantaged students. Colvin responded that the argument would be the same, that the numbers were not important, but rather "it is the principle of keeping a man out because of his race that is important."[16] Colvin must have recognized the complexity of citing such a principle in dialogue with Thurgood Marshall.

Marshall went on to pinpoint the difficulty of the case, a difficulty that was inherent in a diverse society that had systematically distributed opportunity based on race but was beginning to try to remedy the legacy of discrimination. "You're arguing about keeping somebody out and the other side is arguing about getting somebody in," he stated, getting Colvin to agree that the principle he relied upon depended on which way one looked at the problem. Then, following a brief exchange in which Marshall acted incredulous that the principle might depend on the circumstances ("It does?"), the justice offered his final comment: "You're talking about your client's rights; don't these underprivileged people have some rights?"[17] Colvin continued in dialogue with the other justices for another eighteen minutes, but Marshall had made his point. The wisdom of the plan, a question independent of its constitutionality, depended on how highly one valued the right of applicants who had experienced educational or economic disadvantage to have access to medical school: to Marshall, the program represented an effort to get such students *in*, and not a program designed to keep Allan Bakke out. Marshall's challenge, however, was translating that position into a constitutional argument.

Justice Marshall kept unusually detailed notes in his *Bakke* case file, perhaps as he sensed that his frustrating losses in *Rodriguez* and *Milliken* five years earlier might be repeated. In some ways, more was at stake in *Bakke*.[18] While *Milliken* limited how much discretion federal courts had in crafting desegregation remedies, it did not touch the underlying equal protection principle that government action that resulted in segregation was unconstitutional. Similarly, *Rodriguez* was a case about what the government could be *required* to do to create equal opportunities: although the Supreme Court had refused to order Texas to fund its school districts equally, Texas could certainly choose to do so on its own. In contrast, *Bakke* presented a case that might establish a limit on what a government *could* do. After centuries of discrimination against African Americans, Justice Marshall was troubled at the possibility that the Constitution might now prohibit discrimination in their favor.

While the justices' initial deliberations concerned technical questions about the record, much of the discussion centered on political and social considerations, rather than legal ones. Justice Marshall's own memorandum to the Court reflected this, and as the only African American involved in the deliberations, he offered a particularly forceful perspective:

> As a result of our last discussion on this case, I wish also to address the question of whether Negroes have "arrived." Just a few examples illustrate that Negroes most certainly have not. In our own Court, we have had only three Negro law clerks, and not so far have we had a Negro Officer of the Court. . . . The dream of America as a melting pot has not been realized by Negroes—either the Negro did not get into the pot, or he did not get melted down.

Marshall went on, referring to racial disparities cited in many of the briefs and noting that "that gulf was brought about by centuries of slavery and then by another century in which, with the approval of this Court, states were permitted to treat Negroes 'specially.'"[19]

While Marshall lamented the "lousy record" and "poorly reasoned lower court opinion," he understood that the Court was stuck with the case. He saw the allure of the principle of colorblindness—indeed, earlier in his career in some of his most famous cases, he had argued that race was an invalid factor to be considered when it came to student assignment. But he reminded his colleagues that colorblindness had only appeared in the dissent in *Plessy v. Ferguson*; it was not the law: "If only the principle of colorblindness had been accepted by the majority in *Plessy* in 1896, we would not be faced with this problem in 1978." In a preview of his published opinion, he continued: "It would be the cruelest irony for this Court to adopt the dissent in *Plessy* now and hold that the University must use color-blind admissions."[20]

From the outset, it seemed that four justices (Burger, Rehnquist, Stewart, and Stevens) wished to invalidate the UC Davis policy, while three (Brennan, White, Marshall) wanted the reverse. That left Lewis Powell, the one-time Richmond school board president, and Harry Blackmun, who was increasingly drifting away ideologically from his fellow Minnesotan on the Court, Chief Justice Burger. In his own memorandum to the Court, Justice Blackmun had noted the tension between fixed principles and pragmatism presented in the *Bakke* case:

> This is not an ideal world. It probably never will be. It is easy to give legislative language a literal construction when one assumes that the factual atmosphere is idealistic. But we live in a real world.

The literal construction Blackmun referred to was the principle of a colorblind Constitution that permitted no classifications based on race. But the real world in which the justices lived was, as Marshall had argued, decidedly not colorblind. Blackmun ultimately sided with those who would uphold the school's policy.[21]

In a reflection of the novelty and difficulty of the case, six justices wrote opinions in *Bakke*, none of which commanded a majority. Justice Powell authored what would be the controlling opinion, though he managed to both please and anger all of his colleagues in doing so. While Powell rejected the idea that the Constitution permitted no consideration of race in admissions (which Justices Brennan, White, Marshall, and Blackmun joined), he concluded that the UC Davis policies at issue in the case were indeed improper because they explicitly set aside seats based on race (which Justices Burger, Rehnquist, Stewart, and Stevens joined).

CRUEL IRONY

In his own opinion, Justice Marshall disagreed with nearly everything Justice Powell wrote. As he would a decade later in the context of the Constitution's bicentennial, he offered a thorough history lesson amid his disbelief that his colleagues could conclude that a school could not legally seek to right historic wrongs in this way.

Beginning with the "dragging" of Africans to America more than 350 years prior, Marshall documented the disconnect between the nation's professed "self-evident" ideals and its treatment of African Americans. Marshall then traced the subjugation of African Americans despite the amendments in the aftermath of the Civil War, specifically indicting the Supreme Court for its role in legitimizing racial discrimination, before citing the Court's work—largely through lawyer Marshall's advocacy—in confronting segregation. But those decisions "did [not] move Negroes from a position of legal inferiority to one of equality."[22]

Next, Marshall connected the history to the present, listing statistics on life expectancy, employment, and socioeconomic status to demonstrate that "meaningful equality remains a distant dream for the Negro." Given that the connection between past and present "cannot be denied," Marshall thundered that "bringing the Negro into the mainstream of American life should be a state interest of the highest order." This was precisely what the medical school's program sought to do. Striking down that effort would help "ensure that America will forever remain a divided society."[23]

Marshall found it "inconceivable" that the Fourteenth Amendment, adopted in the wake of emancipation, could be read to prohibit race-conscious relief measures. After all, the same Congress that passed the Fourteenth Amendment had also passed the 1866 Freedmen's Bureau Act, which provided many benefits only to African Americans. Marshall argued that barring government use of race to remedy the effects of discrimination "would pervert the intent of the Framers by substituting abstract equality for the genuine equality the Amendment was intended to achieve." To Marshall, "colorblindness" offered an "abstract equality" that was not only disconnected from the disparity-riddled reality of the nation, but also incompatible with the "genuine equality" promised by the amendment. He subsequently clarified his view of what such genuine equality would look like: "a fully integrated society, one in which the color of a person's skin will not determine the opportunities available to him or her."[24]

Allan Bakke, of course, had made precisely the same request—that the color of his skin not determine how many seats were open to him in his quest to attend medical school. His argument had been rooted in the belief that the equal protection clause protected individuals rather than groups, and that therefore excluding an individual based on race violated the Constitution. Whatever the merits of a group-based remedy to historic discrimination, it could not be imposed through classification and exclusion of individuals based on race. But, as he had at oral argument, Marshall viewed the rights from the perspective of those who would be aided by the program rather than those who might be negatively affected. For those individuals, including African Americans who had suffered a history of "special treatment" against them, "we must be willing to open those doors."[25]

Marshall was flabbergasted, though perhaps not surprised, that several of his colleagues felt otherwise:

> It is more than a little ironic that, after several hundred years of class-based discrimination against Negroes, the Court is unwilling to hold that a class-based remedy for that discrimination is permissible. In declining to so hold, today's judgment ignores the fact that for several hundred years Negroes have been discriminated against, not as individuals, but rather solely because of the color of their skins. It is unnecessary in 20th-century America to have individual Negroes demonstrate that they have been victims of racial discrimination; the racism of our society has been so pervasive that none, regardless of wealth or position, has managed to escape its impact. The experience of Negroes in America has been different in kind, not just in degree, from that of other ethnic groups. It is not merely the history of slavery alone but also that a whole people were marked as inferior by the law. And that mark has endured. The dream

of America as the great melting pot has not been realized for the Negro; because of his skin color he never even made it into the pot.[26]

Marshall saw a Court that had come full circle. The Court had neutered the equal protection clause before—in *Plessy* and the *Civil Rights Cases*—and now threatened to do so again. After all, he reminded his colleagues, the "colorblind" interpretation of the Constitution had come in a dissent. However wonderful the ideal, it had never been the law.

PROTECTING DIVERSITY

The jumble of opinions in the *Bakke* case reflected the extent to which affirmative action was forcing the justices to consider a new problem. *Brown* and the collection of race discrimination cases had established that the equal protection clause did not permit *exclusion* or disadvantage based upon race. But what about the opposite? Would the clause permit *inclusion* based on race?

In doing the constitutional analysis, the justices could not even form a consensus on the initial question of how much scrutiny to apply. In the controlling opinion, Powell argued that

> the guarantee of equal protection cannot mean one thing when applied to one individual and something else when applied to a person of another color. If both are not accorded the same protection, then it is not equal.

Powell sought to apply the same level of judicial scrutiny to the UC Davis program as would apply to government policies that had excluded individuals on the basis of race. In dissent, Justice Brennan (joined by Justice Marshall) had argued against such fixed interpretation of equal protection. Noting that the medical school's policy was fundamentally different from race-based laws rooted in a presumption of Black inferiority, Brennan demanded that the two be treated differently. "Claims that law must be 'color-blind' or that the datum of race is no longer relevant to public policy must be seen as aspiration rather than as description of reality," Justice Brennan wrote.[27]

For nearly two decades, the Court would continue to struggle with even this initial question of scrutiny, with neither side able to claim victory. In his effort to affirm the ability of governments to work to remedy racial disparities, Marshall consistently made the point that "Such programs should not be subjected to conventional 'strict scrutiny'—scrutiny that is strict in theory, but fatal in fact." He fleshed out his position most thoroughly in a dissent in the middle of the decade, also joined by Justices Blackmun and Brennan, about a school district's efforts to maintain the diversity of its teaching force.[28]

The school district in Jackson, Michigan, had come to an agreement with the local teachers' union to help preserve the percentage of African American teachers in an increasingly diverse district. In the early 1970s, prompted by increasing racial tensions that had led to violence at Jackson High School, the district took action to increase the number of Black teachers, doubling the percentage between 1969 and 1971. The district and union came to an agreement in 1972 that in the event of layoffs, the percentage of Black teachers would be required to be maintained. Thus, rather than relying solely on seniority—which would have disproportionately impacted the newly hired Black teachers—the district also took race into account when making layoff decisions. The compromise did not insulate minority teachers from being laid off, but it did freeze the percentage of the teaching force. If teachers from minority groups represented 8.5 percent of the staff, then no more than 8.5 percent of the teachers laid off would be teachers from minority groups, regardless of seniority.[29]

When layoffs were required later in the decade and into 1981, the district followed the agreement, laying off white teachers who had greater seniority than Black teachers who were retained and prompting several groups of white teachers to sue. The case, *Wygant v. Jackson Board of Education*, was somewhat unusual among affirmative action cases. As an initial matter, the provision was about protecting diversity that had already been achieved instead of the more typical efforts to remedy prior racial dispar-

ities by increasing employment or educational opportunities to members
of underrepresented groups: this was not a case about hiring members of
minority groups, but a case about *not firing* them. At oral argument in
November 1985, Justice Marshall pressed the point that the provision had
been included in a contract that the union, with a membership that was
80 percent white, had negotiated and approved. In response, the lawyer
representing the white teachers asserted that no amount of negotiation and
compromise could override the constitutional rights of his clients not to be
discriminated against based upon race. This argument was consistent with
that taken in a brief filed by the Reagan administration (and worked on by
future justice Samuel Alito) that urged the Court to adopt strict scrutiny
and strike down the layoff provision as unconstitutional.[30]

While the Court ultimately struck down the provision, it still failed to
reach consensus on the appropriate level of scrutiny to apply. Justice Powell
again wrote for a plurality (including Chief Justice Burger and Justices
Rehnquist and O'Connor) and reiterated his position from *Bakke* that all
racial classifications should receive the Court's highest degree of scrutiny
and that "the level of scrutiny does not change merely because the challenged classification operates against a group that historically has not been
subject to governmental discrimination." He warned that allowing past
societal discrimination to justify the use of race could allow "benign" discrimination to continue in perpetuity, a result that, if carried to its logical
extreme, could "lead to the very system the Court rejected in *Brown*."[31] The
invocation of *Brown* as a weapon *against* protecting diversity evinced a very
different reading of that case than the one Justice Marshall held.

In his own opinion, Marshall reminded that Court that "unfairness
ought not be confused with constitutional injury." The harm suffered by
the white teachers was fundamentally different, in Marshall's mind, to the
exclusion at issue in *Brown*. He urged that decisions about how to allo-
cate harm—after all, *someone* was going to lose their job whenever the district instituted layoffs—could not "be fairly assessed in a vacuum." As in
Bakke, he urged consideration of context in determining how much scrutiny to apply when the government considered race in different ways, and

he accused the Court of blinding itself to historical realities and doing a grave injustice "to individuals and governments committed to the goal of eliminating all traces of segregation throughout the country." Rather than forcing the Jackson school board to watch the "hard-won benefits of its integration efforts vanish," Justice Marshall would have found the district's efforts to preserve diversity in its teaching force, which benefited all of the district's students, sufficient to satisfy the demands of the Constitution.[32]

In *Bakke* and *Wygant*, Justice Marshall offered a flexible interpretation of the Constitution's equal protection clause that rejected the principle of absolute colorblindness and neutrality toward which his colleagues were moving. In equal protection, Marshall saw a tool for inclusion and against subjugation, not a command that forced courts to pretend that what Black students had faced during the era of segregation was the same as what Allan Bakke confronted in the 1970s. The skirmishes on the Court about the proper degree of scrutiny for affirmative action represented the judicial manifestation of the broader societal debate about the value of diversity and the responsibility of government to remedy past exclusions.

In addition, these clashes demonstrated the moment's competing methods for interpretating the Constitution. Just as he had rejected the idea that the Constitution's framers had created a fixed document to be celebrated at the 1987 bicentennial, Marshall rejected a fixed application of the principles of the equal protection clause in undeniably differing contexts. At the bicentennial, Marshall was willing to celebrate a "living document" that was perpetually being nurtured as it encountered societal efforts to grapple with a diverse citizenry. And in *Bakke* and *Wygant*, he sought to empower the continuation of those efforts. But as the Court worked through the 1980s, Marshall's vision was being met with a contrasting one.

FOURTEEN

FIXED OR FLEXIBLE

While Clarence Thomas was a student at Yale law school in the early 1970s, a Yale professor delivered a lecture in Indiana criticizing "a persistently disturbing aspect of constitutional law." The professor was concerned with the phenomenon that the nature of the Constitution seemed to change along with the personnel of justices on the Court, with "no principled way to prefer any claimed human value to any other" in situations where constitutional materials did not clearly identify which value ought be preferred. As a solution, the professor offered a principle he felt could keep judges from simply projecting their preferred values into constitutional interpretation: "the judge must stick close to the text and the history, and their fair implications, and not construct new rights." The starting point for any principle must be the understanding of the intent and meaning of the text at the time of its adoption. The lecture was entitled "Neutral Principles and Some First Amendment Problems," and the professor was Robert Bork.[1]

In the lecture, Bork took particular offense to the recently decided case of *Griswold v. Connecticut*, in which the Court found there to be a constitutionally protected zone of privacy that prohibited the government from outlawing contraception. In short order, *Griswold* would yield *Roe v. Wade*, the case that would consume much of the ideological struggles of the Court for decades. But Bork also critiqued the lack of neutral principles that might explain equal protection cases such as *Brown* and *Shelley v. Kraemer*, both of which had been argued by Thurgood Marshall.

According to Bork, the Fourteenth Amendment "can require formal procedural equality, and, because of its historical origins, it does require that government not discriminate along racial lines." But that was where the clear principles of the text stopped. "The Supreme Court has no principled way of saying which non-racial inequalities are permissible."² In the Indiana lecture, Bork did not grapple with the idea that the Court might treat different types of racial discrimination differently, but it was not difficult to extrapolate that just as neutral principles of equality could not justify when inequality was constitutionally impermissible outside of race, according to Bork, they could also not distinguish between "good" and "bad" racial discrimination.

Bork spent the 1970s bouncing between academia and government service, including a stint as solicitor general within the Nixon administration (the same position Thurgood Marshall had held under Lyndon Johnson), but he remained a chief champion of the argument that a judiciary untethered by constitutional text and history posed the danger of creating a government "by judiciary." He was appointed by President Reagan to the DC Circuit Court of Appeals in 1982 and was a top candidate for a Supreme Court vacancy during Reagan's second term. When Reagan nominated him to the Court in 1987, the nominee confronted a Senate controlled by a Democratic majority for the first time during Reagan's tenure. His confirmation hearings were historically contentious as groups lined up in opposition to his frank and unapologetic ideology. Democrats flexed their power within the Senate; Senator Ted Kennedy took to the Senate floor immediately upon announcement of the Bork nomination to denounce the nominee, and Senate Judiciary Chairperson Joe Biden delayed hearings for over two months. In the end, the anti-Bork forces prevailed, and the nominee was rejected by the full Senate. Ultimately, Reagan would appoint the less controversial and more moderate Anthony Kennedy to the Court.³ For his part, Bork was sufficiently scarred by the experience that he resigned from the DC Circuit in February 1988. It took more than two years for a replacement to be appointed and confirmed, but in March 1990, Clarence Thomas took the oath as a federal judge on the Court of Appeals.

Clarence Thomas did not encounter Robert Bork as a professor during their shared time at Yale, but the two would share more than simply a seat on the Court of Appeals for the Federal Circuit. Both would endure historically contentious Supreme Court confirmation hearings, setting the bar for modern nominees. But before that, Bork was a leading figure in a movement of conservative legal thinkers that Thomas would come to inhabit and lead himself. Over time, Thomas would adopt and build on Bork's admonition that judges stick closely to constitutional text, and it would be Thomas's ascension to the Supreme Court that would tip the balance of the Court, however slowly, toward Bork's preferred outcomes.

THE LIFE OF THE CONSTITUTION

The constitutional questions of affirmative action and the appropriate amount of scrutiny to apply to racial classifications that sought to benefit members of minority groups mapped onto broader ideological and interpretive struggles on the Court in the 1970s and 80s. In the early 1970s, it had largely been the backlash to the Court's involvement in schools through desegregation that had driven President Nixon's desire to reshape the Court. More than a decade later, that effort had yielded mixed results. Chief Justice Burger and Justice Rehnquist had proven to be largely reliable on conservative interests, but Justice Powell had proven to be somewhat unpredictable, and Justice Blackmun had migrated away from his fellow Nixon appointees in the aftermath of his majority opinion in *Roe v. Wade*. Gerald Ford's lone nominee, Justice Stevens, seemed to be similarly moving away from the Court's more conservative justices. In *Wygant*, Stevens had argued that race might be a valid consideration and dissented along with Marshall, noting "it is quite obvious that a school board may reasonably

conclude than an integrated faculty will be able to provide benefits to the
student body that could not be provided by an all-white, or nearly all-white,
faculty."[4] The fractured opinions on affirmative action were but a symptom
of the failure of these five Republican-appointed justices of the late 60s and
70s to achieve what conservative politicians had hoped for.

One problem was that several goals of the conservative movement within
the courts ran counter to the increasing inclusion of a more diverse range
of Americans into the nation's schools, workplaces, and halls of leadership.
For those unconcerned about the minutiae of constitutional jurisprudence,
many (especially women and African Americans) were alienated by opposition to the *Roe* decision protecting a woman's right to choose whether to
continue a pregnancy and to affirmative action. In previous generations, con-
flating jurisprudential methods (such as increased power to states within the
American federal system) with racism and sexism had run against the tide of
history. The call for states' rights could be a defensible, neutral position in the
abstract, but when the primary state right being defended was the right to
continue slavery or segregation—or, more recently, to prohibit abortions—
the abstract principles were obscured by their real-world applications. The
same could be said about the principle of colorblindness and strict prohibitions on racial classifications—admirable principles in the abstract. Yet the
application of those principles within a society where the legacy of prior col-
or-consciousness remained rendered the principles vulnerable to the critique
of being employed to perpetuate inequality.

Conservative politicians had been successful in deploying arguments
less connected to specific issues to adjust the public view on the judiciary in
the past. For example, Nixon had lauded the principle of judicial restraint to
contrast the "activist" Supreme Court of Earl Warren with his own vision
of the proper role of the judiciary, where judges did not "legislate from the
bench." This was a perspective far easier to defend than direct attacks on
any particular decision of the Warren Court; it was a critique more of the
Court's process than its substance. Judicial restraint was a highly successful *political* argument for conservative politicians who could then appoint
more conservative judges.

In the early years of the Reagan administration, buoyed by the success of Reagan's open rejection of the Great Society ideas of liberalism, conservatives began constructing a mechanism for systematically framing and implementing a broader legal agenda. One step in this process occurred in April 1982 at a conference for conservative law students from Yale, Harvard, and the University of Chicago that birthed the Federalist Society. Among the speakers at the three-day symposium were two Reagan nominees for the Supreme Court: Antonin Scalia (who was confirmed in 1986) and Bork. Through its chapters on law school campuses and among local members of the bar, the Federalist Society would grow into an organizational network for conservative lawyers and judges. Indeed, in the twenty-first century, Federalist Society membership would be virtually a prerequisite to anyone seeking a judicial nomination in a Republican administration.

As Nixon had in the 1960s, Reagan's administration sought ways not only to influence the work of the Court but also the public perception of it. In July 1985, Reagan's Attorney General Edwin Meese summarized the recently concluded Supreme Court term as "incoherent" and "ad hoc," lacking in any clear jurisprudential principle and therefore susceptible to the taint of ideological predilection. Though more than sixteen years had passed since Chief Justice Earl Warren had retired, Meese continued to raise the specter of the Warren Court as he declared the imperative not to "drift back to the radical egalitarianism and expansive civil libertarianism of the Warren Court." He built on Bork's call for fixed principles, articulating a "jurisprudence of original intention" that would base constitutional analysis in the document's text and the intentions of its drafters.[5]

Meese was among the inner circle within the Reagan administration with whom Clarence Thomas had occasionally butted heads during his time at the Department of Education and the EEOC, but the two collaborated later in the summer of 1985 after Meese's speech. Thomas, then chairperson of the EEOC, worked with Meese on a proposed change in an executive order that would free federal contractors from having to document their efforts to hire women and members of minority groups. Though their motivations might have been different, Thomas and the administration converged in the belief that such efforts, and the numerical targets that inevitably followed, were inconsistent with principles of fairness that required persons to be judged individually and not based on any group membership. During his tenure, Thomas described his philosophy to Juan Williams, the *Washington Post* journalist who had first pushed Thomas into the national consciousness, claiming that though he might be tempted to "cheat in favor of those of us who were cheated," he could not do so. "You have to ask yourself whether, in doing that, you do violence to the safe harbor, and that is the Constitution, which says you are to protect an individual's rights no matter what."[6] Thomas was not speaking the language of a jurisprudence of original intention, but he, like Meese, was framing the Constitution as one that had a fixed meaning with unchanging principles that must be applied even if he might personally be tempted to do otherwise.

It was into this milieu that Justice Marshall had delivered his speech on the bicentennial of the Constitution, reminding listeners of the limitations of the framers' perspectives. The framers not only did not reflect a diverse cross section of American citizenry, but the document they produced had allowed millions of those citizens to be denied basic rights. Two years earlier, Marshall's judicial ally, William Brennan, had taken direct aim at Meese's speech and the proposed jurisprudence of original intention, noting that Meese's position was "a choice no less political than any other" and "a view that feigns self-effacing deference . . . [but] is little more than arrogance cloaked as humility." The greatest failure, according to Marshall and Brennan, was the idea that constitutional principles could be frozen in time. The Constitution had been intended to create a new society rather than preserve an existing one. Its genius, according to Brennan, "rests not in any static meaning it might have had in a world that is dead and gone, but in the adaptability of its great principles to cope with current problems and needs."[7]

The debate was not merely rhetorical. Meese continued to challenge the very authority of the Supreme Court, and the Reagan Administration began to make espousal of an originalist (as it was coming to be called) interpretation of the Constitution a key criterion in appointments of federal judges.[8] Reagan's first appointment to the Supreme Court had been Sandra Day O'Connor in

1981, the Court's first woman and a justice who would prove nimbly pragmatic over nearly a quarter-century tenure. But when Chief Justice Burger resigned in 1986 and took over the constitutional bicentennial project, Reagan nominated Antonin Scalia to join the Court (in addition to elevating William Rehnquist to the position of chief justice). Scalia had spoken at the founding conference for the Federalist Society and, less than two weeks before being nominated, had delivered an address at Meese's request on the contours of originalism.[9] Scalia's confirmation to the Court ensured an originalist would be present as constitutional decisions were made. Then, in 1987, after Marshall's nemesis Lewis Powell retired, Reagan nominated Robert Bork to fill his seat. That the Bork nomination failed (and the more moderately conservative Anthony Kennedy ultimately seated) revealed the conflict surrounding the Court. The stakes of the Court's makeup had rarely been higher.

CONFLICTING MESSAGES FROM THE COURT

The drama surrounding the Court was reflected within it as well, and the justices continued to encounter the question of affirmative action. As the 1980s came to a close, the Court offered seemingly conflicting decisions, failing to reach consensus on even the level of scrutiny to apply when government sought to use race to overcome a history of discrimination. In 1989, all three Reagan appointees embraced the highest level of scrutiny, and Justice O'Connor dismissed Marshall's call for anything else as "watered down equal protection review."[10]

However, the following year, the Court appeared to do an about-face. Whereas the Court had utilized strict scrutiny in 1989, a different majority embraced the lower standard of review for affirmative action in a similar case. After twelve years, Brennan, Marshall, and Blackmun had finally amassed a majority for the position that "benign race-conscious measures" need not be held to the Court's highest standard prohibiting discrimination based on race. Justices White and Stevens joined Brennan's majority, while Justice O'Connor penned the primary dissent.[11]

Thus, the Court entered the 1990s still divided on the question of the proper evaluation of government efforts to use racial classifications to over-come inequalities. In *Bakke* and *Wygant,* among other cases, no one view on how to apply the equal protection clause to the use of race in this manner car-ried a majority of the justices. In 1989, a majority seemed ready to definitively apply the Court's strictest scrutiny, but the following year, a different majority had come to the precise opposite conclusion: the context in which race was being used mattered, and the "benign" use of race by the government should be treated differently. Though Justice Marshall's position had prevailed in the Court's latest case, the divided nature of the Court's jurisprudence suggested that it had yet to reach denouement. Five years and four new justices later, the Court encountered yet another affirmative action case and resolved the ques-tion: again, it would be Marshall's replacement who proved decisive.

SETTLING THE QUESTION OF SCRUTINY

When Clarence Thomas was nominated to the Supreme Court in 1991, anyone who was paying any attention knew his position on affirmative action. At the EEOC, he had drawn the ire of many civil rights groups for his disavowal of group-based remedies that required employers to utilize timetables and numerical goals to remedy charges of discrimination. There was a substantial record of public comments, dating back to his first na-tional feature in the *Washington Post* in 1980, that demonstrated Thomas's belief that affirmative action, however benignly motivated, did more harm than good. In 1987, Juan Williams published another profile of Thomas, in which the head of the EEOC reiterated his position:

> There is no governmental solution. It hasn't been used on any group. And
> I will ask those who proffer a governmental solution to show me which
> group in the history of this country was pulled up and put into the main-
> stream of the economy with governmental programs.[12]

Those who had benefited from the work of the Freedmen's Bureau or the initiatives of the New Deal might have raised their hands.

As EEOC chair, Thomas had guided the organization away from look-ing at discrimination as a group-based problem and toward considering in-dividual complaints that merited individual remedies. He sought a review of what he considered the overuse of statistics in guiding EEOC decisions, arguing that looking only at numbers and imposing targets seemed "to assume some inherent inferiority of blacks, Hispanics, other minorities, and women, by suggesting that they should not be held to the same stan-dards as other people, even if those standards are race and sex neutral." On the other hand, Thomas refused the urging of some, including Ed Meese, to eliminate all use of timetables and numerical targets, instead continuing to enforce EEOC settlements that had previously been agreed to. He used this point to rebut criticism during his 1986 confirmation hearings to con-tinue as EEOC chair, claiming that the targets were the law, whether he liked it or not. "Whatever reservations I have are purely personal. They're subversive literature now," he quipped.[13]

Those reservations were based on a deep skepticism of government and a deep commitment to certain fixed principles. These were staunchly con-servative values. He may have been reluctant to take a job with a Republi-can attorney general in John Danforth in Missouri when he graduated law school, but the years since had led Thomas into strong alliance with con-servative thinking and the Republican Party, even if from a substantially different motivation. From chairing the EEOC to judge to justice, Thomas was given a platform from which he could build on those reservations to influence the law of the land.

Thus, when the Court considered a case challenging a federal program that gave contractors on federal projects financial incentives for utilizing subcontractors controlled by "socially and economically disadvantaged groups" and used race as a proxy for disadvantage, it was unsurprising that Justice Thomas voted to strike it down. The case, *Adarand Constructors, Inc. v. Pena*, explicitly reconsidered the 1990 conclusion that the federal government be given some leeway in pursuing affirmative action and, by a 5–4 margin, reversed it. In a majority opinion that relied heavily on her dissent in that 1990 case, Justice O'Connor traced the Court's conflicting interpretations of affirmative action. But this time, O'Connor had an additional vote to employ the Court's strictest scrutiny to "all racial classifications, imposed by whatever federal, state, or local governmental actor."[14]

The fifth vote, definitively settling the issue seventeen years after *Bakke*, was Justice Thomas. In his final dissent as a justice, Thurgood Marshall had lamented that a mere change in the makeup of the Supreme Court had led to a change in interpretation of the Constitution. In *Adarand*'s 1995 reversal of the outcome from five years prior, the same thing had happened. As shown in Table 2, while five justices had voted to apply only intermediate scrutiny to a form of affirmative action in 1990, a new majority of five justices had emerged in 1995 to apply the Court's highest level of scrutiny to such cases. Further, as the table shows, while there had been several Court appointments in that half decade, only one resulted in a change in vote. A decision less than five years old was rejected primarily because Clarence Thomas had replaced Thurgood Marshall.

In her opinion, Justice O'Connor emphasized that the government could take actions to confront the lingering effects of racial discrimination, but it must only do so in the narrowest of circumstances and for the most compelling of reasons. The equal protection clause protected persons, not groups, O'Connor insisted, and therefore use of racial classifications of any sort required deep skepticism, as well as consistency, regardless of the race of an individual burdened by a racial classification. The plaintiff contractor in *Adarand*—like the laid off teachers of Jackson, Michigan, in *Wygant*, and Allan Bakke—was as protected from racial discrimination as anyone else. This was a principle Justice Thomas could agree with.

Thomas offered a brief concurrence in *Adarand*, in which he offered his own rationale for why "government-sponsored racial discrimination based on benign prejudice is just as noxious as discrimination inspired by malicious prejudice." Thomas drew on his own experiences to argue that even the consideration of race with good intentions could be "poisonous and pernicious," doing harm to the very individuals it aimed to benefit:

So-called "benign" discrimination teaches many that because of chronic

Metro Broadcasting v. FCC (1990)	Adarand Constructors v. Pena (1995)
Strict Scrutiny (dissent)	*Strict Scrutiny (majority)*
O'Connor	O'Connor
Rehnquist	Rehnquist
Scalia	Scalia
Kennedy	Kennedy
	Thomas (replaced Marshall)
Intermediate Scrutiny (majority)	*Intermediate Scrutiny (dissent)*
Brennan	Souter (replaced Brennan)
White	Ginsburg (replaced White)
Blackmun	Breyer (replaced Blackmun)
Stevens	Stevens
Marshall	

TABLE 2. Comparison of constitutional scrutiny applied by each justic in *Metro Broadcasting v. FCC* and *Adarand Constructors v. Pena*. Made by author.

and apparently immutable handicaps, minorities cannot compete with them without their patronizing indulgence. Inevitably, such programs engender attitudes of superiority or, alternatively, provoke resentment among those who believe that they have been wronged by the government's use of race. These programs stamp minorities with a badge of inferiority and may cause them to develop dependencies or to adopt an attitude that they are "entitled" to preferences.[15]

Here, Thomas offered several of the arguments he had regularly made about the harm affirmative action had done to African Americans, including an implication of inferiority that required preferences or incentives, the danger of dependency and entitlement among beneficiaries, and, of perhaps most personal impact, the stamp of inferiority.

On this final point, Thomas might have had in mind an incident from a decade earlier, when, at his swearing in for his second term as head of the EEOC, Assistant Attorney General Brad Reynolds raised a glass for a toast. "Clarence Thomas is the epitome of the right kind of affirmative action working the right way," Reynolds had said.[16] Thomas flinched at the comment. Presumably, Reynolds had intended to say something nice, but he had done so in a way that suggested that but for his race, Clarence Thomas might not have been sworn in as head of the EEOC. That suggestion seemed to trail Clarence Thomas everywhere, and he took the opportunity in *Adarand* to incorporate it into the Court's annals while, from his perspective, protecting others from the same fate. He would have far more to say in the future.

FIFTEEN

COLORBLINDNESS ASCENDANT

Despite being accused of pulling the ladder of Black progress up behind him through his opposition to affirmative action, Clarence Thomas made a point to reach out to promising African American students in Washington, DC. In 1994, after reading a *Wall Street Journal* article about Cedric Jennings, just such a student at Ballou High School, Thomas invited Jennings to his chambers. Jennings had been a focus of a series of articles written by the journalist Ron Suskind, who accompanied the young man on his trip to the Court. Though Jennings lived only two miles away, he had never visited the building before the visit with Justice Thomas during the spring of his senior year. Inside the chambers, Thomas shared stories of his childhood before asking Jennings about his own plans for the future.[1]

"I'm off to Brown University," Jennings said, eliciting a frown from Thomas.

"Well, that's fine, but I'm not sure if I would have selected an Ivy League school," Thomas responded. He went on:

"No doubt, one thing you'll find when you get to a school like Brown is a lot of classes and orientation on race relations. Try to avoid them. Try to say to yourself, 'I'm not a black person, I'm just a person.'"

Thomas was relieved to learn of Jennings's plan to major in math:

"That's what I look for in hiring my clerks—the cream of the crop. I look for the maths and the sciences, real classes, none of that Afro-American studies stuff. If they've taken that stuff as an undergraduate, I don't want them. You want to do that, do it in your spare time."[2]

The justice and the high school senior met for nearly three hours that afternoon. Thomas warned that Jennings would have to outwork other students and would not have time for going out and partying. As the meeting ended, Thomas seemed to sense that he might have frightened Jennings with his gusto and advice, and he offered a gentler sentiment:

"I'm sure you'll do just fine. It's just that I understand, in a very personal way, how big a step you're taking. When you get on that plane, or train, at the end of the summer and leave home, you won't ever really be able to go back. But you may find you're never really accepted up ahead either, that you've landed between worlds. That's the way I feel sometimes, even now, and it can make you angry. But you just have to channel that anger, to harness it."[3]

Jennings shook the justice's hand and responded, "Well, you know, I guess I'm just hoping I won't have a reason to become an angry person. That I'll be accepted up ahead for who I am." According to Suskind, Thomas simply smiled a warm and melancholy smile.[4]

The afternoon with Cedric Jennings revealed a fury in Clarence Thomas.

Meeting with a promising student heading for a prestigious institution, Thomas spoke of his own pain and isolation. He often wore this isolation as a badge of honor. In a 2001 speech to the American Enterprise Institute, he remarked that "we are required to wade into those things that matter to our country, no matter what the disincentives are, and no matter the personal cost." To shy away from controversial positions in the face of vile attacks was a form of "cowardice, or well-intentioned self-deception at best."[5]

No issue better defines the need for Clarence Thomas to withstand personal criticism than affirmative action. The chasm between Thomas and the African American community has largely been defined by this issue that legal scholar (and former law clerk to Justice Marshall) Randall Kennedy has described as the litmus test, "the third rail of Black American politics." "Were he to have taken a different position on *that* issue," Kennedy wrote, "his relationship to other African Americans would be altogether different."[6] At the root of the criticism has been the sense that having at times benefited in his career from racial considerations, Thomas's opposition to the continuation of such policies constituted an act of betrayal. For the multitude of critics of Justice Thomas's position on affirmative action, it was not only that Thomas was taking a contrary position, but that he seemed to be denying others the opportunities that played a role in his own rise to the highest court in the nation. For this, he has been subjected to bitter insults and hatred not only from leaders, lawyers, and scholars but from the full range of Black Americans.

Yet, just as Thurgood Marshall was dumbfounded that anyone could look at American history and conclude that efforts to *aid* African Americans could be unconstitutional, Clarence Thomas expressed astonishment that anyone with knowledge of how affirmative action played out could think it was actually good for African Americans. Rather than settling for token, short-term gains in the form of opportunities for some African Americans, Thomas argued for stricter adherence to an absolute principle of non-discrimination. Anything short would simply prolong the prevalence of race in determining opportunities in the United States.

In a series of opinions, Thomas laid out a view of constitutional color-

blindness that reflected many of his core beliefs. Rather than consideration
of African Americans primarily as members of a group, Thomas argued for
the right for individuals to be judged by their effort and merit instead of
their skin color. Contrary to claims that affirmative action would provide
greater opportunity for African Americans, Thomas asserted—drawing
on his own schooling experiences—that racial preferences undermined the
ability of Black students to prove themselves. Thus, affirmative action was
not only constitutionally suspect, but ineffective.

These were positions identified with Thomas from his first exposure
on the national scene in the *Washington Post* and through his stewardship
of the EEOC during the 1980s. They had brought him into conflict not
only with African Americans, but with what he would describe as white
intellectual elites who were not genuinely concerned with the welfare of
African Americans. While his disillusionment with these groups might
have been borne during his own years in higher education, the bitterness
of his confirmation widened the breach so that it became irreconcilable.
Thomas's affirmative action opinions, then, provided an opportunity not
only to apply his beliefs, but also to strike new blows in the ongoing feud
with his detractors. In them, he brought the same fury with which he addressed young Cedric Jennings.

A BLISTERING AND PERSONAL DISSENT

In 1978, the same year *Bakke* was decided, a woman named Barbara Grutter
graduated from Michigan State University. Grutter went on to have two
children and start her own small business as a health care IT consultant.
In 1996, having decided on a career change and with a goal of becoming a
health law lawyer, she applied to law school at the University of Michigan.
Like Allan Bakke, Barbara Grutter was older than the typical applicant.
Like Allan Bakke, Barbara Grutter was white. Like Allan Bakke, Barbara
Grutter was not admitted to graduate school. And like Allan Bakke, Barbara Grutter ultimately filed a lawsuit. Among her motivations were her
children: "I was most concerned by what I would teach them if I did noth-

ing in the face of a formal policy of discrimination by a public institution."[7] So it was that twenty-five years after *Bakke,* the Supreme Court confronted affirmative action in higher education yet again.

Seven of the nine justices who had heard the *Bakke* case were no longer on the Court and had passed away. The two who remained—now Chief Justice William Rehnquist and Justice John Paul Stevens—had both agreed that Bakke must be admitted to medical school but disagreed with Justice Powell's opinion that race was a valid consideration in admissions. Justice Stevens had penned the primary dissent on this point. However, another thing that had changed in the quarter century was Justice Stevens himself.[8]

Gerald Ford's only Court appointment, Stevens had arrived on the Court in 1975 and wrote in *Bakke* that "Race cannot be the basis of excluding anyone from participation in a federally funded program."[9] Yet, as early as 1980, Stevens cited Justice Marshall's *Bakke* opinion and suggested that "tragic class-based discrimination" might justify remedies that considered race. By 1990, he was declaring that promoting diversity was a valid rationale for race-based affirmative action. When Barbara Grutter's case reached the Court along with a companion case on undergraduate admissions at the University of Michigan in 2003, Justice Stevens was ready to uphold the law school's policy.[10]

A result of Justice Stevens's evolution was that Barbara Grutter did not get from the Court what Allan Bakke had: a 5–4 majority upheld the law school's admissions policy. In this instance, the transition from Justice Marshall to Justice Thomas had not been determinative, at least not in the outcome. Five justices *did* believe the Court's highest degree of scrutiny must be applied, but in *Grutter v. Bollinger,* the Court held that the law school had a compelling reason for its use of race: namely, capturing the educational benefits of diversity. According to Justice O'Connor's majority opinion, "these benefits are not theoretical, but real."[11] While this was not quite the position Marshall had articulated—after all, he thought UC Davis's policy was valid because of its aim of inclusion to overcome historical discrimination—the *Grutter* Court reached a result Marshall would have supported. Justice Thomas was left writing in dissent.

"The majority upholds the Law School's racial discrimination not by interpreting the people's Constitution, but by responding to a faddish slogan of the cognoscenti," Thomas wrote in fiery opening paragraphs.[12] Throughout, he dismissed both the law school and the majority as wrong in their application of the Constitution and dishonest in their motivations. While he claimed shared sympathies with those who implemented affirmative action out of a wish to see all students succeed regardless of race, Thomas systematically refuted the arguments in favor of affirmative action. It was a practice that, in Thomas's view, was pernicious, unnecessary, and ineffective, aside from being unconstitutional.

As he had the year prior in *Zelman,* Thomas began his opinion with reference to Frederick Douglass, whose portrait Cedric Jennings had noticed in Thomas's office, citing Douglass's 1865 plea for independence from government ("Do nothing with us!"). From this sentiment, Thomas argued for strict adherence to the principle of colorblindness. "The Constitution abhors classifications based on race," he wrote,

> not only because those classifications can harm favored races or are based on illegitimate motives, but also because every time the government places citizens on racial registers and makes race relevant to the provision of burdens or benefits, it demeans us all.[13]

The majority had found that the law school had presented a compelling interest in using race in admissions to realize the educational benefits of diversity in its student body, but Thomas scornfully dismissed the law school's motivations. "Attaining 'diversity,' whatever it means," Thomas argued, was really an effort to impact "classroom aesthetics." Diversity was simply a "fashionable catchphrase" and the pursuit of a critical mass of students from underrepresented groups merely a devious version of a quota.[14]

Worse still, the law school's distribution of benefits based solely on race would do nothing for the most disadvantaged in society: those too poor or uneducated to participate in higher education at all. Moreover, even if the law school's aims were genuine, Thomas argued that the use of race was not necessary to achieve them. Citing the experience in California in the years since voters prohibited consideration of race in admissions, Thomas observed that the enrollment of students from underrepresented groups exceeded 1996 levels. "Apparently the [Michigan] Law School cannot be counted on to be as resourceful."[15]

Returning to a theme first explored in *Fordice* in 1992 about higher education in Mississippi, Thomas used the success of HBCUs to turn the law school's argument on its head. If there were educational benefits to racial *homogeneity*, those might be cited as justification for maintaining racial *segregation*. Educational benefits could no more countenance the consideration of race to achieve diversity than they might to justify racial exclusions. A decade later, Thomas would return to this point in another affirmative action case:

> No court would accept the suggestion that segregation is permissible because historically black colleges produced Booker T. Washington, Thurgood Marshall, Martin Luther King, Jr., and other prominent leaders.[16]

But Thomas left his most vociferous—and personal—critique for the premise that diversity was beneficial to Black students at all. He criticized the majority for ignoring growing evidence that racial diversity actually *impaired* learning for Black students. Thomas lamented that "unprepared students" were "tantalized . . . with the promise of a University of Michigan degree." Such "overmatched students" often find they cannot succeed, creating a crisis in which Black students find themselves in schools where there is a "mismatch" between their abilities and those of their peers.[17]

For someone who had himself succeeded in predominantly white institutions and who claimed that he, like Frederick Douglass, "believe[d] blacks can achieve in every avenue of American life without the meddling of university administrators," this argument evinced a profound lack of faith that other Black students could accomplish what Thomas had. Thomas then implicitly drew a distinction between himself and some of the students aided by the University of Michigan's policies, again echoing the sting of isolation evident in his encounter with Cedric Jennings. "Who can differentiate between those who belong and those who do not?" Thomas asked about the Black students at the University of Michigan law school, acknowledging that some would have been admitted regardless of affirmative action. But that policy "tarred [all] as undeserving," Thomas wrote, since no one could tell who had been a beneficiary. "The question itself is the stigma."[18]

Who knew better than Thomas the persistence of the question of qualification? As he reached the pinnacle of the American legal profession, standing outside the Bush family retreat in Maine, Thomas had to answer a question about how he would respond to the charge that he was appointed merely because he was Black. Later, on the Court, he would have to deal with accusations that he was intellectually unfit to serve on the Court as shown by his failure to ask questions. Thomas had never escaped the qualification issue, and he blamed affirmative action, a policy devised by "aestheticists" not concerned about real problems, like the crisis of Black male underperformance, but only about the law school's image among "know-it-all elites."[19]

In his *Grutter* opinion, Thomas converted this pain into a principle of racial non-discrimination that would not tolerate any consideration of race. A decade later, both pain and principle had only hardened further. In a 2013 concurrence in another affirmative action case, Thomas compared the arguments of those favoring affirmative action to similar arguments made by enslavers and segregationists. All three had argued that oppressive practices benefited their African American victims, but, to Thomas, the history lesson was clear: "Racial discrimination is never benign."[20] This later opinion evinced Thomas's increasing willingness to explicitly connect conservative positions (such as opposition to affirmative action) to the quest for racial justice, arguing that it was his critics who were racist. Though stuck in dissent in *Grutter*, Thomas's vision of colorblindness would ultimately prevail in another case that evinced the full scope of the Court's evolution from *Brown v. Board of Education* to what seemed to be becoming "the Thomas Court."

PROTECTING DIVERSITY

At the dawn of the twenty-first century, the leaders of Jefferson County Public Schools (JCPS) in Louisville, Kentucky, found themselves at a crossroads. For nearly fifty years, the school district had worked toward compliance with both the letter and spirit of the Supreme Court's decision in *Brown v. Board of Education*. In the 1970s, Louisville had defied the national trend of division of urban and suburban school districts present in *Milliken*; instead, the county's two districts consolidated into one through a local court order and action from the Kentucky legislature despite the Supreme Court's directive that district lines remain sacrosanct. The local court had then overseen a desegregation plan in which each school in JCPS served a percentage of African American students within a proscribed range, ultimately settling in the 1990s on a range of between 15 and 50 percent in a district with an African American enrollment approximating one third of students. The early consolidation and adherence to the desegregation plan had helped JCPS emerge as an exemplar of sustained integration even as many school districts grew increasingly homogeneous. Toward the end of the century, the court dissolved the district's desegregation decree since it had achieved desegregation "to the extent practicable."[21]

However, even as it released the district from oversight, the lower court revived Justice Marshall's warning from *Dowell* a decade earlier that *maintaining* integration remained crucial. The court quoted Marshall on the need for preserving the school district's integration because "the reemergence of racial separation in such schools may revive the message of racial inferiority implicit in the former policy of state-enforced segregation."[22] In *Dowell*, Marshall had predicted that ending court supervision of desegregation would undo any gains achieved. This had occurred in many places, and the leadership of JCPS faced the choice of whether to actively work to avoid such a fate in Louisville.

The JCPS leadership, with substantial community support, opted to try to maintain the diversity in its schools that would represent the diversity of the district. The board adopted a complex plan that utilized geography and choice, but it maintained the strict racial guidelines requiring African American enrollments of between 15 and 50 percent in non-magnet schools (there were no racial parameters placed on the district's magnet schools).[23]

While this might have garnered an enthusiastic endorsement from the now-deceased Justice Marshall, the JCPS plan was a bold move. The district was in somewhat unchartered legal territory. There were mountains of precedent for considering the race of students in making school assignments within the context of a desegregation decree, but JCPS was doing something different. Having been released from court supervision, the district had satisfied its obligations under *Brown*. It was now proposing to utilize race to voluntarily maintain integration, even though it no longer had to by law.

The Supreme Court had never spoken directly on the topic. In *Brown*, the Court had declared that consideration of race for the purposes of segregating was not constitutional; and in *Bakke* and *Grutter*, the Court had determined that race might be used in a limited way to voluntarily achieve diversity in higher education. The plan in JCPS was distinguishable from *Brown* in its purpose and from the graduate school cases in its context. Could a school district consider race to maintain diversity in primary and secondary schools?

The same year that the Court decided the *Grutter* case, a white mother in Louisville, Crystal Meredith, tried to enroll her young son in the elementary school closest to their home. However, because the schools in Jefferson County sought to maintain racial diversity and did so with strict parameters, Meredith's son was assigned to a different school. Like Allan Bakke and Barbara Grutter before her, Crystal Meredith sued.

A WAY TO STOP DISCRIMINATION

By the time Crystal Meredith's case reached the Supreme Court in 2007, it had been combined with a related case from Seattle, known as *Parents Involved in Community Schools v. Seattle School District, No. 1*, or *PICS*. As in Louisville, the Seattle schools had considered the race of individual students in making school assignments in order to maintain student body diversity. Since Seattle had never been ordered by a court to desegregate its schools and Louisville had been released from court order in 2000, both plans were voluntary in that local school boards were acting affirmatively to attain diversity rather than acting under orders of a court. In so doing, the school districts in Louisville and Seattle sought to avoid a situation where schools would remain racially identifiable a half century after *Brown*.

The efforts in Louisville and Seattle represented a move to spread opportunities more evenly within a diverse community. In a sense, they were small versions of a test the United States had faced from its founding: how to provide individuals with equal opportunities in a pluralistic society, particularly one with a history of identity-based discrimination. *Brown* had delegitimized that identity-based discrimination; the half century that followed had shown the difficulty of taking the next step toward *Brown*'s ideal of educational opportunities as a "right made available to all on an equal basis." The post-*Brown* cases like *Swann*, *Milliken*, and *Jenkins* represented one element of that effort. The Great Society and educational assistance legislation of the 1960s and 70s represented another. Affirmative action policies in employment, contracting, and higher education, such as those considered by the Supreme Court and the EEOC, provided a new direction to the work, shifting the focus from outlawing exclusion to mandating inclusion. And the collective bargaining agreement in Jackson, Michigan, demonstrated a move to protect that inclusion from vanishing. But no case more directly connected to the legacy of *Brown* than did the one considering the school assignment policies of Louisville and Seattle.

In *Brown*, a student had been denied assignment to a school based on her race; in Louisville, a student had been denied assignment to a school based on his race. The contexts were different: in *Brown*, the race was being used to maintain racial separation in all the district's schools, while in Louisville, race was taken into account out of a desire to maintain racial diversity in all the district's schools. The case presented the question of whether this difference in context made any constitutional difference. This was a version of the question the Court—and society—had been grappling with for nearly three decades in other affirmative action cases.

The Court that considered *PICS* had two new members, both of whom had worked in Republican administrations during previous affirmative action cases (Chief Justice John Roberts had served as acting solicitor general and argued for strict race neutrality in *Metro Broadcasting* in 1990, while Justice Samuel Alito had participated in crafting a similar brief in *Wygant* in 1986). Having replaced Chief Justice Rehnquist and Justice O'Connor, the new justices further solidified the conclusion that all racial classifications, regardless of alleged motivation, demanded the Court's strictest scrutiny. The fractured *Bakke* Court had not even reached consensus on this initial question, but since Thomas had replaced Marshall, the Court had consistently applied strict scrutiny when confronting affirmative action. In *PICS,* Chief Justice Roberts simply stated the conclusion as a "well-established" truism.[24]

The determinative question in *PICS*, then, was whether the school districts had a sufficiently compelling justification for the racial consideration, as the law school had in *Grutter*. Roberts answered the question simply: "The way to stop discrimination on the basis of race is to stop discriminating on the basis of race." The school districts had argued that there were educational and community benefits to diverse schools, but Roberts felt that the mechanics of the plan belied such a goal. "In design and operation," he wrote, "the plans are directed only to racial balance, pure and simple, an objective this Court has repeatedly condemned as illegitimate."[25] Since the school-level targets in each district were not connected to any needed critical mass to achieve such benefits, but rather were pegged to each district's racial makeup, Roberts and the Court's majority smelled improper quotas rather than a careful consideration of how best to achieve diversity's alleged benefits.

The chief dissent was authored by Justice Stephen Breyer, who provided a thorough analysis of both the facts and law that he felt justified the districts' use of race and dictated the Court's affirmation of it. Among other points, Breyer argued that the districts were due deference given their benign motivations—after all, the Court in *Rodriguez, Milliken,* and other cases had lauded the importance of local decision making in schools. But local control was not a priority of the majority's opinion in *PICS.*

The task of refuting Breyer was taken up by Justice Thomas, who just as thoroughly offered his own interpretation of the district's actions and the Constitution's requirements. Breyer had argued that the districts' use of race could be permissible in order to avoid a return to segregation, but Thomas drew a firm distinction between segregation and racial imbalance. "Segregation," Thomas explained, "is the deliberate operation of a school system to carry out a government policy to separate pupils in schools solely on the basis of race." It was thus an intentional government act of enforced racial segregation. In contrast, "racial imbalance is the failure of a school district's individual schools to match or approximate the demographic makeup of the student population at large." Racial imbalance *might* result from segregation, but it also might result from other causes, including residential segregation or "any number of innocent private decisions." Indeed, according to Thomas, "the further we get from the era of state-sponsored racial segregation, the less likely it is that racial imbalance has a traceable connection to any prior segregation."[26]

From this distinction, Thomas arrived at a very different conclusion than had Breyer. Remedying segregation was a constitutional imperative, but remedying racial imbalance was only permissible if the imbalance had actually resulted from segregation. From Justice Thomas's perspective, the school districts in both Louisville and Seattle were simply seeking to avoid racial imbalance. This was not only not required by the Constitution, but violated it, since the districts were utilizing racial classifications.

As he had in *Grutter,* Thomas characterized the districts' efforts at maintaining racial balance as "faddish" and merely an interest in "classroom aesthetics" born of "hypersensitivity to elite sensibilities." Thomas next turned to the districts' claims that their assignment policies were justified by educational benefits. Specifically, Breyer had endorsed the districts' argument that racially diverse student bodies provided both educational benefits and improvements in racial attitudes and therefore justified consideration of race in much the same way as educational benefits had justified the University of Michigan law school's consideration of applicants' race. Thomas, of course, had covered this ground in *Grutter* and built on it in *PICS*. "It is far from apparent that coerced racial mixing has any educational benefits," he wrote.[27]

Thomas was no more confident that the districts' assignment plans would lead to improved racial attitudes. He pointed to tracking within schools that often separated students by race and the fact that "students of different races within the same school may separate themselves socially."[28] One result was that some studies found that racial attitudes actually deteriorated in more diverse schools. If the districts' hoped to justify using race in making student assignments based on such a hope, Thomas demanded far more convincing proof that actual benefits would accrue. In the absence of any provable benefits, Thomas saw the districts' plans as merely an experiment that could not be justified by a Constitution that prohibited consideration of race in all but the narrowest circumstances.

What was really wrong with Breyer's perspective, Thomas argued, was its rejection of "the colorblind Constitution." He quoted Justice Harlan's dissent from *Plessy v. Ferguson* in offering his conclusion: "Because 'our Constitution is color-blind, and neither knows nor tolerates classes among citizens,' [such] race-based decisionmaking is unconstitutional." To the charge that the local districts should be trusted due to their benign motivations, Thomas wondered just how one could know that any racial consideration was truly benign. While Thomas cast no doubt on Justice Breyer's intentions, he claimed himself unwilling to make constitutional decisions on an assumption that school boards' intentions will remain as good as his colleague's. "If our history has taught us anything," he quipped, "it has taught us to beware of elites bearing racial theories."[29]

Marshall well understood that race-based decision making could be devastating, and in *Bakke*, looked forward to a day "in which the color of a person's skin will not determine the opportunities available to him or her."[30] But as he left the Court in 1991, he knew that day had yet to arrive. In his blustery press conference on the day following his retirement, Marshall did offer one extended anecdote. After disclaiming any involvement in issues of civil rights since he accepted his appointment to the Second Circuit Court of Appeals in 1962, Marshall responded to a question referencing Martin Luther King's hope that African Americans would one day be "free at last":

> I'm not free. All I know is that years ago, when I was a youngster, a Pullman porter told me that he had been in every city in this country, he was sure, and he had never been in a city in the United States where he had to put his hand up in front of his face to find out he was a Negro. I agree with it.[31]

The world African Americans encountered was not colorblind. And Marshall felt that until that context shifted, the Constitution need not be interpreted in a colorblind way either.

Thomas was no less aware that the world he lived in was far from colorblind. He had felt the stings of racism as a child and as a student. He had endured race-based doubts all the way to his seat on the Supreme Court. Indeed, he had even raised the charge of racism in the throes of his nasty confirmation fight and its accusations of sexual harassment, using decidedly *not* colorblind language, referring to the hearings as "a high-tech lynching for uppity blacks who in any way deign to think for themselves, to do for themselves, to have different ideas."[32] But Thomas arrived at a different conclusion in a world that continued to see race. Instead of finding justification for the further use of race to undo the sins of the past, Thomas believed in a Constitution that must prohibit any use of race to prevent similar sins in the future.

RETURNING TO BATTLE OVER 'BROWN'

That the legacy of *Brown*, and indirectly of Thurgood Marshall, was at stake in *PICS* was obvious from the number of justices who had invoked that landmark decision. Chief Justice Roberts concluded his opinion drawing an equivalence to the arguments of the *Brown* plaintiffs. "Before *Brown*, schoolchildren were told where they could and could not go to school based on the color of their skin," he wrote. Roberts even quoted an argument made by Marshall's colleague, Robert Carter, in the *Brown* oral arguments: "[N]o state has any authority under the equal protection clause of the Fourteenth Amendment to use race as a factor in affording educational opportunities among its citizens."[33] Roberts, and the Court, concluded that neither Seattle nor Louisville had sufficiently demonstrated that using race, deemed illegitimate in *Brown*, could be revived.

Robert Carter, who was still a federal judge a half century after his contributions to *Brown v. Board of Education*, rebuked the Court's misuse of the *Brown* arguments, noting that there had only been one way race was being used at the time: exclusion. To take his statements from that context and use them to condemn efforts to bring students together turned the argument on its head.[34] The one member of the Court who had served with Thurgood Marshall also saw something different in the Court's invocation of *Brown*. Justice Stevens, by 2007 the senior justice on the Court, saw "cruel irony" and chided the chief justice for rewriting history. While it was true, as the chief justice said, that before *Brown*, schoolchildren were told which school to attend based on the color of their skin, Justice Stevens reminded his colleagues "that it was only black schoolchildren who were so ordered; indeed, the history books do not tell stories of white children struggling to attend black schools." Looking back on more than three decades on the Court, including his own evolution, Justice Stevens lamented his "firm conviction that no Member of the Court that I joined in 1975 would have agreed with today's decision."[35] Certainly, his colleague Justice Marshall would not have.

But Justice Thomas, too, sought to claim the mantle of *Brown*. In an extended section of his concurrence, complete with extensive footnotes referencing the briefs and arguments in *Brown*, Thomas identified multiple ways in which the arguments made by the districts in Louisville and Seattle echoed those made by the defendant school districts in *Brown*. The districts' calls for deference to local expertise, pleas for avoiding disruption, and concerns about the practical effects of judicial interference with local school assignment all had been raised during the *Brown* case. "What was wrong in 1954 cannot be right today," Thomas concluded.[36]

"I am quite comfortable in the company I keep," he claimed, directly claiming that his view of a Constitution that mandated a fixed principle of colorblindness "was the rallying cry for the lawyers who litigated *Brown*." The lawyer he had in mind most prominently was Thurgood Marshall. Thomas cited to a speech made by Judge Constance Baker Motley, one of Marshall's colleagues from his time at the NAACP, on the occasion of Justice Marshall's 1993 death. Motley had said:

> Marshall had a "Bible" to which he turned during his most depressed moments. The "Bible" would be known in the legal community as the first Mr. Justice Harlan's dissent in *Plessy v. Ferguson*. I do not know of any opinion which buoyed Marshall more in his pre-*Brown* days.

Harlan had first introduced the concept of colorblindness in that dissent.[37]

But Thomas need not have excavated the comments of Judge Motley to learn what Marshall thought about the colorblind Constitution. He had written on the very topic in *Bakke*. There, he had lamented the Court's failure to adopt the principle that the equal protection clause forbade differences in treatment based on race in 1896, but he reminded his colleagues that that principle had appeared only in dissent. For sixty years, the Constitution permitted racial considerations to be utilized, and Marshall asserted that this shameful history was precisely what justified the use of race to remedy the persisting disparities that were that history's legacy:

> It is because of a legacy of unequal treatment that we now must permit the institutions of this society to give consideration to race in making decisions about who will hold the positions of influence, affluence, and prestige in America.[38]

Had Marshall seen the Court citing one of his greatest triumphs to reach the opposite conclusion would have been a cruel irony indeed.

While the root of this disagreement between justices on the Supreme Court was about the purpose of the Constitution's equal protection clause, the more fundamental question encompassed the central American challenge of coexistence within a democracy made up of an increasingly diverse body of citizens. Both justices recognized the centrality of education to that challenge in the ways schools prepared the citizens of future generations. In their writings, each justice wrote passionately about that project, while also drawing attention to real problems facing vulnerable students, such as lack of quality educational options for poor students, persistent racial achievement gaps, and varied educational and psychological harms students suffered from disparate opportunities.

But Marshall's and Thomas's own schooling experiences had set them on distinct paths that informed their work as lawyers and judges. They would continue to utilize the harms they suffered as students to suffuse their work with contradictory perspectives on the best path for Black uplift, the correct equilibrium between a government and its citizens, the proper balance of the role of state and federal government, the appropriate scope of judicial power in the American system, and the best method for interpreting the Constitution. In this, they gave judicial voice to enduring debates that ran alongside the nation's ideological, political, and racial diversity. The transition from Marshall to Thomas represented an impactful turning point in the outcome of those debates on the Supreme Court.

In 1954, Marshall had convinced the justices of the Supreme Court to reject the Constitution's acquiescence to racial segregation in *Brown v. Board of Education*. This had been a crucial moment in the nation's efforts to extend its ideals of citizenship more broadly among its diverse population. On the Court, Marshall struggled to convince his colleagues to accept the affirmative use of race to expand that promise even further. He had argued that the best way to a colorblind world was to remain cognizant of the context of a discriminatory past and work tirelessly to eliminate its continuing effects. Once there was "true integration," then the nation could enjoy the luxury of a colorblind Constitution.

During Marshall's final decade, the Court wavered and fractured in resolving these constitutional questions. Though the Court would continue to encounter similar cases, following the arrival of Justice Thomas, it did so with a clearer directive that all considerations of race would receive the Court's highest judicial scrutiny. This reflected Thomas's firm belief that the mandates of the Constitution were fixed and that the equal protection clause must mean the same thing regardless of context. According to Thomas, the best way to a colorblind world began with a colorblind Constitution. It was not the Constitution that must change, but the world it governed.

Marshall may have won a unanimous victory in 1954 and enjoyed success during his earlier tenure on the Court, but Thomas's arrival reconstituted the Court. And by 2007, in *PICS,* Thomas had something supporting his vision that had eluded Marshall as he pursued his: a majority on the Supreme Court who agreed with him.

CONCLUSION

THE RULE OF LAW

After losing in the first three primary contests in his quest for the Democratic Party's nomination for president in February 2020, former Vice President Joe Biden made a commitment to the Democratic voters of South Carolina, many of whom were African American. "I'm looking forward to making sure there's a Black woman on the Supreme Court to make sure we in fact get everyone represented," Biden said in a debate in Charleston.[1]

This was a decidedly different strategy than that pursued by President George H. W. Bush in 1991, when he insisted that race had not been considered in his selection of Clarence Thomas to be Thurgood Marshall's successor. Here was a presidential candidate explicitly acknowledging the importance of varied experiences and perspectives in the nation's judiciary, highlighting the fact that the experience of Black women was one that was both distinct and underrepresented, and committing to take steps to address the situation.

Undoubtedly, Biden's motivations were primarily political—his presidential ambitions rested almost entirely on his performance in the South

Carolina primary—and the promise would have been largely forgotten had Biden not gone on to win the primary, catapulting him toward the Democratic nomination and, ultimately that November, to winning the presidency. But even before that future had come to pass over the course of the year, in merely making the declaration as a candidate, Biden had not only provided a rare transparency into how race might play a role in decisions by national political figures, but also highlighted the undeniable fact that Black women had not yet cracked the highest echelons of American law. Thurgood Marshall's colleague at the NAACP LDF, Constance Baker Motley, had been the first Black woman appointed as a federal judge, taking a seat as a district court judge in New York in 1966. In 1979, Amalya Lyle Kearse was appointed to the Second Circuit Court of Appeals, but few Black women had been considered top candidates for a Supreme Court appointment, creating the void Biden identified. At the time of Biden's promise, there were only 4 African American women serving on any of the federal courts of appeals out of over 175 such judgeships. Several of the circuits had never had a Black female appellate judge.[2]

At the time of the promise, some commentators pushed against the idea of limiting Supreme Court candidates based on race and sex, but as long as Biden was merely a candidate, such engagement was limited. However, with Biden as president, Justice Stephen Breyer's retirement announcement in January 2022 made the abstract real. To that point in Biden's presidency, four additional Black women had been confirmed to judgeships on the courts of appeals: Tiffany Patrice Cunningham (Federal Circuit), Ketanji Brown Jackson (DC Circuit), Candace Rae Jackson-Akiwumi (Seventh Circuit), and Eunice Cheryl Lee (Second Circuit). This doubled the number of Black women at the level of the judiciary just beneath the Supreme Court. But with an open seat on the Supreme Court, the idea that the president had predetermined that his pick would be a Black woman attracted much attention from Biden's critics, at least until his nomination of Judge Ketanji Brown Jackson to Breyer's seat. Senator Roger Wicker raised a specter that had haunted the Thomas nomination more than thirty years earlier, noting that whoever Biden nominated would be "the beneficiary of this sort of quota."³ The implication was that whomever the president nominated would not be as "qualified" as would have been the case had he cast a wider net. This perspective ignored the fact that being a Black woman had been a *dis*qualifying factor for most of American history to that point.

When Biden announced Judge Jackson as the nominee to succeed Breyer, it became difficult to take arguments about qualification too seriously. Jackson had already served as both a district court and court of appeals judge, had clerked at all three levels of federal court (including at the Supreme Court for Justice Breyer), and had a varied legal practice that included work in private practice, as a public defender, and on the United States Sentencing Commission. She had excelled in every setting she entered, including as a high school debater like Thurgood Marshall. Her high school in Miami had been more diverse than the high schools of Justices Marshall and Thomas, though she still was among the minority of Black students in a school that was nearly three-quarters white. How, if at all, her schooling might inform her work on the Court remains to be seen. However, upon being nominated, Judge Jackson highlighted the "steadfast and courageous commitment to equal justice under law" of a foremother with whom she shared a birthday, Constance Baker Motley. "Judge Motley's life and career has been a true inspiration to me."⁴

Jackson's stellar qualifications did not dissuade some senators from subjecting her to openly partisan questioning, which had increasingly become a feature of confirmation hearings since Robert Bork's failed nomination in 1987. Despite (or perhaps because of) this, the nomination and ultimate confirmation of Justice Jackson also provided inspiration for many, including 16-year-old Samiya Williams, who noted that her "dreams have gotten so much bigger, it seems overnight."⁵

But the transition from Stephen Breyer to Ketanji Brown Jackson was unlikely to disrupt the balance of the Supreme Court in 2022. Unlike the transition from Thurgood Marshall to Clarence Thomas or the Court's most recent transition from Justice Ruth Bader Ginsburg to Amy Coney Barrett in 2020, the Breyer-to-Jackson transition would bring a new justice with similar ideological leanings to the bench. In her opening remarks at her confirmation hearings, Jackson thanked Breyer for his mentorship and declared that she hoped "to carry on his spirit" if confirmed, highlighting his belief that law aimed to allow

> all people to live together in a society, where they have so many different views . . . in a way that is more harmonious, that is better, so that they can work productively together.[6]

But the Supreme Court that Justice Jackson would join would be one that, like the nation it served, had been transformed in the two years between Joe Biden's promise to nominate a Black woman and the confirmation of Ketanji Brown Jackson. The nation was dealing with an unprecedented global pandemic and a revival of demands for racial justice, and it had endured a historically contentious presidential election that had led to an assault on the nation's Capitol on January 6, 2021. In this extraordinary period, the themes that animated the work of Thurgood Marshall and Clarence Thomas as well as the effects of the transition from one to the other were consistently evident.

CONTEMPORARY COURT TRANSITIONS

The Supreme Court transition that preceded the confirmation of the nation's first Black female justice was the one that perhaps most resembled the 1991 Marshall-to-Thomas transition in both symbolism and impact. Thomas had confirmed a conservative majority on the Court that had proved durable, but not dominant. The Court had moved definitively in a more conservative direction over the years, but the moderation of several of the conservative-leaning justices (most notably Sandra Day O'Connor and Anthony Kennedy) and the thin margins of a 5–4 Court ensured that, for the most part, the Court was not deciding cases using the most extreme arguments favored by conservative advocates, arguments that were often made by Justice Thomas in solo concurrences.

But the passing of Justice Ruth Bader Ginsburg in September 2020 created an opportunity to shift that balance. Like Marshall, before her appointment, Ginsburg had been a fierce and successful advocate at the Supreme Court. She had even been referred to as "the Thurgood Marshall of Women's Equality."[7] On the Court, she had developed a reputation as a passionate dissenter on cases where she found the Court's outcomes unjust, and, like Marshall, she had achieved unusual fame and adulation from her admirers that transcended that of the typical Supreme Court justice. And like Marshall, she suffered from declining health late in her career that forced her to confront a decision about whether or not to stay on the Court.[8]

In 1991, as Marshall struggled with his health, he understood that retirement would provide a president, with whom he did not often agree, with the opportunity to name his successor. But at the time, President George H. W. Bush was riding a wave of popularity as the nation engaged in the Gulf War with Iraq, and Marshall might have concluded that the prospect of a Democratic president being elected again in his lifetime seemed slim—after all, only a single Democrat had been elected in the preceding six presidential elections. With the prospect of a second Bush term seeming likely, Marshall retired despite the prospect of being replaced by a justice who would tip the balance of the Court; given his health, that result seemed inevitable. Of course, Bill Clinton ultimately defeated Bush in the 1992 election, though it is not clear that even had Marshall stayed an additional term and a half to potentially be replaced by Clinton, the outcome would have been different. Marshall passed away on January 24, 1993, four days after Clinton was inaugurated.

For her part, Ginsburg faced a decision in the waning months of Barack Obama's presidency in 2015 and 2016. However, Ginsburg had seen Democrats win four of the prior six presidential elections (plus the popular vote in 2000), and the prospects for the presumptive Democratic nominee, Hillary Clinton, seemed strong. Still, given Ginsburg's tenuous health amid her multiple battles with cancer, some urged her retirement to assure Obama would name her replacement. In response, Ginsburg felt that even Obama could not get someone who shared her fierce ideology so late in his presidency, given the makeup of the Senate—a concern that seemed prescient given the Senate's obstinacy in even holding hearings for Obama's 2016 nomination of Merrick Garland to replace Justice Antonin Scalia, who had recently passed away.

The circumstances of Scalia's vacancy were markedly different than a hypothetical 2016 Ginsburg retirement because replacing Scalia carried the potential of undoing the conservative majority on the Court for the first time since 1991. Given these stakes, Republican senators held firm for months, arguing that justices should not be replaced during an election year. After Donald Trump defeated Clinton for the presidency, he was able to appoint Neil Gorsuch to succeed Scalia, thus maintaining the Court's ideological makeup. However, when Ginsburg passed away in the waning months of Trump's first term, the reverse prospect of strengthening the conservative majority presented itself. Though votes in the 2020 election were already being cast, Trump and the Republican majority in the Senate disregarded the argument from 2016 about replacing justices during an election year and confirmed Judge Amy Coney Barrett less than two weeks before the November election. Thus, like Marshall before her, Ginsburg would be replaced by a successor with a vastly different ideology who solidified a conservative tilt to the Court's work. It did not take long to see the effect of replacing Justice Ginsburg with Justice Barrett.

THE PANDEMIC AND THE COURT

In the history of the Supreme Court, the arrival of the COVID-19 pandemic will be found in a simple press release issued March 16, 2020. "In keeping with public health precautions recommended in response to COVID-19," the press release read, "the Supreme Court is postponing the oral arguments currently scheduled for the March session."[9] Ever mindful of precedent, the release noted that arguments had been impacted on two occasions in the late 1700s for yellow fever and had been postponed in 1918 due to the Spanish flu epidemic. Two weeks later, the Court also postponed its April arguments as the nation grappled with how to continue operating amid stay-at-home orders aimed at slowing the spread of the coronavirus.[10] Like much of the rest of the country, the Court's building was closed to the public, and most personnel began to work remotely.

In the months that followed, the Court changed its protocols, shifting to remote telephonic arguments, instituting a strict justice-by-justice format for questioning, and, for the first time, allowing the public to listen to arguments in real time when they resumed in May. More substantively, in the summer of 2020, the Court was called upon to consider questions of religious freedom in the context of public health mandates instituted to confront the pandemic. Prior to Justice Ginsburg's passing, Justice Thomas was on the losing end of two 5–4 decisions allowing pandemic regulations limiting capacity to apply to places of worship. The Court stood by prior First Amendment holdings ensuring that religious institutions were not exempt from adherence to generally applicable laws. But only a month after Justice Barrett's confirmation, the Court seemed to reverse itself, voting 5–4 to *grant* injunctions against application of pandemic regulations to religious entities.[11] Though none of the dissenters said so as directly as Justice Marshall had in his dissent in *Payne*, the most significant change from the summer to the fall had merely been to the personnel of the Court.

Even as new faces arrived at the Supreme Court, Justice Thomas—now the Court's senior justice—built on the limited government philosophy he had been advancing since his appointment three decades prior. As the Court entered its new phase, and as the leadership of the Republican Party grew less restrained in advancing more extreme positions, Thomas's positions found more fertile soil and appeared more undisputedly partisan in the increasingly frayed national political climate.

Indeed, the pandemic forced broader questions of the role of government to restrict the liberty of individuals, the answers to which might literally be a matter of life and death. These were questions of the highest order in a representative democracy built upon respect for the rule of law. To what extent would citizens respect or accept government decisions with which they might disagree? While respect might be strengthened in a representative democracy where government action could be traceable to the will of the people, what might happen if the people felt that democracy itself was defective? Reactions to the 2020 pandemic and the divisive presidential election in which it unfolded would help answer these queries, but in a way that raised further questions about the status of the rule of law in American democracy.

ELECTIONS AND THE LEGITIMACY OF DEMOCRACY

As Americans across the racial and ideological spectrum took to the streets in 2020, they did so under divergent banners Thurgood Marshall and Clarence Thomas would have embraced. Marshall's commitment to combating racial injustice infused the passions of those demanding Black Lives Matter, while Thomas's skepticism of government was amplified by those resistant to health mandates and taken a step further in claims of a stolen election.

From the earliest days of the pandemic, religious groups were not the only groups challenging government authority. Demonstrators in many states confronted their governments as state and local health officials began to impose mask mandates, occupancy limits, and stay-at-home orders. For example, in April, protestors in Michigan began an "Unlock Michigan" campaign, honking horns and circling the state capitol while several hundred others gathered outside. Two weeks later, another group, including several people carrying automatic weapons, stormed into the state's capitol building and demanded entry into a live legislative session.[12]

At the root of these protests were arguments about freedom from government tyranny; several of the demonstrators in Michigan carried signs charging Governor Gretchen Whitmer's imposition of pandemic regulations as tyrannical. The pandemic intensified the clash, but the resistance to government regulation had been developing into an increasingly potent element of conservative ideology for some time and had roots as deep as the nation's founding. Rejection of gun control regulation and opposition to the government mandates in the Affordable Care Act championed by Barack Obama had become central to conservative orthodoxy, building on the theme articulated by President Ronald Reagan in his 1981 inaugural address: "Government is not the solution to our problem, government *is* the problem."[13] By 2020, the antigovernment theme had coalesced into an increasingly confrontational movement with Donald Trump at its center. Trump, as head of the federal government, had tweeted "Liberate Michigan" in the days leading up to the protests at the state capitol and regularly used his platform to foment antigovernment fervor.

Clarence Thomas had bought into antigovernment ideas long before Donald Trump did. Rooted in his experience that government efforts to aid African Americans had not only failed, but backfired, Thomas was drawn to the themes of limited and restrained government that Reagan had articulated. Through his years in government and on the Supreme Court, his beliefs only seemed to harden. While this further alienated him from much of the nation's Black community, it made him a sort of patron saint of twenty-first-century conservatism, particularly the brand tapped into by Trump. Indeed, on the campaign trail in 2015, Trump identified Thomas as his favorite justice, and during Trump's presidency, Justice Thomas's former clerks were appointed to a number of administration positions and federal judgeships.[14]

From his chambers at the Supreme Court, Thomas could not actively participate in any protests against pandemic regulations even if he had wanted to; his dissenting votes in the summer 2020 cases constituted the extent of his public objection to health mandates. By the time he voted with a newly constituted majority (including Justice Barrett) to strike down similar regulations in November 2020, many of those who had protested pandemic regulations throughout the year had transitioned to a different cause that struck not only at the authority of government but to the heart of democracy itself.

Despite certified election results confirming Joe Biden as the winner of the presidential election, supporters of Donald Trump engaged in a multifaceted effort to declare Trump the winner. The foundation for these efforts had been laid even before the election: Trump supporters claimed that expanded access to mail-in voting in the midst of the pandemic would increase opportunities for fraud. On the eve of the election, the Supreme Court had declined (over the objections of Justice Thomas and two other justices) to weigh in on a challenge brought by the Trump campaign against Pennsylvania's handling of mail-in ballots.[15]

Following the election, Trump aggressively promoted a narrative, rejected as baseless in numerous courts, that widespread fraud across states and government conspiracy had denied him a second term. Protestors gathered in numerous states as election officials certified results, and subsequent reporting revealed that Thomas's wife, Ginni Thomas, was actively involved in promoting the idea that Trump had been wrongfully denied victory and encouraging the Trump team to fight to stay in office.[16] For his part, Justice Thomas joined a statement noting his belief that a pro-Trump lawsuit brought by the state of Texas against the state of Pennsylvania should be allowed to continue. However, the Court rejected the suit, unwilling to intervene on Trump's behalf.[17]

But more broadly, the antigovernment jurisprudence Thomas had fostered over the years was a central component of Trump's unrestrained attack on government as both candidate and president. These arguments each pointed toward assaults on democracy itself as a logical endpoint. After all, a rejection of the legitimacy of a democratic government's actions was ultimately a rejection of the people's collective ability to express its will through government. It was only a short additional step to dismiss the will of the people itself.

The cries for liberty that were uttered in response to the pandemic regulations would have been familiar to Thurgood Marshall, who was aware of the perils of this path. As both a lawyer and a justice, he had encountered direct challenges to the authority of government and was forced to contemplate the consequences of citizens' loss of faith in democracy. Marshall's triumph in *Brown v. Board of Education* activated a resistance to government authority, with opponents offering obstruction and defiance, openly flouting Supreme Court decisions, federal statutes, and presidential directives. And they promoted alternative facts aimed at discrediting the government's position. Members of Congress signed the Southern Manifesto, and state leaders, such as Governors Orval Faubus and George Wallace, stood in the schoolhouse door. At root, segregationists were arguing for the freedom to maintain existing racial hierarchies without federal government interference. The demand for freedom from alleged tyranny during the COVID-19 pandemic similarly rejected justifications for government authority as "fake" and unabashedly flouted legal directives deemed illegitimate.

In his time, Thurgood Marshall recognized the hazard of eroding the rule of law and argued that such defiance of the law could not be permitted. In *Cooper v. Aaron*, the case determining whether the Little Rock school board could delay implementation of desegregation after a traumatic first year, Marshall identified the stakes if delay were tolerated. "Democracy is hard!" he thundered before the Court. And he worried about the message the nation's next generation of citizens would take from an outcome tolerating delay:

> I worry about the white children in Little Rock who are told as young people that the way to get your rights is to violate the law and defy the lawful authorities. I'm worried about their future.[18]

Though Marshall prevailed in *Cooper v. Aaron*, the decades that followed held numerous examples of communities circumventing orders for desegregation rather than defying them outright. The Supreme Court ultimately blessed such evasion, making itself an accomplice to an erosion of the rule of law by nourishing the belief that avoidance of court orders might be tolerated. Communities wishing to avoid substantial change might take the lesson Marshall feared, concluding that the way to get a desired result was to defy the lawful authorities. And unlike civil rights protestors who were willing to accept jail for their own defiance of laws they found unjust, the lesson for those circumventing desegregation was that defiance would not trigger accountability.

Resistance to desegregation under a banner of freedom attracted many to Ronald Reagan's limited government message in the 1970s and 1980s. By the 2010s, "limited government" had become "antigovernment," and Donald Trump emboldened the belief that open defiance of norms and laws was a form of righteous resistance to government tyranny. The children of Little Rock had learned their lesson well through the decades: compliance with inconvenient laws could be avoided without accountability. Thus, when pandemic mandates and election results were unsatisfactory, resistance would be righteous in the minds of the resistors.

Though he would not have been sympathetic to the ways it was manifesting itself in 2020, Thurgood Marshall understood such indignation. However, as evidenced by his words before the Court in *Cooper v. Aaron* and by actions throughout his career, a foundational belief in the authority and power of the rule of law was central to his view of citizenship. Marshall also understood that the legitimacy of elections was central to the rule of law in the American system. He had represented Black voters as an NAACP lawyer and had defended the Voting Rights Act of 1965 against some of its earliest challenges during his tenure as U.S. solicitor general. On the Court (and in contrast to his successor), Marshall was a frequent voice for an expansive reading of the act.[19] Voting was "the right preservative of all other rights," he wrote in 1980.[20]

In that case, which concerned alterations to Mobile, Alabama's electoral system, Marshall had argued in dissent that the Court was again sanctioning action that undermined the purposes and authority of law, just as it had in the later school desegregation cases. Marshall thought requiring intent to prove voting discrimination—as opposed to more broadly prohibiting actions that had disparate racial *effects* on voting—would enable officials "to adopt policies that are the products of discriminatory intent so long as they sufficiently mask their motives through the use of subtlety and illusion."[21] By allowing such subterfuge, the Court was "an accessory to the perpetuation of racial discrimination" and by undercutting efforts to combat voting discrimination, it was undermining American democracy. He concluded with a warning:

If this Court refuses to honor our long-recognized principle that the Constitution nullifies sophisticated as well as simple-minded modes of discrimination, it cannot expect the victims of discrimination to respect political channels of seeking redress.[22]

Voting was thus the lynchpin upon which the entire constitutional system turned. Its illegitimacy, Marshall warned, might lead to channels of redress outside of the constitutional system. After all, if political channels were being led by officials elected illegitimately, why should citizens turn to the government to see problems rectified? Frustrated citizens might see no choice but to defy the rule of law—an outcome Marshall, a fierce believer in the power and responsibility of government and an American whose entire worldview depended on respect for the rule of law, abhorred.

In the 1980 case, Marshall was worried that the frustrated citizens would be victims of surreptitious racial discrimination in voting. But his premonition of a breakdown in the rule of law due to perceived illegitimacy of elections would play itself out four decades later, fueled by a very different category of frustrated citizens.

LIBERTY, JUSTICE, AND CITIZENSHIP

Though they had struck out in numerous courts, including the Supreme Court, those believing the 2020 election had been stolen from Donald Trump continued to push to have the election results reversed. Trump refused to concede defeat into the new year, and the protests culminated on January 6 when a pro-Trump mob he had addressed earlier in the day stormed the U.S. Capitol while members of Congress oversaw the formal tallying of electoral college votes. Five people were killed, and more than a hundred were injured in the chaos.[23]

The insurrection was precisely the kind of extra-political channel for redress Marshall had warned frustrated citizens might pursue if faith in the democratic system were lost. He might have dismissed this particular group's frustrations as baseless: all of his arguments had been made in the context of protecting the voting rights of groups that had been legally excluded from democracy for centuries, citizens demanding respect for their rights. There was no history of legal disenfranchisement against those who made up Trump's political base. But Marshall could understand how frustration, even frustration he might have deemed illegitimate, might lead to open defiance—after all, he had had a front-row view of the antigovernment resistance stemming from *Brown v. Board of Education*. Marshall had understood the lessons people would take from tacit acceptance of defiance of the rule of law: people would feel entitled to bend the law to suit their own desires. This was precisely what those who stormed the Capitol sought to accomplish.

Clarence Thomas took a different view. Donald Trump and Clarence Thomas were very different people, but they had found common cause in an antigovernment ideology that Thomas patiently pushed throughout his career as a Supreme Court justice and that Trump weaponized in his rise to political power. Each tapped into a longstanding American sentiment that freedom from government was the highest form of liberty. When Thomas wrote of the limited powers of the federal government or the need for judges to restrain from making policy or that the Supreme Court need not feel bound by its own prior decisions, he furthered a vision that saw government efforts to regulate society as an infringement on individual liberty.[24] The protestors against pandemic regulations shared this vision, and Trump had built a passionate base of supporters by casting himself as the ultimate thumb in the eye of government. Even after the insurrection, Thomas signaled his solidarity with those supporters, a group that included his wife and some of his former law clerks, with his votes on election-related cases that amplified the discredited claims of election fraud that fueled the post-election protests. Further, when the Court required the Trump administration to turn over documents to the congressional commission investigating the January 6 insurrection, only Thomas dissented.[25]

Thomas had found in the conservative movement and the Republican Party, particularly from the most extreme pro-Trump elements within it, an acceptance that had always eluded him from the majority of the nation's Black community. This despite elements of white supremacist zeal animating many of Trump's most enthusiastic supporters, an ideology difficult to reconcile with Thomas's claim that his antigovernment sentiments were born of his loss of faith in government to address the needs of African Americans. Thomas had even begun to directly tie race to conservative causes, casting his rejection of abortion rights as a form of anti-racism. Yet in an extraordinary moment when protests for racial justice flooded American streets alongside protests against government regulations, Thomas consistently prioritized the latter.[26]

On criminal justice, the topic most directly igniting those protests, Thomas had remained an obstacle to Black defendants in recent terms on topics from juror selection to the death penalty.[27] And on voting, Thomas had been calling for invalidation of the Voting Rights Act for years prior to the Court's scaling back of that landmark statute in *Shelby County v. Holder* in 2013. Further, in the same term in which he amplified Trump's claims of election fraud, Thomas and the Court further restricted portions of the act, rejecting claims that continued aggressive oversight remained necessary.[28]

The alleged and disproved fraud surrounding the 2020 election seemed to merit greater concern from Thomas than allegations of racial discrimination in voting. A lone exception to this pattern could be found in Thomas's writings on "qualified immunity," in which his limited government inclinations led him to call for limits on immunity for police officers accused of violating the rights of citizens. Yet, even on this topic, Thomas's position was rooted in distrust of government as opposed to a denunciation of police violence against Black citizens that had fueled calls among racial justice protestors in 2020 to call for an end to qualified immunity. These were the kinds of positions that led to doubts about Thomas's sincerity on issues affecting African Americans.[29]

Such questions had hounded Thomas since before his appointment in 1991, but by 2020, the consistency and intensity of his alignment with a political party seemed to belie his claims of fierce independence of thought. His vehement distrust of institutions had led him to implicit—or perhaps explicit—endorsement of a coordinated effort to override election results that included both those who stormed the U.S. Capitol and others, including Thomas's wife, who explored other options behind the scenes. This was certainly a radical position for a Supreme Court justice, but its roots had been there all along in Thomas's work.

From the idealized independence of his grandfather in mid-century Savannah, Thomas had embraced an extreme version of individualism that drove him away from positions popular within the Black community and toward a limited or antigovernment worldview that prized freedom from government. Thanks in part to the work of Thurgood Marshall, Thomas had not experienced legal exclusions from full citizenship to the same extent as his predecessor, but his experiences as an African American navigating white-dominated spaces taught him to distrust the motivations of even those who claimed to be allies, including some African Americans themselves. He felt a subtler form of racism that nonetheless delivered a message that African Americans were not worthy of full inclusion in society. This led to his understanding that the Constitution did its best work when protecting citizens from the power of government. That view showed itself in his work at the EEOC as he eschewed systemic interventions in employment discrimination and in judicial opinions advocating limited judicial power to remedy historic inequities and a weak federal government. It was present in his demands for a colorblind Constitution that must be interpreted based on its text and must consider citizens as individuals rather than as members of racial or other groups. And it showed in his embrace of independent institutions, such as private schools or HBCUs, over institutions that served a broader range of the community. For Thomas, citizenship was independence, and it was up to each citizen to do with that independence what they would.

But for Marshall, citizenship demanded inclusion. Only if the rights of citizenship were equally accessible could the promises of the nation's founding documents be fully realized. Whereas Thomas offered a negative freedom from government, Marshall championed a positive freedom to participate fully that must be protected by government and courts. This, too, had been there all along.

Marshall had taken his experience in segregated Baltimore and utilized the scars of his legalized exclusion from full citizenship to mount a crusade against systems of disenfranchisement. Marshall demanded that the Constitution be compelled to deliver on its principles of equality regardless of the nation's shameful history of excluding those who looked like him, and he believed that change was possible. "The progress has been dramatic, and it will continue," he told the audience in his speech on the Constitution's bicentennial.[30] Indeed, his own work as a lawyer had caused much of that progress, an effort that took place in courtrooms hostile to his very presence and in communities where he was more likely to be lynched than served a meal.

Marshall was never shy in acknowledging the distance still to travel toward full citizenship, but he also never lost faith in the power of law to push toward that goal. This meant that the Constitution must continue to evolve to combat the evolving efforts to undermine the ideal of inclusion and that both governments and judges must have greater discretion to protect and promote robust rights for all citizens. And while the work of Mr. Civil Rights will always be associated with the pursuit of African American rights, this view was not limited based on race. The obstacles to full citizenship were most severe for African Americans, making Marshall's work the ultimate test of his ideals. Further, as Marshall saw it, the way the nation treated African Americans reflected rights more broadly. "History teaches that when the Supreme Court has been willing to shortchange the equality rights of minority groups," Justice Marshall told a conference of judges in 1989, "other basic personal civil liberties like the rights of free speech and to personal security against unreasonable searches and seizures are also threatened."[31]

Because his retirement was made contingent on the confirmation of his successor, Justice Marshall continued as a member of the Supreme Court for several months after penning his dissent in *Payne v. Tennessee*. Though he did not speak publicly during the contentious confirmation of his successor, Marshall watched some of the hearings with an old colleague from the NAACP, William Coleman, who had made his own history in 1948 when he became the first Black law clerk at the Supreme Court, working with Justice Felix Frankfurter.[32] Coleman described the experience as a "most miserable time," while Marshall's colleague at the time, Antonin Scalia, noted that watching the confirmation "could not have been a pleasant experience for him to see his seat filled by someone who did not have his view on the matters that were closest to his heart." Still, Scalia said, "Marshall handled it with dignity and with class, as he did everything else."[33]

When Thomas was ultimately confirmed in October, Marshall's tenure officially concluded. The incoming justice paid a courtesy call on his predecessor. According to Thomas's autobiography, the visit lasted two-and-a-half hours, with Marshall the storyteller presiding one final time. "I did in my time what I had to do," Thomas recalled Marshall telling him. "You have to do in your time what you have to do."[34]

What Marshall had done was work to force the justices on the nation's court of last resort to redefine citizenship in ways that revolutionized the Constitution. But during his own tenure on the Supreme Court, that vision began to erode. After years of expanding protections and demanding inclusion, the Court began to embrace a more limited view of government and citizenship. Marshall's retirement was a massive turning point in that redefinition, the most impactful single transition on the Court over a period of at least seventy years. The Court's emerging vision emphasized different priorities, such as strict colorblindness, and deemphasized efforts to remedy historical inequities. For thirty years, Clarence Thomas offered a consistent vision encapsulating these views and, with further changes on the Court, led the way toward their ultimate embrace. The prevailing answers from the Court seem as far from Marshall's vision as they have ever been: his work took decades to build and has taken decades to transform.

What the next decades hold for the Court's definition of citizenship will be of enormous consequence to a nation that continues to grow more diverse. As they have always been, these are urgent questions, their significance demonstrated by the intensity of their contestation. And their resolution will depend to a great extent on the transitions that remain in the Court's future.

ACKNOWLEDGMENTS

It is difficult to even begin to acknowledge all of the people and forces that gave me the materials to complete this book. Since I am a teacher by trade, I will begin in my classrooms.

As mentioned in the Preface, my middle school social studies and history teacher, Mr. Jackson, provided a model for critical thinking and boldness that I continue to admire. Later, I was fortunate to have professors who inspired and pushed me, including Michael Stoff (for history) and Dorothea Barrett (for writing) during college, and Randall Kennedy, Gary Orfield, Samantha Power, and Jon Hanson during law school. In my own classrooms, I am forever indebted to the hundreds of students who have taken my Education and Civil Rights course at the University of Memphis Cecil C. Humphreys School of Law over the years. The conversations that began in those classes and the engagement of those students prompted me to continue along the path that led to this book. My students' enthusiasm and curiosity are the fuel that keep my own enthusiasm and curiosity from waning. I am particularly grateful to the students who participated in my Winter Break Book Club 2021, during which they reviewed an early version of this book and provided invaluable guidance and feedback: Demarcus Davis, Hailey Townsend, Kylie Ronnow, David McIntyre, Alex McWhirter, Jake Stoner, and Skkye Moreno.

So many friends and colleagues provided a word of encouragement or interest throughout this project. These helped ensure that the most difficult or discouraging moments did not last too long. I am thankful to all who have had to listen to me ramble on this topic over the years and who have provided a kind word at just the right time. Early on, Aram Goudsouzian and Charles McKinney helped convince me that I could indeed do this. As I explored how the project might come together, Randall Kennedy, James Forman Jr., Tomiko Brown-Nagin, Derek Black, Michelle Adams, Justin Driver, and Noah Feldman each offered notes or conversations that kept me on track. Tim Huebner provided an essential boost at a particularly important moment. Demetria Frank, Kevin Smith, Daphene McFerren, and Adriane Johnson-Williams may not recall our brief conversations, but each provided me valuable insight into both the challenges and potential of this book. Mike Cody and Jef Feibelman read portions of early drafts and played a significant role in that daunting task of freeing the work from the confines of my computer and sharing it with a wider world. (Speaking of my computer, I am grateful for my laptop, a reliable companion on this journey. At some point in the past three years, I got a new laptop that didn't spontaneously shut down Microsoft Word, which made the entire enterprise that much less frustrating, a reminder that a writer's tools are as crucial to the process as the ideas, perhaps more so.)

This book would not be possible without the incredible work of so many others that have explored the work of Justices Marshall and Thomas and the various subjects considered here. I am grateful to have learned from those cited throughout the book and many others as well, and I hope that I have built something interesting from those who have been in this space before me. My own research was aided greatly by my research assistants, Hailey Townsend and Kylie Ronnow, as well as the eager assistance of Jan Stone at my home library and several librarians at the Library of Congress who assisted in my work through the Thurgood Marshall papers. In addition, research support from the University of Memphis Research Fund made it possible for me to take the time in the summers that I needed to get this work done.

Thank you to Jim Levine, who helped me believe in the potential for this book and succeeded in navigating the frightening world of publishers. Thank you, also, to Courtney Paganelli at LGR for making everything work along the way.

From the first time I spoke with Marcela Maxfield at Stanford University Press, I knew that she got it! She understood precisely what I wanted to say and helped guide me toward doing so in a crisper, more accessible way. It means so much to have someone you can trust as an editor, and I came away from every conversation with Marcela overwhelmed by her care for the project and commitment to seeing it come to life. Jennifer Gordon offered detailed copyediting with a gentle hand that helped with precision and clarity of language, while Tim Roberts steered the production process with skill. I am grateful that each of you put so much care into this project. Thank you, also, to the staff members at SUP who have helped make the book real, the editorial board who gave it a green light, and the readers who offered important and valuable feedback.

My close family has lived with this book alongside me. If you are reading this, then the answer to the question you have been asking for some time ("When is the book coming out?") has been answered. While your encouragement and support of this project has been essential, it is nothing compared to the foundation you provide in everything I do. Mom and Dad, you helped nurture my curiosity and interest in history throughout my childhood and ensured that I had every opportunity to follow my heart. The model of Dad reading drove my own love of learning, and I can't wait to see a copy of this on your wall of books. Carly, your writing excellence offers a standard of crispness and wit I'll never reach but can continue to strive for. Joseph and Brian, your belief in me helps me believe in myself. Warren and Jeanne, thank you for your unadulterated support as well as for a forum for endless debate (you know who does which).

And then there are those who have had to live alongside me as I've worked through this book. First, thank you to Ginger and Hazel for being in the room where most of this book happened, squeaking away and providing a consistent symphony as I worked through difficult passages. Toby and Pippa, while you may have thought the early afternoon walks around the block were for your exercise, they were just as often to provide me with the necessary mental health break to allow me to continue working productively—thank you for seeing the best in me. Sadie and Ben, I am sorry that you will remember this portion of your lives as the part where every conversation led in some way to Thurgood Marshall or Clarence Thomas. But it all does somehow. Are you convinced yet? Your presence in my life pushes me to always be better, and I thank y'all for that. Keep asking questions and believing in magic. Meggan, for every doubt I had, you had confidence I could get this done in the way I imagined. That you think I can provides the foundation for every time I've stretched beyond my comfort zone. I am so lucky to be on this journey with you as a partner—so happy to be stuck with you.

NOTES

PREFACE

1. *Adams v. United States*, 319 U.S. 312 (1943).

2. *Payne v. Tennessee*, 501 U.S. 808, 844, 856 (1991) (Marshall, dissenting).

3. *Payne*, 501 U.S. at 856 (Marshall, dissenting).

4. *Payne,* 501 U.S. at 844 (Marshall, dissenting).

5. See *Payne v. State*, 2007 WL 4258178 (Tenn. Ct. Crim. App. 2007) (denying DNA testing).

6. *Tennessee v. Payne*, Nos. 87-04409 & 87-04410, Order (Tenn. Sup. Ct. Feb. 24, 2020) (setting execution date); Daniel Kiel, "Avoiding *Atkins*: How Tennessee Is on the Verge of Unconstitutionally Executing an Individual with Intellectual Disabilities," *Law and Inequality (Inequality Inquiry)* (2020), see footnotes 36, 74, 75, accessed July 7, 2022, https://lawandinequality.org/2020/11/18/avoiding-at-kins-how-tennessee-is-on-the-verge-of-unconstitutionally-executing-an-individu-al-with-intellectual-disabilities/#

7. *Atkins v. Virginia*, 536 U.S. 304 (2002).

8. Katherine Burgess, "Shelby County District Attorney Abandons Pursuit of Death Penalty in Pervis Payne Case," *The Commercial Appeal* (November 18, 2021).

INTRODUCTION

1. *City of Los Angeles v. Lyons*, 461 U.S. 95 (1983).

2. *Lyons*, 461 U.S. at 137 (Marshall, dissenting) ("The federal judicial power is now limited to levying a toll for such systematic constitutional violation" because

only damages and not injunctions are available unless a plaintiff can show that they will suffer the violation again in the future); *Lyons*, 461 U.S. at 115–116 and n.3 (Marshall, dissenting).

3. *Patton v. Mississippi*, 332 U.S. 463 (1947); *Taylor v. Alabama*, 335 U.S. 252 (1948) (confession coerced by threats and physical violence); *Watts v. Indiana*, 338 U.S. 49 (1949) (confession obtained after four days in solitary confinement); *Tinsley v. City of Richmond*, 368 U.S. 18 (1961) (due process claim of individual arrested for loitering while protesting outside of a department store); *Lyons v. Oklahoma*, 322 U.S. 596 (1944) (the Court did find that the confession was not admissible, but since Lyons had also confessed without coercion, his conviction was upheld).

4. See *Furman v. Georgia*, 408 U.S. 238, 363 (1972) (Marshall, concurring); *Lyons,* 461 U.S. at 116–118 (Marshall, dissenting). "The victim experiences extreme pain. His face turns blue as he is deprived of oxygen, he goes into spasmodic convulsions, his eyes roll back, his body wriggles, his feet kick up and down, and his arms move about wildly." *Id.* Eric Garner was also killed by a chokehold from police in 2015.

5. *PICS v. Seattle School District*, 551 U.S. 701 (2007); *Ricci v. Destefano*, 557 U.S. 557 (2009); *Shelby County v. Holder*, 570 U.S. 529 (2013) at 590 (Ginsburg, dissenting).

6. *Northwest Austin Municipal District v. Holder*, 557 U.S. 193, 216 (2009) (Thomas, concurring in part and dissenting in part); *Shelby County v. Holder*, 570 U.S. at 557 (Thomas, concurring); *Brnovich v. DNC*, 594 U.S. ___, 141 S.Ct. 2321 (2021); *Mississippi v. Flowers*, 588 U.S. ___, 139 S.Ct. 2228, 2252 (2019) (Thomas, dissenting).

7. Daniel Kiel, "A Bolt of Lightning: Measuring the Impact of Modern Transitions on the Supreme Court," 42 *Cardozo Law Review* 2813, 2828 (2021); see Figure 4, noting the difference in average Martin-Quinn score of justices on either side of a Court transition. See Andrew D. Martin and Kevin M. Quinn, "Dynamic Ideal Point Estimation via Markov Chain Monte Carlo for the U.S. Supreme Court, 1953–1999," 10 *Political Analysis* 134 (2002). See also "Measures," *Martin-Quinn Scores*, accessed July 7, 2022, https://perma.cc/DMB5-4P6N

8. The durability of the majority Thomas solidified can be seen in the fact that Justice Thomas's first term (1991–92) was also the first term in which Justice Sandra Day O'Connor occupied the ideological median of the Court (utilizing Martin-Quinn scores). Either Justice O'Connor or Justice Anthony Kennedy, both ideologically conservative during their tenures, occupied the median seat until both had retired by 2018. See generally Kiel, "A Bolt of Lightning."

9. Alexis de Tocqueville, *Democracy in America,* trans. George Lawrence (New York: Perennial Classics, 2000), 270.

10. *Mahanoy Area School District v. B.L.*, 594 U.S. __, 141 S.Ct. 2038, 2046 (2021); *Brown v. Board of Education*, 347 U.S. 483, 493 (1954).

11. Justin Driver, *The School House Gate: Public Education, The Supreme Court, and the Battle for the American Mind* (New York: Pantheon, 2018), 9.

12. *Holder v. Hall*, 512 U.S. 874, 892–893 (1994) (Thomas, concurring); *Brnovich v. DNC*, 594 U.S. ___, 141 S.Ct. 2321 (2021) at 2356 (Kagan, dissenting).

13. *Lyons*, 461 U.S. at 137 (Marshall, dissenting).

CHAPTER 1

1. See "National Bar Association (1925–)." *BlackPast,* accessed July 14, 2022, https://www.blackpast.org/african-american-history/national-bar-association-1925/ and "History," *National Bar Association*, accessed July 14, 2022, https://www.nationalbar.org/NBA/History.aspx. In an ironic twist, after his unsuccessful nomination to the nation's highest court, Judge Parker would remain seated on the federal Fourth Circuit Court of Appeals and would be one of three judges assigned in 1950 to a school desegregation case from Clarendon County, South Carolina, *Briggs v. Elliott.* Judge Parker would write the opinion in the *Briggs* case, rejecting the arguments of NAACP attorney Thurgood Marshall that South Carolina's segregation laws violated the U.S. Constitution. Upon appeal to the Supreme Court, *Briggs* would be consolidated with school desegregation cases from other states and heard under the heading of *Brown v. Board of Education.*

2. Gary Lee, "Black Lawyers' Group Divided on Thomas," *Washington Post* (August 5, 1991).

3. Neil A. Lewis, "Invitation to Justice Thomas Creates Furor," *New York Times* (May 29, 1998). Neil A. Lewis, "Justice Thomas Declines to Drop Speech to Bar," *New York Times* (June 17, 1998).

4. Lewis, "Invitation to Justice Thomas."

5. See Randall Kennedy, *Sellout: The Politics of Racial Betrayal* (New York: Pantheon, 2008) (devoting an entire chapter to "The Case of Clarence Thomas"), 87–143.

6. Kennedy, *Sellout,* 92.

7. Andrew Kaczynski, "Democratic Congressman Makes Shocking Racial Comments About Republicans, Clarence Thomas, Mitch McConnell," *BuzzFeed News* (April 29, 2014), accessed July 7, 2022, https://www.buzzfeednews.com/article/andrewkaczynski/democratic-congressman-makes-shocking-racial-comments-about; Catalina Camia, "Congressman Stands By Calling Clarence Thomas 'Uncle Tom,'" *USA Today* (April 30, 2014).

8. Kennedy, *Sellout,* 87–88.

9. Kennedy, *Sellout,* 96 n.27 (referencing an essay by Angelou in the *Black Scholar*).

10. A. Leon Higginbotham Jr., "Clarence Thomas in Retrospect," 45 *Hastings Law Journal* 1405, 1412 (1993).

11. Kevin Merida and Michael Fletcher, *Supreme Discomfort: The Divided Soul of Clarence Thomas* (New York: Broadway, 2007), 25. Thomas remarked "It's ridiculous that so-called black leaders in Savannah would jeopardize the future of young black children because they don't like me or my political leanings or my decisions." See also, Emma Whitford, "College Urged to Strip Clarence Thomas's Name from Building," *Inside Higher Ed* (October 15, 2018), accessed July 14, 2022, https://www.insidehighered.com/quicktakes/2018/10/15/college-urged-strip-clarence-thomass-name-building

12. "Black Judges and Lawyers: Arbiters and Advocates for Human Rights, Civil Justice and Economic Power" (Preliminary Agenda of the Judicial Council for the National Bar Association, August 7–11, 1988), *National Bar Association Digital Collection: Drake University Law Library,* accessed July 7, 2022, http://content.library.drake.edu/digital/collection/p16331coll9/id/2065

13. Gilbert King, *Devil in the Grove* (New York: Perennial, 2012), 2–5.

14. "Congress Names Building for Thurgood Marshall in Record Two Days," *Jet* (February 22, 1993).

15. *Furman v. Georgia*, 408 U.S. 238 (1972).

16. See, e.g., King, *Devil in the Grove,* 153–154 (describing disagreements between Marshall and William Patterson, leader of the Civil Rights Congress of the 1940s, about tactics for civil rights advocacy).

17. "Justice Marshall Receives National Bar Association Award." *C-SPAN* (August 10, 1988), accessed July 7, 2022, https://www.c-span.org/video/?3962-1/justice-marshall-receives-national-bar-association-award

18. Clarence Thomas, "Supreme Court Justice Speech," *C-SPAN* (July 29, 1998), accessed July 7, 2022, https://www.c-span.org/video/?109490-1/supreme-court-justice-speech; Robert D. McFadden, "Damon Keith, Federal Judge Who Championed Civil Rights, Dies at 96," *New York Times* (April 28, 2019).

19. Thomas, "Supreme Court Justice Speech."

20. Thomas, "Supreme Court Justice Speech."

21. Thomas, "Supreme Court Justice Speech."

22. And Justice Thomas's opinions on the subject do not seem to have softened either. Speaking of President Barack Obama, Thomas said that he had always believed that there would be a Black President:

"[T]he thing that I always knew is that it would have to be a Black President who was approved by the elites and the media, because anybody they didn't agree with, they would take apart. . . . You pick your person. Any Black person who says something that is not the prescribed things that they expect from a Black person will be picked apart."

Quoted in Nick Wing, "Clarence Thomas: Obama Only President Because He's What Elites Expect from a Black Person," *Huffington Post* (May 3, 2013) (describing comments from Justice Thomas at Duquesne University law school).

23. Adam Liptak, "Clarence Thomas Breaks 10 Years of Silence at Supreme Court," *New York Times* (February 29, 2016); see *Voisine v. U.S.*, 579 U.S. 686 (2016); "Oral Argument: Voisine v. United States," *Oyez*, accessed July 7, 2022, https://www.oyez.org/cases/2015/14-10154; Adam Liptak, "Justice Clarence Thomas Breaks His Silence," *New York Times* (January 14, 2013).

24. Jena McGregor, "Justice Thomas's Supreme Silence," *Washington Post* (January 17, 2013); Josh Gerstein, "Clarence Thomas Defends Silence in Supreme Court Health Care Arguments," *Politico* (April 6, 2012).

25. Robert Barnes, "Supreme Court Takes Modest but Historic Step with Teleconference Hearings," *Washington Post* (May 4, 2020) ("The day's surprise was Thomas, who at times on the court has gone a decade without asking a question"); see also Pete Williams, "Supreme Court Makes History with Oral Arguments by Phone. But It's Business as Usual for the Justices," *NBC News* (May 4, 2020) ("It was a day of firsts . . . ," such as the first time the justices were not together for oral argument, the first time audio of the argument was available live, and the first questions since March 2019 from Clarence Thomas).

26. See, e.g., Dahlia Lithwick, "Hands Off Thomas," *Slate* (May 30, 2009).

27. Steve Kroft, "Clarence Thomas: The Justice Nobody Knows," *CBS News: 60 Minutes* (September 27, 2007).

28. Juan Williams, *Thurgood Marshall: American Revolutionary* (New York: Three Rivers, 1998), 68.

29. Matt Ford, "Thurgood Marshall's Patient, but Relentless War," *The Atlantic* (September 6, 2007); Bob Woodward and Scott Armstrong, *The Brethren: Inside the Supreme Court* (New York: Simon & Shuster, 1979), 197.

30. Merida and Fletcher, *Supreme Discomfort,* 329–330.

31. Howard Ball, *A Defiant Life: Thurgood Marshall and the Persistence of Racism* (New York: Crown, 1999), 211; Edward V. Heck, "Justice Brennan and the Heyday of Warren Court Liberalism," 20 *Santa Clara Law Review* 841, 872 (1980) (indicating that Marshall and Brennan voted alike in 95 percent of cases over a two-year period early in Marshall's tenure).

32. Donna Coltharp, "Writing in the Margins: Brennan, Marshall, and the Inherent Weakness of Liberal Judicial Decision-Making," 29 *St. Mary's Law Journal* 1 (1997).

33. Merida and Fletcher, *Supreme Discomfort,* 323–328.

34. Carl Rowan, "Thomas Is Far from 'Home,'" *Chicago Sun-Times* (July 4, 1993).

35. Adam White, "Just, Wise, and Constitutional: Justice Thomas's Legacy in Law and Politics," *Law & Liberty* (April 17, 2014).

36. Merida and Fletcher, *Supreme Discomfort,* 328.

37. Coltharp, "Writing in the Margins," 35–40 (citing Hunter Clark's view that Brennan viewed Marshall as highly intelligent but uninterested in debating many matters before Court).

38. Merida and Fletcher, *Supreme Discomfort,* 333.

39. Nina Totenburg, "Justice Scalia, the Great Dissenter, Opens Up," *NPR Morning Edition* (April 28, 2008).

40. "General Convention," *Journal of the General Convention of . . . The Episcopal Church, Anaheim, 2009,* at 782, accessed July 7, 2022, https://episcopalarchives. org/cgi-bin/acts/acts_resolution.pl?resolution=2009-B020

41. Ian Schwartz, "Pence on Gorsuch: We Want to Give Clarence Thomas an Aid in His Lonely Fight," *Real Clear Politics* (February 5, 2017).

42. Emma Green, "The Clarence Thomas Effect," *The Atlantic* (July 10, 2019).

43. John Lewis, *Walking with the Wind* (New York: Harcourt Brace, 1998), 107.

CHAPTER 2

1. Juan Williams, *Thurgood Marshall: American Revolutionary* (New York: Three Rivers, 1998), 44, 52, 59.

2. Columbia Oral History Project, "The Reminiscences of Thurgood Marshall," in *Thurgood Marshall: His Speeches, Writings, Arguments, Opinions, and Reminiscences,* ed. Mark Tushnet (Chicago: Lawrence Hill, 2001), 413.

3. Williams, *Thurgood Marshall,* 22–23.

4. Williams, *Thurgood Marshall,* 17, 19.

5. Williams, *Thurgood Marshall,* 17–20.

6. Williams, *Thurgood Marshall,* 21–23.

7. Williams, *Thurgood Marshall,* 34.

8. Williams, *Thurgood Marshall,* 27–30.

9. "Public School No. 103," *Explore Baltimore Heritage,* accessed July 7, 2022, https://explore.baltimoreheritage.org/items/show/75

10. "Old Frederick Douglass High School (1924)," *Baltimore Places,* accessed July 7, 2022, http://places.baltimoreheritage.org/old-douglass-high-school/; Williams, *Thurgood Marshall,* 34.

11. Williams, *Thurgood Marshall,* 34–41.

12. Williams, *Thurgood Marshall,* 41–46.

13. Williams, *Thurgood Marshall,* 48–49.

14. Williams, *Thurgood Marshall,* 53.

15. Genna Rae McNeil, *Groundwork: Charles Hamilton Houston and the Struggle for Civil Rights* (Philadelphia: University of Pennsylvania Press, 1983), 64–65.

16. McNeil, *Groundwork,* 71.

17. Rawn James Jr., *Root and Branch: Charles Hamilton Houston, Thurgood Marshall, and the Struggle to End Segregation* (New York: Bloomsbury, 2010), 30.

18. Williams, *Thurgood Marshall,* 57, 59; James, *Root and Branch,* 32.

19. Williams, *Thurgood Marshall,* 55–56.

20. James, *Root and Branch,* 51.

21. Williams, *Thurgood Marshall,* 59.

22. McNeil, *Groundwork,* 114; James, *Root and Branch,* 56–58.

23. James, *Root and Branch*, 62.

24. McNeil, *Groundwork*, 134.

25. *Plessy v. Ferguson*, 163 U.S. 537 (1896) at 544, 551. Justice Brewer did not participate in the decision and Justice Harlan dissented.

26. *Plessy*, 163 U.S. at 551–552.

27. *Missouri, ex rel Gaines v. Canada*, 305 U.S. 337, 345–346 (1938); *Sipuel v. Bd of Regents of Univ of Oklahoma*, 332 U.S. 631 (1948); *Sweatt v. Painter*, 339 U.S. 629, 634 (1950).

28. *McLaurin v. Okla State Board of Regents*, 339 U.S. 637 (1950).

29. *McLaurin*, 339 U.S. at 642.

CHAPTER 3

1. Richard Kluger, *Simple Justice* (New York: Vintage, 1975), 4–6.

2. Kluger, *Simple Justice*, 8, 14–15.

3. Kluger, *Simple Justice*, 16–18.

4. Kluger, *Simple Justice*, 23, 302.

5. Kluger, *Simple Justice*, 291–294, 302; see also Robert Carter, *A Matter of Law* (New York: New Press, 2005), 96–97 (noting that the context of this meeting was making sure that southern NAACP leaders had the support for a frontal assault on segregation laws). In June 1950, Marshall had pushed a group of dozens of NAACP lawyers and leaders to endorse a resolution declaring that education cases "be aimed at obtaining education on a non-segregated basis."

6. Carter, *A Matter of Law*, 94.

7. Carter, *A Matter of Law*, 99.

8. Kluger, *Simple Justice*, 315–319, 336.

9. Kluger, *Simple Justice*, 318.

10. Kluger, *Simple Justice*, 330–331.

11. Kluger, *Simple Justice*, 334–335, 345, quote at 334. Incidentally, Byrnes had served for a year on the Supreme Court more than a decade earlier and perhaps understood the legal requirement of equalization under *Plessy* and the need for actual equalization in order to rebut constitutional challenges. In addition, he had served as secretary of state for President Truman and was aware that the nation's despicable treatment of Black citizens had a significant international public relations impact.

12. Kluger, *Simple Justice*, 335, 345, 347.

13. Carter, *A Matter of Law*, 103.

14. Kluger, *Simple Justice*, 348.

15. Kluger, *Simple Justice*, 353–354.

16. Kluger, *Simple Justice*, 363.

17. Kluger, *Simple Justice*, 363.

18. *Briggs v. Elliott*, 98 F.Supp. 529, at 532, 536 (E.D. S.C. 1951) ("*Briggs District Ct 1951*"). Because the constitutionality of a state law was at issue, federal court pro-

cedure required impaneling three judges rather than the typical single judge for trials in the district court. Marshall had attempted to avoid the three-judge panel when the case was first assigned to Judge Waties Waring, whom Marshall thought would be sympathetic to the plaintiffs' case and indeed proved to be the dissenter in the first hearing.

19. *Briggs District Ct 1951*, 98 F.Supp. at 531.

20. *Briggs v. Elliott*, 342 U.S. 350 (1952). Two justices, Justice Black and Justice Douglas, appeared ready to hear the case absent the additional evidence from the December report on the grounds that new facts were "wholly irrelevant to the constitutional questions presented." *Id.*, at 352. This suggests that these two justices, at least, were ready as early as 1952 to directly consider the constitutionality of segregation laws, a position the rest of the Court would arrive at two terms later with the *Brown* cases. See also, *Briggs v. Elliott*, 103 F.Supp. 920, 922 (E.D. S.C. 1952); *Brown v. Board of Education*, 98 F.Supp. 797 (D. Kan. 1951).

21. "1952 Argument: Briggs v. Elliott," in *Brown v. Board: The Landmark Oral Argument Before the Supreme Court*, ed. Leon Friedman (New York: New Press, 2004), 37.

22. Kluger, *Simple Justice*, 555–556 (with some referring to the evidence as "crap" or a "gimmick"); "1952 Argument: Briggs v. Elliott," 42, 63, 66–68.

23. Kluger, *Simple Justice*, 588–591, 656, 664 (Warren's appointment was on an interim basis; he would not actually be confirmed by the Senate until after the *Brown* oral argument, but before releasing the decision).

24. "1953 Argument: Briggs v. Elliott," in *Brown v. Board: The Landmark Oral Argument Before the Supreme Court*, ed. Leon Friedman (New York: New Press, 2004), 199–200, 239–240.

25. *Brown v. Board of Education*, 347 U.S. 483, 492–493 (1954) ("*Brown I*").

26. *Brown I*, 347 U.S. at 494 n.11.

27. *Brown I*, 347 U.S. at 495.

28. Juan Williams, *Thurgood Marshall: American Revolutionary* (New York: Three Rivers, 1998), 229.

CHAPTER 4

1. Clarence Thomas, *My Grandfather's Son* (New York: Perennial, 2007), 86.

2. Thomas, *My Grandfather's Son*, 87.

3. Thomas, *My Grandfather's Son,* 87–88.

4. Thomas, *My Grandfather's Son*, 99–100.

5. Thomas, *My Grandfather's Son*, 2–3.

6. Thomas, *My Grandfather's Son*, 1–3; Kevin Merida and Michael Fletcher, *Supreme Discomfort: The Divided Soul of Clarence Thomas* (New York: Broadway, 2007), 46.

7. Thomas, *My Grandfather's Son*, 4–5.

8. *Brown v. Board of Education*, 347 U.S. 483, 493 (1954) (*"Brown I"*).

9. Florance Street School," *Historical Marker Database,* accessed July 7, 2022, https://www.hmdb.org/marker.asp?marker=12088

10. Thomas, *My Grandfather's Son*, 6–8; Kevin Merida and Michael Fletcher, *Supreme Discomfort: The Divided Soul of Clarence Thomas* (New York: Broadway, 2007), 57.

11. Thomas, *My Grandfather's Son,* 8, 13.

12. Thomas, *My Grandfather's Son,* 12.

13. Thomas, *My Grandfather's Son,* 10–12; Merida and Fletcher, *Supreme Discomfort,* 78–81.

14. Thomas, *My Grandfather's Son,* 10–15, 20–21; Merida and Fletcher, *Supreme Discomfort,* 59.

15. Merida and Fletcher, *Supreme Discomfort,* 53.

16. Thomas, *My Grandfather's Son,* 27.

17. "1953 Argument: Briggs v. Elliott," in *Brown v. Board: The Landmark Oral Argument Before the Supreme Court*, ed. Leon Friedman (New York: New Press, 2004), 234, 237.

18. Congressional Record, 84th Congress Second Session, vol. 102, part 4 (March 12, 1956), 4459–4460 ("Southern Manifesto").

19. *Cooper v. Aaron*, 358 U.S. 1, 16 (1958); *Aaron v. McKinley*, 173 F.Supp. 944 (E.D. Ark. 1959).

20. Tomiko Brown-Nagin, *Courage to Dissent* (Oxford: Oxford University Press, 2011), 312, 315.

21. Merida and Fletcher, *Supreme Discomfort*, 16; Brown-Nagin, *Courage to Dissent*, 71; *Heyward v. Public Housing Administration*, 238 F.2d 689, 691 (5th Cir. 1956).

22. *Briggs v. Elliott,* 132 F. Supp. 776, 777 (E.D. S.C. 1955) (*"Briggs on Remand"*).

23. *Stell v. Savannah-Chatham County Board of Education*, 220 F.Supp. 667, 669–675, 683 (1963).

24. *Stell*, 220 F.Supp. at 674, 679–680, 683.

25. Jan Skutch, "1963, Desegregation Changed the Lives of 19 Savannah Teens, Society," *Savannah Morning News* (August 18, 2013).

CHAPTER 5

1. Kevin Merida and Michael Fletcher, *Supreme Discomfort: The Divided Soul of Clarence Thomas* (New York: Broadway, 2007), 68–69.

2. Jane Mayer, "Is Ginni Thomas a Threat to the Supreme Court?" *The New Yorker* (January 21, 2022); Bob Woodward and Robert Costa, "Virginia Thomas Urged White House Chief to Pursue Unrelenting Efforts to Overturn the 2020 Election, Texts Show," *Washington Post* (March 24, 2022); Emma Brown, "Ginni Thomas, Wife of Supreme Court Justice, Pressed Ariz. Lawmakers to Help Reverse Trump's Loss, Emails Show," *Washington Post* (May 20, 2022).

3. Clarence Thomas, *My Grandfather's Son* (New York: Perennial, 2007), 33.

4. Thomas, *My Grandfather's Son,* 36; Merida and Fletcher, *Supreme Discomfort,* 72–73.

5. Thomas, *My Grandfather's Son,* 33.

6. Thomas, *My Grandfather's Son,* 42–43.

7. Thomas, *My Grandfather's Son,* 43, 48; Diane Brady, *Fraternity* (New York: Spiegel & Grau, 2012).

8. Thomas, *My Grandfather's Son,* 50–54

9. Thomas, *My Grandfather's Son,* 51, 55.

10. Thomas, *My Grandfather's Son,* 54, 58, 63–64.

11. Thomas, *My Grandfather's Son,* 75.

12. Thomas, *My Grandfather's Son,* 70, 80–81 ("the point of becoming a lawyer was to help my people . . .").

13. Thomas, *My Grandfather's Son,* 75, 78.

14. Sonia Sotomayor, *My Beloved World* (New York: Knopf, 2013), 188–191.

15. Thomas, *My Grandfather's Son,* 56.

CHAPTER 6

1. *Smith v. Allwright,* 321 U.S. 649 (1944).

2. David Levering Lewis, *W. E. B. Du Bois: The Fight for Equality and the American Century, 1919–1963* (New York: Henry Holt, 2000), 498.

3. Lewis, *W. E. B. Du Bois,* 55–56.

4. Lewis, *W. E. B. Du Bois,* 337.

5. Lewis, *W. E. B. Du Bois,* 337.

6. W. E. B. Du Bois, *The Souls of Black Folk* (New York: Bantam Classic, 1989), 7.

7. Juan Williams, *Thurgood Marshall: American Revolutionary* (New York: Three Rivers, 1998), 49.

8. Lewis, *W. E. B. Du Bois,* 342.

9. Lewis, *W. E. B. Du Bois,* 335, 342–348.

10. W. E. B. Du Bois, "Does the Negro Need Separate Schools?" 4 *Journal of Negro Education* 328, 328–333 (1935).

11. Du Bois, "Does the Negro Need Separate Schools?" 335.

12. Lewis, *W. E. B. Du Bois,* 497.

13. Du Bois, "Does the Negro Need Separate Schools?" 332 ("The NAACP and other Negro organizations have spent thousands of dollars to prevent the establishment of segregated Negro schools, but scarcely a single cent to see that the division of funds between white and Negro schools, North and South, is carried out with some faint approximation of justice").

14. Richard Kluger, *Simple Justice* (New York: Vintage, 1975), 362 (re *Briggs* case at trial), 416 (*Brown* case at trial), 546 (Supreme Court brief), 574 (Supreme Court oral argument).

15. James Baldwin, *The Fire Next Time* (New York: Vintage International, 1963), 93–94.

16. Russell Rickford, *We Are an African People: Independent Education, Black Power, and the Radical Imagination* (Oxford: Oxford University Press, 2016), 82.

17. Martin Luther King Jr., "Our God Is Marching On," in *A Testament of Hope*, ed. James M. Washington (San Francisco: Harper, 1986), 227.

18. Jerome Morris, "Malcolm X's Critique of the Education of Black People," 25(2) *The Western Journal of Black Studies* 126, 130 (2001) (quoting a 1964 speech).

19. Rickford, *We Are an African People*, 2.

20. Rickford, *We Are an African People*, 3–6.

21. Rickford, *We Are an African People*, 40–41.

22. Du Bois, "Does the Negro Need Separate Schools?" 335.

23. Quoted in Michael Lackey, "A Brief History of the Haverford Group," in *The Haverford Discussions: A Black Integrationist Manifesto for Racial Justice*, ed. Michael Lackey (Charlottesville: University of Virginia Press, 2013), xxxix.

24. See, e.g., James Ryan, "Schools, Race, and Money," 109 *Yale Law Journal* 249, 258 (1999).

25. *Aaron v. Cooper*, 163 F.Supp. 13, 32 (E.D. Ark. 1958); *Aaron v. Cooper*, 257 F.2d 33, 40 (8th Cir. 1958).

26. "Oral Argument: Cooper v. Aaron," *Oyez*, accessed July 7, 2022, https://www.oyez.org/cases/1957/1_misc ("I don't see how anybody under the sun could say that after those children, those families, went through that for a year to tell them 'All you have done is gone. You fought for what you consider to be democracy and you lost. And you go back to the segregated school from which you came'").

27. "Oral Argument: Cooper v. Aaron."

28. *Cooper v. Aaron*, 358 U.S. 1, 4, 17 (1958) at 22 (Frankfurter concurring); see U.S. Constitution, Article VI.

29. Nick Kotz, *Judgment Days: Lyndon Baines Johnson, Martin Luther King Jr., and the Laws That Changed America* (New York: Houghton Mifflin, 2005).

CHAPTER 7

1. "Retirement of Justice Marshall," *C-SPAN* (June 28, 1991), accessed July 7, 2022, https://www.c-span.org/video/?18679-1/retirement-justice-marshall

2. See *Shelby County v. Holder*, 570 U.S. 529 (2013); *Brnovich v. DNC*, 594 U.S. ___, 141 S.Ct. 2321 (2021).

3. *Harrison v. Day*, 106 S.E.2d 636, 646 (Va. 1959).

4. *Green v. County School Board of New Kent County*, 391 U.S. 430, 432–434 (1968).

5. *Green*, 391 U.S. at 435 (1968).

6. *Green*, 391 U.S. at 437–438 (1968).

7. *Green*, 391 U.S. at 439 (1968).

8. *Alexander v. Holmes County Board of Education*, 396 U.S. 1218 (1969) (denying stay of 417 F.2d 852 (5th Cir. 1969)); cert granted and final opinion against school board at *Alexander v. Holmes County Board of Education*, 396 U.S. 19 (1969). Justice Black: "[T]here is no longer any excuse for permitting the 'all deliberate speed' phrase to delay the time when Negro children and white children will sit together and learn together in the same public schools."

9. "Oral Argument: Green v. County School Board of New Kent County," *Oyez*, accessed July 7, 2022, https://www.oyez.org/cases/1967/695

10. *Green*, 391 U.S. at 440 n.5. The report also identified the efforts being made to equalize all-Negro schools as working to discourage Black families from "choosing" to attend formerly all-white schools.

11. *Swann v. Charlotte-Mecklenburg Board of Education*, 402 U.S. 1, 6–7 (1971); *Swann v. Charlotte-Mecklenburg Board of Education*, 306 F.Supp. 1299, 1312 (W.D. N.C. 1969).

12. *Swann*, 402 U.S. at 15–17.

13. Juan Williams, *Thurgood Marshall: American Revolutionary* (New York: Three Rivers, 1998), 350 n.32.

14. *Board of Education of Oklahoma City v. Dowell*, 498 U.S. 237, 252–253 (1991) (Marshall, dissenting).

15. *Dowell*, 498 U.S. at 240 (Marshall, dissenting)..

16. *Dowell*, 498 U.S. at 241–242, at 254 (Marshall, dissenting).

17. *Dowell*, 498 U.S. at 255 (Marshall, dissenting).

18. *Dowell*, 498 U.S. at 244, 249–250 (Marshall, dissenting). Justice Souter did not participate in the case as he was confirmed to the Court between the argument in October 1990 and the decision in January 1991.

19. *Dowell*, 498 U.S. at 251 (Marshall, dissenting).

20. *Dowell*, 498 U.S. at 257–258 (Marshall, dissenting).

21. *Dowell*, 498 U.S. at 257, 259–260 (Marshall, dissenting).

22. *Dowell*, 498 U.S. at 251, 257, 261 (Marshall, dissenting) ("the majority's standard ignores how the stigmatic harm identified in *Brown I* can persist even after the state ceases actively to enforce segregation").

23. *Dowell*, 498 U.S. at 260 n.5, 262 (Marshall, dissenting).

24. *Dowell*, 498 U.S. at 268 (Marshall, dissenting).

25. *Dowell v. Okla City Bd of Educ*, 778 F.Supp. 1144 (W.D. Okla. 1991), aff'd by 8 F.3d 1501 (10th Cir. 1993). Between the tenures of the two justices, the Court further eased the path for school districts to be released from court supervision in *Freeman v. Pitts*, 503 U.S. 467 (1992).

CHAPTER 8

1. Gretchen Keiser, "Photo Inspires Look Back at Era When Catholic Schools Segregated," *Georgia Bulletin* (January 9, 2014) (newsletter of Atlanta's archdiocese).

2. Gary McDonogh, *Black and Catholic in Savannah, Georgia* (Knoxville: University of Tennessee Press, 1993), 120; Andria Segedy, "St. Pius X History: Savannah Churches, Community Opened Doors to Classical Education During Segregation," *Savannah Morning News* (September 15, 2018).

3. McDonogh, *Black and Catholic in Savannah,* 122–127.

4. McDonogh, *Black and Catholic in Savannah,* 127 ("The clash of two distinct if well-meaning paradigms produced a tragic process that scars the black and Catholic community to this day").

5. Heather Andrea Williams, *Self-Taught: African American Education in Slavery and Freedom* (Chapel Hill: University of North Carolina Press, 2005), 174–175; Jeanita W. Richardson and J. John Harris III, *"Brown* and Historically Black Colleges and Universities (HBCUs): A Paradox of Desegregation Policy," 73(3) *Journal of Negro Education,* 365, 371 (2004).

6. Bobby L. Lovett, *America's Historically Black Colleges and Universities: A Narrative History* (Atlanta: Mercer University Press, 2015), xi, 12–13.

7. *Murray v. Pearson,* 182 A. 590 (Md. 1935); *Missouri ex rel Gaines v. Canada,* 305 U.S. 337 (1938); *Sweatt v. Painter,* 339 U.S. 629, 634 (1950).

8. William B. Harvey, Adia M. Harvey, and Mark King, "The Impact of the Brown v. Board of Education Decision on Postsecondary Participation of African Americans," 73(3) *Journal of Negro Education* 328 (2004).

9. Taylor Branch, *Parting the Waters: America in the King Years, 1954–63* (New York: Simon & Schuster, 1988), 386.

10. Tomiko Brown-Nagin, *Civil Rights Queen: Constance Baker Motley and the Struggle for Equality* (New York: Pantheon, 2022), 141.

11. *Meredith v. Fair,* 305 F.2d 343, 344 (5th Cir. 1962).

12. See, generally, *Meredith v. Fair,* 305 F.2d 343; *Meredith v. Fair,* 83 S.Ct. 10 (1962); *Fair v. Meredith,* 371 U.S. 828 (1962) (denying cert).

13. Gene Roberts and Hank Klibanoff, *The Race Beat: The Press, the Civil Rights Struggle, and the Awakening of a Nation* (New York: Knopf, 2007), 274, 288 (political points, frenzy of resistance), 290 (marshals), 291 (rock throwing), 297 (forms at registrar's office).

14. *Ayers v. Allain,* 674 F.Supp. 1523, 1530 (N.D. Miss. 1987).

15. *U.S. v. Fordice,* 505 U.S. 717, 725 (1992).

16. *Ayers,* 674 F.Supp. at 1524, 1526–1529, 1554; *Ayers v. Allain,* 914 F.2d 676 (5th Cir. 1990); *Fordice,* 505 U.S. at 724–725. The five historically white institutions are University of Mississippi, Mississippi State University; Mississippi University for Women, University of Southern Mississippi, and Delta State University; the three historically Black institutions are Alcorn State University, Jackson State University, and Mississippi Valley State University.

17. *Fordice,* 505 U.S. at 729. Although all nine justices concurred in the ultimate outcome, Justice Scalia dissented in part from the majority opinion. 505 U.S. at 749 (Scalia, dissenting).

18. *Fordice,* 505 U.S. at 734–742 (Scalia, dissenting). For example, in the aftermath of James Meredith's enrollment at Ole Miss, three of the state's historically white institutions had adopted a minimum ACT score of 15 for admission. The effect was to disqualify the vast majority of Black applicants. By the time of trial in *Fordice,* the state still granted automatic admission to its formerly white institutions based on ACT scores, a policy that had a segregative effect in 1985: 72 percent of Mississippi's white high school seniors scored a 15 or above, but only 30 percent of Black seniors did.

19. Clarence Thomas, *My Grandfather's Son* (New York: Perennial, 2007), 42–43.

20. NAACP, "Editorial," *The Crisis* (January 1917); *Fordice,* 505 U.S. at 745 (Thomas, concurring).

21. *Fordice,* 505 U.S. at 746 (Thomas, concurring) (emphasis in original).

22. *Fordice,* 505 U.S. at 747–748 (Thomas, concurring) (emphasis in original).

23. *Fordice,* 505 U.S. at 748–749 (Thomas, concurring).

24. *Fordice,* 505 U.S. at 748–749 (Thomas, concurring); see also, Kevin Merida and Michael Fletcher, *Supreme Discomfort: The Divided Soul of Clarence Thomas* (New York: Broadway, 2007), 67.

25. *Missouri v. Jenkins,* 515 U.S. 70, 114, 121–122 (1995) (Thomas, concurring).

26. *Jenkins,* 515 U.S. at 120–122 (Thomas, concurring).

CHAPTER 9

1. "Junction School," *National Park Service,* accessed July 7, 2022, https://www.nps.gov/lyjo/planyourvisit/junctionschool.htm

2. Lyndon B. Johnson, "Signing of the Elementary and Secondary Education Act, 4/11/65," *LBJ Library,* accessed July 7, 2022, https://www.youtube.com/watch?v=QQzCViUdPLc

3. Christopher R. Berry, "School Consolidation and Inequality (September 2006)," *ResearchGate* (January 2007), accessed July 21, 2022, https://www.researchgate.net/profile/Christopher-Berry-8/publication/5091300_School_Consolidation_and_Inequality/links/54d243bb0cf25017917da65d/School-Consolidation-and-Inequality.pdf There were more than 120,000 school districts in 1930; by 2000, there were fewer than 20,000 districts. *Id.* at 27 (fig. 3).

4. Noah Feldman, *The Three Lives of James Madison* (New York: Picador, 2017), 101–105.

5. Joel Richard Paul, *Without Precedent: Chief Justice John Marshall and His Times* (New York: Riverhead, 2018), 93.

6. H. W. Brands, *Heirs of the Founders* (New York: Doubleday, 2018), 27, 149–150. Calhoun claimed that federal tariffs were making farmers of the South "serfs of the system, out of whose labor is raised not only the money paid into the Treasury, but the funds out of which are drawn the rich rewards of the manufacturer and his associates in interest" (149).

7. Feldman, *The Three Lives of James Madison*, 224.

8. Carol Anderson, *The Second: Race and Guns in a Fatally Unequal America* (New York: Bloomsbury, 2021); see also U.S. Constitution, Ninth Amendment.

9. Brands, *Heirs of the Founders,* 82–85.

10. U.S. Constitution, Article 1, Section 2. Though the three-fifths clause is often pointed to as evidence that the Constitution denied full humanity to African Americans held in bondage, the true abolitionist position would have been to not count such individuals at all for purposes of apportionment, as such a complete exclusion would have denied any representative power derived in slave states from the presence of entirely disenfranchised individuals.

11. See *Scott v. Emerson*, 15 Mo. 576 (Mo. 1852). Scott's initial case was dismissed due to the exclusion of evidence crucial to his case; though he won a subsequent case at trial, the Missouri Supreme Court reversed the decision and denied Scott's claim.

12. *Dred Scott v. Sandford*, 60 U.S. 393, at 404 (1857).

13. *Dred Scott*, 60 U.S. at 451–452. By the time of the *Dred Scott* decision, the Kansas–Nebraska Act (1854) had largely superseded the Missouri Compromise.

14. David D. Blight, *Frederick Douglass* (New York: Simon & Schuster, 2018), 425. Douglass, like Marshall, was from Maryland and spent some of his early years in bondage in Baltimore.

15. "Freedmen's Bureau Acts of 1865 and 1866," *U.S. Senate*, accessed July 7, 2022, https://www.senate.gov/artandhistory/history/common/generic/FreedmensBureau.htm

16. Blight, *Frederick Douglass*, 425.

17. See Paul Cimbala and Randall Miller, eds., *The Freedmen's Bureau and Reconstruction: Reconstructing America* (New York: Fordham University Press, 1999). See https://www.history.com/topics/black-history/freedmens-bureau:

There was no tradition of government responsibility for a huge refugee population and no bureaucracy to administer a large welfare, employment and land reform program.... Congress and the army and the Freedmen's Bureau were groping in the dark. They created the precedents.

Ron Chernow, *Grant* (New York: Penguin, 2017), 644:

Federal power had expanded immeasurably, testing the president's ability to manage the change. The National Bank Acts, the Homestead Act, the Morrill Acts setting up land-grant universities—such war-time measures dramatically broadened Washington's authority. Boasting 53,000 employees, the federal government ranked as the nation's foremost employer. Before the war, it had touched citizens' lives mostly through the postal system. Now it taxed citizens directly, conscripted them into the army, oversaw a national economy, and managed a giant national debt.

18. U.S. Constitution, Amendments Thirteen, Fourteen, Fifteen.

19. See, e.g., Chernow, *Grant,* 789 (regarding terrorism in Mississippi that intim-

idated Black voters and eventually led to the replacement of elected Black leaders: "The Vicksburg vote showed the fundamental weakness of a political revolution that had relied heavily on force applied by outsiders in Washington—something that couldn't be maintained indefinitely").

20. *Civil Rights Cases,* 109 U.S. 3, 11, 25 (1883). Among the five cases that make up the *Civil Rights Cases,* the Missouri case was *U.S. v. Nichols.* The Civil Rights Act of 1875:

That all persons within the jurisdiction of the United States shall be entitled to the full and equal enjoyment of the accommodations, advantages, facilities, and privileges of inns . . . subject only to the conditions and limitations established by law and applicable alike to citizens of every race and color, regardless of any previous condition of servitude.

Civil Rights Cases, at 9.

21. *Plessy v. Ferguson,* 163 U.S. 537, 552 (1896).

22. Nicholas Lemann, "Hating on Herbert Hoover," *The New Yorker* (October 16, 2017).

23. See, e.g., *Hammer v. Dagenhart,* 247 U.S. 251 (1918); *U.S. v. Darby,* 312 U.S. 100 (1941).

24. Richard Rothstein, *The Color of Law* (New York: Livewright, 2017); *Shelley v. Kraemer,* 334 U.S. 1 (1948).

25. Lyndon B. Johnson, "Commencement Address at Howard University: 'To Fulfill These Rights' (June 4, 1965)," *Teaching American History,* accessed July 7, 2022, https://teachingamericanhistory.org/library/document/commencement-address-at-howard-university-to-fulfill-these-rights/ /

26. See Nicholas Buccola, *The Fire Is Upon Us* (Princeton: Princeton University Press, 2019), 84.

27. Alexander Hamilton, "No. 78: The Judiciary Department," in *The Federalist Papers,* ed. Charles R. Kesler (New York: Signet Classic, 1961), 463.

28. Buccola, *The Fire Is Upon Us,* 84.

29. Ronald Reagan, "A Time for Choosing (October 27, 1964)," *Ronald Reagan Presidential Library,* accessed July 7, 2022, https://www.youtube.com/watch?v=qXBswFfh6AY

30. Adam Cohen, *Supreme Inequality: The Supreme Court's Fifty-Year Battle for a More Unjust America* (New York: Penguin, 2020), xvii.

31. Cohen, *Supreme Inequality,* 26–27.

32. Cohen, *Supreme Inequality,* 36; see "Supreme Court Nominations (1789–Present)," *U.S. Senate,* accessed July 7, 2022, https://www.senate.gov/legislative/nominations/SupremeCourtNominations1789present.htm

Washington appointed all initial members of the Court in 1789. Andrew Jackson had two appointments in his first twelve months. Ulysses Grant had two appointments confirmed in his thirteenth month, though one was for a newly created seat. William Howard Taft had two in first thirteen months. Harry Truman had two in his first fourteen months.

33. Cohen, *Supreme Inequality*, 56–59.

34. Richard Kluger, *Simple Justice* (New York: Vintage, 1975) 605–606.

35. Cohen, *Supreme Inequality*, 61.

CHAPTER 10

1. Joyce A. Baugh, *The Detroit School Busing Case* (Lawrence: University Press of Kansas, 2011), 68–69. The committee included Judge Damon Keith, the person who introduced Clarence Thomas at the NBA speech in Memphis in the 1990s. *Id.*, at 74.

2. Paul A. Sracic, *San Antonio v. Rodriguez and the Pursuit of Equal Education* (Lawrence: University Press of Kansas, 2006), 20.

3. Wil Haygood, *Showdown: Thurgood Marshall and the Supreme Court Nomination That Changed America* (New York: Knopf, 2015), 261–262; Isabel Wilkerson, *The Warmth of Other Suns* (New York: Vintage, 2010), 131.

4. Richard Rothstein, *The Color of Law* (New York: Livewright, 2017), 74 (includes a picture of the wall at 58).

5. See *Shelley v. Kraemer*, 334 U.S. 1 (1948). Marshall served as counsel at the Supreme Court in the companion case from Detroit, entitled *Sipes v. McGhee*. See *Sipes v. McGhee*, 316 Mich. 614 (1947) (reversed by *Shelley v. Kraemer*).

6. Baugh, *The Detroit School Busing Case*, 29, 37. See Lorraine Hansberry, *A Raisin in the Sun* (New York: Vintage, 1958).

7. Wilkerson, *The Warmth of Other Suns*, 378; see also Rothstein, *The Color of Law*, 146–147 (quoting a Michigan Civil Rights Commission report: "our experience has been that nearly all attempts by black families to move to Detroit's suburbs have been met with harassment").

8. Baugh, *The Detroit School Busing Case*, 25–26, 38 (speaking about Dearborn, Livonia, and Warren; also notes that in only 2 of 27 suburbs with more than 35,000 people was the Black population more than 3 percent).

9. Haygood, *Showdown*, 262–263, 275, 279. Senator John McClellan of Arkansas commented, "I cannot support the nomination of anybody . . . who I think will not sustain the right of the sovereign to protect itself against internal danger, especially with the Constitution authorizing a reasonable search and seizure" (275).

10. U.S. Department of Justice, "National Advisory Commission on Civil Disorders, Report" (1967) (Kerner Commission Report), at 1, accessed on July 7, 2022, https://www.ncjrs.gov/pdffiles1/Digitization/8073NCJRS.pdf

11. *Rodriguez v. San Antonio ISD*, 337 F.Supp. 280, 281 (W.D. Tex. 1971) (noting that in addition to the seven districts within San Antonio, there were five additional rural districts within Bexar County) ("*Rodriguez-District Court*"); *San Antonio ISD v. Rodriguez*, 411 U.S. 1, 12 (1973).

12. *Rodriguez*, 411 U.S. at 12–13.

13. *Rodriguez-District Court*, 337 F.Supp. 280 (W.D. Tex. 1971). Because this was a three-judge panel (due to the constitutionality of a state statute being at issue), the appeal went directly from the district court to the Supreme Court.

14. Baugh, *The Detroit School Busing Case*, 70–74, 80–83.

15. *Bradley v. Milliken*, 338 F.Supp. 582, 586 (E.D. Mich. 1971) (*"Milliken-District Ct. 1971"*). In addition, Detroit experienced the largest increase in the percentage of Black students among large northern school districts between 1968 and 1970.

16. *Milliken-District Ct. 1971*, 338 F.Supp. at 585; *Bradley v. Milliken*, 345 F.Supp. 914, 916 (E.D. Mich. 1972) (*"Milliken-District Ct. 1972"*).

17. *State Ice Co. v. Liebmann*, 285 U.S. 262, 311 (1932) (Brandeis, dissenting).

18. *Rodriguez*, 411 U.S. at 49–50.

19. *Milliken v. Bradley*, 418 U.S. 717, 741–742 (1974).

20. *Rodriguez*, 411 U.S. at 43.

21. *Milliken*, 418 U.S. at 743–744.

22. *Rodriguez*, 411 U.S. at 32.

23. *Milliken*, 418 U.S. at 782 (Marshall, dissenting) ("I cannot subscribe to this emasculation of our constitutional guarantee of equal protection of the laws and must respectfully dissent"); see also *Rodriguez*, 411 U.S. at 98 (Marshall, dissenting) ("I cannot accept such an emasculation of the Equal Protection Clause in the context of this case"); at 70–71 (1973) (Marshall, dissenting) ("Most unfortunately, though, the majority's holding can only be seen as a retreat from our historic commitment to equality of educational opportunity and as unsupportable acquiescence in a system which deprives children in their earliest years of the chance to reach their full potential as citizens"); *Milliken*, 418 U.S. at 782 (Marshall, dissenting).

24. *Milliken*, 418 U.S. at 756, note 2 (Stewart, concurring); *Milliken*, 418 U.S. at 806 (Marshall, dissenting). It may be worth noting that Marshall used the word "interposition" in describing the use of district boundaries as barriers to effective desegregation. "Interposition" was the word used by Jefferson in arguing that Kentucky could simply ignore state law and that Faubus had used in arguing that Arkansas need not abide by *Brown*. *Milliken*, 418 U.S. at 783 (Marshall, dissenting) ("I perceive no basis either in law or in the practicalities of the situation justifying the state's imposition of school district boundaries as absolute barriers to the implementation of an effective desegregation remedy").

25. *Rodriguez*, 411 U.S. at 84, 128–129 (Marshall, dissenting).

26. *Milliken*, 418 U.S. at 805, 808 (Marshall, dissenting).

27. *Rodriguez*, 411 U.S. at 132 (Marshall, dissenting).

28. *Rodriguez*, 411 U.S. at 71 (Marshall dissenting).

29. *Milliken*, 418 U.S. at 783 (Marshall, dissenting).

CHAPTER 11

1. *Milliken v. Bradley,* 418 U.S. 717, 804 (1974) (Marshall, dissenting); Kevin Fox Gotham, "Missed Opportunities, Enduring Legacies: Segregation and Desegregation in Kansas City, Missouri," 43(2) *American Studies* 5, 18 (Summer 2002).

2. Gotham, "Missed Opportunities, Enduring Legacies," 17 (table 4). The same pattern held for high schools. *Id.,* at 19 (table 5). Monroe Billington, "Public School Integration in Missouri, 1954–64," 35(3) *Journal of Negro Education* 252, 261 (Summer 1966).

3. Gotham, "Missed Opportunities, Enduring Legacies," 24.

4. Clarence Thomas, *My Grandfather's Son* (New York: Perennial, 2007), 107.

5. See Kennell Jackson Jr., "Review: *Black Education: Myths and Tragedies,*" 5(7) *Change* 58, 59 (September 1973).

6. Thomas, *My Grandfather's Son,* 107.

7. Thomas, *My Grandfather's Son,* 104–105.

8. Thomas, *My Grandfather's Son,* 106 (quoting Sowell's *Race and Economics*).

9. Thomas, *My Grandfather's Son,* 106.

10. Thomas, *My Grandfather's Son,* 107, 122–123; Corey Robin, *The Enigma of Clarence Thomas* (New York: Metropolitan, 2019), 84–103.

11. Robin, *The Enigma of Clarence Thomas,* 84.

12. Juan Williams, "Black Conservatives, Center Stage," *Washington Post* (December 16, 1980).

13. Thomas, *My Grandfather's Son,* 133–135.

14. Gareth Davies, *See Government Grow: Education Politics from Johnson to Reagan* (Lawrence: University Press of Kansas, 2007), 75–76, 246–247.

15. Davies, *See Government Grow,* 248–249, 258.

16. Thomas, *My Grandfather's Son,* 146.

17. Thomas, *My Grandfather's Son,* 146–147.

18. Kevin Merida and Michael Fletcher, *Supreme Discomfort: The Divided Soul of Clarence Thomas* (New York: Broadway, 2007), 154, 159–163 (detailing some disagreements during Thomas's tenure at the EEOC); Robin, *The Enigma of Clarence Thomas,* 87 (noting that a colleague within the Reagan administration called Thomas "a radical, almost a black nationalist").

19. Davies, *See Government Grow,* 257–258, 267.

20. *Milliken v. Bradley,* 433 U.S. 267, 272–273, 277 (1977) ("*Milliken II*"); at 291 (Marshall, concurring).

21. In Missouri, a court had ordered districts consolidated due to a finding that each had committed constitutional violations. Among the consolidated districts was Ferguson, the site of the murder of Michael Brown and significant Black Lives Matter demonstrations in 2015. See *U.S. v. Missouri,* 515 F.2d 1365 (8th Cir. 1975).

22. *Jenkins v. Missouri,* 593 F.Supp. 1485, 1494 (W.D. Mo. 1984); *Jenkins v. Mis-*

souri, 639 F.Supp. 19, 30–33 (W.D. Mo. 1985). See *Missouri v. Jenkins,* 495 U.S. 33, 40 (1990) (summarizing district court decisions in 1985 and 1986) (*"Jenkins 1990"*); at 60 (Kennedy, concurring).

23. *Jenkins 1990,* 495 U.S. at 38–41.

24. *Jenkins 1990,* 495 U.S. at 51–55.

25. See *Keyes v. Denver School District, No. 1,* 413 U.S. 189 (1973); *Jenkins 1995,* 515 U.S. at 80.

26. *Jenkins 1995,* 515 U.S. at 78–79.

27. *Missouri v. Jenkins,* 515 U.S. 70, 121–123 (1995) (Thomas, concurring) (*"Jenkins 1995"*).

28. *Jenkins 1995,* 515 U.S. at 124–126 (Thomas, concurring).

29. *Jenkins 1995,* 515 U.S. at 128–129 (Thomas, concurring).

30. *Jenkins 1995,* 515 U.S. at 125, 132–133 (Thomas, concurring).

31. *Milliken,* 418 U.S. at 782, 802 (Marshall, dissenting).

32. *Jenkins 1995,* 515 U.S. at 114–117 (Thomas, concurring). In this, Justice Thomas echoed similar arguments made in Justice Stewart's *Milliken* concurrence.

33. *Jenkins 1995,* 515 U.S. at 120–121 (Thomas, concurring); also see 119–120 and n.2 ("Such assumptions and any social science research upon which they rely certainly cannot form the basis upon which we decide matters of constitutional principle." The note begins: "The studies cited in *Brown I* have received harsh criticism").

34. *Jenkins 1995,* 515 U.S. at 138 (Thomas, concurring).

35. See *Reed v. Rhodes,* 422 F.Supp. 708, 795–796 (N.D. Ohio 1976) (noting the "direction of the future is to wholly separate school districts, rather than integrated suburban school districts"); *Reed v. Rhodes,* 179 F.3d 453, 458 (6th Cir. 1999) (noting that the district court had overseen two decades of busing to ensure that each school had a racial makeup within 15 percent of the district's overall makeup); *Reed v. Rhodes,* 934 F.Supp. 1533 (N.D. Ohio 1996) (releasing the district from its desegregation order under the lowered standard articulated in *Dowell*); *Zelman v. Simmons-Harris,* 536 U.S. 639, 644–647, 653 (2002) (noting that 96 percent of the 3,700 Cleveland students who utilized vouchers during the 1999–2000 school year enrolled in religious schools).

36. *Zelman,* 536 U.S. at 676 (Thomas, concurring).

37. *Zelman,* 536 U.S. at 680–682 (Thomas, concurring) (citing statistics on public opinion toward vouchers compiled by Terry Moe, one of the earliest and strongest supporters of voucher programs).

38. *Zelman,* 536 U.S. at 682–683 (Thomas, concurring).

39. *Milliken,* 411 U.S. at 71 (Marshall, dissenting).

40. See Clarence Page, "Thomas' Sister Gives Lie to Welfare Fable," *Chicago Tribune* (July 24, 1991); Karen Tumulty, "Sister of High Court Nominee Traveled Different Road," *Los Angeles Times* (July 5, 1991).

CHAPTER 12

1. Noah Feldman, *The Three Lives of James Madison* (New York: Picador, 2017).

2. H. W. Brands, *Heirs of the Founders* (New York: Doubleday, 2018), 225–226 (describing the reactions of English writer Harriet Martineau, who observed great variety among those gathered in the U.S. Congress).

3. U.S. Constitution, First Amendment.

4. *Abrams v. U.S.*, 250 U.S. 616, 630 (1919) (Holmes, dissenting).

5. Thurgood Marshall, "Reflections on the Bicentennial of the United States Constitution," in *Thurgood Marshall: His Speeches, Writings, Arguments, Opinions, and Reminiscences*, ed. Mark Tushnet (Chicago: Lawrence Hill, 2001), 281.

6. *U.S. v. Carolene Products*, 304 U.S. 144, 152 n.4 (1938).

7. "Retirement of Justice Marshall," *C-SPAN* (June 28, 1991), accessed July 7, 2022, https://www.c-span.org/video/?18679-1/retirement-justice-marshall

8. "Retirement of Justice Marshall."

9. "Retirement of Justice Marshall."

10. "Supreme Court Nomination Announcement," *C-SPAN* (July 1, 1991), accessed July 7, 2022, https://www.c-span.org/video/?18649-1/supreme-court-nomination-announcement

11. "Supreme Court Nomination Announcement."

12. "Supreme Court Nomination Announcement."

13. "Supreme Court Nomination Announcement"; Wil Haygood, *Showdown: Thurgood Marshall and the Supreme Court Nomination That Changed America* (New York: Knopf, 2015).

14. "Supreme Court Nomination Announcement."

15. "Retirement of Justice Marshall"; "Supreme Court Nomination Announcement."

16. "Supreme Court Nomination Announcement."

17. *Plessy v. Ferguson*, 163 U.S. 537, 559, 563 (1896) (Harlan, dissenting) ("there would remain a power in the states, by sinister legislation, to interfere with the full enjoyment of the blessings of freedom . . . and to place in a condition of legal inferiority a large body of American citizens").

18. Civil Rights Act of 1964 §7, 42 U.S.C. §2000e et seq. (1964).

19. *Griggs v. Duke Power*, 401 U.S. 424, 429–430 (1971).

20. *Watson v. Fort Worth Bank and Trust*, 487 U.S. 977, 993 (1988) (plurality opinion). See also *Connecticut v. Teal*, 457 U.S. 440, 463 (1982) (Powell, dissenting) (for employers with limited funds, the result "may well be the adoption of simple quota hiring").

21. *Wards Cove Packing Co. v. Atonio*, 490 U.S. 642 (1989). See *id.*, at 652 (Justice Kennedy noting that the only practical option for many employers "would be to

adopt racial quotas, insuring that no portion of their work forces deviated in racial composition").

22. See Gary A. Moore and Michael K. Braswell, "Quotas and the Codification of the Disparate Impact Theory: What Did *Griggs* Really Say and Not Say?" 55 *Albany Law Review* 459, 472 (1991); *City of Richmond v. J.A. Croson, Co.*, 488 US 469, 528, 551–552 (1989) (Marshall dissenting).

23. *Croson,* 488 U.S. at 549–452, 558 (Marshall dissenting).

24. *Croson,* 488 U.S. at 493. Note, however, that the Court had approved set-asides in federal contracts in 1980. *Fullilove v. Klutznick*, 448 U.S. 448 (1980).

25. Clarence Thomas, "Affirmative Action Goals and Timetables: Too Tough? Not Tough Enough!" 5 *Yale Law & Policy Review* 402, 403 n.3 (1987).

26. Thomas, "Affirmative Action Goals and Timetables," 404, 406–407. See *id.*, at n.6 (noting a Statement of Enforcement Policy from 1984 setting forth this EEOC enforcement goal).

27. Thomas, "Affirmative Action Goals and Timetables," 410–411.

28. William M. Welch, "Thomas Presided over Shift in Policy at EEOC, Records Show," *Associated Press* (July 25, 1991).

29. Welch, "Thomas Presided over Shift in Policy at EEOC."

30. "Supreme Court Nominations (1789–Present)," *U.S. Senate*, accessed July 7, 2022, https://www.senate.gov/legislative/nominations/SupremeCourtNominations1789present.htm

31. *Croson,* 488 U.S. at 561 (Marshall, dissenting).

32. Thomas, "Affirmative Action Goals and Timetables," 405.

CHAPTER 13

1. U.S. Commission on the Bicentennial of the U.S. Constitution, "We the People" (1976), vi–viii, 10-14. The commission included senators, members of Congress, federal judges, scholars, and others. It included Senator Strom Thurmond of South Carolina, who had signed the Southern Manifesto, had run for president on an avowedly racist platform in 1948, and had denigrated Marshall at his 1967 confirmation hearings. It also included Phyllis Schlafly, who had opposed the Equal Rights Amendment for women. There were two African Americans on the initial commission in 1985: E. V. Hill, a pastor at Mount Zion Missionary Baptist Church in Los Angeles who had delivered the prayer at Richard Nixon's inauguration and was aligned with Republican politicians, and William Lucas, the chief executive of Wayne County (Detroit), Michigan, who had recently switched parties and would be the Republican candidate for governor of Michigan in 1986. Judge Damon Keith was eventually appointed to the commission in 1990 to replace Lucas.

2. Thurgood Marshall, "Reflections on the Bicentennial of the United States Constitution," in *Thurgood Marshall: His Speeches, Writings, Arguments, Opinions, and Reminiscences*, ed. Mark Tushnet (Chicago: Lawrence Hill, 2001), 281.

3. Marshall, "Reflections on the Bicentennial of the United States Constitution."

4. Marshall, "Reflections on the Bicentennial of the United States Constitution."

5. Stuart Taylor Jr., "Marshall Sounds Critical Note on Bicentennial," *New York Times* (May 7, 1987).

6. Ronald Reagan, "Address Before a Joint Session of Congress on the State of the Union—1987," *Ronald Reagan Presidential Library and Museum*, accessed August 24, 2022, https://www.reaganlibrary.gov/archives/speech/address-joint-session-congress-state-union-1987

7. Michael Selmi, "The Life of *Bakke:* An Affirmative Action Retrospective," 87 *Georgetown Law Journal* 981, 984–985 (1998); see also Joel Dreyfuss and Charles Lawrence III, *The Bakke Case: The Politics of Inequality* (New York: Harcourt, 1979); *Bakke v. Regents of the Univ. of California*, 553 P.2d 1152, 1157 (Cal. 1976) ("*Bakke–California*").

8. See Brief of the National Medical Association, et al., in *Bakke v. Regents of the Univ. of California*, 1977 WL 189515, 26, 28 (1977) ("NMA Brief").

9. NMA Brief, 54.

10. NMA Brief, 42–43 (quoting David Saxon, president of the University of California, in testimony before the California legislature on March 2, 1977).

11. *Bakke–California*, 553 P.2d at 1158–1159.

12. *Korematsu v. U.S.*, 323 U.S. 214, 216 (1944).

13. *Washington v. Davis*, 426 U.S. 229 (1976). See also *Village of Arlington Heights v. Metropolitan Housing Corp.*, 429 U.S. 252 (1977). In later years, the Court extended this reading of discrimination as requiring intent from its constitutional disparate impact cases to claims brought under employment statutes. In that context, Justice O'Connor wrote that "a contrary ruling on this point would almost inexorably lead to the use of numerical quotas in the workplace." *Wards Cove Packing Co. v. Atonio*, 490 U.S. 642, 653 (1989) (*Wards Cove* was a 5–4 decision with Marshall in dissent with Blackmun, Stevens, and Brennan).

14. Selmi, "The Life of *Bakke*," 987, 989. *Bakke* was not the first case of its kind to reach the Court. In 1974, the Court had punted on the substantive questions raised in dismissing the case of Martin DeFunis for being moot since DeFunis had ultimately been admitted to the defendant institution and was about to graduate. In that case, Justice Brennan had noted (in a dissent joined by Justice Marshall) that the issues would "inevitably return to the federal courts, and ultimately again to this Court." *DeFunis v. Odegaard*, 416 U.S. 312, 350 (1974) (Brennan, dissenting). The *Bakke* case proved Brennan right. In *DeFunis*, Justice William Douglas was the only justice to grapple with the scrutiny question. His dissent, particularly Part III, is a fascinating exploration of the law and policy behind affirmative action. *Id.* at 331–344 (Douglas, dissenting).

15. "Oral Argument: Regents of the Univ. of California v. Bakke," *Oyez*, accessed July 7, 2022, https://www.oyez.org/cases/1979/76-811

16. Selmi, "The Life of *Bakke*," 98; "Oral Argument: Bakke."

17. "Oral Argument: Bakke."

18. "Thurgood Marshall Papers, 1949–1991," Library of Congress, Manuscript Division, Washington, DC, catalog record: https://lccn.loc.gov/mm92081427. The *Bakke* case file is Box 203 in the "Supreme Court File"; Selmi, "The Life of Bakke," 990–991 (noting that the Bakke file spans seven folders and is "unusually rich").

19. Selmi, "The Life of *Bakke*," 991–993. It seems also that at least one justice was influenced by not wanting to appear to have ducked the affirmative action issue twice, after *DeFunis*.

20. Selmi, "The Life of *Bakke*," 993.

21. Selmi, "The Life of *Bakke*," 994.

22. *Regents of the Univ. of California v. Bakke,* 438 U.S. 265, 394 (1978) (Marshall, separate opinion) ("*Bakke–Supreme*").

23. *Bakke–Supreme,* 438 U.S. at 395–396 (Marshall, separate opinion).

24. *Bakke–Supreme,* 438 U.S. at 396–398, 401 (Marshall, separate opinion)

25. *Bakke–Supreme,* 438 U.S. at 401–402 (Marshall, separate opinion).

26. *Bakke–Supreme,* 438 U.S. at 400–401 (Marshall, separate opinion).

27. *Bakke–Supreme,* 438 U.S. at 289, 291; Id., at 327, 357–358 (Brennan, concurring in part and dissenting in part).

28. *Fullilove v. Klutznick,* 448 U.S. 448, 519 (1980) (Marshall, concurring). In the *Fullilove* opinions, there were at least three distinct arguments for the amount of scrutiny to be applied: Justices Burger and White called for "close examination," while Justices Stewart, Rehnquist, and Stevens called for traditional strict scrutiny, the colorblindness approach. Marshall wrote for himself, Brennan, and Blackmun for the intermediate standard Brennan had advocated for in *Bakke* and that had been developing in the context of sex-based discrimination.

29. *Wygant v. Jackson Board of Education*, 546 F.Supp. 1195, 1197 (E.D. Mich. 1982) ("*Wygant–District*").

30. *Wygant–District,* 546 F.Supp. at 1198–1199; "Oral Argument: Wygant v. Jackson Board of Education," *Oyez*, accessed July 7, 2022, https://www.oyez.org/cases/1985/84-1340; Brief for the United States as Amicus Curiae Supporting Petitioners, *Wygant v. Jackson Board of Education*, 1985 WL 669739 (1985).

31. *Wygant v. Jackson Board of Education*, 476 U.S. 267, 273 (1986) ("*Wygant–Supreme*"). In *Wygant*, Justice O'Connor wrote a concurrence that attempted to find some middle ground between Powell's strict scrutiny and Marshall's heightened scrutiny. She argued, as she would later in *Grutter,* that strict scrutiny did not mean automatic invalidation (though it would invalidate the provision in *Wygant*). *Id.*, at 275 (O'Connor, concurring). At the root of Powell's opinion was the assertion that the Jackson school district could not employ racial classifications in its layoff decisions unless and until it had been found to have previously discriminated. Rather than relying on vague claims of societal discrimination or the value of Black role

models to allow race, Justice Powell sought a specific finding of prior discrimination before a school district could use a racial classification for a remedial purpose. Since there was no such finding in the case, he found the district's use of race improper. He also noted that terminating someone from their job was a more significant burden than that which resulted from a hiring preference that included racial considerations. *Id.,* at 282–283.

32. *Wygant–Supreme,* 476 U.S. at 296, 306–307, 312 (Marshall, dissenting).

CHAPTER 14

1. Robert Bork, "Neutral Principles and Some First Amendment Problems," 47 *Indiana Law Journal* 1, 1, 8 (1971).

2. Bork, "Neutral Principles," 15.

3. See Erwin Gilkes and Robert Bork, "Address: Erosion of the President's Power in Foreign Affairs," 68 *Washington University Law Quarterly* 693 (1990). Anthony Kennedy was actually Reagan's third choice for the Court seat; a second nominee, Douglas Ginzburg, withdrew amid personal scandal.

4. Michael Graetz and Linda Greenhouse, *The Burger Court and the Rise of the Judicial Right* (New York: Simon & Schuster, 2016); Linda Greenhouse, *Becoming Justice Blackmun* (New York: Times, 2005); *Wygant v. Jackson Board of Education,* 476 U.S. 267, 315 (1986) (Stevens, dissenting).

5. Edwin Meese, "A Jurisprudence of Original Attention," *American Bar Association* (July 9, 1985), 6–7, accessed July 7, 2022, https://www.justice.gov/sites/default/files/ag/legacy/2011/08/23/07-09-1985.pdf

6. Juan Williams, "A Question of Fairness," *The Atlantic* (February 1987).

7. William Brennan, "Speech to the Text and Teaching Symposium," *Georgetown University* (October 12, 1985), accessed July 7, 2022, https://fedsoc.org/commentary/publications/the-great-debate-justice-william-j-brennan-jr-october-12-1985; See also Jonathan K. Van Patten, "The Partisan Battle over the Constitution: Meese's Jurisprudence of Original Intention and Brennan's Theory of Contemporary Ratification," 70 *Marquette Law Review* 389 (1987).

8. See, e.g., Edwin Meese, "The Law of the Constitution," *Tulane University* (October 21, 1986), accessed July 7, 2022, https://www.justice.gov/sites/default/files/ag/legacy/2011/08/23/10-21-1986.pdf

9. Lawrence Solum, "What Is Originalism? The Evolution of Contemporary Originalist Theory," *Georgetown University Law Center* (2011) (citing speech by Antonin Scalia before the Attorney General's Conference on Economic Liberties in Washington, DC, on June 14, 1986), accessed July 7, 2022, https://scholarship.law.georgetown.edu/cgi/viewcontent.cgi?article=2362&context=facpub

10. *City of Richmond v. J.A. Croson, Co.,* 488 U.S. 469, 495 (1989); *id.* at 521 (Scalia, concurring); *id.,* at 518 (Kennedy, concurring).

11. *Metro Broadcasting, Inc. v. FCC,* 497 U.S. 547, 564–565 (1990). The measures

in *Metro Broadcasting* had been mandated by Congress (who had the power under the Fourteenth Amendment to adopt legislation), whereas in *Croson*, it had merely been local (Richmond) government, and in *Wygant*, the local school board.

12. Williams, "A Question of Fairness."

13. Williams, "A Question of Fairness." Thomas also moved the EEOC away from "comparable worth" considerations that affected women substantially.

14. *Adarand Constructors, Inc. v. Pena*, 515 U.S. 200, 227 (1995).

15. *Adarand*, 515 U.S. at 241 (Thomas, concurring).

16. Williams, "A Question of Fairness."

CHAPTER 15

1. Ron Suskind, *A Hope in the Unseen: An American Odyssey from the Inner City to the Ivy League* (New York: Broadway, 1998), 116.

2. Suskind, *A Hope in the Unseen*, 120–121.

3. Suskind, *A Hope in the Unseen*, 122.

4. Suskind, *A Hope in the Unseen*, 122–123.

5. Clarence Thomas, "Be Not Afraid," *American Enterprise Institute* (February 13, 2001), accessed July 7, 2022, https://www.aei.org/research-products/speech/be-not-afraid/

6. Randall Kennedy, *Sellout: The Politics of Racial Betrayal* (New York: Pantheon, 2008), 87–95 (includes a collection of such references, including hopes for his death, lobs of "Uncle Tom," and equating Thomas with the devil).

7. Wendy Parker, "The Story of *Grutter v. Bollinger:* Affirmative Action Wins," *Wake Forest Legal Studies Research Paper* (2006), 1, 7, accessed July 7, 2022, http://users.wfu.edu/mcclanas/bookchapter.pdf

8. *Regents of the Univ. of California v. Bakke*, 438 U.S. 265, 408 (1978) (Stevens, concurring in part). For the sake of clarity, Justice Stevens actually argued that the case should be decided on the grounds of Title VI's prohibition on discrimination since UC Davis received federal funds. He thus would not have even reached the equal protection question. See Diane Marie Amann, "John Paul Stevens and Equally Impartial Government," 43 *U.C. Davis Law Review* 885 (2010). Amann notes that the break from the absolute position of Rehnquist (and eventually Thomas) that the Constitution does not tolerate any racial classifications occurred as early as 1980 in *Fullilove v. Klutznick*, where Stevens cited to Marshall's *Bakke* dissent in an effort to claim that some class-based remedies might be appropriate, even if the one in *Fullilove* was not.

9. *Bakke*, 438 U.S. at 418 (Stevens, concurring in part).

10. Amann, "John Paul Stevens and Equally Impartial Government," 904, 908 (citing *Fullilove v. Klutznick*, 448 U.S. 448, 537, 548 (1980) (Stevens, dissenting)). See *Metro Broadcasting v. FCC*, 497 U.S. 547, 602 n.6 (1990) (Stevens, concurring).

11. *Grutter v. Bollinger*, 539 U.S. 306, 323 (2003) ("Since this Court's splintered

decision in *Bakke,* Justice Powell's opinion announcing the judgment of the Court has served as the touchstone for constitutional analysis of race-conscious admissions policies"). The same day, the Court rejected Michigan's undergraduate admissions program as too mechanical. *Gratz v. Bollinger,* 539 U.S. 244 (2003). *Grutter,* 539 U.S. at 330–333 ("These benefits are not theoretical, but real"). In the Michigan cases, it was Justice Ruth Bader Ginsburg who came closest to channeling Justice Marshall: "It is well documented that conscious and unconscious race bias, even rank discrimination based on race remains alive in our land, impeding realization of our highest values and ideas." *Grutter,* 539 U.S. at 345 (Ginsburg, concurring). In the undergraduate case, *Gratz v. Bollinger,* she admonished in Marshall-like prose that "We are not far distant from an overtly discriminatory past, and the effects of law-sanctioned inequality remain painfully evident in our communities and schools." *Gratz v. Bollinger,* 539 U.S. 244, 298 (2003) (Ginsburg, dissenting).

12. *Grutter,* 539 U.S. at 349 (Thomas, dissenting).

13. *Grutter,* 539 U.S. at 349–350, 353 (Thomas, dissenting).

14. *Grutter,* 539 U.S. at 354 n.3 (Thomas, dissenting).

15. *Grutter,* 539 U.S. at 354 n.3, 367 (Thomas, dissenting).

16. *Fisher v. University of Texas,* 570 U.S. 297, 323 (2013) (Thomas, concurring).

17. *Grutter,* 539 U.S. at 364, 372 (Thomas, dissenting) (citing the work of Sowell here).

18. *Grutter,* 539 U.S. at 350, 373 (Thomas, dissenting).

19. *Grutter,* 539 U.S. at 372, n.11 (Thomas, dissenting).

20. *Fisher,* 570 U.S. at 330 (Thomas, concurring). See also *Box v. Planned Parenthood of Indiana and Kentucky,* 587 U.S. ___, 139 S.Ct. 1780, 1782 (2019) (Thomas, concurring); *Flowers v. Mississippi,* 588 U.S. ___, 139 S.Ct. 2228, 2252 (2019) (Thomas, dissenting).

21. See Daniel Kiel, "Accepting Justice Kennedy's Dare," 78 *Fordham Law Review* 2873, 2879–2881 (2010) (citing various cases); see *Hampton v. Jefferson County Board of Education,* 102 F.Supp.2d 358, 369 (W.D. Ky. 2000) (citing Marshall's *Dowell* dissent regarding district good faith), at 360 (using "to the extent practicable" standard). The JCPS dissolution decree was the ultimate result of a suit brought by Black parents complaining that the demographic guidelines were resulting in a cap being placed on Black enrollment in the district's magnet schools.

22. *Hampton,* 102 F.Supp.2d at 375 (citing Marshall's *Dowell* dissent).

23. At the time, the district served 97,000 students, 34 percent of whom were Black. Kiel, "Accepting Justice Kennedy's Dare," 2881–2882.

24. *PICS v. Seattle School District,* 551 U.S. 701, 720 (2007).

25. *PICS,* 551 U.S. at 726, 748.

26. *PICS,* 551 U.S. at 749, 756 (Thomas, concurring).

27. *PICS,* 551 U.S. at 750 n.3, 761 (Thomas, concurring).

28. *PICS,* 551 U.S. at 768–770 (Thomas, concurring).

29. *PICS*, 551 U.S. at 778–812, n.27, n.30 (Thomas, concurring).

30. *Bakke*, 438 U.S. at 401 (Marshall, separate opinion).

31. "Retirement of Justice Marshall," *C-SPAN* (June 28, 1991), accessed July 7, 2022, https://www.c-span.org/video/?18679-1/retirement-justice-marshall

32. "High Tech Lynching: Thomas Denies Anita Hill Harassment Allegations," *Washington Post* (October 11, 1991), accessed July 7, 2022, https://www.washingtonpost.com/video/politics/high-tech-lynching-thomas-denies-anita-hill-harassment-allegations/2018/09/18/370097aa-bbae-11e8-adb8-01125416c102_video.html

33. *PICS v. Seattle School District*, 551 U.S. at 747 (Roberts plurality) ("The school districts in these cases have not carried the heavy burden of demonstrating that we should allow this once again—even for very different reasons").

34. Adam Liptak, "The Same Words, but Differing Views," *New York Times* (June 29, 2007) (quoting Carter as saying that "All that race was used for at that point in time was to deny equal opportunity to black people").

35. *PICS*, 551 U.S. at 798–799 (Stevens, dissenting).

36. *PICS*, 551 U.S. at 774–776 n.21–24, 778 (Thomas, concurring).

37. *PICS*, 551 U.S. at 772–773 (Thomas, concurring) (citing remarks of Judge Motley).

38. *Bakke*, 438 U.S. at 401 (Marshall, separate opinion).

CONCLUSION

1. Michael Shear, "Biden Made a Campaign Pledge to Put a Black woman on the Supreme Court," *New York Times* (January 26, 2022). As a candidate for president in 1980, Ronald Reagan had made a similar pledge to appoint a woman to the Court, a pledge he delivered on in 1981 with the nomination of Justice Sandra Day O'Connor. Lou Cannon, "Reagan Pledges He Would Name a Woman to the Supreme Court," *Washington Post* (October 15, 1980).

2. "Biographical Directory of Article III Federal Judges, 1789–Present," *Federal Judicial Center,* accessed July 7, 2022, https://www.fjc.gov/history/judges/search/advanced-search

3. Sonnet Swire and Veronica Stracqualursi, "GOP Senator Says Black Woman Supreme Court Pick Would Be 'Beneficiary' of Affirmative Action," *CNN* (January 29, 2022). See also Tomiko Brown-Nagin, *Civil Rights Queen: Constance Baker Motley and the Struggle for Equality* (New York: Pantheon, 2022).

4. Patricia Mazzei, "How a High School Debate Team Shaped Ketanji Brown Jackson," *New York Times* (February 26, 2022); "Supreme Court Nominee Judge Ketanji Brown Jackson," *C-SPAN* (February 25, 2022), accessed July 7, 2022, https://www.c-span.org/video/?c5003288/supreme-court-nominee-judge-ketanji-brown-jackson-statement

5. Brandon Tensley, "The Many Joys of Ketanji Brown Jackson's Historic Confirmation," *CNN* (April 7, 2022).

6. Ketanji Brown Jackson, "Opening Statement for Supreme Court Hearings," *Politico* (March 21, 2022), accessed July 7, 2022, https://www.politico.com/news/2022/03/21/kentaji-brown-jackson-opening-statement-supreme-court-00018980

7. See Linda Hirshman, *Sisters in Law: How Sandra Day O'Connor and Ruth Bader Ginsburg Went to the Supreme Court and Changed the World* (New York: Harper Perennial, 2016), xvi.

8. Jessica Weisberg, "Remembering Ruth Bader Ginsburg in Her Own Words," *Elle* (September 21, 2020).

9. U.S. Supreme Court, "Press Release" (March 16, 2020), accessed July 7, 2022, https://www.supremecourt.gov/publicinfo/press/pressreleases/pr_03-16-20

10. U.S. Supreme Court, "Press Release" (April 3, 2020), accessed July 7, 2022, https://www.supremecourt.gov/publicinfo/press/pressreleases/pr_04-03-20

11. See *Calvary Chapel Dayton Valley v. Sisolak*, 591 U.S. ___, 140 S.Ct. 2603 (2020) (denying injunctive relief to church in Nevada); *South Bay United Pentecostal Church v. Newsom*, 590 U.S. ___, 140 S.Ct. 1613 (2020) (denying injunctive relief to church in California); *Roman Catholic Diocese of Brooklyn v. Cuomo*, 592 U.S. ___, 141 S.Ct. 63 (2020).

12. Jason Slotkin, "Protesters Swarm Michigan Capitol amid Showdown over Governor's Emergency Powers," *NPR* (May 1, 2020).

13. Ronald Reagan, "Inaugural Address," *Ronald Reagan: Presidential Foundation and Institute* (January 20, 1981), accessed July 7, 2022, https://www.reaganfoundation.org/ronald-reagan/reagan-quotes-speeches/inaugural-address-2/

14. Dahlia Lithwick and Mark Joseph Stern, "The Clarence Thomas Takeover," *Slate* (August 2, 2017); Eugene Scott, "Trump Hits Scalia over Comments on Black Students," *CNN* (December 13, 2015); Joan Biskupic, "Clarence Thomas Has Found His Moment," *CNN* (May 11, 2020); Emma Green, "The Clarence Thomas Effect," *The Atlantic* (July 10, 2019).

15. *Republican Party of Pennsylvania v. Boockvar*, 592 U.S. ___, 141 S.Ct. 643 (2020) (denying motion to expedite consideration of the matter before the election, against which Justices Alito, Thomas, and Gorsuch dissented).

16. Emma Brown, "Ginni Thomas, Wife of Supreme Court Justice, Pressed Ariz. Lawmakers to Help Reverse Trump's Loss, Emails Show," *Washington Post* (May 20, 2022); Bob Woodward and Robert Costa, "Virginia Thomas Urged White House Chief to Pursue Unrelenting Efforts to Overturn the 2020 Election, Texts Show," *Washington Post* (March 24, 2022).

17. *Texas v. Pennsylvania*, 592 U.S. ___, 141 S.Ct. 1230 (2020) (denying Texas's motion to file complaint due to lack of standing; Justice Alito, joined by Justice Thomas, made a statement noting their belief that the complaint should have been allowed, but that they would not grant any other relief).

18. "Oral Argument: Cooper v. Aaron," *Oyez,* accessed July 7, 2022, https://www.oyez.org/cases/1957/1_misc

19. See *South Carolina v. Katzenbach,* 383 U.S. 301 (1966); *Allen v. State Board of Elections*, 393 U.S. 544, 594–595 (1969) (Marshall, concurring in part); *Beer v. U.S.*, 425 U.S. 130, 145 (1976) (Marshall, dissenting) (accusing the Court majority of adopting a cumbersome analysis that allows a blatantly discriminatory redistricting plan in New Orleans to remain); *City of Richmond v. U.S.*, 429 U.S. 358 (1975) (joining dissent of Brennan); *Dunn v. Blumstein,* 405 U.S. 330 (1972) (in which Marshall authored the majority opinion in a Fourteenth Amendment case striking down certain state residency requirements for votes); *City of Rome v. U.S.*, 446 U.S. 156, 177 (1980) ("Congress could rationally have concluded that, because electoral changes by jurisdictions with a demonstrable history of intentional racial discrimination in voting create the risk of purposeful discrimination, it was proper to prohibit changes that have a discriminatory impact"); *City of Mobile v. Bolden,* 446 U.S. 55, 123 (1980) (Marshall, dissenting) ("the protection against vote dilution recognized by our prior cases serves as a minimally intrusive guarantee of political survival for a discrete political minority that is effectively locked out of governmental decisionmaking processes").

20. *City of Mobile v. Bolden*, 446 U.S. at 135 (Marshall, dissenting).

21. *City of Mobile v. Bolden*, 446 U.S. at 135 (Marshall, dissenting).

22. *City of Mobile v. Bolden*, 446 U.S. at 141 (Marshall, dissenting) (noting that the decision might produce only a "superficial tranquility" that would be "short-lived").

23. Chris Cameron, "These Are the People Who Died in Connection with the Capitol Riot," *New York Times* (January 5, 2022).

24. See *U.S. v. Lopez,* 514 U.S. 549, 584 (1995) (Thomas, concurring) (arguing for very narrow reading of the commerce clause); *Gamble v. U.S.,* 587 U.S. ___, 139 S.Ct. 1960, 1980 (2019) (Thomas, concurring).

25. *Republican Party of Pennsylvania v. Degraffenreid,* 592 U.S. ___, 141 S.Ct. 732 (2021) (Thomas, dissenting from denial of cert) (continuation of the *Boockvar* case the Court declined to expedite in the days before the 2020 election); *Trump v. Thompson*, 595 U.S. ___, 142 S.Ct. 680 (2022) (rejecting stay of injunction over Thomas disagreement); Jacqueline Alemany, Emma Brown, Tom Hamburger, and Jon Swaine, "Ahead of Jan. 6, Willard Hotel in Downtown D.C. Was a Trump Team 'Command Center' for Effort to Deny Biden Presidency," *Washington Post* (October 23, 2021) (noting that former Thomas clerk John Eastman was among those who developed the legal arguments for impeding certification of the election).

26. *Box v. Planned Parenthood of Indiana and Kentucky*, 587 U.S. ___, 139 S.Ct. 1780, 1782 (2019) (Thomas, concurring).

27. On juror selection, see *Georgia v. McCollum*, 505 U.S. 42, 60 (1992) (Thomas, concurring); *Snyder v. Louisiana*, 552 U.S. 472, 486 (2008) (Thomas, dissenting); *Foster v. Chatman*, 578 U.S. 488, 524 (2016) (Thomas, dissenting); *Flowers v. Mississippi*, 588 U.S. ___, 139 S.Ct. 2228, 2252 (2019) (Thomas, dissenting).

28. On voting, see *Northwest Austin Municipal District v. Holder*, 557 U.S. 193, 212 (2009) (Thomas, concurring in part and dissenting in part); *Evenwel v. Abbott*, 578 U.S. 54, 75 (2016) (Thomas, concurring).

29. On qualified immunity, see *Ziglar v. Abbasi*, 582 U.S. ___, 137 S.Ct. 1843, 1869 (2017) (Thomas, concurring) (Thomas expressing "growing concern" with the Court's qualified immunity jurisprudence); *Baxter v. Bracey*, 590 U.S. ___, 140 S.Ct. 1862 (2020) (Thomas, dissenting from denial of cert) (Thomas expressing "strong doubts" about qualified immunity).

Indeed, there are strong reasons to believe that Justice Thomas was not particularly sympathetic to the Black Lives Matter demonstrations of 2020. In November, Thomas dissented (without commentary) when the Court returned a case involving a suit brought by a police officer injured during a 2016 Black Lives Matter protest, vacating a Louisiana court's decision to allow the case to proceed. The implication of the dissent was that Thomas believed the officer *should* be able to sue the leader of a protest during which the officer was injured. *McKesson v. Doe*, 592 U.S. ___, 141 S.Ct. 48 (2020).

Further, Thomas's spouse criticized the Virginia town where she kept her professional offices for displaying a banner that read "Welcome to Clifton Where Black Lives Matter." In an email to town officials, Virginia (Ginni) Thomas wrote that

BLM is a bit of a dangerous Trojan Horse and they are catching well-meaning people into dangerous posturing that can invite mob rule and property looting. . . . Let's not be tricked into joining cause with radical extremists seeking to foment a cultural revolution because they hate America.

Patricia Sullivan, "A Small, Mostly White Virginia Town Put up a 'Black Lives Matter' Banner. Ginni Thomas Denounced It," *Washington Post* (July 10, 2020).

30. Thurgood Marshall, "Reflections on the Bicentennial of the United States Constitution," in *Thurgood Marshall: His Speeches, Writings, Arguments, Opinions, and Reminiscences*, ed. Mark Tushnet (Chicago: Lawrence Hill, 2001), 281.

31. Thurgood Marshall, "Remarks at the Annual Conference of the Second Circuit, Sept. 8, 1989," in *Thurgood Marshall: His Speeches, Writings, Arguments, Opinions, and Reminiscences*, ed. Mark Tushnet (Chicago: Lawrence Hill, 2001), 217.

32. "William T. Coleman Jr.," *The History Makers*, accessed July 7, 2022, https://www.thehistorymakers.org/biography/william-t-coleman-jr

33. Juan Williams, *Thurgood Marshall: American Revolutionary* (New York: Three Rivers, 1998), 394.

34. Clarence Thomas, *My Grandfather's Son* (New York: Perennial, 2007), 286.

BIBLIOGRAPHY

Alemany, Jacqueline, Emma Brown, Tom Hamburger, and Jon Swaine. "Ahead of Jan. 6, Willard Hotel in Downtown D.C. Was a Trump Team 'Command Center' for Effort to Deny Biden Presidency." *Washington Post* (October 23, 2021).

Amann, Diane Marie. "John Paul Stevens and Equally Impartial Government." 43 *U.C. Davis Law Review* 885 (2010).

Anderson, Carol. *The Second: Race and Guns in a Fatally Unequal America* (New York: Bloomsbury, 2021).

Baldwin, James. *The Fire Next Time* (New York: Vintage International, 1963).

Ball, Howard. *A Defiant Life: Thurgood Marshall and the Persistence of Racism* (New York: Crown, 1999).

Barnes, Robert. "Supreme Court Takes Modest but Historic Step with Teleconference Hearings." *Washington Post* (May 4, 2020).

Baugh, Joyce A. *The Detroit School Busing Case* (Lawrence: University Press of Kansas, 2011).

Berry, Christopher R. "School Consolidation and Inequality (September 2006)." *ResearchGate* (January 2007). Accessed July 21, 2022. https://www.researchgate.net/profile/Christopher-Berry-8/publication/5091300_School_Consolidation_and_Inequality/links/54d243bb0cf25017917da65d/School-Consolidation-and-Inequality.pdf

Billington, Monroe. "Public School Integration in Missouri, 1954–64." 35(3) *Journal of Negro Education* 252 (Summer 1966).

"Biographical Directory of Article III Federal Judges, 1789–Present." *Federal Judicial Center.* Accessed July 7, 2022. https://www.fjc.gov/history/judges/search/advanced-search

Biskupic, Joan. "Clarence Thomas Has Found His Moment." *CNN* (May 11, 2020).

"Black Judges and Lawyers: Arbiters and Advocates for Human Rights, Civil Justice and Economic Power" (Preliminary Agenda of the Judicial Council for the National Bar Association, August 7–11, 1988). *Digital Collection, National Bar Association Archives at Drake University.* Accessed July 7, 2022. http://content.library.drake.edu/digital/collection/p16331coll9/id/2065

Blight, David D. *Frederick Douglass* (New York: Simon & Schuster, 2018).

Bloch, Susan Low. "Celebrating Thurgood Marshall: The Prophetic Dissenter." 52 *Howard Law Journal* 667 (2009).

Bork, Robert. "Neutral Principles and Some First Amendment Problems." 47 *Indiana Law Journal* 1 (1971).

Brady, Diane. *Fraternity* (New York: Spiegel & Grau, 2012).

Branch, Taylor. *Parting the Waters: America in the King Years, 1954–63* (New York: Simon & Schuster, 1988).

Brands, H. W. *Heirs of the Founders* (New York: Doubleday, 2018).

Brennan, William. "Speech to the Text and Teaching Symposium." *Georgetown University* (October 12, 1985). Accessed July 7, 2022. https://fedsoc.org/commentary/publications/the-great-debate-justice-william-j-brennan-jr-october-12-1985

Brief for the United States as Amicus Curiae Supporting Petitioners, *Wygant v. Jackson Board of Education*, 1985 WL 669739 (1985).

Brief of the National Medical Association, et al., *Bakke v. Regents of the Univ. of California*, 1977 WL 189515 (1977).

Brown, Emma. "Ginni Thomas, Wife of Supreme Court Justice, Pressed Ariz. Lawmakers to Help Reverse Trump's Loss, Emails Show." *Washington Post* (May 20, 2022).

Brown-Nagin, Tomiko. *Civil Rights Queen: Constance Baker Motley and the Struggle for Equality* (New York: Pantheon, 2022).

———. *Courage to Dissent* (Oxford: Oxford University Press, 2011).

Brown-Scott, Wendy. "Justice Thurgood Marshall and the Integrative Ideal." 26 *Arizona State Law Journal* 535 (1994).

Buccola, Nicholas. *The Fire Is Upon Us* (Princeton: Princeton University Press, 2019).

Burgess, Katherine. "Shelby County District Attorney Abandons Pursuit of Death Penalty in Pervis Payne Case." *The Commercial Appeal* (November 18, 2021).

Burns, Cynthia. "The Fading of the *Brown* Objective: A Historical Perspective of the Marshall Legacy in Education." 35 *Howard Law Journal* 95 (1991).

Cameron, Chris. "These Are the People Who Died in Connection with the Capitol Riot." *New York Times* (January 5, 2022).

Camia, Catalina. "Congressman Stands by Calling Clarence Thomas 'Uncle Tom.'" *USA Today* (April 30, 2014).

Cannon, Lou. "Reagan Pledges He Would Name a Woman to the Supreme Court." *Washington Post* (October 15, 1980).

Carter, Robert. *A Matter of Law* (New York: New Press, 2005).

Cashin, Sheryll. "Justice Thurgood Marshall: A Race Man's Race-Transcending Jurisprudence." 52 *Howard Law Journal* 507 (2009).

Chabot, Christine Kexel, and Benjamin Remy Chabot. "Mavericks, Moderates, or Drifters? Supreme Court Voting Alignments, 1838–2018." 76 *Missouri Law Review* 999 (2011).

Chambers, Julius. "Thurgood Marshall's Legacy." 44 *Stanford Law Review* 1249 (1992).

Chernow, Ron. *Grant* (New York: Penguin, 2017).

Cimbala, Paul, and Randall Miller, eds. *The Freedmen's Bureau and Reconstruction: Reconstructing America* (New York: Fordham University Press, 1999).

Civil Rights Act of 1964 §7, 42 U.S.C. §2000e et seq. (1964).

Clemon, U. W., and Stephanie Y. Moore. "Justice Clarence Thomas: The Burning of Civil Rights Bridges." 1 *Alabama Civil Rights and Civil Liberties Law Review* 49 (2011).

Cohen, Adam. *Supreme Inequality: The Supreme Court's Fifty-Year Battle for a More Unjust America* (New York: Penguin, 2020).

Coltharp, Donna. "Writing in the Margins: Brennan, Marshall, and the Inherent Weakness of Liberal Judicial Decision-Making." 29 *St. Mary's Law Journal* 1 (1997).

Columbia Oral History Project. "The Reminiscences of Thurgood Marshall." In *Thurgood Marshall: His Speeches, Writings, Arguments, Opinions, and Reminiscences*, ed. Mark Tushnet (Chicago: Lawrence Hill Books, 2001), 413.

Congressional Record, 84th Congress Second Session. Vol. 102, part 4 (March 12, 1956) 4459–4460 ("Southern Manifesto").

"Congress Names Building for Thurgood Marshall in Record Two Days." *Jet* (February 22, 1993).

Consovoy, William S., and Nicole Stelle Garnett. "'To Help, Not to Hurt': Justice Thomas's Equality Canon." 127 *Yale Law Journal Forum* 221 (2017).

Cook Jr., Julian Abele. "Thurgood Marshall and Clarence Thomas: A Glance at Their Philosophies." 73 *Michigan Bar Journal* 298 (1994).

Davies, Gareth. *See Government Grow: Education Politics from Johnson to Reagan* (Lawrence: University Press of Kansas, 2007).

De Tocqueville, Alexis. *Democracy in America*, trans. George Lawrence (New York: Perennial Classics, 2000).

Dreyfuss, Joel, and Charles Lawrence III. *The Bakke Case: The Politics of Inequality* (New York: Harcourt, 1979).

Driver, Justin. *The School House Gate: Public Education, the Supreme Court, and the Battle for the American Mind* (New York: Pantheon, 2018).

Du Bois, W. E. B. "Does the Negro Need Separate Schools?" 4 *Journal of Negro Education* 328 (1935).

———. *The Souls of Black Folk* (New York: Bantam Classic, 1989).

Entin, Jonathan L. "Justice Thomas, Race, and the Constitution Through the Lens of Booker T. Washington and W. E. B. Du Bois." 88 *University of Detroit Mercy Law Review* 755 (2011).

Feldman, Noah. *The Three Lives of James Madison* (New York: Picador, 2017).

"Florance Street School." *Historical Marker Database.* Accessed July 7, 2022. https://www.hmdb.org/marker.asp?marker=12088

Ford, Matt. "Thurgood Marshall's Patient but Relentless War." *The Atlantic* (September 6, 2007).

"Freedmen's Bureau Acts of 1865 and 1866." *U.S. Senate.* Accessed July 7, 2022. https://www.senate.gov/artandhistory/history/common/generic/Freedmens-Bureau.htm

Garnett, Nicole Stelle. "'But for the Grace of God Go I': Justice Thomas and the Little Guy." 4 *New York University Journal of Law and Liberty* 626 (2009).

"General Convention." *Journal of the General Convention of . . . the Episcopal Church, Anaheim, 2009.* Accessed July 7, 2022. https://episcopalarchives.org/cgi-bin/acts/acts_resolution.pl?resolution=2009-B020

Gerber, Scott D. "Justice for Clarence Thomas: An Intellectual History of Justice Thomas's Twenty Years on the Supreme Court." 88 *University of Detroit Mercy Law Review* 667 (2011).

Gerhardt, Michael J. "Divided Justice: A Commentary on the Nomination and Confirmation of Justice Thomas." 60 *George Washington Law Review* 969 (1992).

Gerstein, Josh. "Clarence Thomas Defends Silence in Supreme Court Health Care Arguments." *Politico* (April 6, 2012).

Gilkes, Erwin, and Robert Bork. "Address: Erosion of the President's Power in Foreign Affairs." 68 *Washington University Law Quarterly* 693 (1990).

Gotham, Kevin Fox. "Missed Opportunities, Enduring Legacies: Segregation and Desegregation in Kansas City, Missouri." 43(2) *American Studies* 5 (Summer 2002).

Graetz, Michael, and Linda Greenhouse. *The Burger Court and the Rise of the Judicial Right* (New York: Simon & Schuster, 2016).

Green, Emma. "The Clarence Thomas Effect." *The Atlantic* (July 10, 2019).

Greenhouse, Linda. *Becoming Justice Blackmun* (New York: Times, 2005).

Hamilton, Alexander. "No. 78: The Judiciary Department." In *The Federalist Papers,* ed. Charles R. Kesler (New York: Signet Classic, 1961), 463.

Hansberry, Lorraine. *A Raisin in the Sun* (New York: Vintage, 1958).

Harvey, William B., Adia M. Harvey, and Mark King. "The Impact of the Brown v. Board of Education Decision on Postsecondary Participation of African Americans." 73(3) *The Journal of Negro Education* 328 (2004).

Haygood, Wil. *Showdown: Thurgood Marshall and the Supreme Court Nomination That Changed America* (New York: Knopf, 2015).

Heck, Edward V. "Justice Brennan and the Heyday of Warren Court Liberalism." 20 *Santa Clara Law Review* 841 (1980).

Higginbotham Jr., A. Leon. "Clarence Thomas in Retrospect." 45 *Hastings Law Journal* 1405 (1993).

"High Tech Lynching: Thomas Denies Anita Hill Harassment Allegations." *Washington Post* (October 11, 1991). Accessed July 7, 2022. https://www.washingtonpost.com/video/politics/high-tech-lynching-thomas-denies-anita-hill-harassment-allegations/2018/09/18/370097aa-bbae-11e8-adb8-01125416c102_video.html

Hill, Ruth Johnson. "Mr. Justice Thurgood Marshall 1908–1993: A Bio-Bibliographic Research Guide." 20 *Southern University Law Review* 113 (1993).

Hirshman, Linda. *Sisters in Law: How Sandra Day O'Connor and Ruth Bader Ginsburg Went to the Supreme Court and Changed the World* (New York: Harper Perennial, 2016).

"History." *National Bar Association. Accessed July 14, 2022.* https://www.national-bar.org/NBA/History.aspx

Jackson Jr., Kennell. "Review: *Black Education: Myths and Tragedies*." 5(7) *Change* 58 (September 1973).

Jackson, Ketanji Brown. "Opening Statement for Supreme Court Hearings." *Politico* (March 21, 2022). Accessed July 7, 2022. https://www.politico.com/news/2022/03/21/kentaji-brown-jackson-opening-statement-supreme-court-00018980

———. "Supreme Court Nominee Judge Ketanji Brown Jackson Statement." *C-SPAN* (February 25, 2022). Accessed July 7, 2022. https://www.c-span.org/video/?c5003288/supreme-court-nominee-judge-ketanji-brown-jackson-statement

James Jr., Rawn. *Root and Branch: Charles Hamilton Houston, Thurgood Marshall, and the Struggle to End Segregation* (New York: Bloomsbury, 2010).

Johnson, Lyndon B. "Commencement Address at Howard University: 'To Fulfill These Rights' (June 4, 1965)." *Teaching American History*. Accessed July 7, 2022. https://teachingamericanhistory.org/library/document/commencement-address-at-howard-university-to-fulfill-these-rights/

———. "Signing of the Elementary and Secondary Education Act, 4/11/1965." *LBJ Library*. Accessed July 7, 2022. https://www.youtube.com/watch?v=QQzCViUdPLc

"Junction School." Lyndon B. Johnson National Historical Park Texas. *National Park Service. Accessed July 7, 2022.* https://www.nps.gov/lyjo/planyourvisit/junctionschool.htm

"Justice Marshall Receives National Bar Association Award." *C-SPAN* (August 10, 1988). Accessed July 7, 2022. https://www.c-span.org/video/?3962-1/justice-marshall-receives-national-bar-association-award

Kaczynski, Andrew. "Democratic Congressman Makes Shocking Racial Comments About Republicans, Clarence Thomas, Mitch McConnell." *BuzzFeed.News* (April 29, 2014). Accessed July 7, 2022. https://www.buzzfeednews.com/article/andrewkaczynski/democratic-congressman-makes-shocking-racial-comments-about

Keiser, Gretchen. "Photo Inspires Look Back at Era When Catholic Schools Segregated." *Georgia Bulletin* (January 9, 2014).

Kennedy, Randall. *Sellout: The Politics of Racial Betrayal* (New York: Pantheon, 2008).

Kiel, Daniel. "Accepting Justice Kennedy's Dare." 78 *Fordham Law Review* 2873 (2010).

———. "Avoiding *Atkins*: How Tennessee Is on the Verge of Unconstitutionally Executing an Individual with Intellectual Disabilities." *Law and Inequality (Inequality Inquiry)* (2020). Accessed July 7, 2022. https://lawandinequality.org/2020/11/18/avoiding-atkins-how-tennessee-is-on-the-verge-of-unconstitutionally-executing-an-individual-with-intellectual-disabilities/#

———. "A Bolt of Lightning: Measuring the Impact of Modern Transitions on the Supreme Court." 42 *Cardozo Law Review* 2813, ~~2828~~ (2021).

King, Gilbert. *Devil in the Grove* (New York: Perennial, 2012).

King Jr., Martin Luther. "Our God Is Marching On." In *A Testament of Hope*, ed. James M. Washington (San Francisco: Harper, 1986), 227.

Kluger, Richard. *Simple Justice* (New York: Vintage, 1975).

Kotz, Nick. *Judgment Days: Lyndon Baines Johnson, Martin Luther King Jr., and the Laws That Changed America* (New York: Houghton Mifflin, 2005).

Kroft, Steve. "Clarence Thomas: The Justice Nobody Knows." *CBS News: 60 Minutes* (September 27, 2007).

Lackey, Michael. "A Brief History of the Haverford Group." In *The Haverford Discussions: A Black Integrationist Manifesto for Racial Justice*, ed. Michael Lackey (Charlottesville: University of Virginia Press, 2013), xi.

Lee, Gary. "Black Lawyers' Group Divided on Thomas." *Washington Post* (August 5, 1991).

Lemann, Nicholas. "Hating on Herbert Hoover." *The New Yorker* (October 16, 2017).

Lewis, David Levering. *W. E. B. Du Bois: The Fight for Equality and the American Century, 1919–1963* (New York: Henry Holt, 2000).

Lewis, John. *Walking with the Wind* (New York: Harcourt Brace, 1998).

Lewis, Neil A. "Invitation to Justice Thomas Creates Furor." *New York Times* (May 29, 1998).

———. "Justice Thomas Declines to Drop Speech to Bar." *New York Times* (June 17, 1998).

Liptak, Adam. "Clarence Thomas Breaks 10 Years of Silence at Supreme Court." *New York Times* (February 29, 2016).

———. "Justice Clarence Thomas Breaks His Silence." *New York Times* (January 14, 2013).

———. "The Same Words, but Differing Views." *New York Times* (June 29, 2007).

Lithwick, Dahlia. "Hands Off Thomas." *Slate* (May 30, 2009).

Lithwick, Dahlia, and Mark Joseph Stern. "The Clarence Thomas Takeover." *Slate* (August 2, 2017).

Lovett, Bobby L. *America's Historically Black Colleges and Universities: A Narrative History* (Atlanta: Mercer University Press, 2015).

Marcus, Marcia L. "Learning Together: Justice Marshall's Desegregation Opinions." 61 *Fordham Law Review* 69 (1992).

Marshall, Thurgood. "Reflections on the Bicentennial of the United States Constitution." In *Thurgood Marshall: His Speeches, Writings, Arguments, Opinions, and Reminiscences*, ed. Mark Tushnet (Chicago: Lawrence Hill, 2001), 281.

———. "Remarks at the Annual Conference of the Second Circuit, Sept. 8, 1989." In *Thurgood Marshall: His Speeches, Writings, Arguments, Opinions, and Reminiscences*, ed. Mark Tushnet (Chicago: Lawrence Hill, 2001), 217.

Martin, Andrew D., and Kevin M. Quinn. "Dynamic Ideal Point Estimation via Markov Chain Monte Carlo for the U.S. Supreme Court, 1953–1999." 10 *Political Analysis* 134 (2002).

Mayer, Jane. "Is Ginni Thomas a Threat to the Supreme Court?" *The New Yorker* (January 21, 2022).

Mazzei, Patricia. "How a High School Debate Team Shaped Ketanji Brown Jackson." *New York Times* (February 26, 2022).

McDonogh, Gary. *Black and Catholic in Savannah, Georgia* (Knoxville: University of Tennessee Press, 1993).

McFadden, Robert D. "Damon Keith, Federal Judge Who Championed Civil Rights, Dies at 96." *New York Times* (April 28, 2019).

McGregor, Jena. "Justice Thomas's Supreme Silence." *Washington Post* (January 17, 2013).

McNeil, Genna Rae. *Groundwork: Charles Hamilton Houston and the Struggle for Civil Rights* (Philadelphia: University of Pennsylvania Press, 1983).

"Measures." *Martin-Quinn Scores*. Accessed July 7, 2022. https://perma.cc/DMB5-4P6N

Meese, Edwin. "A Jurisprudence of Original Attention." *American Bar Association* (July 9, 1985). Accessed July 7, 2022. https://www.justice.gov/sites/default/files/ag/legacy/2011/08/23/07-09-1985.pdf

———. "The Law of the Constitution." *Tulane University* (October 21, 1986). Accessed

July 7, 2022. https://www.justice.gov/sites/default/files/ag/legacy/2011/08/23/10-21-1986.pdf

Merida, Kevin, and Michael Fletcher. *Supreme Discomfort: The Divided Soul of Clarence Thomas* (New York: Broadway, 2007).

Moore, Gary A., and Michael K. Braswell. "Quotas and the Codification of the Disparate Impact Theory: What Did *Griggs* Really Say and Not Say?" 55 *Albany Law Review* 459 (1991).

Morris, Jerome. "Malcolm X's Critique of the Education of Black People." 25(2) *The Western Journal of Black Studies* 126 (2001).

NAACP. "Editorial." *The Crisis* (January 1917).

"National Bar Association (1925–)." *BlackPast. Accessed July 14, 2022. https://www.blackpast.org/african-american-history/national-bar-association-1925/*

"1952 Argument: Briggs v. Elliott." In *Brown v. Board: The Landmark Oral Argument Before the Supreme Court*, ed. Leon Friedman (New York: New Press, 2004), 36.

"1953 Argument: Briggs v. Elliott." In *Brown v. Board: The Landmark Oral Argument Before the Supreme Court*, ed. Leon Friedman (New York: New Press, 2004), 179.

Onwuachi-Willig, Angela. "Just Another Brother on the SCT?: What Justice Clarence Thomas Teaches Us About the Influence of Racial Identity." 90 *Iowa Law Review* 931 (2004).

———. "Using the Master's 'Tool' to Dismantle His House: Why Justice Clarence Thomas Makes the Case for Affirmative Action." 47 *Arizona Law Review* 113 (2005).

"Old Frederick Douglass High School (1924)." *Baltimore Places*. Accessed July 7, 2022. http://places.baltimoreheritage.org/old-douglass-high-school/

"Oral Argument: Cooper v. Aaron." *Oyez* Accessed July 7, 2022. https://www.oyez.org/cases/1957/1_misc

"Oral Argument: Green v. County School Board of New Kent County." *Oyez*. Accessed July 7, 2022. https://www.oyez.org/cases/1967/695

"Oral Argument: Regents of the University of California v. Bakke." *Oyez*. Accessed July 7, 2022. https://www.oyez.org/cases/1979/76-811

"Oral Argument: Voisine v. United States." *Oyez*. Accessed July 7, 2022. https://www.oyez.org/cases/2015/14-10154

"Oral Argument: Wygant v. Jackson Board of Education." *Oyez*. Accessed July 7, 2022. https://www.oyez.org/cases/1985/84-1340

Ossei-Owusu, Shaun. "Racial Revisionism." 119 *Michigan Law Review* 1165 (2021).

Page, Clarence. "Thomas' Sister Gives Lie to Welfare Fable." *Chicago Tribune* (July 24, 1991).

Parker, Wendy. "The Story of *Grutter v. Bollinger*: Affirmative Action Wins." *Wake*

Forest Legal Studies Research Paper (2006). Accessed July 7, 2022. http://users. wfu.edu/mcclanas/bookchapter.pdf

Paul, John Richard. *Without Precedent: Chief Justice John Marshall and His Times* (New York: Riverhead, 2018).

Powell, Cedric Merlin. "Justice Thomas, Brown, and Post-Racial Determinism." 53 *Washburn Law Journal* 451 (2014).

"Public School No. 103." *Explore Baltimore Heritage. Accessed July 7, 2022.* https:// explore.baltimoreheritage.org/items/show/75

Reagan, Ronald. "Address Before a Joint Session of Congress on the State of the Union—1987." *Ronald Reagan Presidential Library and Museum.* Accessed August 24, 2022. https://www.reaganlibrary.gov/archives/speech/ address-joint-session-congress-state-union-1987

———. "Inaugural Address (January 20, 1981)." *Ronald Reagan: Presidential Foundation and Institute.* Accessed July 7, 2022. https://www.reaganfoundation.org/ ronald-reagan/reagan-quotes-speeches/inaugural-address-2/

———. "A Time for Choosing (October 27, 1964)." *Ronald Reagan Presidential Library and Foundation.* Accessed July 7, 2022. https://www.youtube.com/ watch?v=qXBswFfh6AY

"Retirement of Justice Marshall." *C-SPAN* (June 28, 1991). Accessed July 7, 2022. https://www.c-span.org/video/?18679-1/retirement-justice-marshall

Richardson, Jeanita W., and J. John Harris III. *"Brown* and Historically Black Colleges and Universities (HBCUs): A Paradox of Desegregation Policy." 73(3) *Journal of Negro Education* 365 (2004).

Rickford, Russell. *We Are an African People: Independent Education, Black Power, and the Radical Imagination* (Oxford: Oxford University Press, 2016).

Roberts, Gene, and Hank Klibanoff. *The Race Beat: The Press, the Civil Rights Struggle, and the Awakening of a Nation* (New York: Knopf, 2007).

Robin, Corey. *The Enigma of Clarence Thomas* (New York: Metropolitan, 2019).

Rothstein, Richard. *The Color of Law* (New York: Livewright, 2017).

Rowan, Carl. "Thomas Is Far from 'Home.'" *Chicago Sun-Times* (July 4, 1993).

Ryan, James. *"Schools, Race, and Money."* 109 *Yale Law Journal* 249 (1999).

Schwartz, Ian. "Pence on Gorsuch: We Want to Give Clarence Thomas an Aid in His Lonely Fight." *Real Clear Politics* (February 5, 2017).

Scott, Eugene. "Trump Hits Scalia over Comments on Black Students." *CNN* (December 13, 2015).

Segedy, Andria. "St. Pius X History: Savannah Churches, Community Opened Doors to Classical Education During Segregation." *Savannah Morning News* (September 15, 2018).

Selmi, Michael. "The Life of *Bakke*: An Affirmative Action Retrospective." 87 *Georgetown Law Journal* 981 (1998).

Shear, Michael. "Biden Made a Campaign Pledge to Put a Black Woman on the Supreme Court." *New York Times* (January 26, 2022).

Skutch, Jan. "1963, Desegregation Changed the Lives of 19 Savannah Teens, Society." *Savannah Morning News* (August 18, 2013).

Slotkin, Jason. "Protesters Swarm Michigan Capitol amid Showdown over Governor's Emergency Powers." *NPR* (May 1, 2020).

Solum, Lawrence B. "What Is Originalism? The Evolution of Contemporary Originalist Theory." *Georgetown University Law Center* (2011). Accessed July 7, 2022. https://scholarship.law.georgetown.edu/cgi/viewcontent.cgi?article=2362&context=facpub

Sotomayor, Sonia. *My Beloved World* (New York: Knopf, 2013).

Sowell, Thomas. *Black Education: Myths and Tragedies* (New York: McKay, 1972).

———. *Race and Economics* (New York: McKay, 1975).

Sracic, Paul A. *San Antonio v. Rodriguez and the Pursuit of Equal Education* (Lawrence: University Press of Kansas, 2006).

Starkey, Brando Simeo. "Uncle Tom and Justice Clarence Thomas: Is the Abuse Defensible?" 4 *Georgetown Journal of Law and Modern Critical Race Perspectives* 101 (2012).

Sullivan, Patricia. "A Small, Mostly White Virginia Town Put up a 'Black Lives Matter' Banner. Ginni Thomas Denounced It." *Washington Post* (July 10, 2020).

"Supreme Court Nomination Announcement." *C-SPAN* (July 1, 1991). Accessed July 7, 2022. https://www.c-span.org/video/?18649-1/supreme-court-nomination-announcemen

"Supreme Court Nominations (1789–Present)." *U.S. Senate.* Accessed July 7, 2022. https://www.senate.gov/legislative/nominations/SupremeCourtNominations1789present.htm

Suskind, Ron. *A Hope in the Unseen: An American Odyssey from the Inner City to the Ivy League* (New York: Broadway, 1998).

Swire, Sonnet, and Veronica Stracqualursi. "GOP Senator Says Black Woman Supreme Court Pick Would Be 'Beneficiary' of Affirmative Action." *CNN* (January 29, 2022).

Taylor Jr., Stuart. "Marshall Sounds Critical Note on Bicentennial." *New York Times* (May 7, 1987).

Tensley, Brandon. "The Many Joys of Ketanji Brown Jackson's Historic Confirmation." *CNN* (April 7, 2022).

Thomas, Clarence. "Affirmative Action Goals and Timetables: Too Tough? Not Tough Enough!" 5 *Yale Law & Policy Review* 402 (1987).

———. "Be Not Afraid." *American Enterprise Institute* (February 13, 2001). Accessed July 7, 2022. https://www.aei.org/research-products/speech/be-not-afraid/

———. "Freedom: A Responsibility, Not a Right." 21 *Ohio Northern University Law Review* 5 (1994).

———. *My Grandfather's Son* (New York: Perennial, 2007).

———. "Supreme Court Justice Speech." *C-SPAN* (July 29, 1998). Accessed July 7, 2022. https://www.c-span.org/video/?109490-1/supreme-court-justice-speech

Totenburg, Nina. "Justice Scalia, the Great Dissenter, Opens Up." *NPR: Morning Edition* (April 28, 2008).

Tumulty, Karen. "Sister of High Court Nominee Traveled Different Road." *Los Angeles Times* (July 5, 1991).

Tushnet, Mark V. "The Jurisprudence of Thurgood Marshall." 1996 *University of Illinois Law Review* 1129 (1996).

———. "The Supreme Court and Race Discrimination, 1967–1991: The View from the Marshall Papers." 36 *William and Mary Law Review* 473 (1995).

U.S. Commission on the Bicentennial of the U.S. Constitution. "We the People" (1976).

U.S. Constitution.

U.S. Department of Justice. "National Advisory Commission on Civil Disorders, Report" (1967). Accessed on July 7, 2022. https://www.ncjrs.gov/pdffiles1/Digitization/8073NCJRS.pdf

U.S. Supreme Court. "Press Release" (March 16, 2020). Accessed July 7, 2022. https://www.supremecourt.gov/publicinfo/press/pressreleases/pr_03-16-20

———. "Press Release" (April 3, 2020). Accessed July 7, 2022. https://www.supremecourt.gov/publicinfo/press/pressreleases/pr_04-03-20

Van Patten, Jonathan K. "The Partisan Battle over the Constitution: Meese's Jurisprudence of Original Intention and Brennan's Theory of Contemporary Ratification." 70 *Marquette Law Review* 389 (1987).

Weisberg, Jessica. *"Remembering Ruth Bader Ginsburg in Her Own Words."* *Elle* (September 21, 2020).

Welch, William M. "Thomas Presided over Shift in Policy at EEOC, Records Show." *Associated Press* (July 25, 1991).

White, Adam. "Just, Wise, and Constitutional: Justice Thomas's Legacy in Law and Politics." *Law & Liberty* (April 17, 2014).

Whitford, Emma. "College Urged to Strip Clarence Thomas's Name from Building." *Inside Higher Ed* (October 15, 2018). Accessed July 14, 2022. https://www.insidehighered.com/quicktakes/2018/10/15/college-urged-strip-clarence-thomass-name-building

Wilkerson, Isabel. *The Warmth of Other Suns* (New York: Vintage, 2010).

Williams, Heather Andrea. *Self-Taught: African American Education in Slavery and Freedom* (Chapel Hill: University of North Carolina Press, 2005).

Williams, Juan. "Black Conservatives, Center Stage." *Washington Post* (December 16, 1980).

———. "A Question of Fairness." *The Atlantic* (February 1987).

———. *Thurgood Marshall: American Revolutionary* (New York: Three Rivers, 1998).

Williams, Pete. "Supreme Court Makes History with Oral Arguments by Phone. But It's Business as Usual for the Justices." *NBC News* (May 4, 2020).

"William T. Coleman, Jr." *The History Makers*. Accessed July 7, 2022. https://www.thehistorymakers.org/biography/william-t-coleman-jr

Wing, Nick. "Clarence Thomas: Obama Only President Because He's What Elites Expect from a Black Person." *Huffington Post* (May 3, 2013).

Woodward, Bob, and Scott Armstrong. *The Brethren: Inside the Supreme Court* (New York: Simon & Shuster, 1979).

Woodward, Bob, and Robert Costa, "Virginia Thomas Urged White House Chief to Pursue Unrelenting Efforts to Overturn the 2020 Election, Texts Show." *Washington Post* (March 24, 2022).

CASES

Aaron v. McKinley, 173 F.Supp. 944 (E.D. Ark. 1959)

Abrams v. U.S., 250 U.S. 616 (1919)

Adams v. United States, 319 U.S. 312 (1943)

Adarand Constructors, Inc. v. Pena, 515 U.S. 200 (1995)

Alexander v. Holmes County Board of Education, 396 U.S. 1218 (1969)

Allen v. State Board of Elections, 393 U.S. 544 (1969)

Atkins v. Virginia, 536 U.S. 304 (2002)

Baxter v. Bracey, 590 U.S. ___, 140 S.Ct. 1862 (2020)

Beer v. U.S., 425 U.S. 130 (1976)

Board of Education of Oklahoma City v. Dowell, 498 U.S. 237 (1991)

Dowell v. Okla City Bd of Educ, 778 F.Supp. 1144 (W.D. Okla. 1991)

Box v. Planned Parenthood of Indiana and Kentucky, 587 U.S. ___, 139 S.Ct. 1780 (2019)

Briggs v. Elliott, 342 U.S. 350 (1952)

Briggs v. Elliott, 98 F.Supp. 529 (E.D. S.C. 1951)

Briggs v. Elliott, 103 F.Supp. 920 (E.D. S.C. 1952)

Briggs v. Elliott, 132 F.Supp. 776 (E.D. S.C. 1955)

Brnovich v. DNC, 594 U.S. ___, 141 S.Ct. 2321 (2021)

Brown v. Board of Education, 347 U.S. 483 (1954)

Brown v. Board of Education, 98 F.Supp. 797 (D. Kan. 1951)

Brown v. Board of Education, 349 U.S. 294 (1955)

Calvary Chapel Dayton Valley v. Sisolak, 591 U.S. ___, 140 S.Ct. 2603 (2020)

City of Los Angeles v. Lyons, 461 U.S. 95 (1983)

City of Mobile v. Bolden, 446 U.S. 55 (1980)

City of Richmond v. J.A. Croson, Co., 488 U.S. 469 (1989)

City of Richmond v. U.S., 429 U.S. 358 (1975)

City of Rome v. U.S., 446 U.S. 156 (1980)

Civil Rights Cases, 109 U.S. 3 (1883)

Connecticut v. Teal, 457 U.S. 440 (1982)

Cooper v. Aaron, 358 U.S. 1 (1958)

Aaron v. Cooper, 163 F.Supp. 13 (E.D. Ark. 1958)

Aaron v. Cooper, 257 F.2d 33 (8th Cir. 1958)

DeFunis v. Odegaard, 416 U.S. 312 (1974)

Dred Scott v. Sandford, 60 U.S. 393 (1857)

Scott v. Emerson, 15 Mo. 576 (Mo. 1852)

Dunn v. Blumstein, 405 U.S. 330 (1972)

Evenwel v. Abbott, 578 U.S. 54 (2016)

Fair v. Meredith, 371 U.S. 828 (1962) (denying cert)

Meredith v. Fair, 83 S.Ct. 10 (1962) (vacating stay)

Meredith v. Fair, 305 F.2d 343 (5th Cir. 1962)

Fisher v. University of Texas, 570 U.S. 297 (2013)

Flowers v. Mississippi, 588 U.S. ___, 139 S.Ct. 2228 (2019)

Foster v. Chatman, 578 U.S. 488 (2016)

Freeman v. Pitts, 503 U.S. 467 (1992)

Fullilove v. Klutznick, 448 U.S. 448 (1980)

Furman v. Georgia, 408 U.S. 238 (1972)

Gamble v. U.S., 587 U.S. ___, 139 S.Ct. 1960 (2019)

Georgia v. McCollum, 505 U.S. 42 (1992)

Gratz v. Bollinger, 539 U.S. 244 (2003)

Green v. County School Board of New Kent County, 391 U.S. 430 (1968)

Griggs v. Duke Power, 401 U.S. 424 (1971)

Griswold v. Connecticut, 381 U.S. 479 (1965)

Grutter v. Bollinger, 539 U.S. 306 (2003)

Hammer v. Dagenhart, 247 U.S. 251 (1918)

Hampton v. Jefferson County Board of Education, 102 F.Supp.2d 358 (W.D. Ky. 2000)

Harrison v. Day, 106 S.E.2d 636 (Va. 1959)

Heyward v. Public Housing Administration, 238 F.2d 689 (5th Cir. 1956)

Holder v. Hall, 512 U.S. 874 (1994)

Keyes v. Denver School District, No. 1, 413 U.S. 189 (1973)

Korematsu v. U.S., 323 U.S. 214 (1944)

Lyons v. Oklahoma, 322 U.S. 596 (1944)

Mahanoy Area School District v. B.L., 594 U.S. __, 141 S.Ct. 2038 (2021)

McKesson v. Doe, 592 U.S. ___, 141 S.Ct. 48 (2020)

McLaurin v. Okla State Board of Regents, 339 U.S. 637 (1950)

Metro Broadcasting, Inc. v. FCC, 497 U.S. 547 (1990)

Milliken v. Bradley, 418 U.S. 717 (1974)

Bradley v. Milliken, 338 F.Supp. 582 (E.D. Mich. 1971)

Bradley v. Milliken, 345 F.Supp. 914 (E.D. Mich. 1972)

Milliken v. Bradley, 433 U.S. 267 (1977)

Mississippi v. Flowers, 588 U.S. ___, 139 S.Ct. 2228 (2019)

Missouri ex rel Gaines v. Canada, 305 U.S. 337 (1938)

Missouri v. Jenkins, 495 U.S. 33 (1990)

Jenkins v. Missouri, 593 F.Supp. 1485 (W.D. Mo. 1984)

Jenkins v. Missouri, 639 F.Supp. 19 (W.D. Mo. 1985)

Missouri v. Jenkins, 515 U.S. 70 (1995)

Murray v. Pearson, 182 A. 590 (Md. 1935)

Northwest Austin Municipal District v. Holder, 557 U.S. 193 (2009)

Patton v. Mississippi, 332 U.S. 463 (1947)

Payne v. Tennessee, 501 U.S. 808 (1991)

Payne v. State, 2007 WL 4258178 (Tenn. Ct. Crim. App. 2007) (denying DNA petition)

Tennessee v. Payne, Nos. 87-04409 & 87-04410, Order (Tenn. Sup. Ct. Feb. 24, 2020) (setting execution date)

PICS v. Seattle School District, 551 U.S. 701 (2007)

Plessy v. Ferguson, 163 U.S. 537 (1896)

Reed v. Rhodes, 179 F.3d 453 (6th Cir. 1999)

Reed v. Rhodes, 422 F.Supp. 708 (N.D. Ohio 1976)

Reed v. Rhodes, 934 F.Supp. 1533 (N.D. Ohio 1996)

Regents of the Univ. of California v. Bakke, 438 U.S. 265 (1978)

Bakke v. Regents of the Univ. of California, 553 P.2d 1152 (Cal. 1976)

Republican Party of Pennsylvania v. Boockvar, 592 U.S. ___, 141 S.Ct. 643 (2020)

Republican Party of Pennsylvania v. Degraffenreid, 592 U.S. ___, 141 S.Ct. 732 (2021)

Ricci v. Destefano, 557 U.S. 557 (2009)

Roe v. Wade, 410 U.S. 113 (1973)

Roman Catholic Diocese of Brooklyn v. Cuomo, 592 U.S. ___, 141 S.Ct. 63 (2020)

San Antonio ISD v. Rodriguez, 411 U.S. 1 (1973)

Rodriguez v. San Antonio ISD, 337 F.Supp. 280 (W.D. Tex.1971)

Shelby County v. Holder, 570 U.S. 529 (2013)

Shelley v. Kraemer, 334 U.S. 1 (1948)

Sipes v. McGhee, 316 Mich. 614 (1947)

Sipuel v. Bd of Regents of Univ of Oklahoma, 332 U.S. 631 (1948)

Smith v. Allwright, 321 U.S. 649 (1944)

Snyder v. Louisiana, 552 U.S. 472 (2008)

South Bay United Pentecostal Church v. Newsom, 590 U.S. ___, 140 S.Ct. 1613 (2020)

South Carolina v. Katzenbach, 383 U.S. 301 (1966)

Stell v. Savannah-Chatham County Board of Education, 220 F. Supp. 667 (1963)

Swann v. Charlotte-Mecklenburg Board of Education, 402 U.S. 1 (1971)

Swann v. Charlotte-Mecklenburg Board of Education, 306 F.Supp. 1299 (W.D. N.C. 1969)

Sweatt v. Painter, 339 U.S. 629 (1950)

Taylor v. Alabama, 335 U.S. 252 (1948)

Texas v. Pennsylvania, 592 U.S. ___, 141 S.Ct. 1230 (2020)

Tinsley v. City of Richmond, 368 U.S. 18 (1961)

Trump v. Thompson, 595 U.S. ___, 142 S.Ct. 680 (2022)

U.S. v. Carolene Products, 304 U.S. 144 (1938)

U.S. v. Darby, 312 U.S. 100 (1941)

U.S. v. Fordice, 505 U.S. 717 (1992)

Ayers v. Allain, 674 F.Supp. 1523 (N.D. Miss. 1987)

Ayers v. Allain, 914 F.2d 676 (5th Cir. 1990)

U.S. v. Lopez, 514 U.S. 549 (1995)

U.S. v. Missouri, 515 F.2d 1365 (8th Cir. 1975)

Village of Arlington Heights v. Metropolitan Housing Corp., 429 U.S. 252 (1977)

Voisine v. U.S., 579 U.S. 686 (2016)

Wards Cove Packing Co. v. Atonio, 490 U.S. 642 (1989)

Washington v. Davis, 426 U.S. 229 (1976)

Watson v. Fort Worth Bank and Trust, 487 U.S. 977 (1988)

Watts v. Indiana, 338 U.S. 49 (1949)

Wygant v. Jackson Board of Education, 476 U.S. 267 (1986).

Wygant v. Jackson Board of Education, 546 F.Supp. 1195 (E.D. Mich. 1982)

Zelman v. Simmons-Harris, 536 U.S. 639 (2002)

Ziglar v. Abbasi, 582 U.S. ___, 137 S.Ct. 1843 (2017)

INDEX